尾田栄一郎

When I was in school, I learned that this man
above was Prince Shotoku, a great figure from
Japan's distant past. But lately, a theory has
surfaced that this illustration wasn't actually
of Shotoku. This ruins my own pet theory that
Prince Shotoku was a glutton who always
carried his own rice-serving paddle around with
him. In that case, who's this glutton?!!
History is still chock-full of mysteries.
Let's get to the bottom of volume 73!!

-Eiichiro Oda, 2014

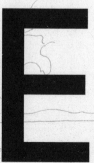iichiro Oda began his manga career at the age of
17, when his one-shot cowboy manga **Wanted!**
won second place in the coveted Tezuka manga
awards. Oda went on to work as an assistant to
some of the biggest manga artists in the industry,
including Nobuhiro Watsuki, before winning the
Hop Step Award for new artists. His pirate
adventure **One Piece**, which debuted in
Weekly Shonen Jump in 1997, quickly became
one of the most popular manga in Japan.

ONE PIECE VOL. 73
NEW WORLD PART 13

SHONEN JUMP Manga Edition

STORY AND ART BY EIICHIRO ODA

Translation/Stephen Paul
Touch-up Art & Lettering/Vanessa Satone
Design/Fawn Lau
Editor/Alexis Kirsch

Printed in the U.S.A.

Published by VIZ Media, LLC
P.O. Box 77010
San Francisco, CA 94107

10 9 8 7 6 5 4 3 2 1
First printing, January 2015

www.viz.com

THE WORLD'S
MOST POPULAR MANGA

www.shonenjump.com

ONE PIECE

Vol. 73

OPERATION DRESSROSA S.O.P.

STORY AND ART BY

EIICHIRO ODA

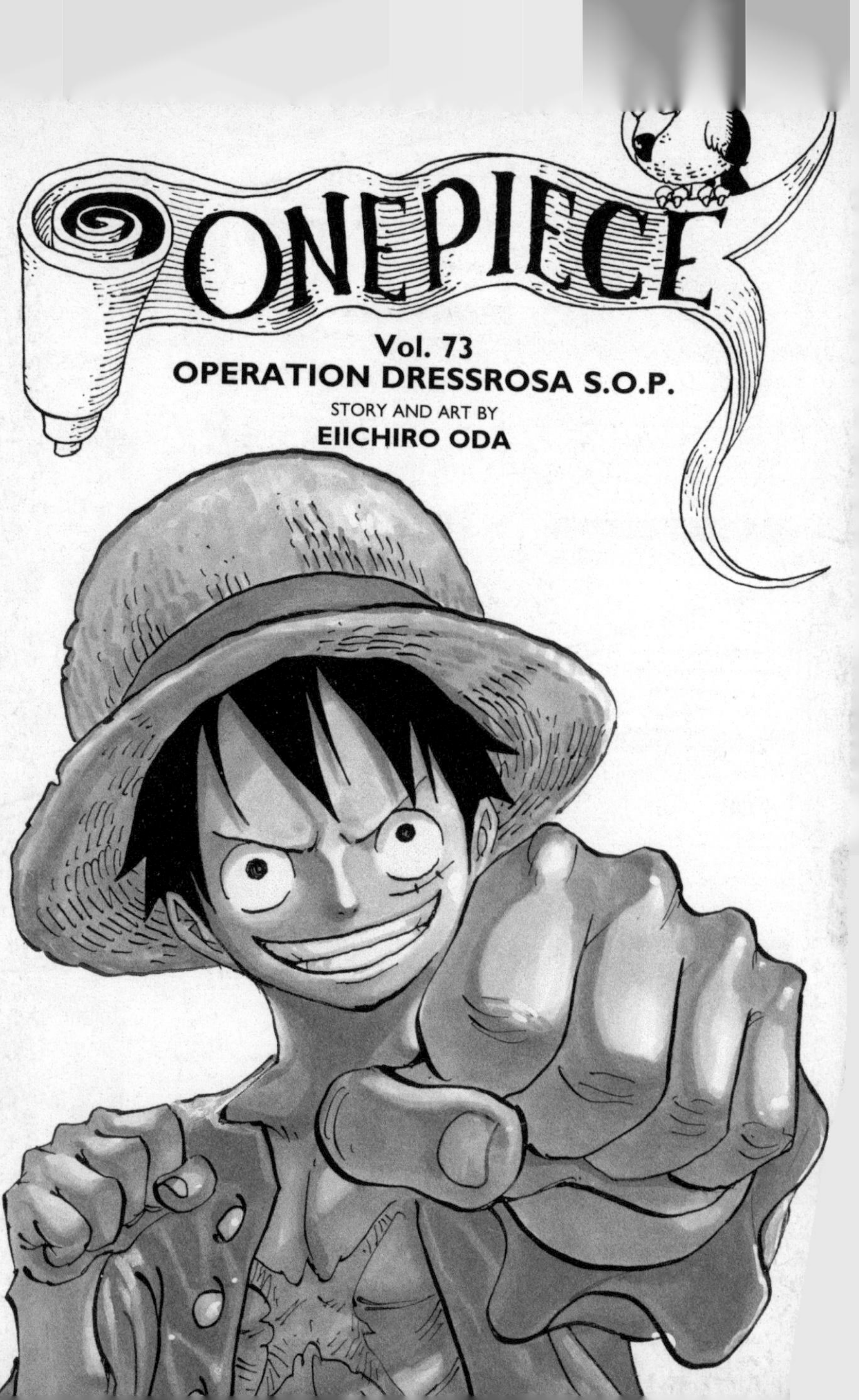

The Straw Hat Crew

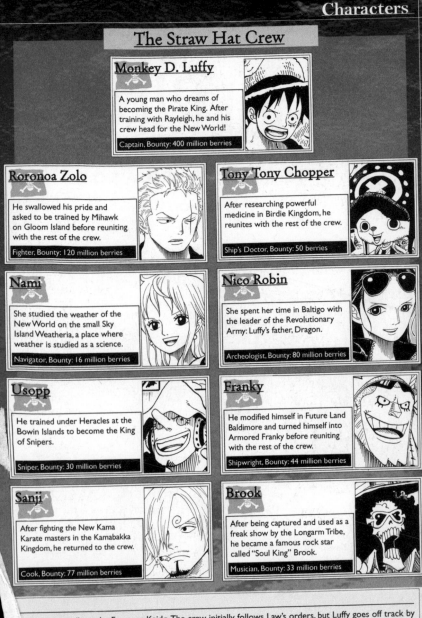

Monkey D. Luffy

A young man who dreams of becoming the Pirate King. After training with Rayleigh, he and his crew head for the New World!

Captain, Bounty: 400 million berries

Roronoa Zolo

He swallowed his pride and asked to be trained by Mihawk on Gloom Island before reuniting with the rest of the crew.

Fighter, Bounty: 120 million berries

Tony Tony Chopper

After researching powerful medicine in Birdie Kingdom, he reunites with the rest of the crew.

Ship's Doctor, Bounty: 50 berries

Nami

She studied the weather of the New World on the small Sky Island Weatheria, a place where weather is studied as a science.

Navigator, Bounty: 16 million berries

Nico Robin

She spent her time in Baltigo with the leader of the Revolutionary Army: Luffy's father, Dragon.

Archeologist, Bounty: 80 million berries

Usopp

He trained under Heracles at the Bowin Islands to become the King of Snipers.

Sniper, Bounty: 30 million berries

Franky

He modified himself in Future Land Baldimore and turned himself into Armored Franky before reuniting with the rest of the crew.

Shipwright, Bounty: 44 million berries

Sanji

After fighting the New Kama Karate masters in the Kamabakka Kingdom, he returned to the crew.

Cook, Bounty: 77 million berries

Brook

After being captured and used as a freak show by the Longarm Tribe, he became a famous rock star called "Soul King" Brook.

Musician, Bounty: 33 million berries

Doflamingo sells to the Emperor, Kaido. The crew initially follows Law's orders, but Luffy goes off track by entering a tournament to win Ace's Flame-Flame Fruit and blasting his way through the prelims. Meanwhile, Law prepares to hand over Caesar, but Doflamingo's clever trap puts him face-to-face with a Naval Admiral! Elsewhere, Usopp's group works with the Tontattas to prepare for the fateful battle with Doflamingo. What will happen next as these storylines collide?

Shanks

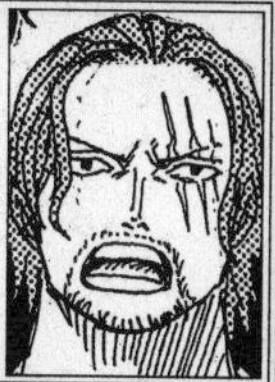

One of the Four Emperors. He continues to wait for Luffy in the second half of the Grand Line, called the New World.

Captain of the Red-Haired Pirates

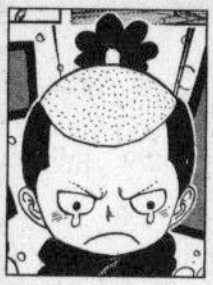

Momonosuke

Kin'emon's Son

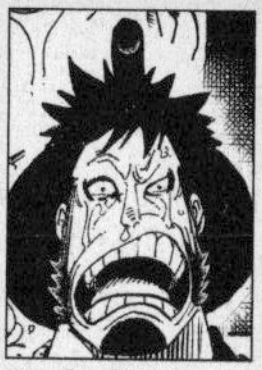

Foxfire Kin'emon

Samurai of Wano

Don Quixote Pirates

Don Quixote Doflamingo (Joker)

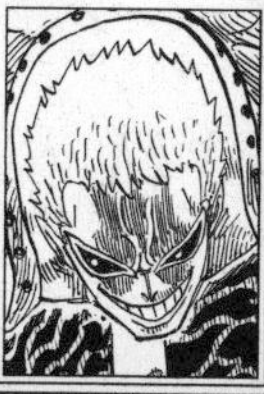

One of the Seven Warlords of the sea and a weapons broker. He works under the alias of "Joker."

Pirate, Warlord (former)

Don Quixote Family

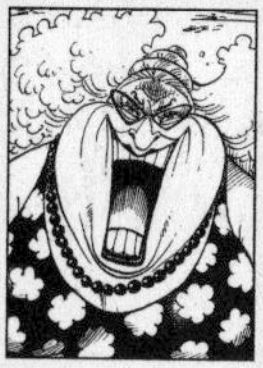

Giolla

♣ Trebol Army

Trafalgar Law

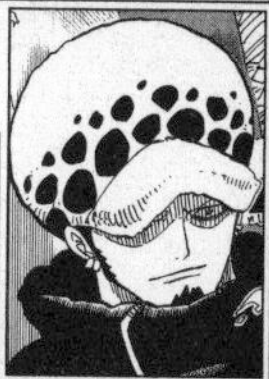

The Surgeon of Death, wielder of the Op-Op Fruit's powers. Currently allied with Luffy.

Pirate, Warlord

Master Caesar Clown

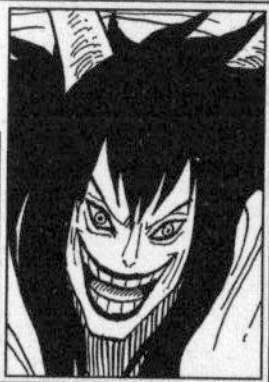

An authority on weapons of mass murder. Kidnapped by Law in an attempt to goad Doflamingo out of hiding.

Former government scientist

Fujitora (Issho)

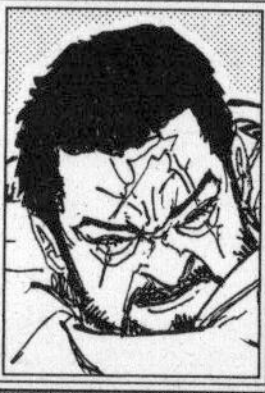

A blind swordsman. One of the Three Admirals after Aokiji's departure.

Naval HQ Admiral

Tontatta Kingdom

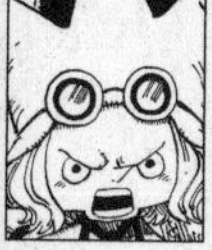

Leo

Warrior

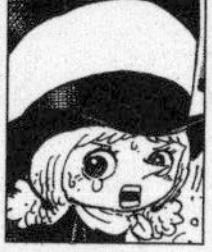

Wicka

Reconnaissance

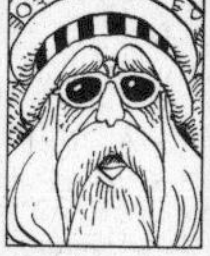

Gancho

King of the Tontattas

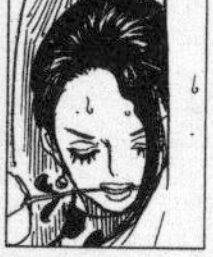

Violet

Dancer

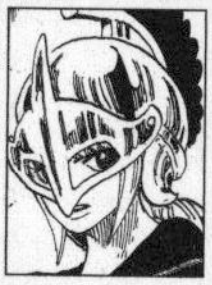

Rebecca

Gladiator

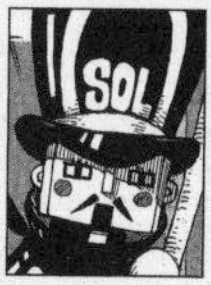
SOL

One-Legged Soldier

Toy

Story

After two years of hard training, the Straw Hat pirates are back together, first at the Sabaody Archipelago and then through Fish-Man Island to their next stage: the New World!!

The crew happens across Trafalgar Law on the island of Punk Hazard, run by Caesar Clown. At his suggestion, they form a new pirate alliance that seeks to take down one of the Four Emperors. In order to draw Doflamingo's attention, they must first capture Caesar, who is producing the artificial Devil Fruit that

Vol. 73
Operation Dressrosa S.O.P.

CONTENTS

Chapter 722:
ROYAL BLOODLINES

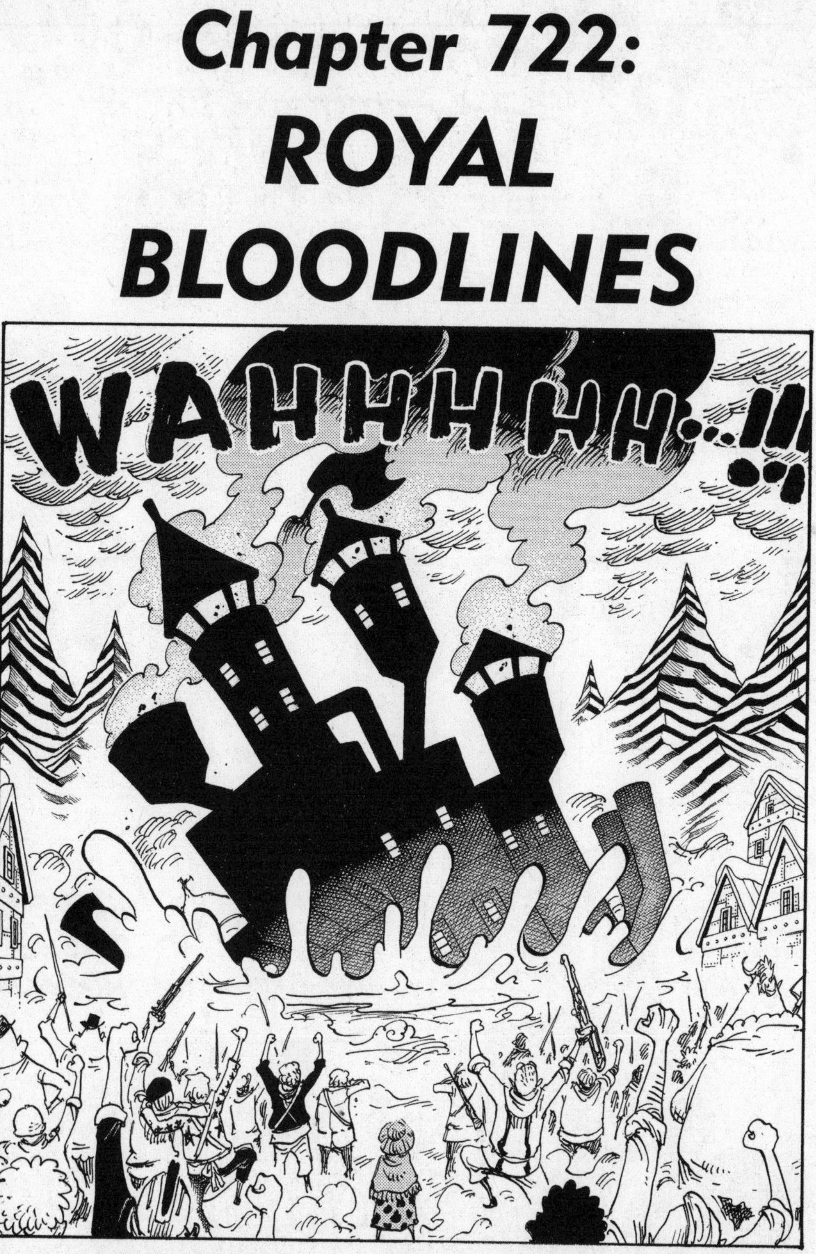
WAHHHHHH...!!!

CARIBOU'S NEW WORLD KEE HEE HEE, VOL. 39:
"TAKE OVER THE FACTORY! NO MORE WORKPLACE!!"

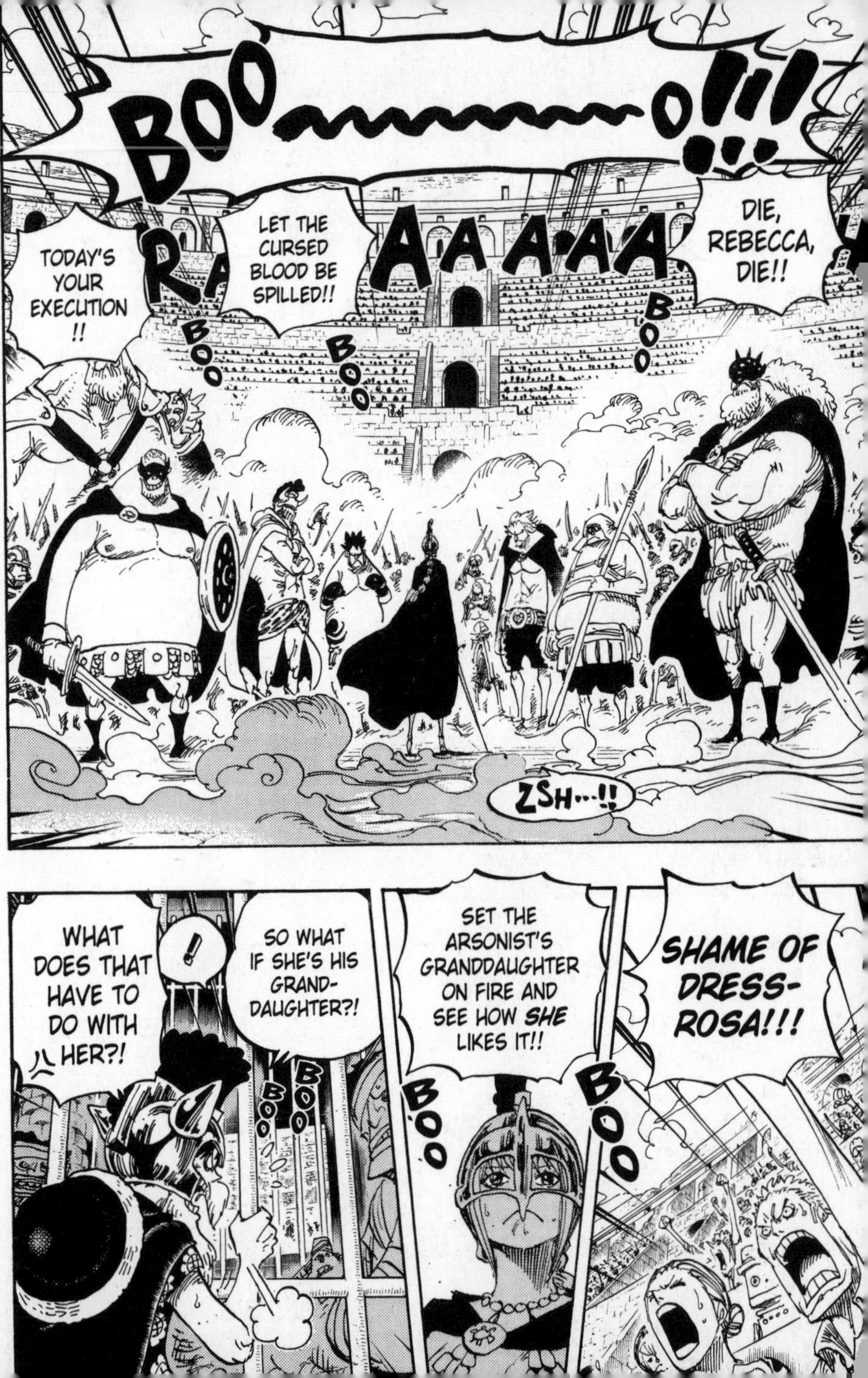
BOOOOOOO!!!
DIE, REBECCA, DIE!!
BOO
AAAAA
LET THE CURSED BLOOD BE SPILLED!!
BOO
RA
BOO
TODAY'S YOUR EXECUTION!!
ZSH...!!
SHAME OF DRESS-ROSA!!!
BOO
SET THE ARSONIST'S GRANDDAUGHTER ON FIRE AND SEE HOW SHE LIKES IT!!
BOO
SO WHAT IF SHE'S HIS GRAND-DAUGHTER?!
BOO
BOO
!
WHAT DOES THAT HAVE TO DO WITH HER?!

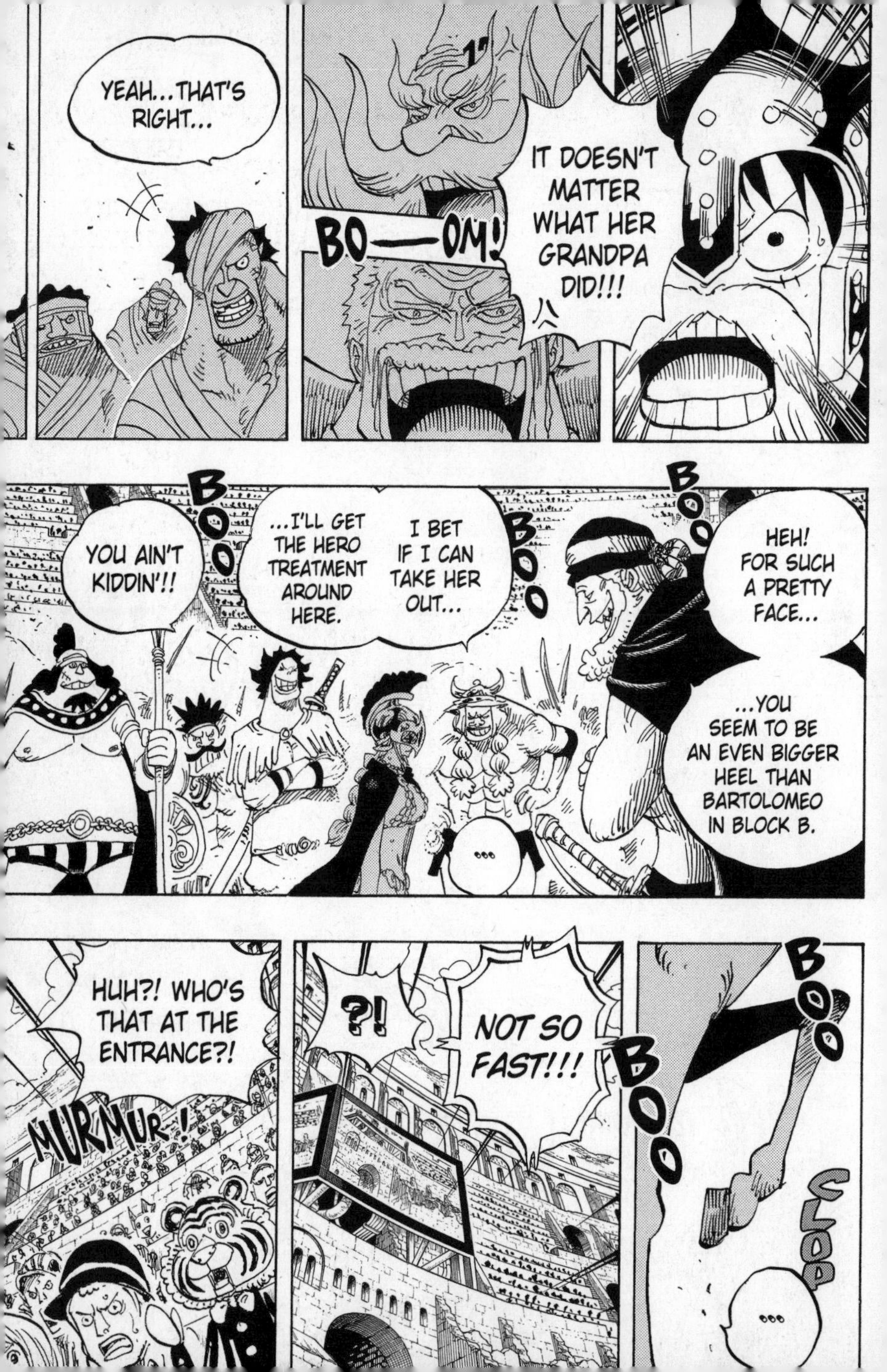
IT DOESN'T MATTER WHAT HER GRANDPA DID!!!
BO—OM!
YEAH...THAT'S RIGHT...
BOOO
HEH! FOR SUCH A PRETTY FACE...
...YOU SEEM TO BE AN EVEN BIGGER HEEL THAN BARTOLOMEO IN BLOCK B.
...
BOOO
I BET IF I CAN TAKE HER OUT...
...I'LL GET THE HERO TREATMENT AROUND HERE.
BOOO
YOU AIN'T KIDDIN'!!
BOOO
BOOO
CLOP
...
NOT SO FAST!!!
?!
HUH?! WHO'S THAT AT THE ENTRANCE?!
MURMUR!

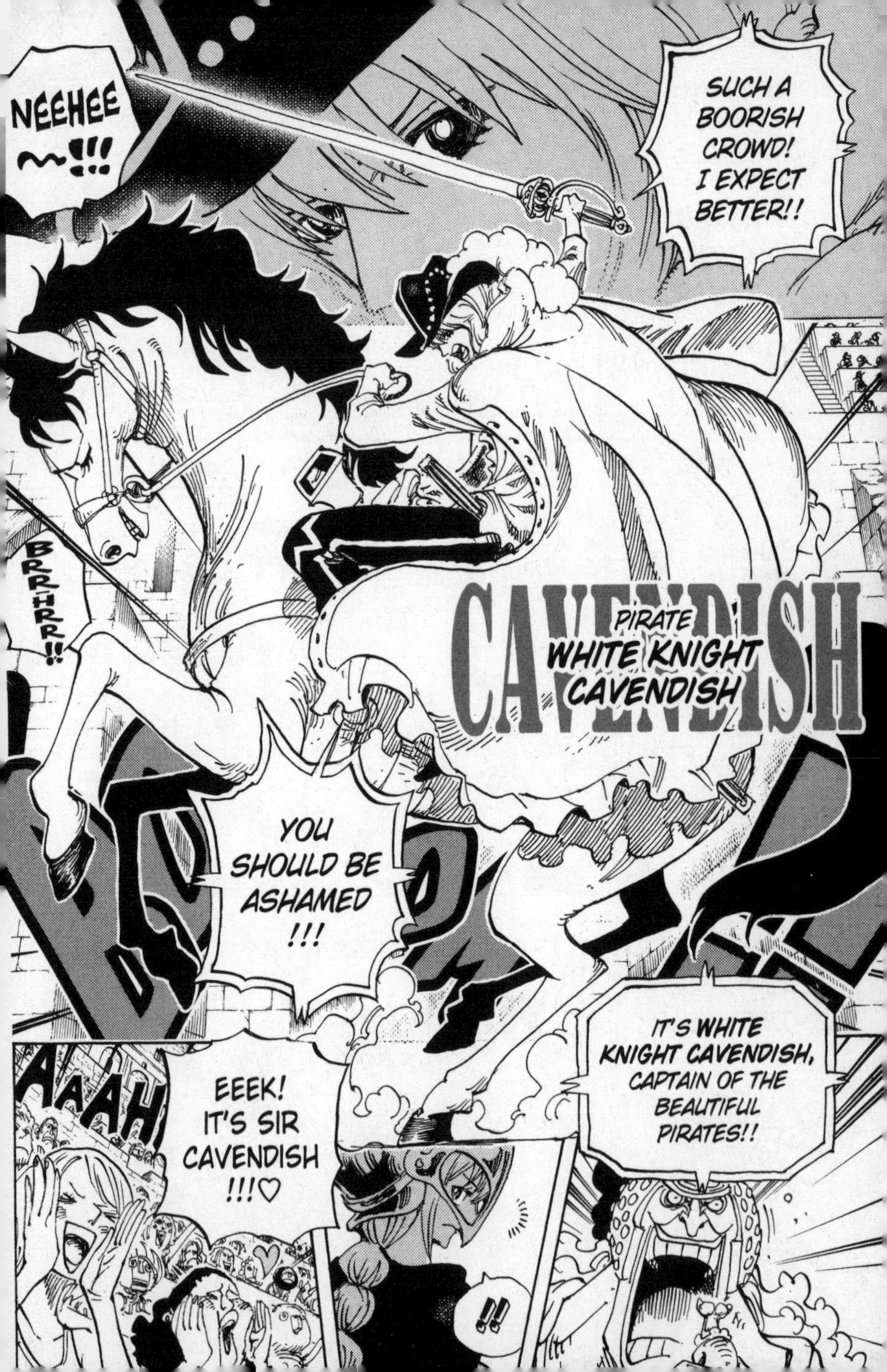
SUCH A BOORISH CROWD! I EXPECT BETTER!!
NEEHEE~!!!
CAVENDISH
PIRATE
WHITE KNIGHT CAVENDISH
BRRRHRR!!
YOU SHOULD BE ASHAMED!!!
IT'S WHITE KNIGHT CAVENDISH, CAPTAIN OF THE BEAUTIFUL PIRATES!!
!!
EEEK! IT'S SIR CAVENDISH!!!♡
AAAH

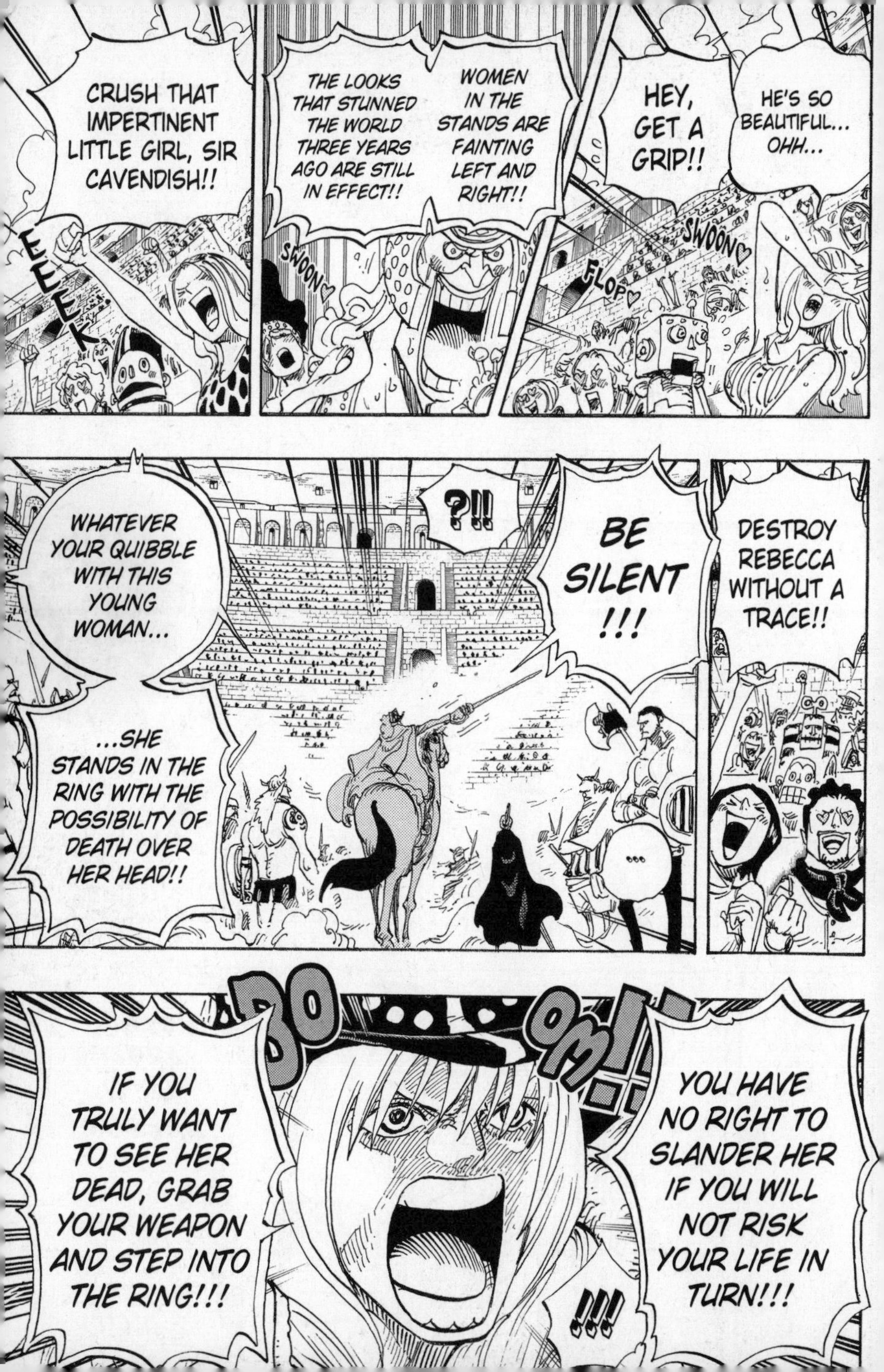
HE'S SO BEAUTIFUL... OHH...
HEY, GET A GRIP!!
SWOON♡
FLOP♡
WOMEN IN THE STANDS ARE FAINTING LEFT AND RIGHT!!
THE LOOKS THAT STUNNED THE WORLD THREE YEARS AGO ARE STILL IN EFFECT!!
SWOON♡
CRUSH THAT IMPERTINENT LITTLE GIRL, SIR CAVENDISH!!
EEEEK
DESTROY REBECCA WITHOUT A TRACE!!
BE SILENT!!!
?!!
WHATEVER YOUR QUIBBLE WITH THIS YOUNG WOMAN...
...SHE STANDS IN THE RING WITH THE POSSIBILITY OF DEATH OVER HER HEAD!!
BOOOM!!
YOU HAVE NO RIGHT TO SLANDER HER IF YOU WILL NOT RISK YOUR LIFE IN TURN!!!
!!!
IF YOU TRULY WANT TO SEE HER DEAD, GRAB YOUR WEAPON AND STEP INTO THE RING!!!

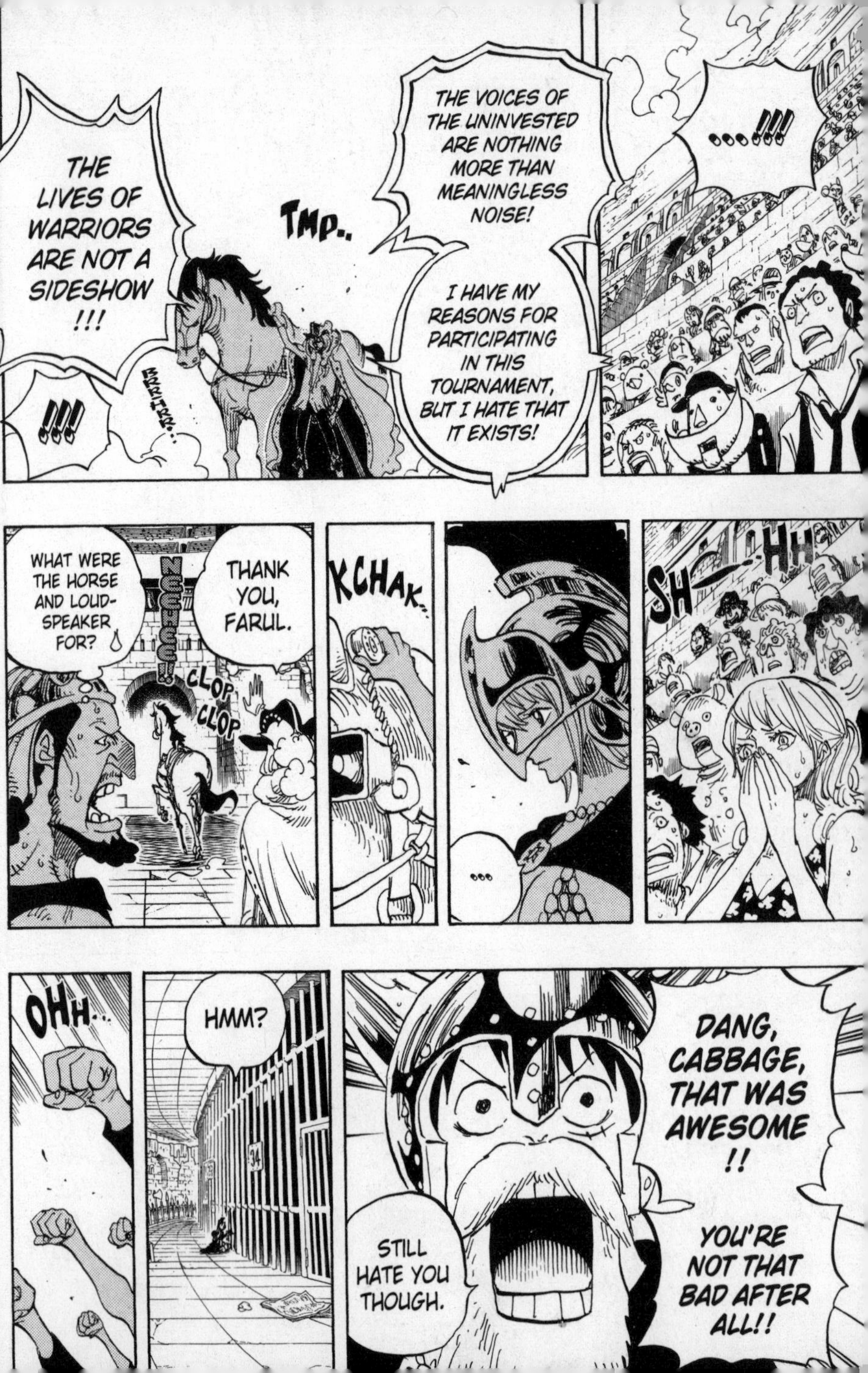
...!!!
THE VOICES OF THE UNINVESTED ARE NOTHING MORE THAN MEANINGLESS NOISE!
I HAVE MY REASONS FOR PARTICIPATING IN THIS TOURNAMENT, BUT I HATE THAT IT EXISTS!
TMP..
THE LIVES OF WARRIORS ARE NOT A SIDESHOW!!!
BRRHRR...
!!!
SH-HH
...
KCHAK...
THANK YOU, FARUL.
NEEHEE!!
CLOP CLOP
WHAT WERE THE HORSE AND LOUD-SPEAKER FOR?
DANG, CABBAGE, THAT WAS AWESOME!!
YOU'RE NOT THAT BAD AFTER ALL!!
STILL HATE YOU THOUGH.
HMM?
OHH...

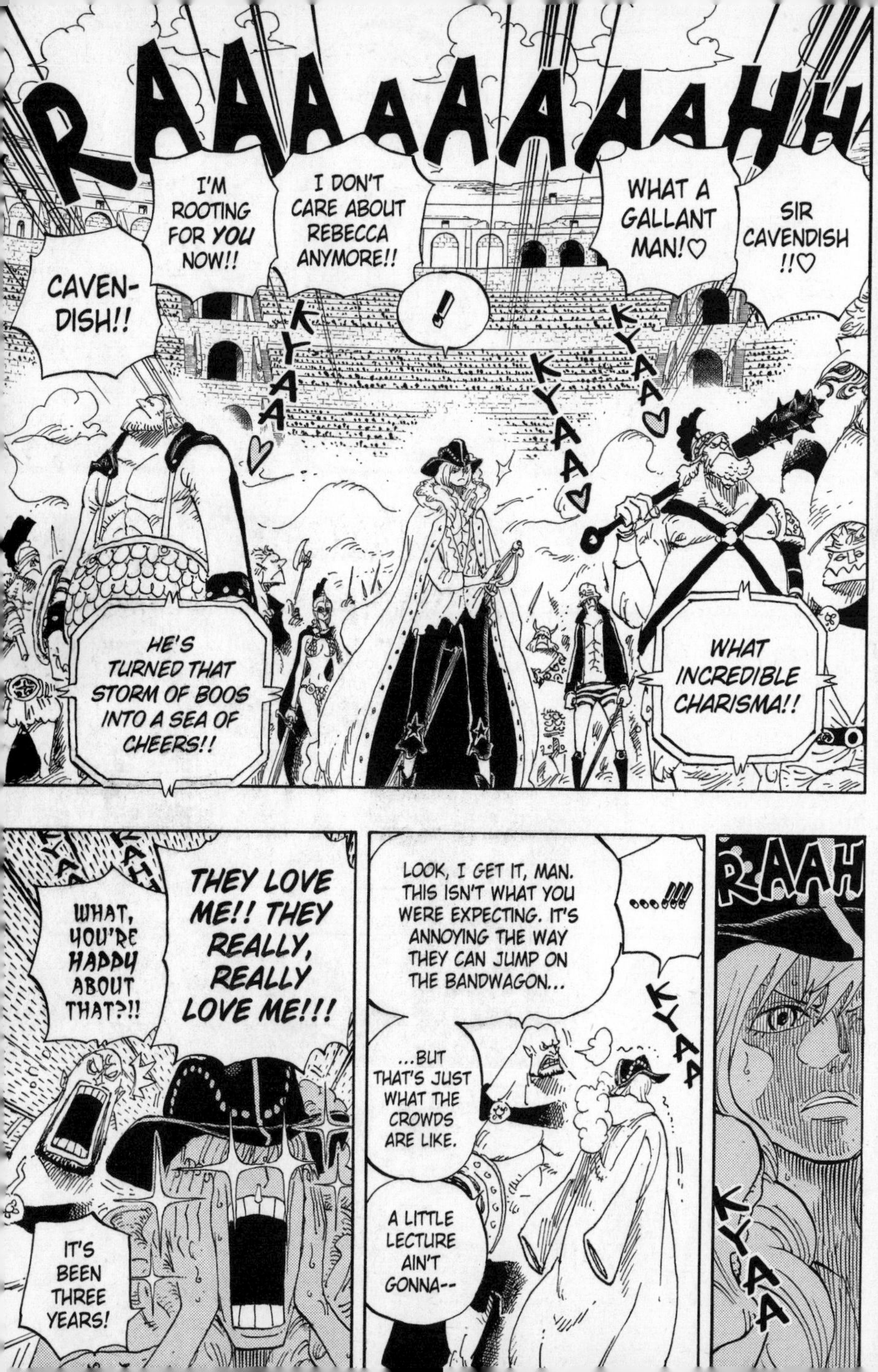
RAAAAAAAAHH
SIR CAVENDISH!!♡
WHAT A GALLANT MAN!♡
I DON'T CARE ABOUT REBECCA ANYMORE!!
I'M ROOTING FOR YOU NOW!!
CAVEN-DISH!!
KYAA KYAA♡
KYAA KYAA♡
KYAA♡
!
WHAT INCREDIBLE CHARISMA!!
HE'S TURNED THAT STORM OF BOOS INTO A SEA OF CHEERS!!
RAAH
KYAA
...!!!
LOOK, I GET IT, MAN. THIS ISN'T WHAT YOU WERE EXPECTING. IT'S ANNOYING THE WAY THEY CAN JUMP ON THE BANDWAGON...
...BUT THAT'S JUST WHAT THE CROWDS ARE LIKE.
KYAA
A LITTLE LECTURE AIN'T GONNA--
THEY LOVE ME!! THEY REALLY, REALLY LOVE ME!!!
WHAT, YOU'RE HAPPY ABOUT THAT?!!
IT'S BEEN THREE YEARS!

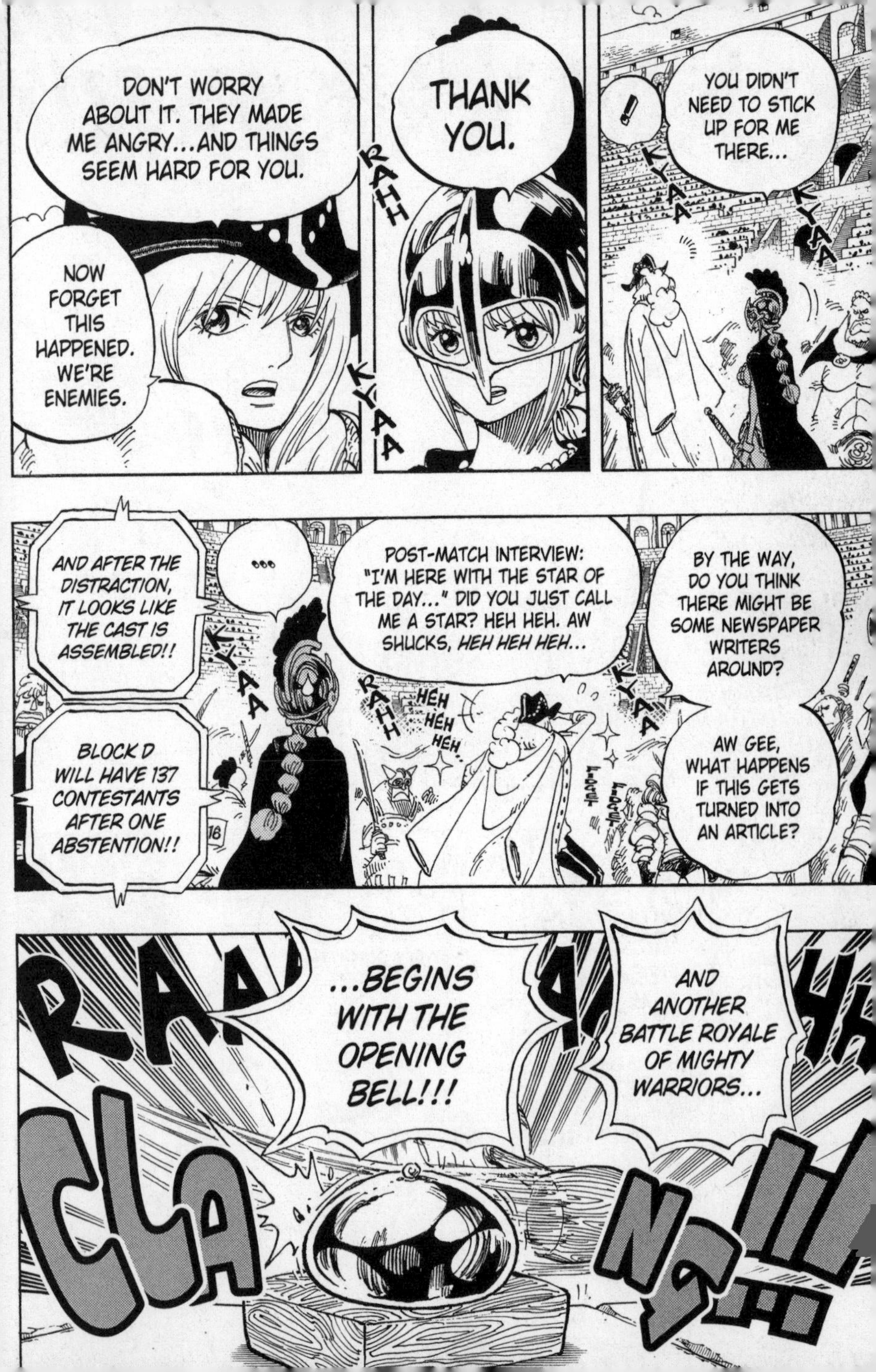
!
YOU DIDN'T NEED TO STICK UP FOR ME THERE...
KYAA
KYAA
THANK YOU.
RAHH
DON'T WORRY ABOUT IT. THEY MADE ME ANGRY...AND THINGS SEEM HARD FOR YOU.
NOW FORGET THIS HAPPENED. WE'RE ENEMIES.
KYAA
BY THE WAY, DO YOU THINK THERE MIGHT BE SOME NEWSPAPER WRITERS AROUND?
AW GEE, WHAT HAPPENS IF THIS GETS TURNED INTO AN ARTICLE?
KYAA
FIDGET
FIDGET
POST-MATCH INTERVIEW: "I'M HERE WITH THE STAR OF THE DAY..." DID YOU JUST CALL ME A STAR? HEH HEH. AW SHUCKS, *HEH HEH HEH...*
HEH HEH HEH
RAHH
...
KYAA
AND AFTER THE DISTRACTION, IT LOOKS LIKE THE CAST IS ASSEMBLED!!
BLOCK D WILL HAVE 137 CONTESTANTS AFTER ONE ABSTENTION!!
AND ANOTHER BATTLE ROYALE OF MIGHTY WARRIORS...
...BEGINS WITH THE OPENING BELL!!!
CLANG!!!

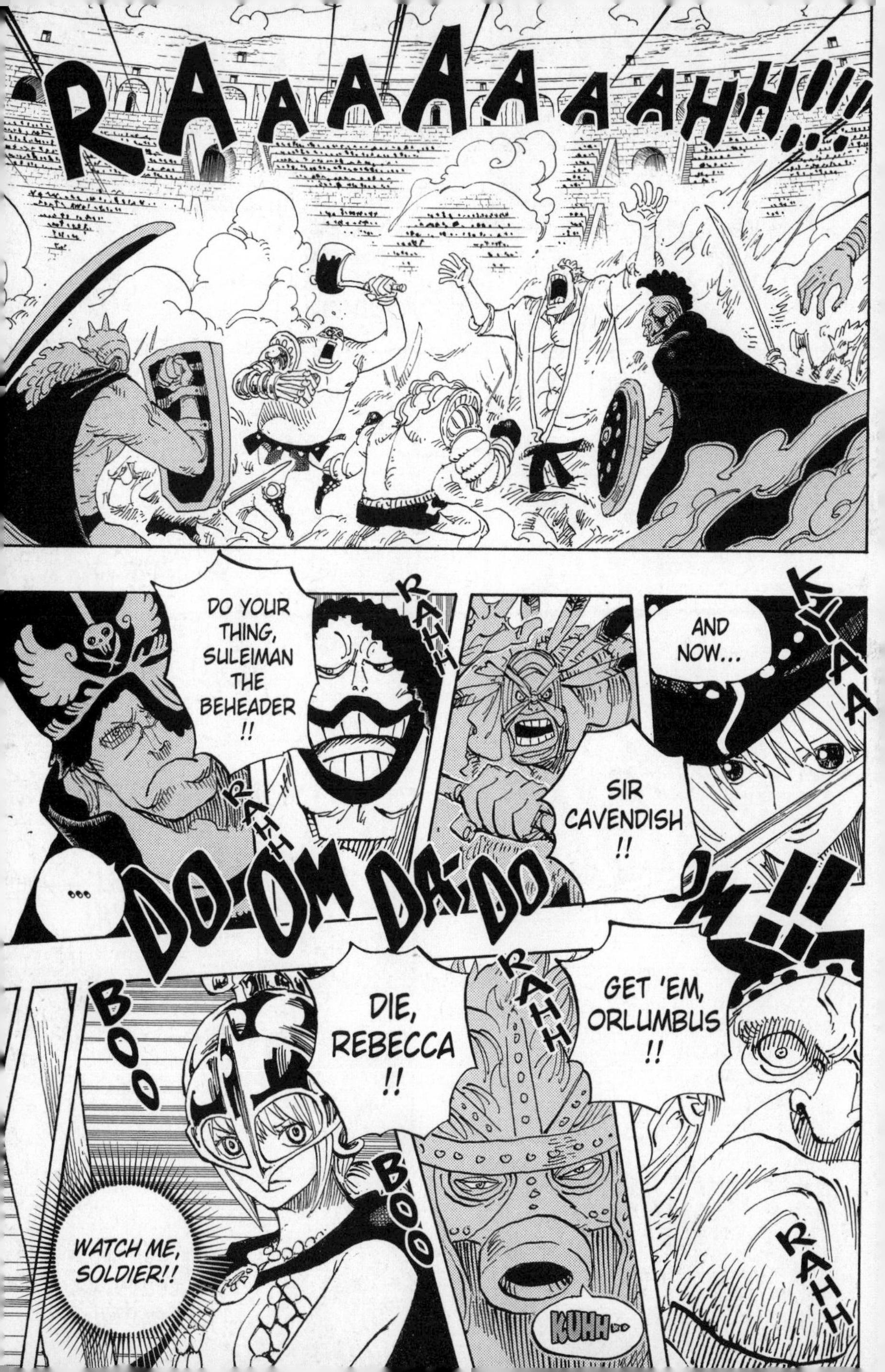
RAAAAAAAAHH!!!
AND NOW...
KYAAA
SIR CAVENDISH!!
RAHH
DO YOUR THING, SULEIMAN THE BEHEADER!!
RAHH
...
DOOM DA-DOOM!!
GET 'EM, ORLUMBUS!!
RAHH
KUHH
RAHH
DIE, REBECCA!!
BOOO
BOOO
WATCH ME, SOLDIER!!

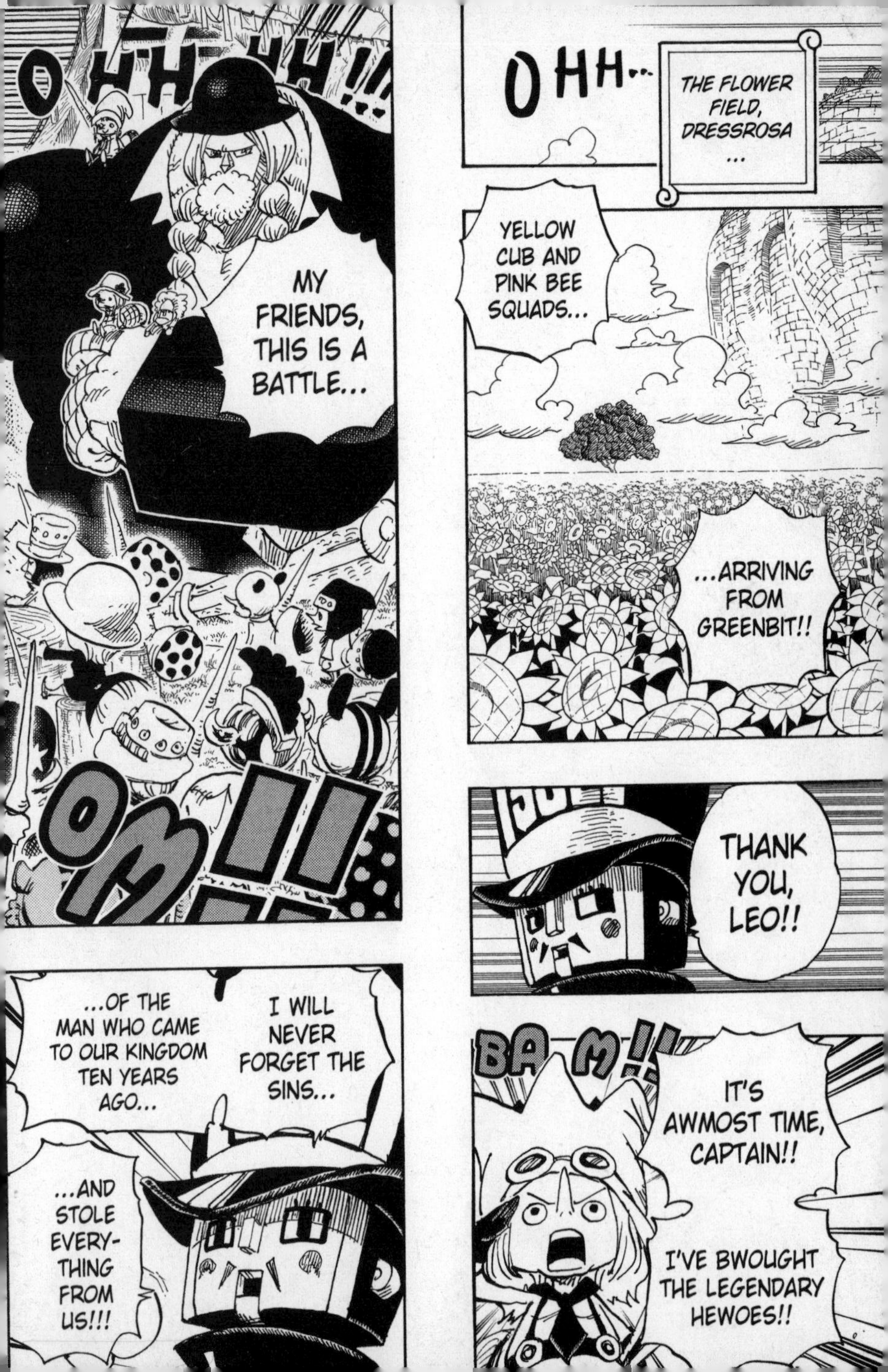
OHH...
THE FLOWER FIELD, DRESSROSA ...
YELLOW CUB AND PINK BEE SQUADS...
...ARRIVING FROM GREENBIT!!
THANK YOU, LEO!!
BA M!!
IT'S AWMOST TIME, CAPTAIN!!
I'VE BWOUGHT THE LEGENDARY HEWOES!!
OHH-UHH!!!
MY FRIENDS, THIS IS A BATTLE...
OM!!
I WILL NEVER FORGET THE SINS...
...OF THE MAN WHO CAME TO OUR KINGDOM TEN YEARS AGO...
...AND STOLE EVERY-THING FROM US!!!

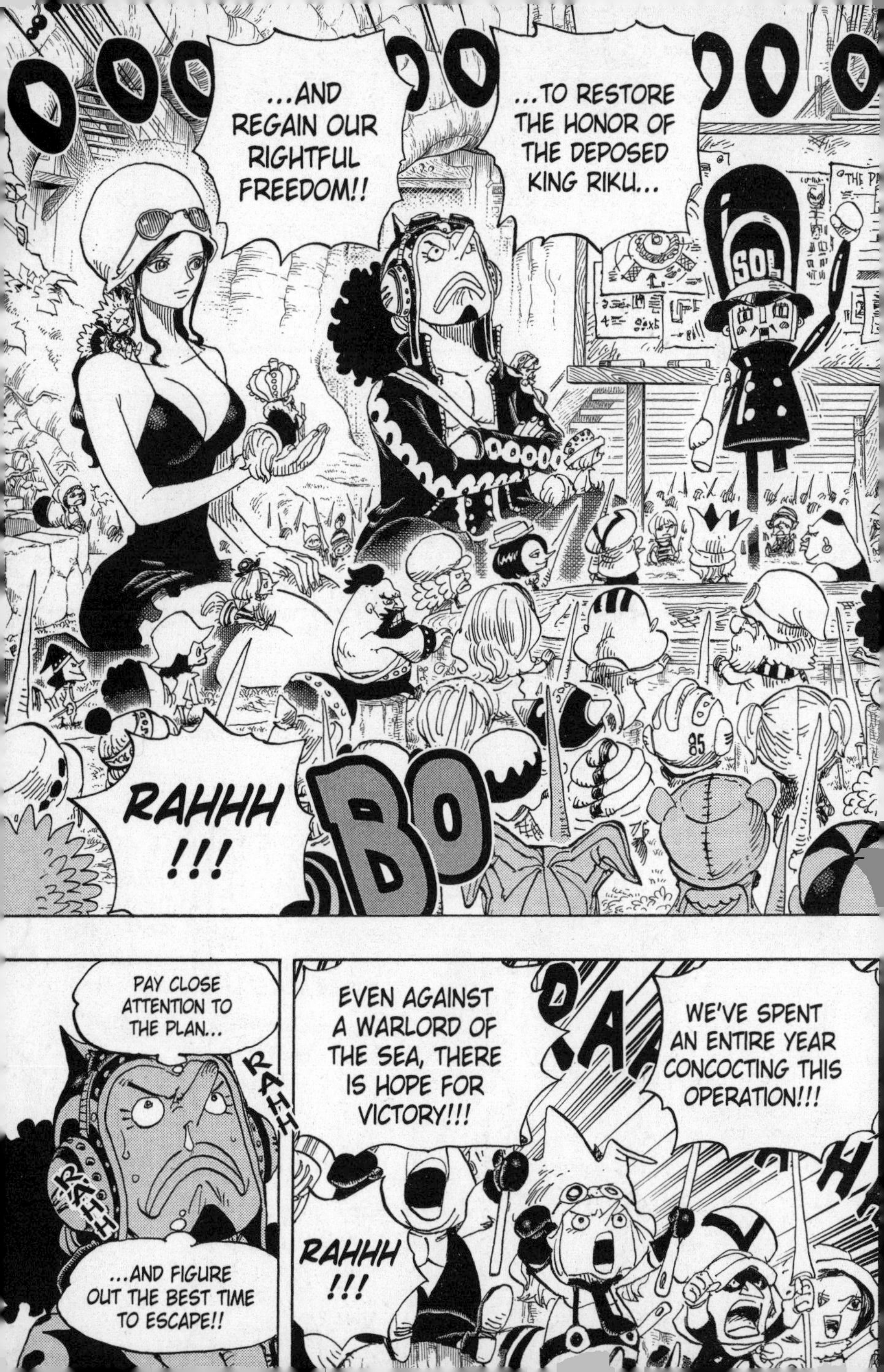
...TO RESTORE THE HONOR OF THE DEPOSED KING RIKU...
...AND REGAIN OUR RIGHTFUL FREEDOM!!
BO
RAHHH!!!
WE'VE SPENT AN ENTIRE YEAR CONCOCTING THIS OPERATION!!!
EVEN AGAINST A WARLORD OF THE SEA, THERE IS HOPE FOR VICTORY!!!
RAHHH!!!
PAY CLOSE ATTENTION TO THE PLAN...
RAHH
RAHH
...AND FIGURE OUT THE BEST TIME TO ESCAPE!!

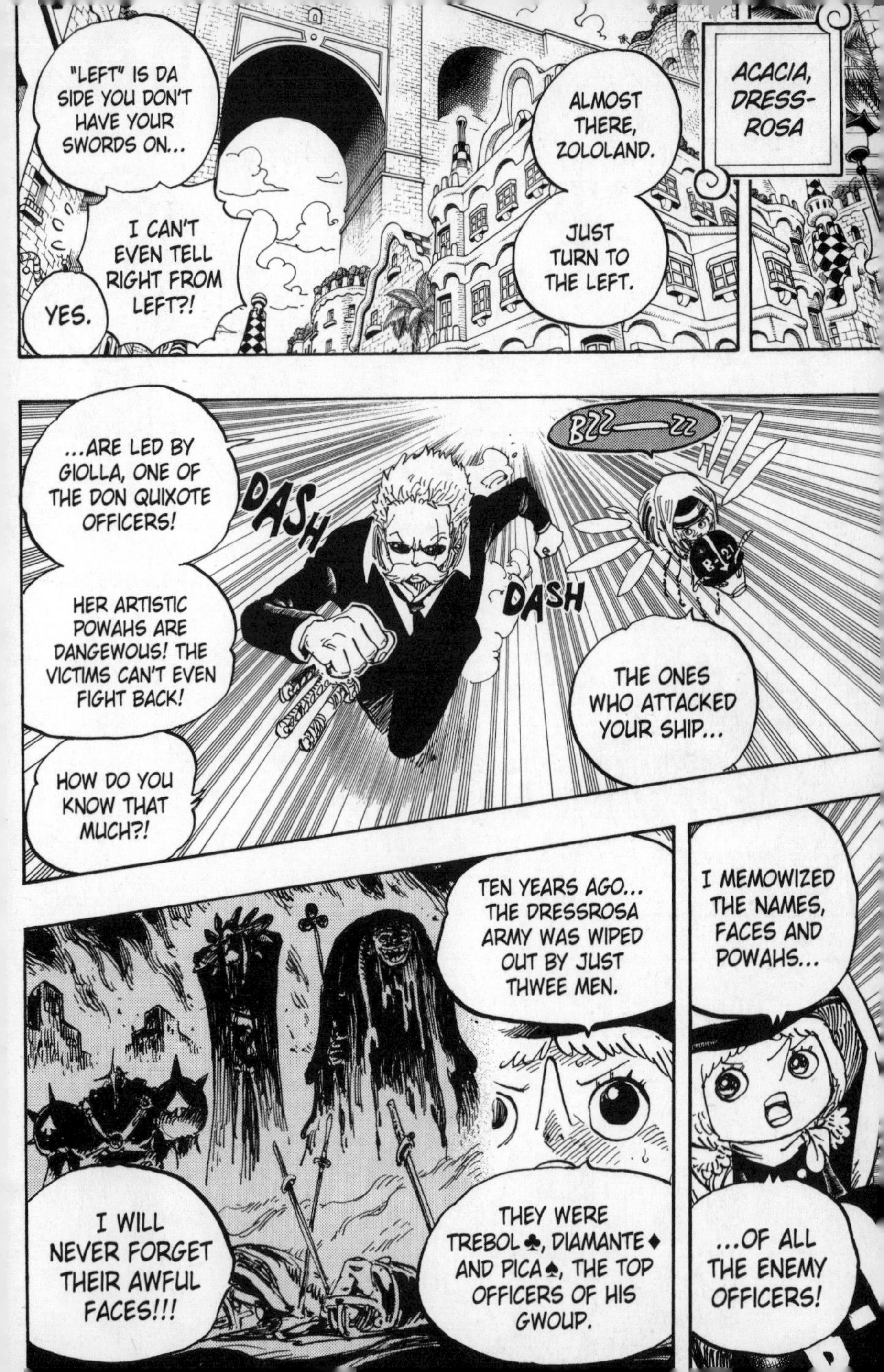
ACACIA, DRESS-ROSA
ALMOST THERE, ZOLOLAND.
JUST TURN TO THE LEFT.
I CAN'T EVEN TELL RIGHT FROM LEFT?!
YES.
"LEFT" IS DA SIDE YOU DON'T HAVE YOUR SWORDS ON...
BZZ—ZZ
DASH
DASH
THE ONES WHO ATTACKED YOUR SHIP...
...ARE LED BY GIOLLA, ONE OF THE DON QUIXOTE OFFICERS!
HER ARTISTIC POWAHS ARE DANGEWOUS! THE VICTIMS CAN'T EVEN FIGHT BACK!
HOW DO YOU KNOW THAT MUCH?!
I MEMOWIZED THE NAMES, FACES AND POWAHS...
...OF ALL THE ENEMY OFFICERS!
TEN YEARS AGO... THE DRESSROSA ARMY WAS WIPED OUT BY JUST THWEE MEN.
THEY WERE TREBOL♣, DIAMANTE♦ AND PICA♠, THE TOP OFFICERS OF HIS GWOUP.
I WILL NEVER FORGET THEIR AWFUL FACES!!!

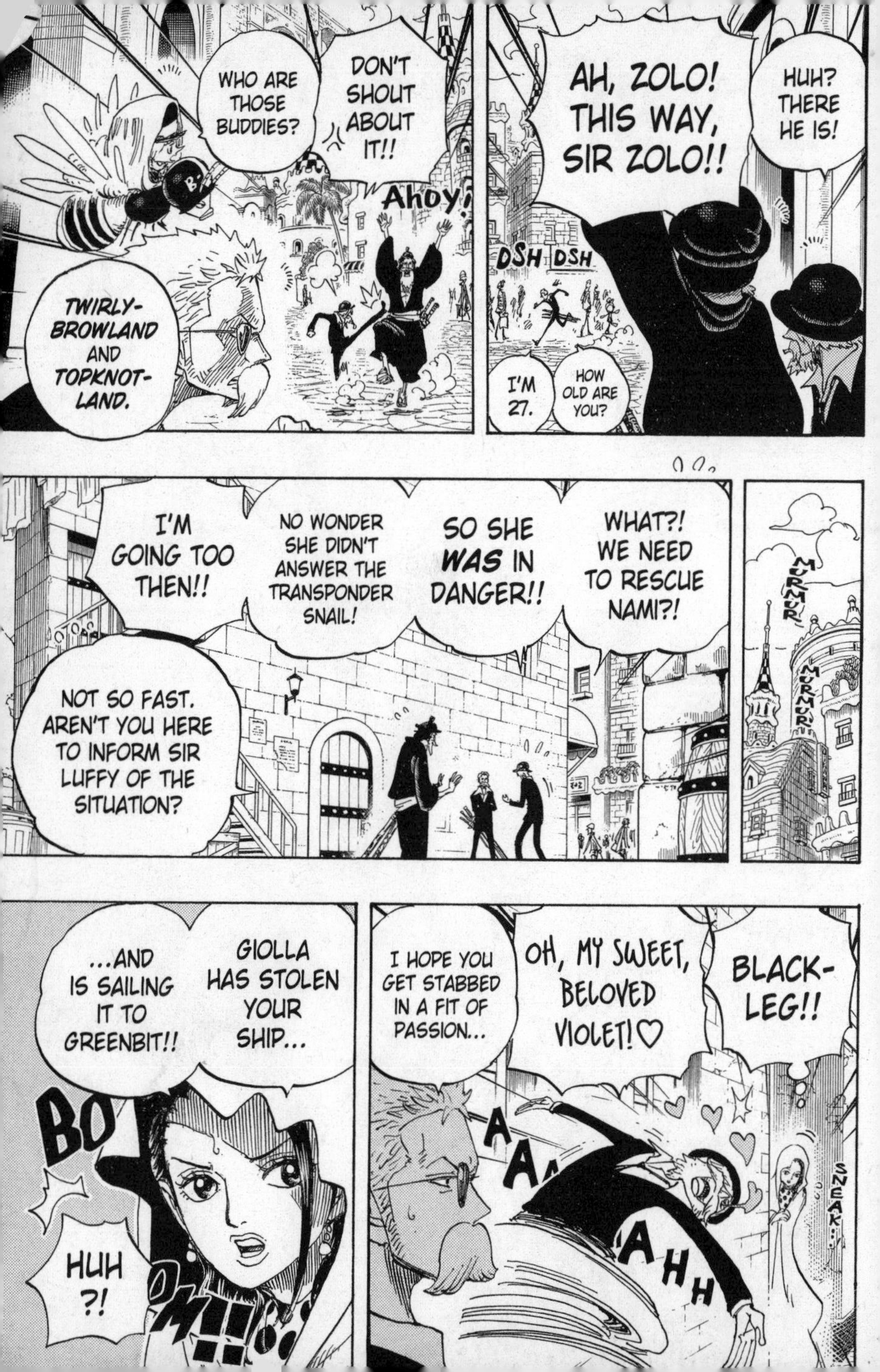
HUH? THERE HE IS!
AH, ZOLO! THIS WAY, SIR ZOLO!!
DSH DSH
HOW OLD ARE YOU?
I'M 27.
DON'T SHOUT ABOUT IT!!
WHO ARE THOSE BUDDIES?
Ahoy!
TWIRLY-BROWLAND AND TOPKNOT-LAND.
MURMUR
MURMUR
WHAT?! WE NEED TO RESCUE NAMI?!
SO SHE WAS IN DANGER!!
NO WONDER SHE DIDN'T ANSWER THE TRANSPONDER SNAIL!
I'M GOING TOO THEN!!
NOT SO FAST. AREN'T YOU HERE TO INFORM SIR LUFFY OF THE SITUATION?
BLACK-LEG!!
OH, MY SWEET, BELOVED VIOLET!♡
I HOPE YOU GET STABBED IN A FIT OF PASSION...
AAAAHH
SNEAK...
GIOLLA HAS STOLEN YOUR SHIP...
...AND IS SAILING IT TO GREENBIT!!
BOOM!!
HUH ?!

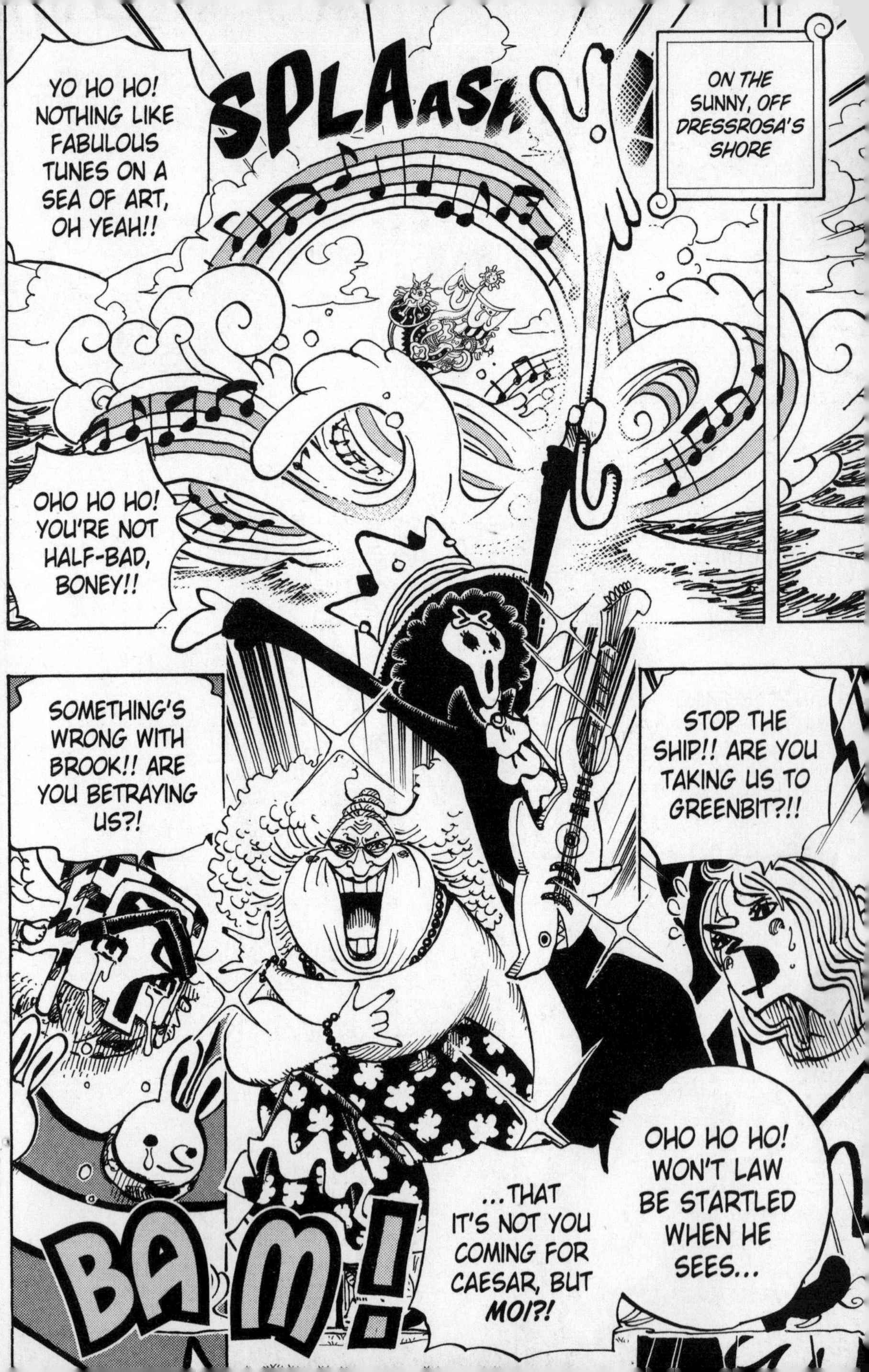
ON THE SUNNY, OFF DRESSROSA'S SHORE
SPLAASH!
YO HO HO! NOTHING LIKE FABULOUS TUNES ON A SEA OF ART, OH YEAH!!
OHO HO HO! YOU'RE NOT HALF-BAD, BONEY!!
STOP THE SHIP!! ARE YOU TAKING US TO GREENBIT?!!
SOMETHING'S WRONG WITH BROOK!! ARE YOU BETRAYING US?!
OHO HO HO! WON'T LAW BE STARTLED WHEN HE SEES...
...THAT IT'S NOT YOU COMING FOR CAESAR, BUT *MOI*?!
BAM!

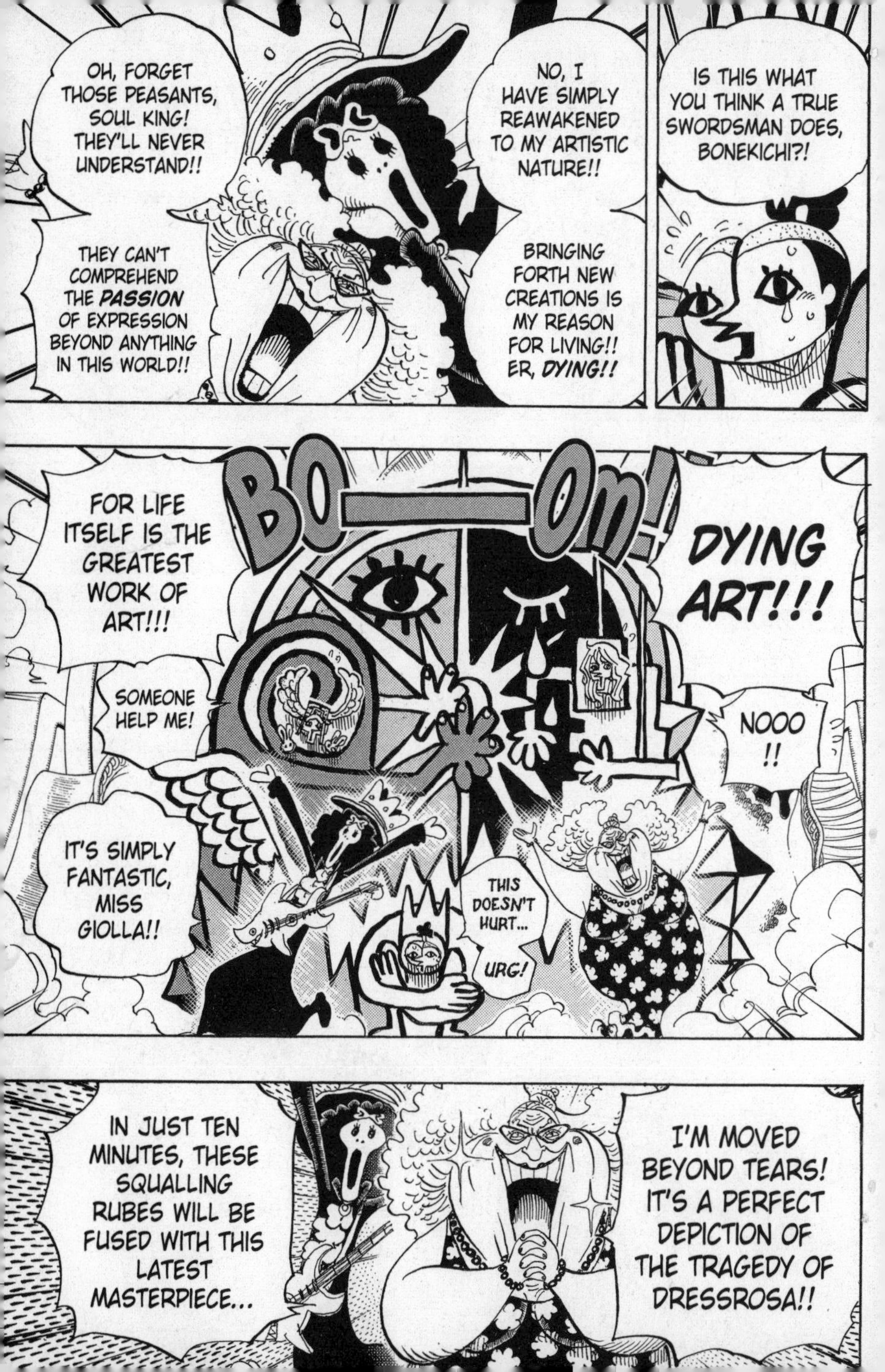
IS THIS WHAT YOU THINK A TRUE SWORDSMAN DOES, BONEKICHI?!
NO, I HAVE SIMPLY REAWAKENED TO MY ARTISTIC NATURE!!
OH, FORGET THOSE PEASANTS, SOUL KING! THEY'LL NEVER UNDERSTAND!!
BRINGING FORTH NEW CREATIONS IS MY REASON FOR LIVING!! ER, DYING!!
THEY CAN'T COMPREHEND THE PASSION OF EXPRESSION BEYOND ANYTHING IN THIS WORLD!!
BO—OM!
DYING ART!!!
FOR LIFE ITSELF IS THE GREATEST WORK OF ART!!!
NOOO !!
SOMEONE HELP ME!
THIS DOESN'T HURT...
URG!
IT'S SIMPLY FANTASTIC, MISS GIOLLA!!
I'M MOVED BEYOND TEARS! IT'S A PERFECT DEPICTION OF THE TRAGEDY OF DRESSROSA!!
IN JUST TEN MINUTES, THESE SQUALLING RUBES WILL BE FUSED WITH THIS LATEST MASTERPIECE...

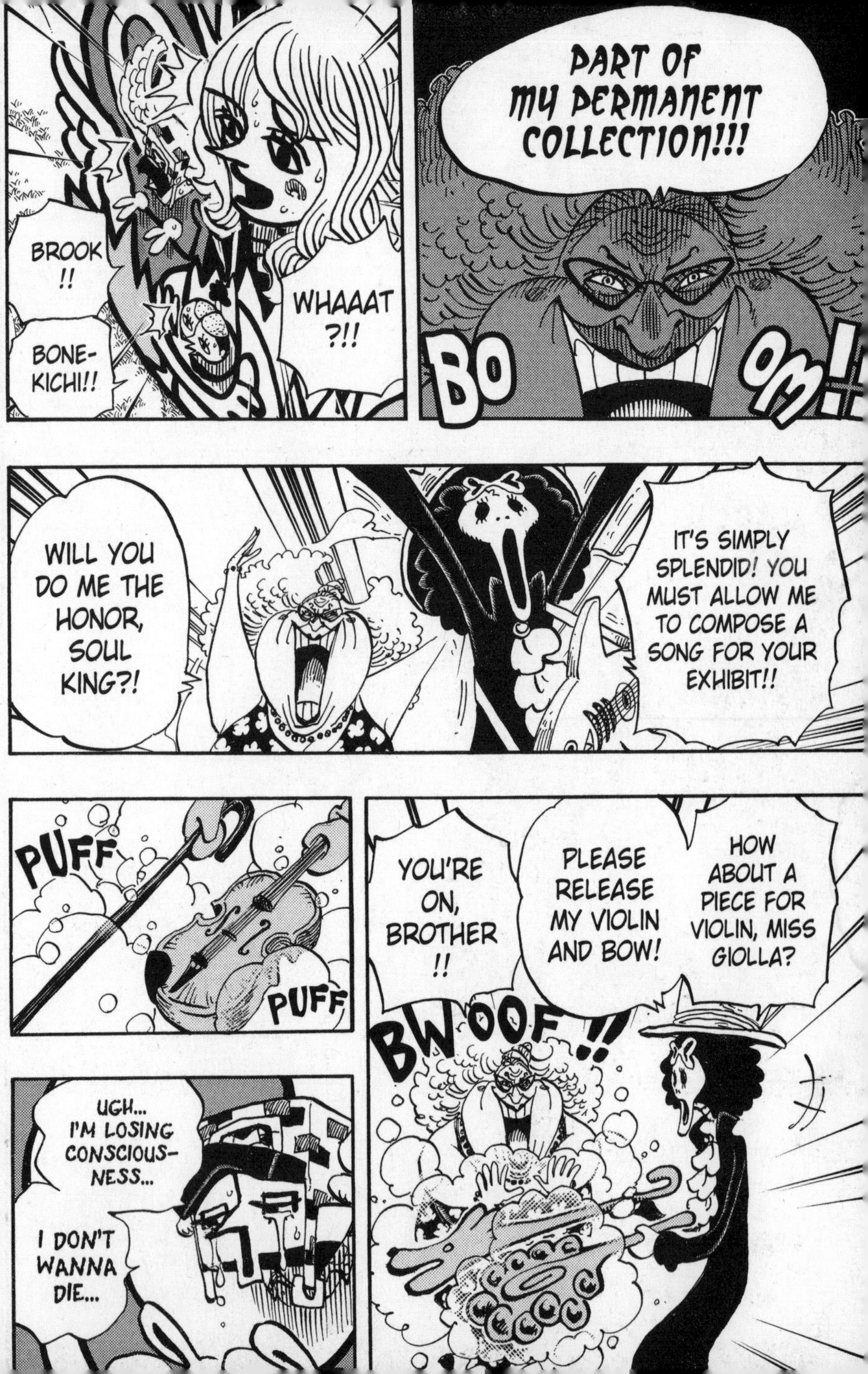
PART OF MY PERMANENT COLLECTION!!!
BOOM!!
WHAAAT?!!
BROOK!!
BONE-KICHI!!
IT'S SIMPLY SPLENDID! YOU MUST ALLOW ME TO COMPOSE A SONG FOR YOUR EXHIBIT!!
WILL YOU DO ME THE HONOR, SOUL KING?!
HOW ABOUT A PIECE FOR VIOLIN, MISS GIOLLA?
PLEASE RELEASE MY VIOLIN AND BOW!
YOU'RE ON, BROTHER!!
BWOOF!!
PUFF
PUFF
UGH... I'M LOSING CONSCIOUSNESS...
I DON'T WANNA DIE...

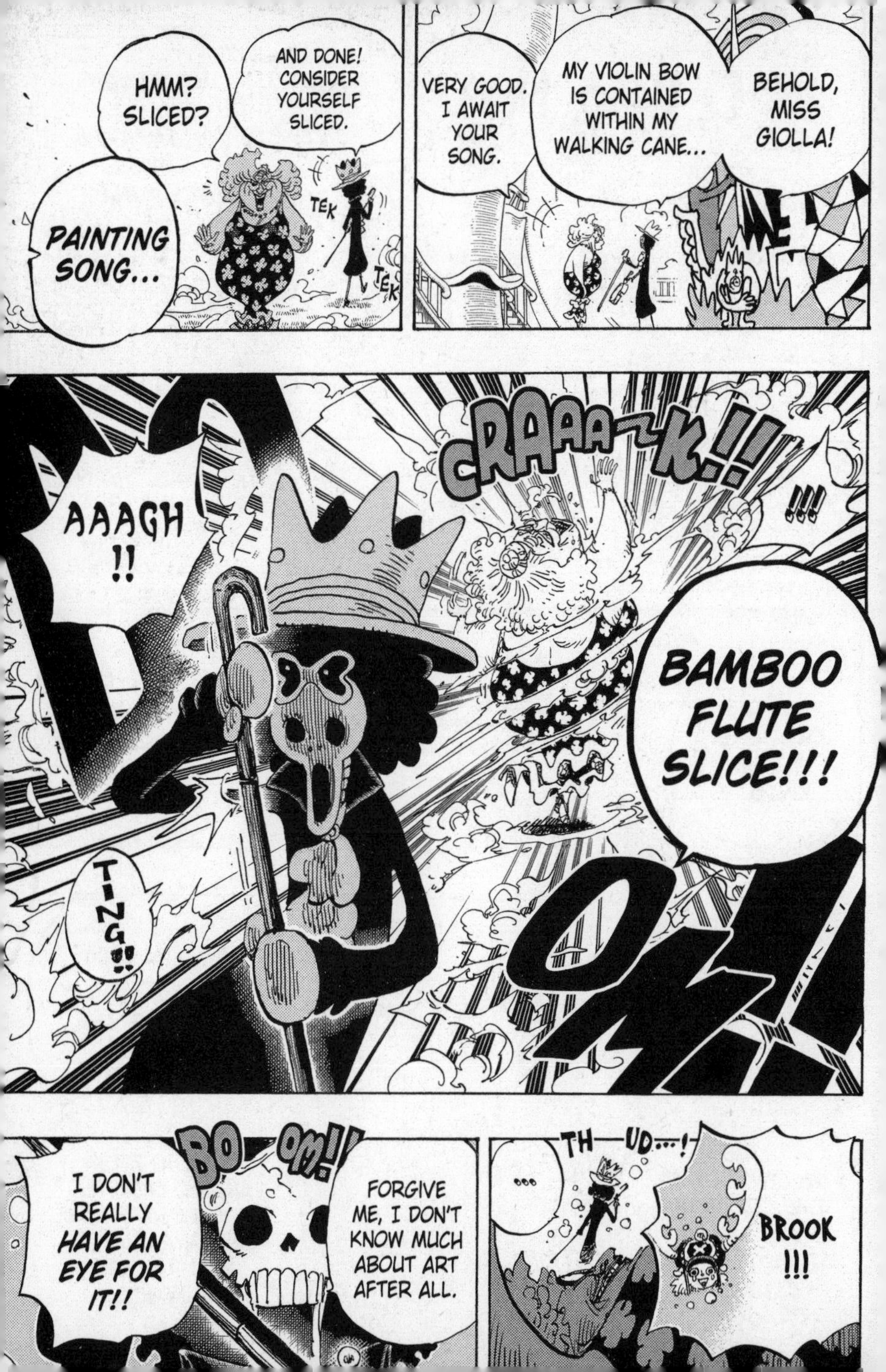
BEHOLD, MISS GIOLLA!
MY VIOLIN BOW IS CONTAINED WITHIN MY WALKING CANE...
VERY GOOD. I AWAIT YOUR SONG.
AND DONE! CONSIDER YOURSELF SLICED.
HMM? SLICED?
TEK
TEK
PAINTING SONG...
CRAAA-K!!!
!!!
AAAGH!!
BAMBOO FLUTE SLICE!!!
TING!!
TH—UD...!
BROOK!!!
...
BO—OM!!
FORGIVE ME, I DON'T KNOW MUCH ABOUT ART AFTER ALL.
I DON'T REALLY HAVE AN EYE FOR IT!!

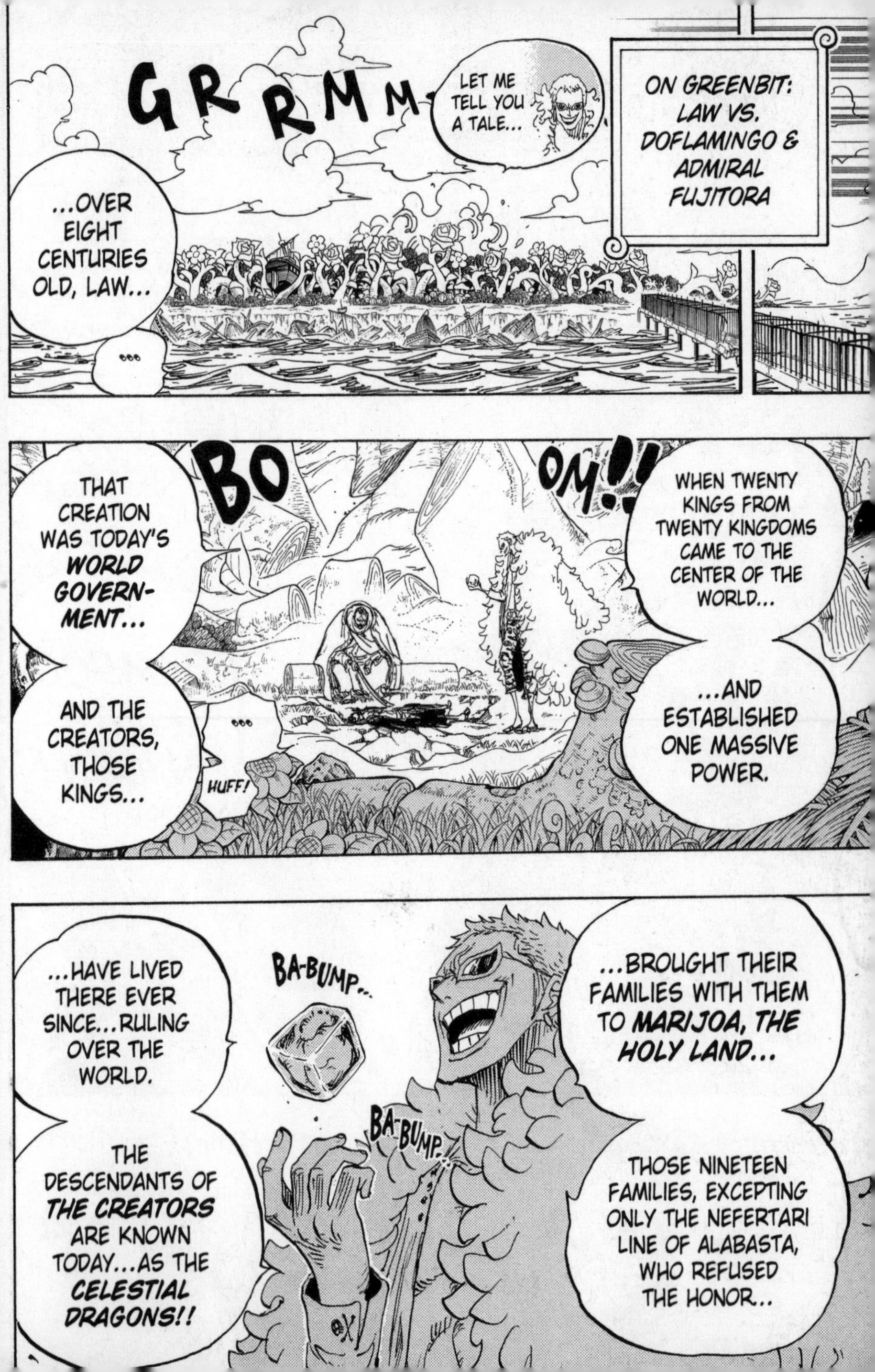
ON GREENBIT: LAW VS. DOFLAMINGO & ADMIRAL FUJITORA
LET ME TELL YOU A TALE...
GRRMM
...OVER EIGHT CENTURIES OLD, LAW...
...
WHEN TWENTY KINGS FROM TWENTY KINGDOMS CAME TO THE CENTER OF THE WORLD...
...AND ESTABLISHED ONE MASSIVE POWER.
BOOM!!
THAT CREATION WAS TODAY'S WORLD GOVERNMENT...
AND THE CREATORS, THOSE KINGS...
...
HUFF!
...BROUGHT THEIR FAMILIES WITH THEM TO MARIJOA, THE HOLY LAND...
THOSE NINETEEN FAMILIES, EXCEPTING ONLY THE NEFERTARI LINE OF ALABASTA, WHO REFUSED THE HONOR..
BA-BUMP..
BA-BUMP..
...HAVE LIVED THERE EVER SINCE...RULING OVER THE WORLD.
THE DESCENDANTS OF THE CREATORS ARE KNOWN TODAY...AS THE CELESTIAL DRAGONS!!

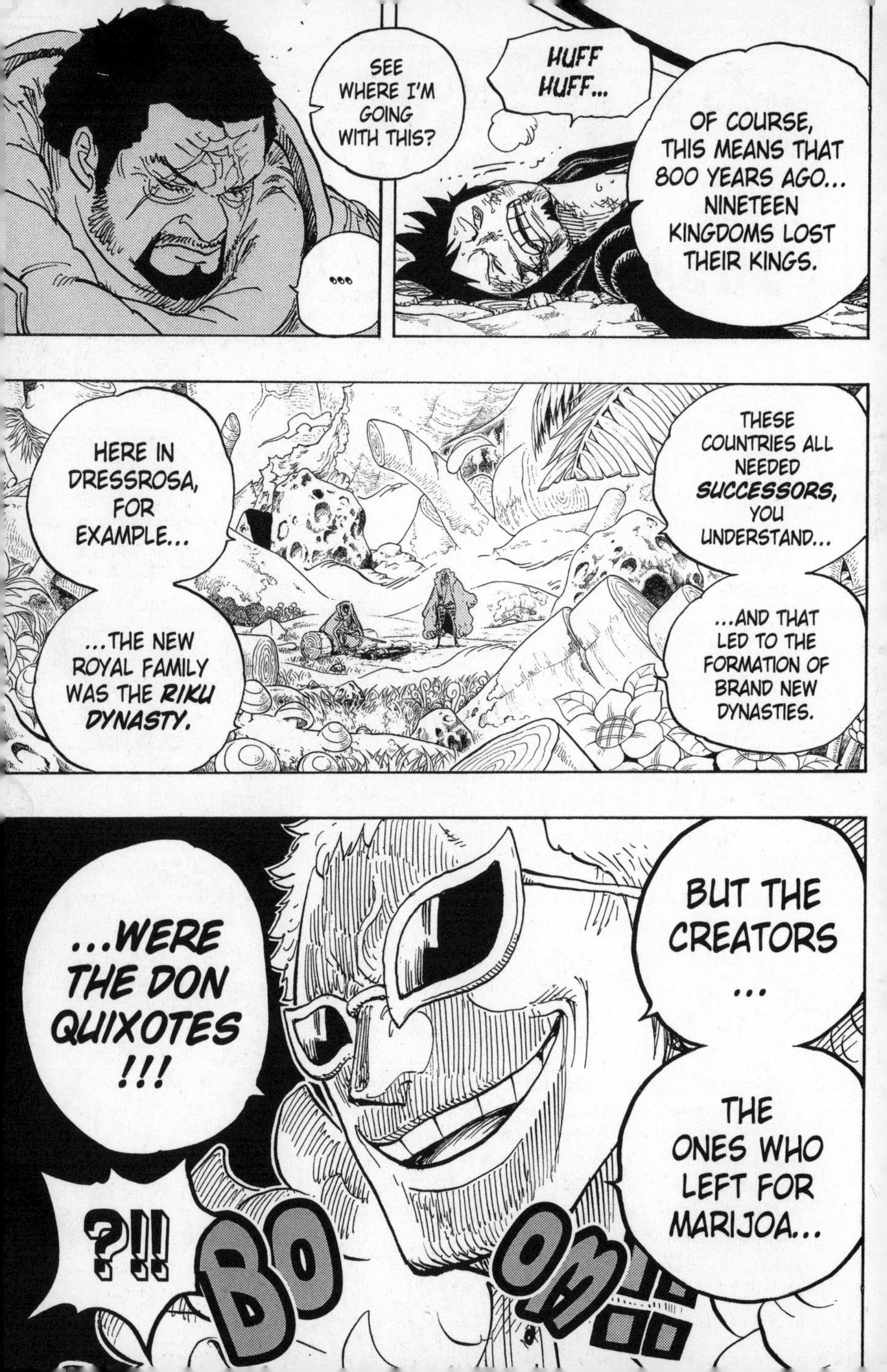
HUFF HUFF...
OF COURSE, THIS MEANS THAT 800 YEARS AGO... NINETEEN KINGDOMS LOST THEIR KINGS.
SEE WHERE I'M GOING WITH THIS?
...
THESE COUNTRIES ALL NEEDED SUCCESSORS, YOU UNDERSTAND...
...AND THAT LED TO THE FORMATION OF BRAND NEW DYNASTIES.
HERE IN DRESSROSA, FOR EXAMPLE...
...THE NEW ROYAL FAMILY WAS THE RIKU DYNASTY.
BUT THE CREATORS ...
THE ONES WHO LEFT FOR MARIJOA...
...WERE THE DON QUIXOTES !!!
?!!
BOOM!!

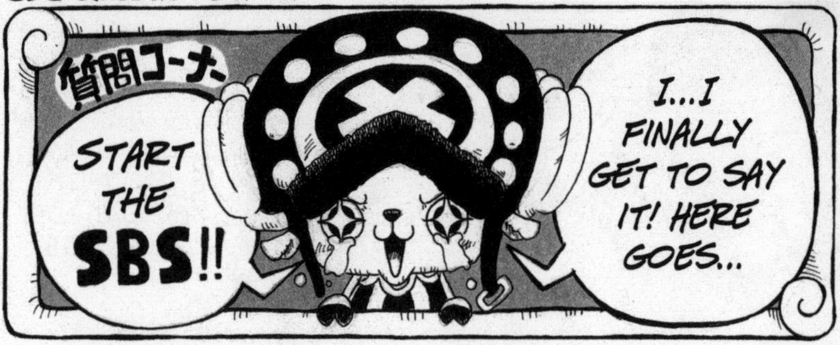
質問コーナー
START THE SBS!!
I...I FINALLY GET TO SAY IT! HERE GOES...

(Takashi Takamatsu, Saitama)

A: **Whaaaaaaat?!! Σ(•□•)**
You can do that? You can start the segment from up there?! ⬆
Well...sure, I guess... Let's begin the SBS...

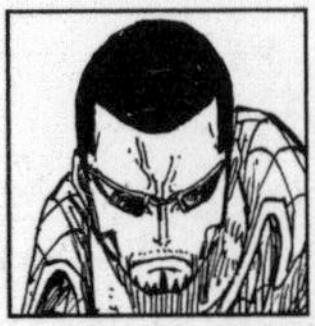

Q: That's Mr. SBS to you.

--Kimurin

A: **Whaaaaaaat?!! Σ(•□•)**
I'm sorry. Start the...Mr. SBS.

Q: My dad can shoot "Land of the Dead" out of his butt. Does he have the power of the Gas-Gas Fruit?

--Okku

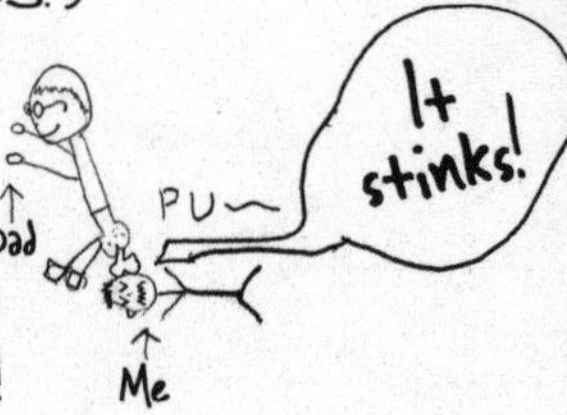
It stinks!
PU~
Dad
Me

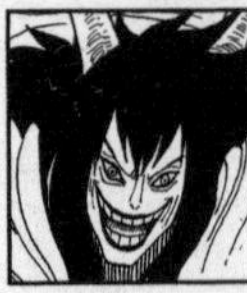

A: Those are **farts. Farts!**
It's "Land of the Farts."

Q: I'm sure you must get letters all the time pointing out that you drew the "Death" tattoos on Law's fingers wrong… In my opinion, whenever this happens, it's because Law is using Chambres on the parts above the knuckles and below the knuckles to switch them around! Wow, that Op-Op Fruit comes in real handy (if you know what I mean)!!

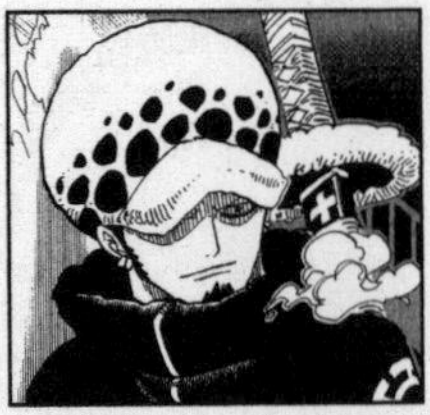

--Kamiki

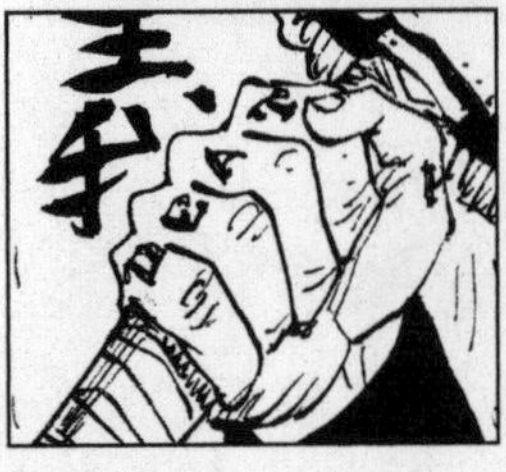

A: Um...yeah. I get a lot of those letters. They all say I screwed up! (cries) That's what everyone says!! But you know what? You're right on the money!! That's right. If they're ever facing the wrong direction or missing entirely...it was all Chambres!!!

Chapter 723:
CHANGE OF PLANS

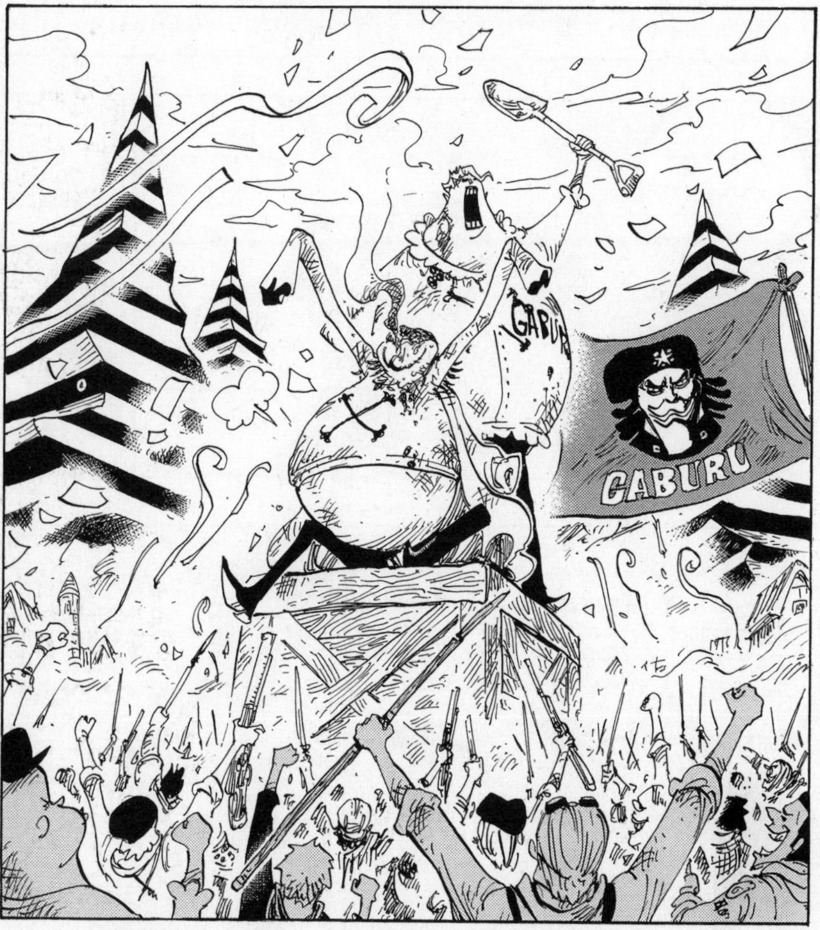
GABURU
GABURU

CARIBOU'S NEW WORLD KEE HEE HEE, VOL. 40:
"GABURU THE HERO"

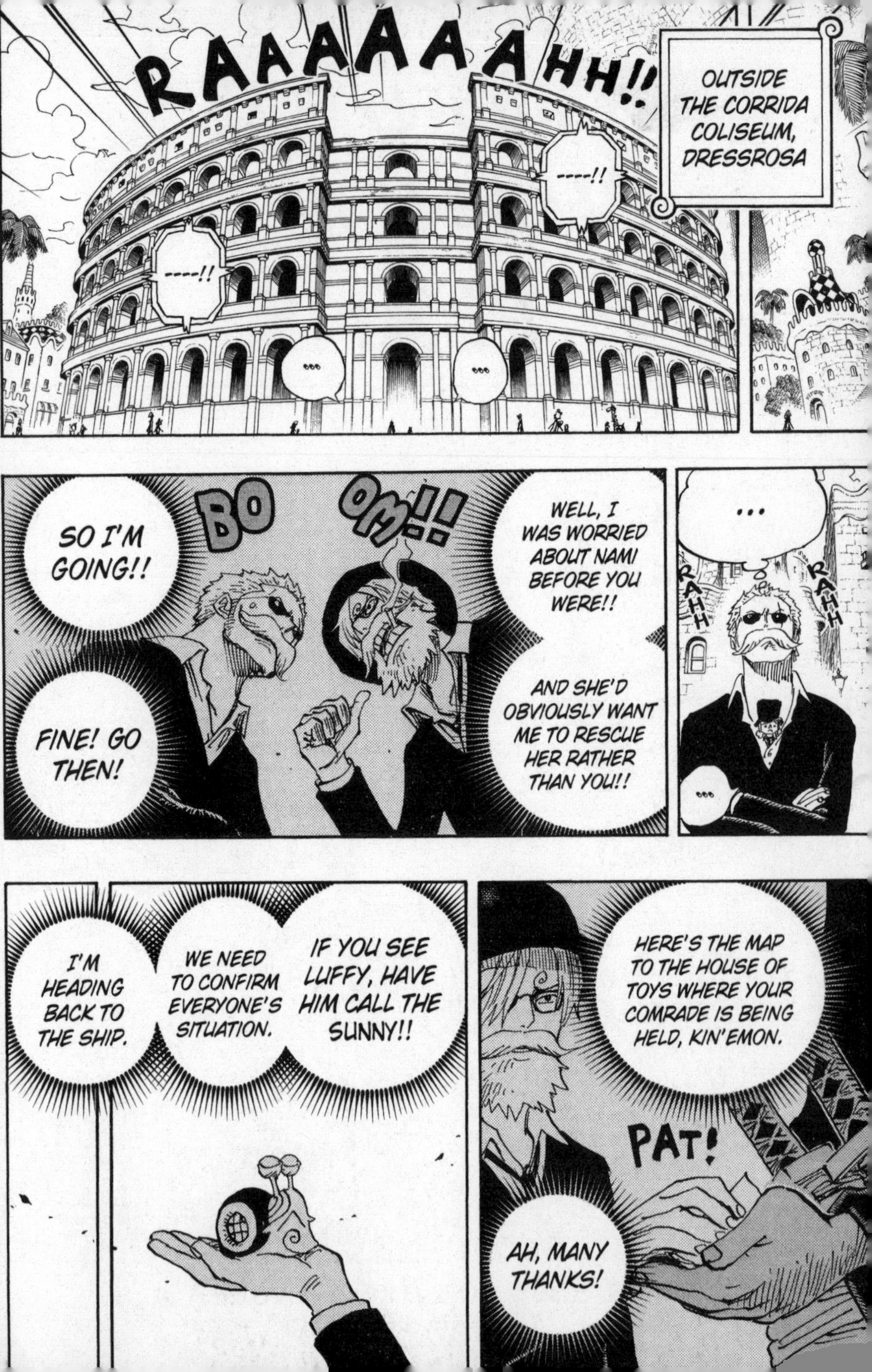
OUTSIDE THE CORRIDA COLISEUM, DRESSROSA
RAAAAAAAHH!!
----!!
----!!
...
...
...
RAHH
RAHH
...
WELL, I WAS WORRIED ABOUT NAMI BEFORE YOU WERE!!
AND SHE'D OBVIOUSLY WANT ME TO RESCUE HER RATHER THAN YOU!!
BOOM!!
SO I'M GOING!!
FINE! GO THEN!
HERE'S THE MAP TO THE HOUSE OF TOYS WHERE YOUR COMRADE IS BEING HELD, KIN'EMON.
PAT!
AH, MANY THANKS!
IF YOU SEE LUFFY, HAVE HIM CALL THE SUNNY!!
WE NEED TO CONFIRM EVERYONE'S SITUATION.
I'M HEADING BACK TO THE SHIP.

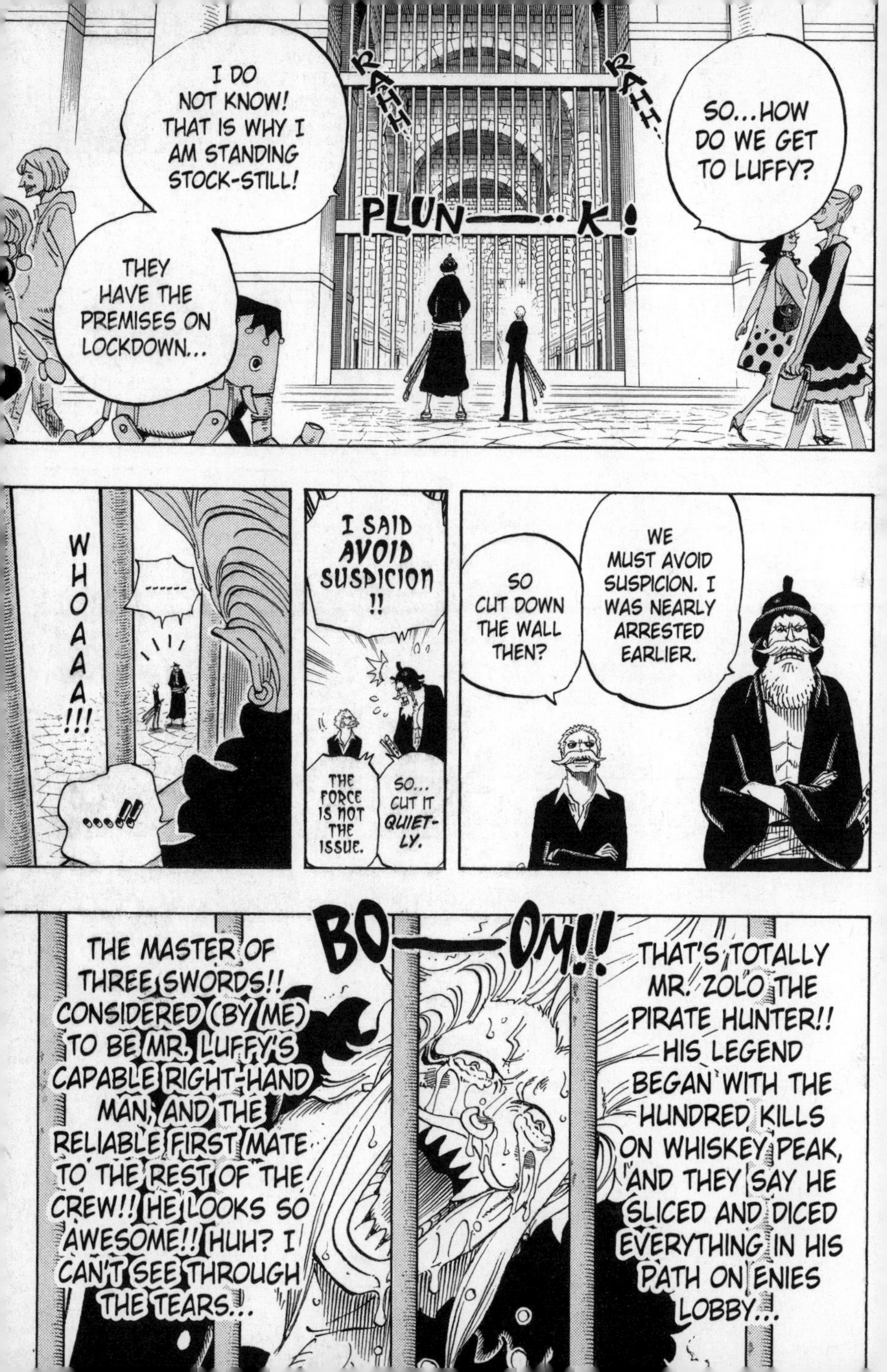
RAHH
SO...HOW DO WE GET TO LUFFY?
RAHH
PLUN—...K!
I DO NOT KNOW! THAT IS WHY I AM STANDING STOCK-STILL!
THEY HAVE THE PREMISES ON LOCKDOWN...
WE MUST AVOID SUSPICION. I WAS NEARLY ARRESTED EARLIER.
SO CUT DOWN THE WALL THEN?
I SAID AVOID SUSPICION!!
SO... CUT IT QUIET-LY.
THE FORCE IS NOT THE ISSUE.

WHOAAAA!!!
...!!
THAT'S TOTALLY MR. ZOLO THE PIRATE HUNTER!! HIS LEGEND BEGAN WITH THE HUNDRED KILLS ON WHISKEY PEAK, AND THEY SAY HE SLICED AND DICED EVERYTHING IN HIS PATH ON ENIES LOBBY...
BO—OM!!
THE MASTER OF THREE SWORDS!! CONSIDERED (BY ME) TO BE MR. LUFFY'S CAPABLE RIGHT-HAND MAN, AND THE RELIABLE FIRST MATE TO THE REST OF THE CREW!! HE LOOKS SO AWESOME!! HUH? I CAN'T SEE THROUGH THE TEARS...

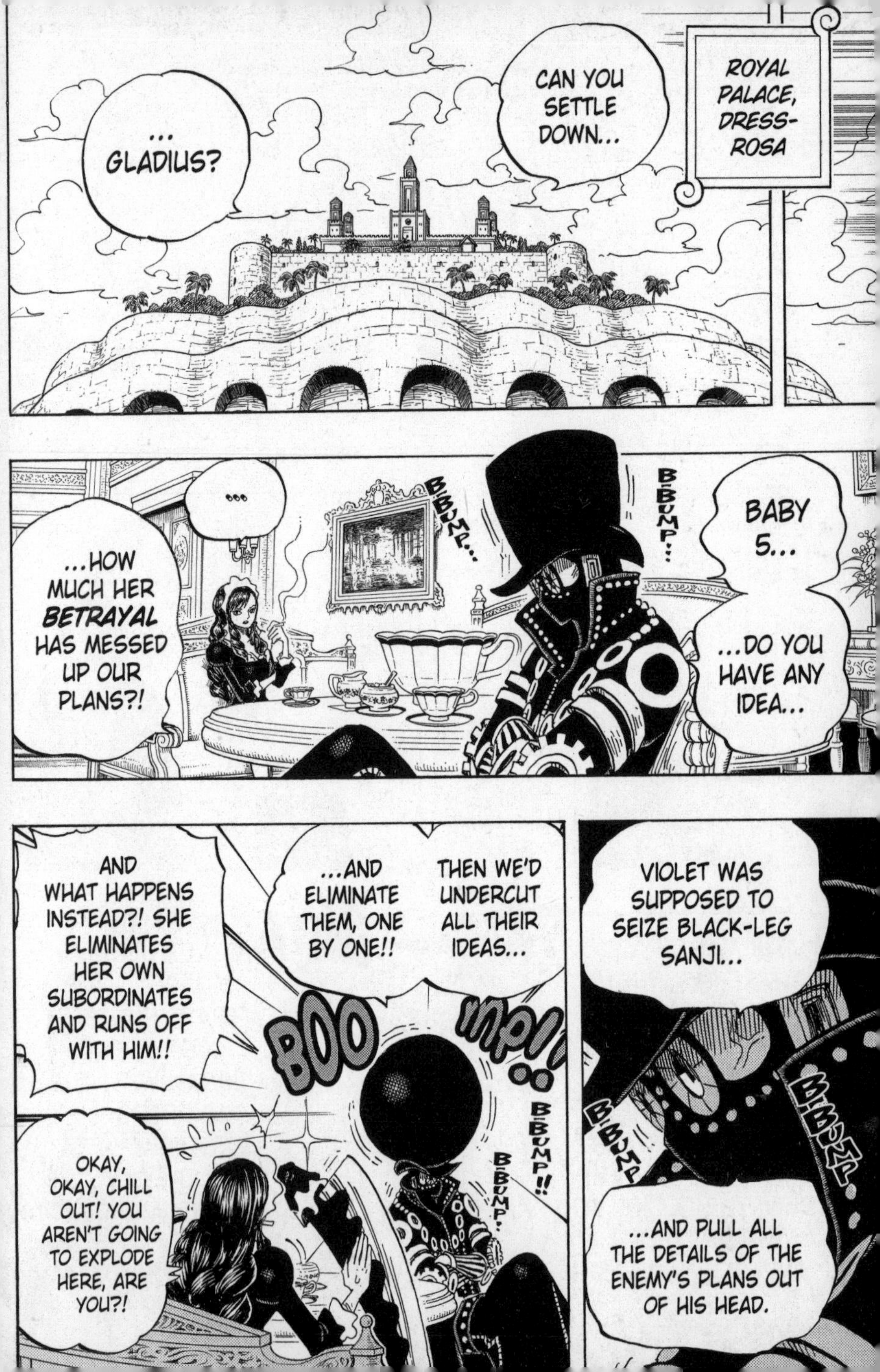
ROYAL PALACE, DRESS-ROSA
CAN YOU SETTLE DOWN...
... GLADIUS?
BABY 5...
...DO YOU HAVE ANY IDEA...
B-BUMP...
B-BUMP...
...HOW MUCH HER BETRAYAL HAS MESSED UP OUR PLANS?!
...
VIOLET WAS SUPPOSED TO SEIZE BLACK-LEG SANJI...
B-BUMP
B-BUMP
...AND PULL ALL THE DETAILS OF THE ENEMY'S PLANS OUT OF HIS HEAD.
THEN WE'D UNDERCUT ALL THEIR IDEAS...
...AND ELIMINATE THEM, ONE BY ONE!!
AND WHAT HAPPENS INSTEAD?! SHE ELIMINATES HER OWN SUBORDINATES AND RUNS OFF WITH HIM!!
BOOM!!
B-BUMP!!
B-BUMP...
OKAY, OKAY, CHILL OUT! YOU AREN'T GOING TO EXPLODE HERE, ARE YOU?!

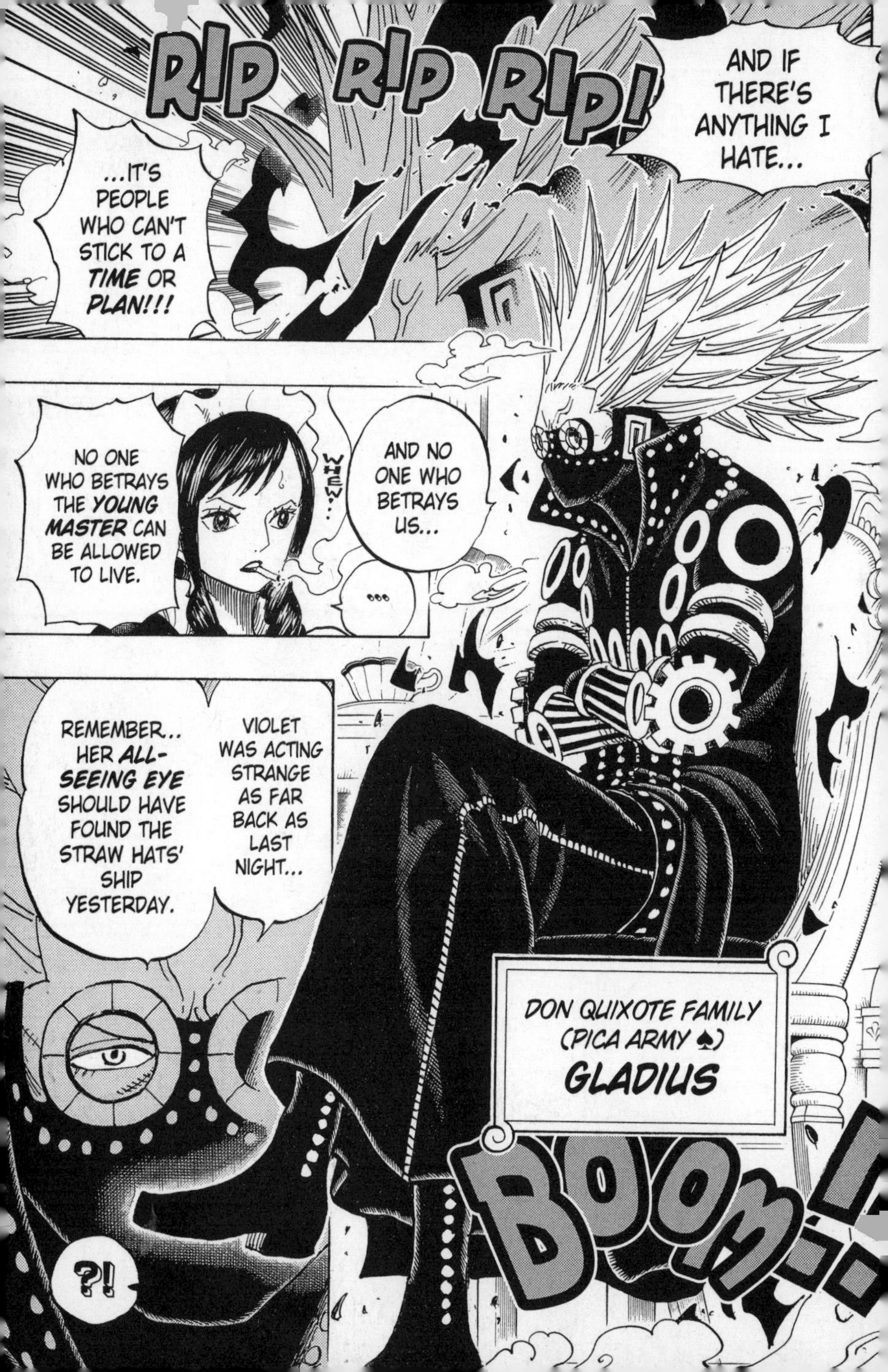
RIP RIP RIP!
AND IF THERE'S ANYTHING I HATE...
...IT'S PEOPLE WHO CAN'T STICK TO A *TIME* OR *PLAN!!!*
NO ONE WHO BETRAYS THE *YOUNG MASTER* CAN BE ALLOWED TO LIVE.
WHEW...
AND NO ONE WHO BETRAYS US...
...
DON QUIXOTE FAMILY (PICA ARMY ♠) GLADIUS
BOOM..!!
VIOLET WAS ACTING STRANGE AS FAR BACK AS LAST NIGHT...
REMEMBER... HER *ALL-SEEING EYE* SHOULD HAVE FOUND THE STRAW HATS' SHIP YESTERDAY.
?!

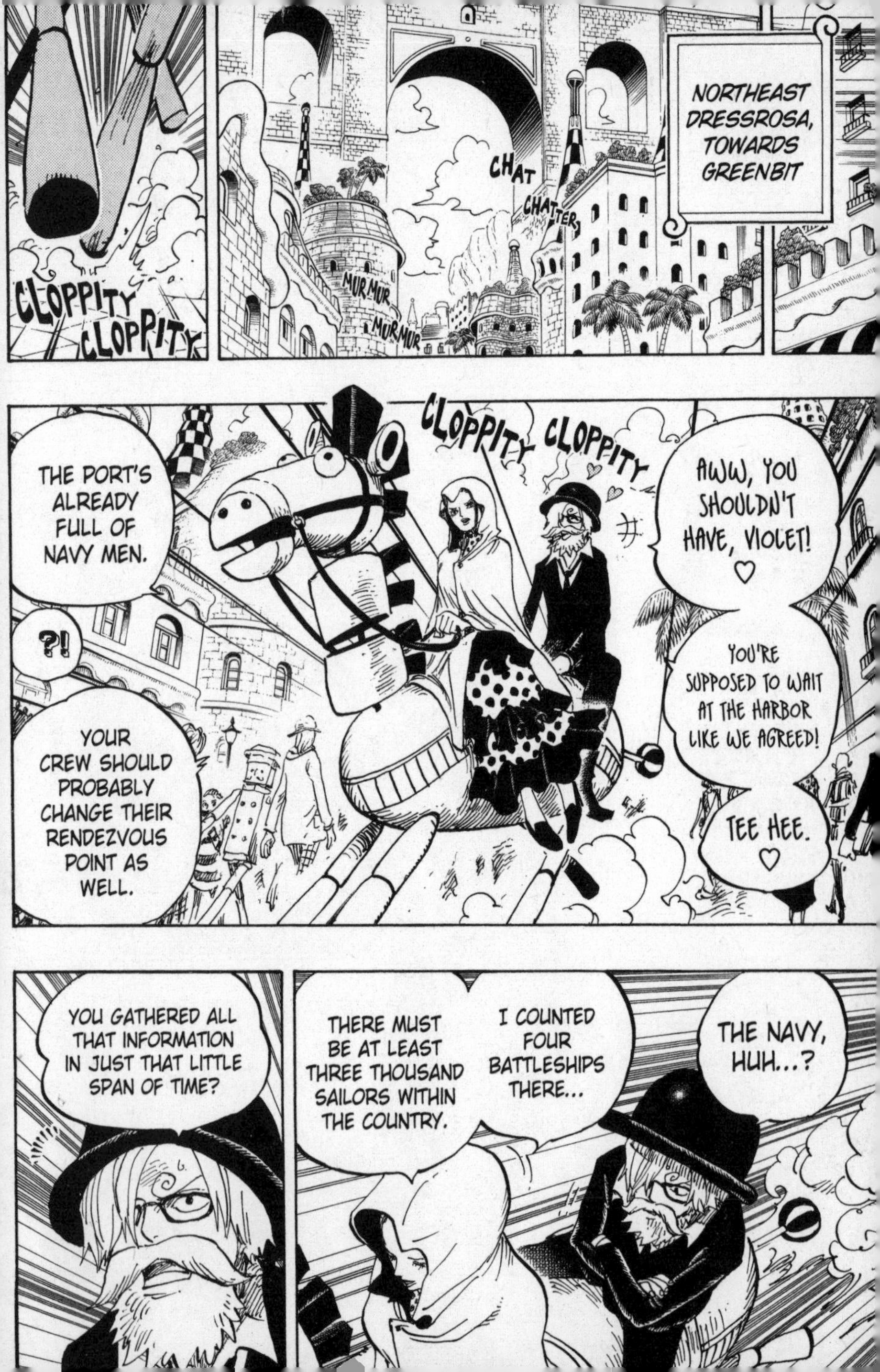
NORTHEAST DRESSROSA, TOWARDS GREENBIT
CHAT
CHATTER
MURMUR
MURMUR
CLOPPITY CLOPPITY
CLOPPITY CLOPPITY
AWW, YOU SHOULDN'T HAVE, VIOLET! ♡
YOU'RE SUPPOSED TO WAIT AT THE HARBOR LIKE WE AGREED!
TEE HEE. ♡
THE PORT'S ALREADY FULL OF NAVY MEN.
?!
YOUR CREW SHOULD PROBABLY CHANGE THEIR RENDEZVOUS POINT AS WELL.
THE NAVY, HUH...?
I COUNTED FOUR BATTLESHIPS THERE...
THERE MUST BE AT LEAST THREE THOUSAND SAILORS WITHIN THE COUNTRY.
YOU GATHERED ALL THAT INFORMATION IN JUST THAT LITTLE SPAN OF TIME?

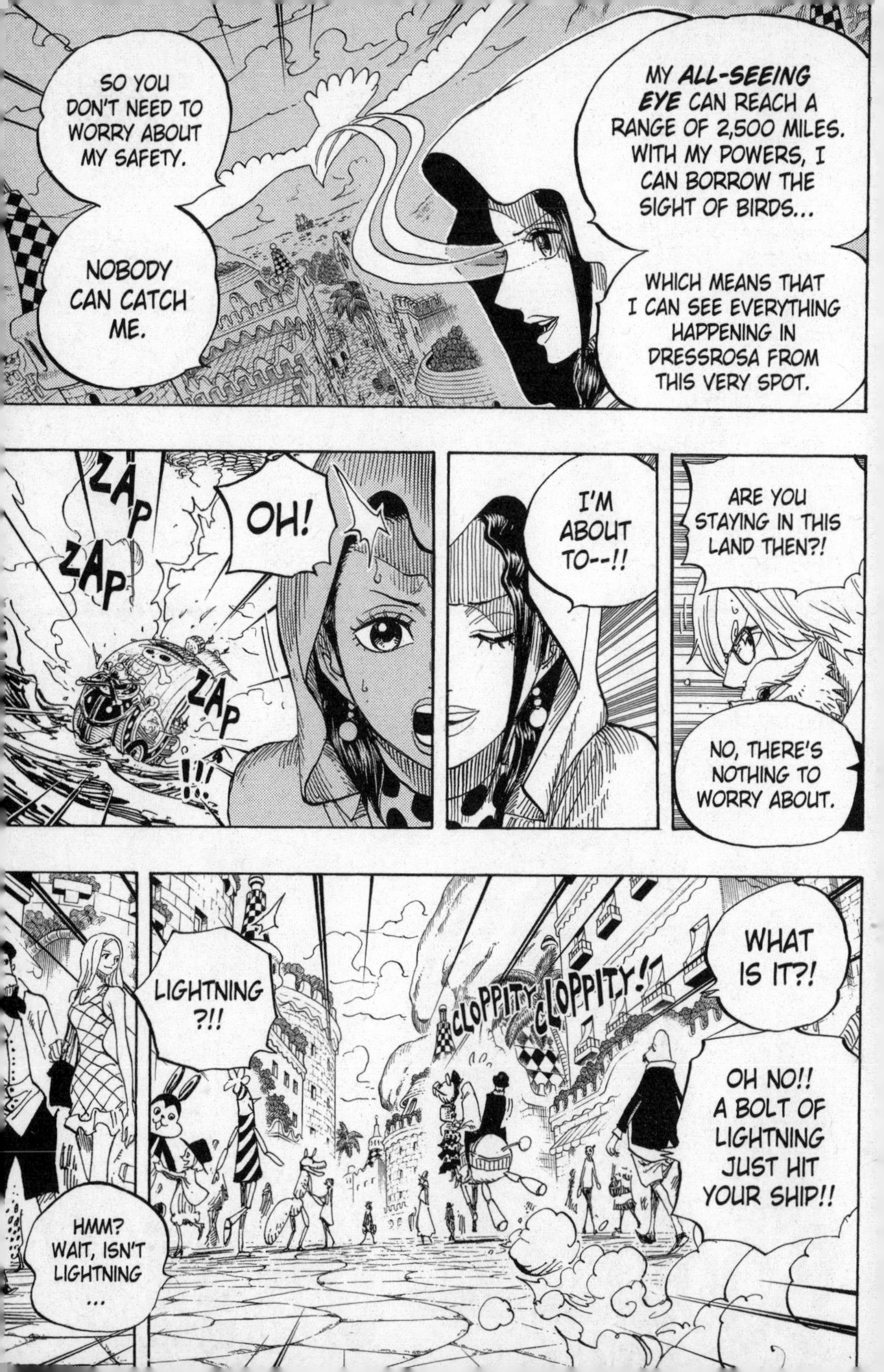
MY ALL-SEEING EYE CAN REACH A RANGE OF 2,500 MILES. WITH MY POWERS, I CAN BORROW THE SIGHT OF BIRDS...
WHICH MEANS THAT I CAN SEE EVERYTHING HAPPENING IN DRESSROSA FROM THIS VERY SPOT.
SO YOU DON'T NEED TO WORRY ABOUT MY SAFETY.
NOBODY CAN CATCH ME.
ARE YOU STAYING IN THIS LAND THEN?!
NO, THERE'S NOTHING TO WORRY ABOUT.
I'M ABOUT TO--!!
OH!
ZAP
ZAP
ZAP
!!!
WHAT IS IT?!
OH NO!! A BOLT OF LIGHTNING JUST HIT YOUR SHIP!!
CLOPPITY CLOPPITY!
LIGHTNING ?!!
HMM? WAIT, ISN'T LIGHTNING ...

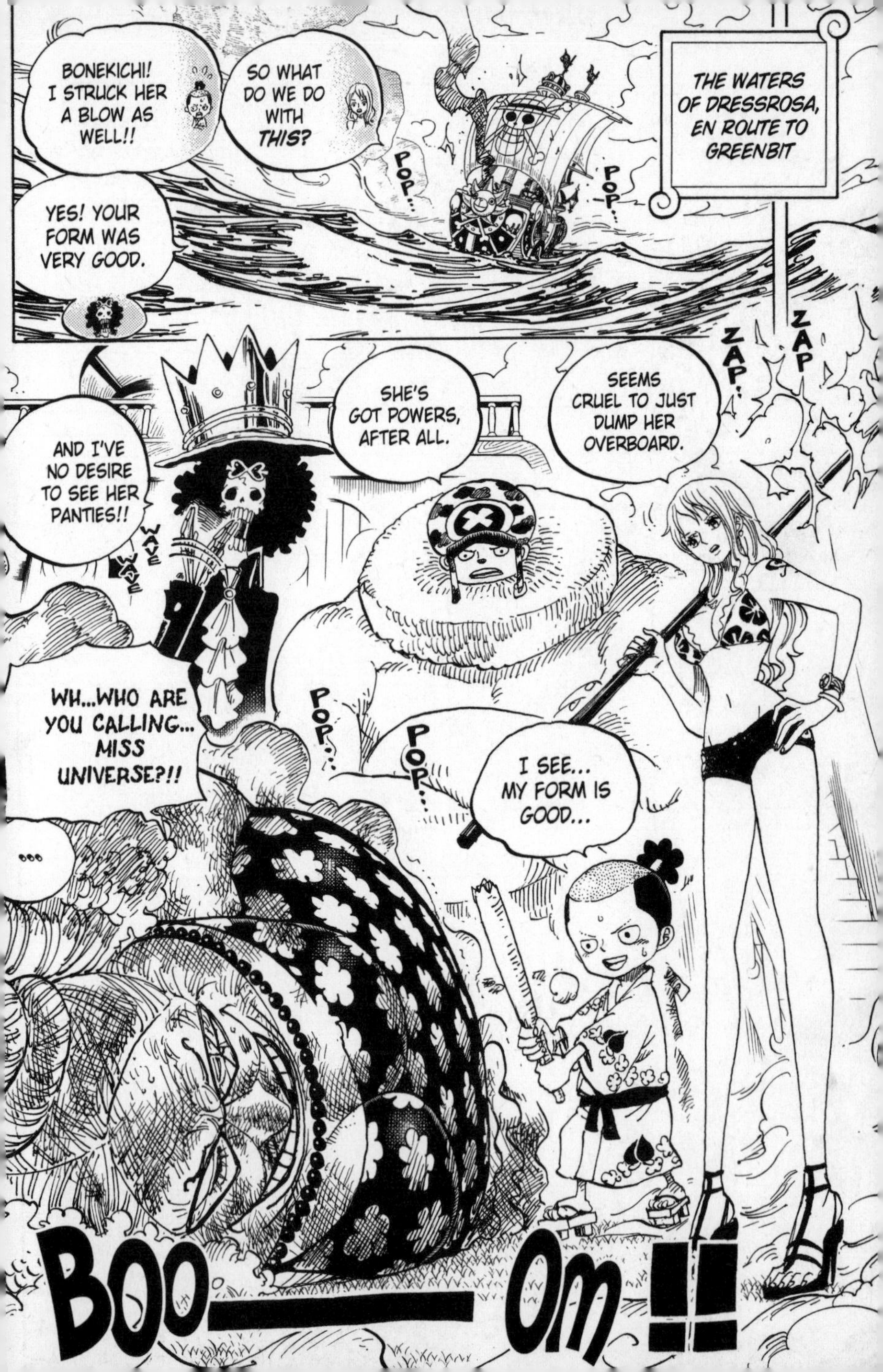
THE WATERS OF DRESSROSA, EN ROUTE TO GREENBIT
POP...
POP...
SO WHAT DO WE DO WITH THIS?
BONEKICHI! I STRUCK HER A BLOW AS WELL!!
YES! YOUR FORM WAS VERY GOOD.
ZAP
ZAP
SEEMS CRUEL TO JUST DUMP HER OVERBOARD.
SHE'S GOT POWERS, AFTER ALL.
AND I'VE NO DESIRE TO SEE HER PANTIES!!
WAVE
WAVE
I SEE... MY FORM IS GOOD...
POP...
POP...
WH...WHO ARE YOU CALLING... MISS UNIVERSE?!!
...
BOO—OM!!

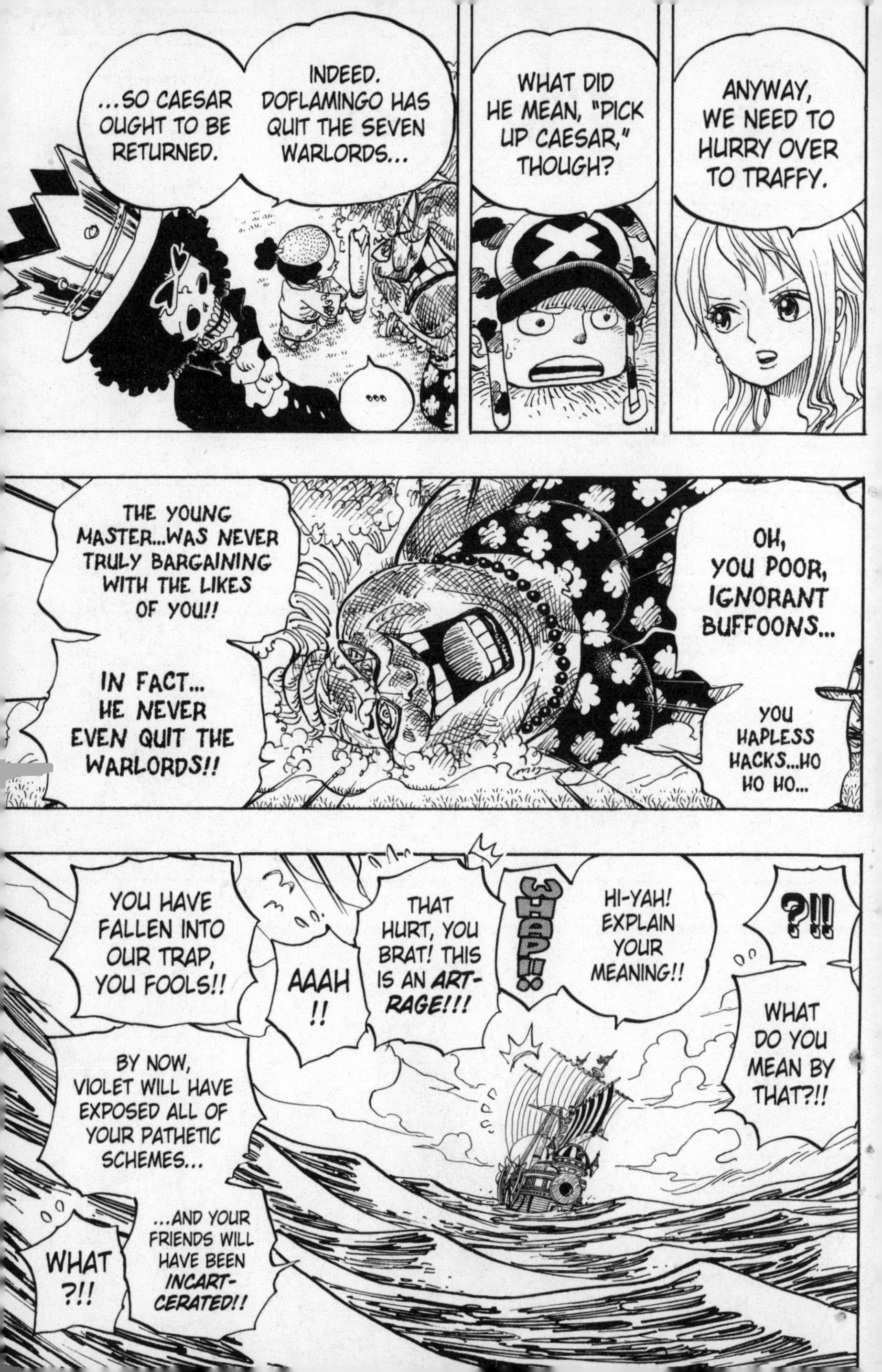
ANYWAY, WE NEED TO HURRY OVER TO TRAFFY.
WHAT DID HE MEAN, "PICK UP CAESAR," THOUGH?
INDEED. DOFLAMINGO HAS QUIT THE SEVEN WARLORDS...
...SO CAESAR OUGHT TO BE RETURNED.
...
OH, YOU POOR, IGNORANT BUFFOONS...
YOU HAPLESS HACKS...HO HO HO...
THE YOUNG MASTER...WAS NEVER TRULY BARGAINING WITH THE LIKES OF YOU!!
IN FACT... HE NEVER EVEN QUIT THE WARLORDS!!
?!!
WHAT DO YOU MEAN BY THAT?!!
HI-YAH! EXPLAIN YOUR MEANING!!
WHAP!!
THAT HURT, YOU BRAT! THIS IS AN *ART-RAGE!!!*
AAAH!!
YOU HAVE FALLEN INTO OUR TRAP, YOU FOOLS!!
BY NOW, VIOLET WILL HAVE EXPOSED ALL OF YOUR PATHETIC SCHEMES...
...AND YOUR FRIENDS WILL HAVE BEEN *INCARCERATED!!*
WHAT?!!

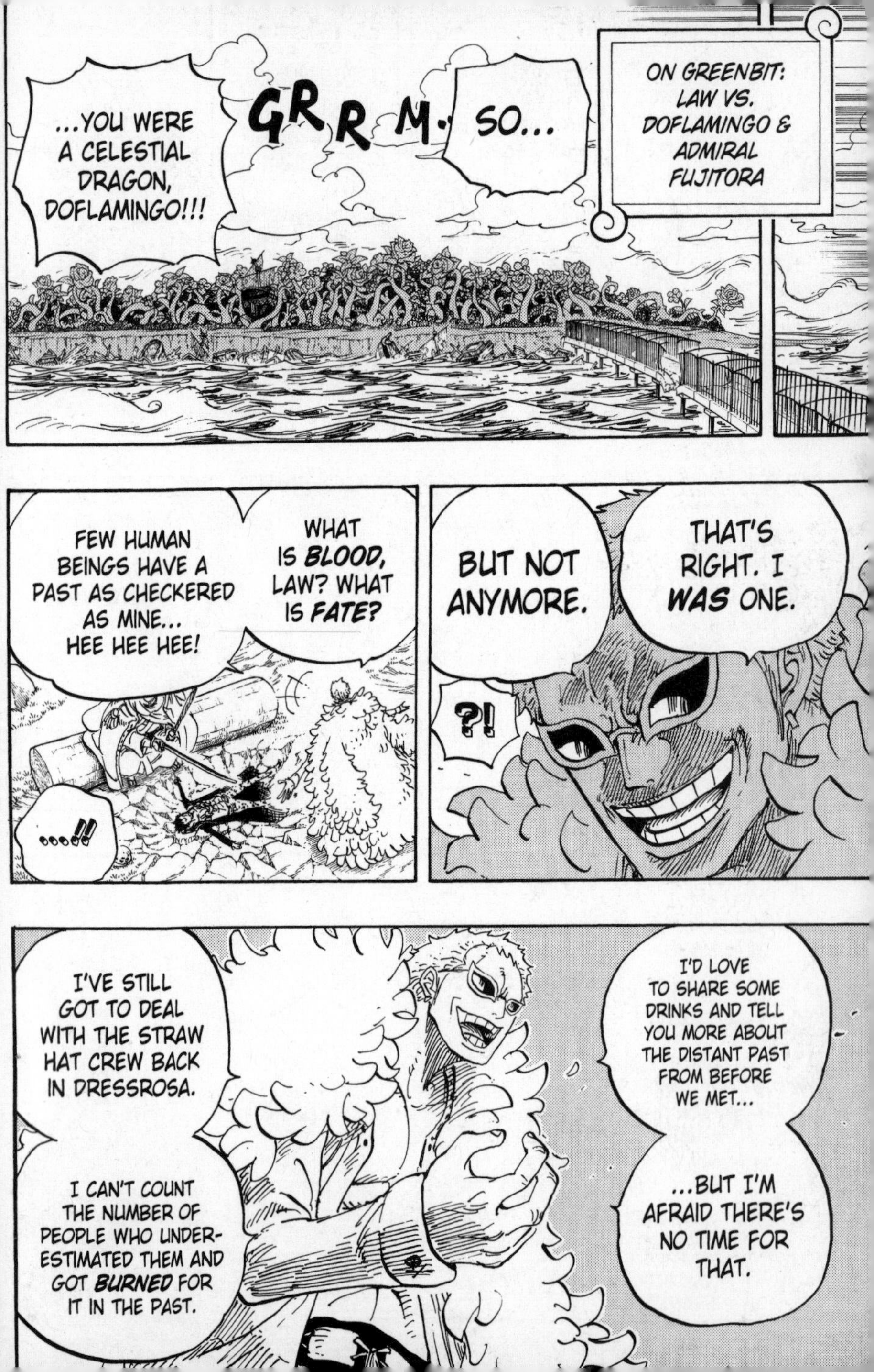
ON GREENBIT: LAW VS. DOFLAMINGO & ADMIRAL FUJITORA
SO...
GRRM.
...YOU WERE A CELESTIAL DRAGON, DOFLAMINGO!!!
THAT'S RIGHT. I WAS ONE.
BUT NOT ANYMORE.
?!
WHAT IS BLOOD, LAW? WHAT IS FATE?
FEW HUMAN BEINGS HAVE A PAST AS CHECKERED AS MINE... HEE HEE HEE!
....!!
I'D LOVE TO SHARE SOME DRINKS AND TELL YOU MORE ABOUT THE DISTANT PAST FROM BEFORE WE MET...
I'VE STILL GOT TO DEAL WITH THE STRAW HAT CREW BACK IN DRESSROSA.
...BUT I'M AFRAID THERE'S NO TIME FOR THAT.
I CAN'T COUNT THE NUMBER OF PEOPLE WHO UNDER-ESTIMATED THEM AND GOT BURNED FOR IT IN THE PAST.

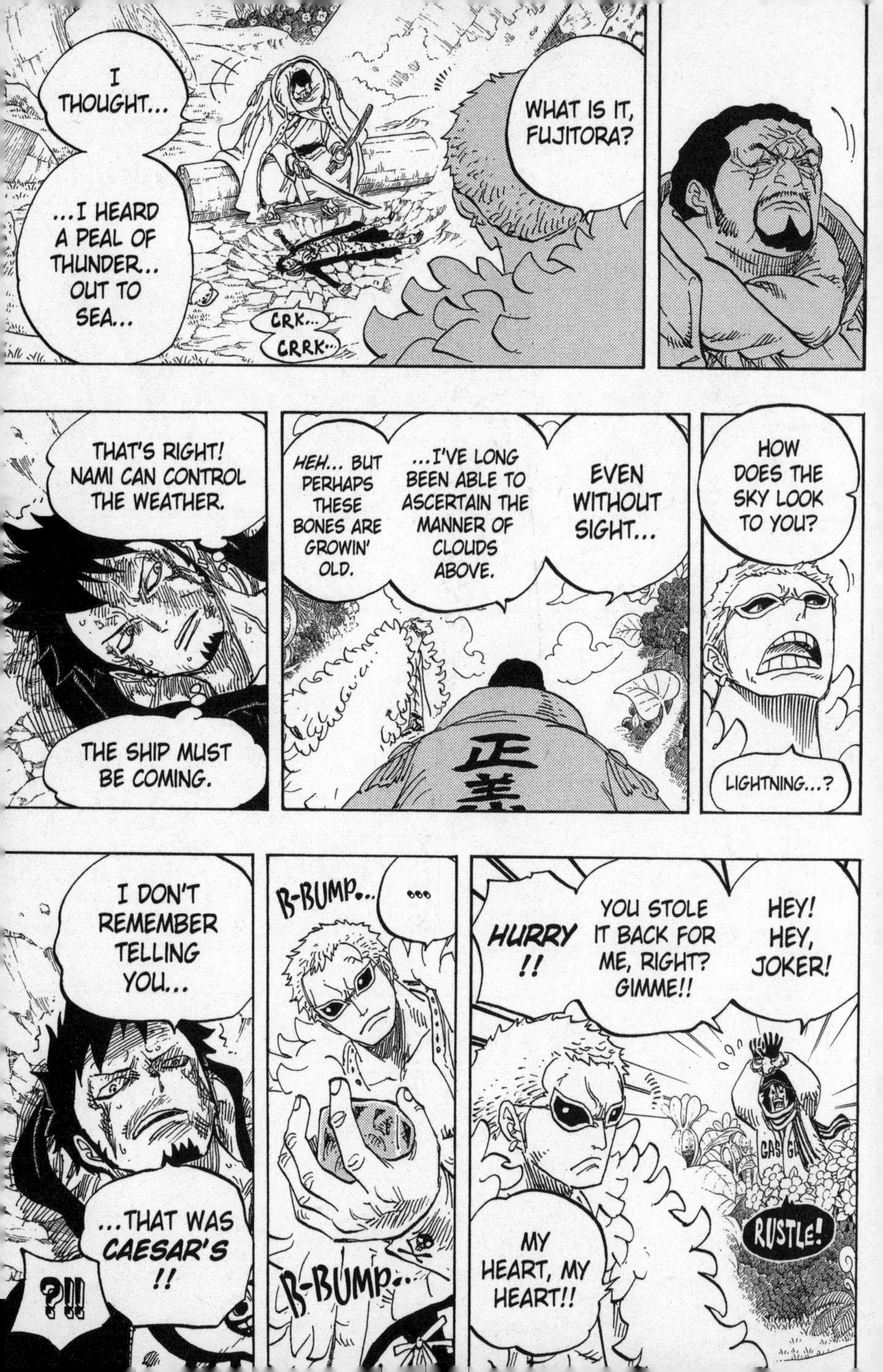
WHAT IS IT, FUJITORA?
I THOUGHT...
...I HEARD A PEAL OF THUNDER... OUT TO SEA...
CRK...
CRRK...
HOW DOES THE SKY LOOK TO YOU?
LIGHTNING...?
EVEN WITHOUT SIGHT...
...I'VE LONG BEEN ABLE TO ASCERTAIN THE MANNER OF CLOUDS ABOVE.
HEH... BUT PERHAPS THESE BONES ARE GROWIN' OLD.
THAT'S RIGHT! NAMI CAN CONTROL THE WEATHER.
THE SHIP MUST BE COMING.
HEY! HEY, JOKER!
YOU STOLE IT BACK FOR ME, RIGHT? GIMME!!
HURRY!!
RUSTLE!
MY HEART, MY HEART!!
B-BUMP...
...
B-BUMP...
I DON'T REMEMBER TELLING YOU...
...THAT WAS CAESAR'S!!
?!!

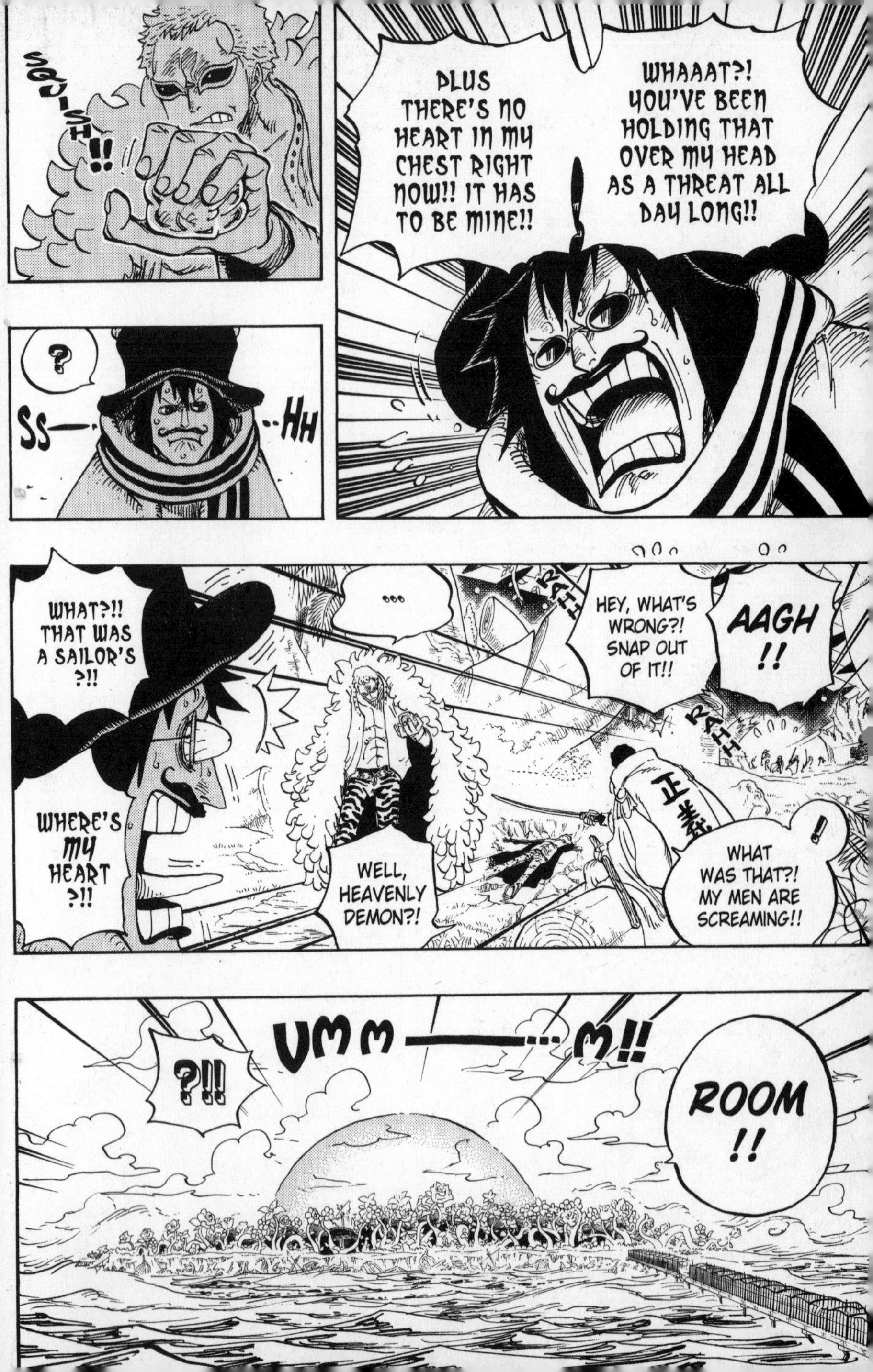
WHAAAT?! YOU'VE BEEN HOLDING THAT OVER MY HEAD AS A THREAT ALL DAY LONG!!
PLUS THERE'S NO HEART IN MY CHEST RIGHT NOW!! IT HAS TO BE MINE!!
SQUISH!!
?
SS—..HH
AAGH!!
HEY, WHAT'S WRONG?! SNAP OUT OF IT!!
...
WHAT?!! THAT WAS A SAILOR'S ?!!
!
WHAT WAS THAT?! MY MEN ARE SCREAMING!!
WELL, HEAVENLY DEMON?!
WHERE'S MY HEART ?!!
ROOM !!
UMM———M!!
?!!

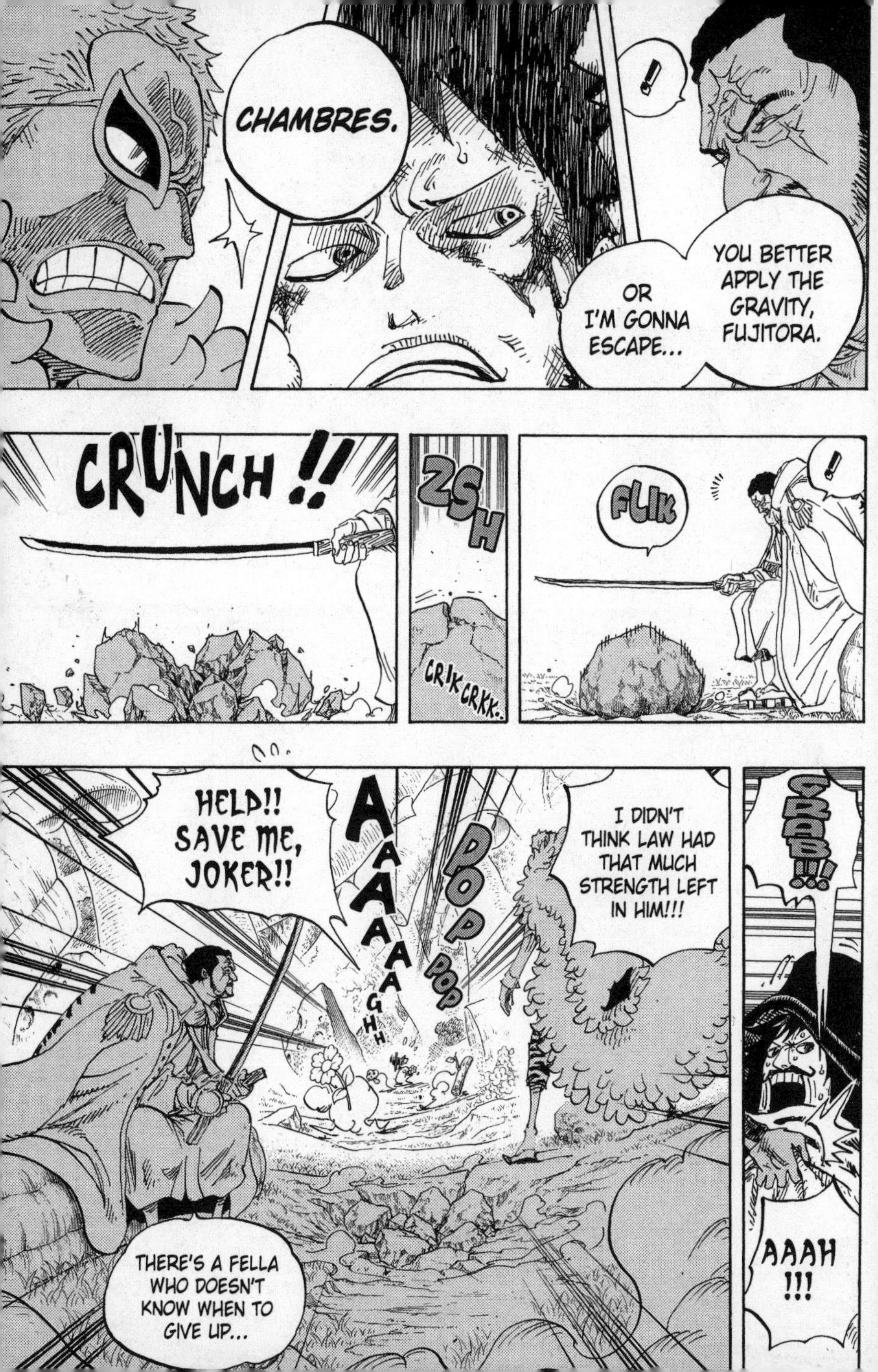
!
YOU BETTER APPLY THE GRAVITY, FUJITORA.
OR I'M GONNA ESCAPE...
CHAMBRES.
!
FLIK
ZSH
CRIK CRKK..
CRUNCH!!
GRAB!!!
AAAH !!!
I DIDN'T THINK LAW HAD THAT MUCH STRENGTH LEFT IN HIM!!!
POP POP
AAAAAAAGHH
HELP!! SAVE ME, JOKER!!
THERE'S A FELLA WHO DOESN'T KNOW WHEN TO GIVE UP...

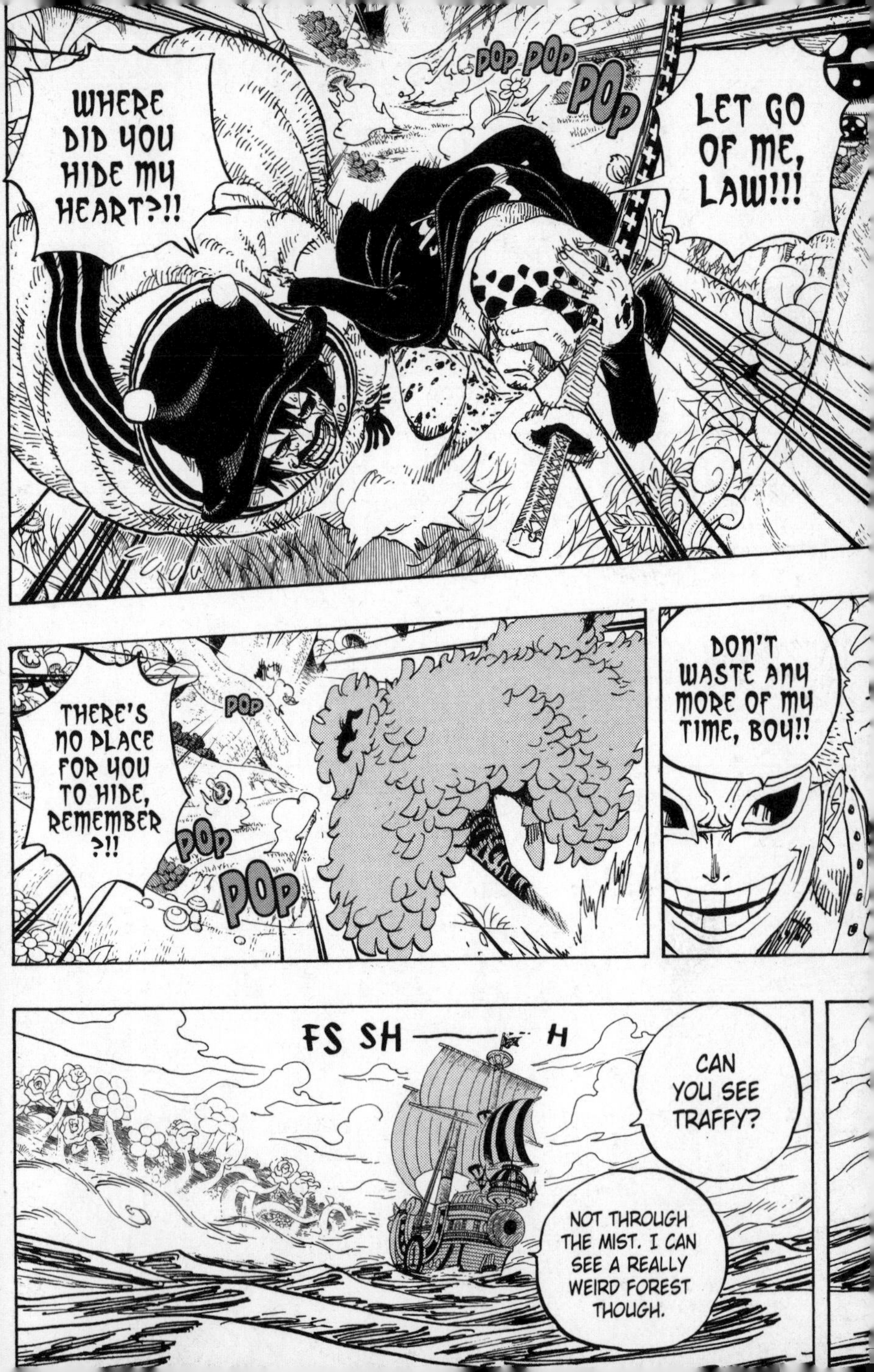
LET GO OF ME, LAW!!!
POP POP POP
WHERE DID YOU HIDE MY HEART?!!
DON'T WASTE ANY MORE OF MY TIME, BOY!!
POP
THERE'S NO PLACE FOR YOU TO HIDE, REMEMBER?!!
POP
POP
FS SH——H
CAN YOU SEE TRAFFY?
NOT THROUGH THE MIST. I CAN SEE A REALLY WEIRD FOREST THOUGH.

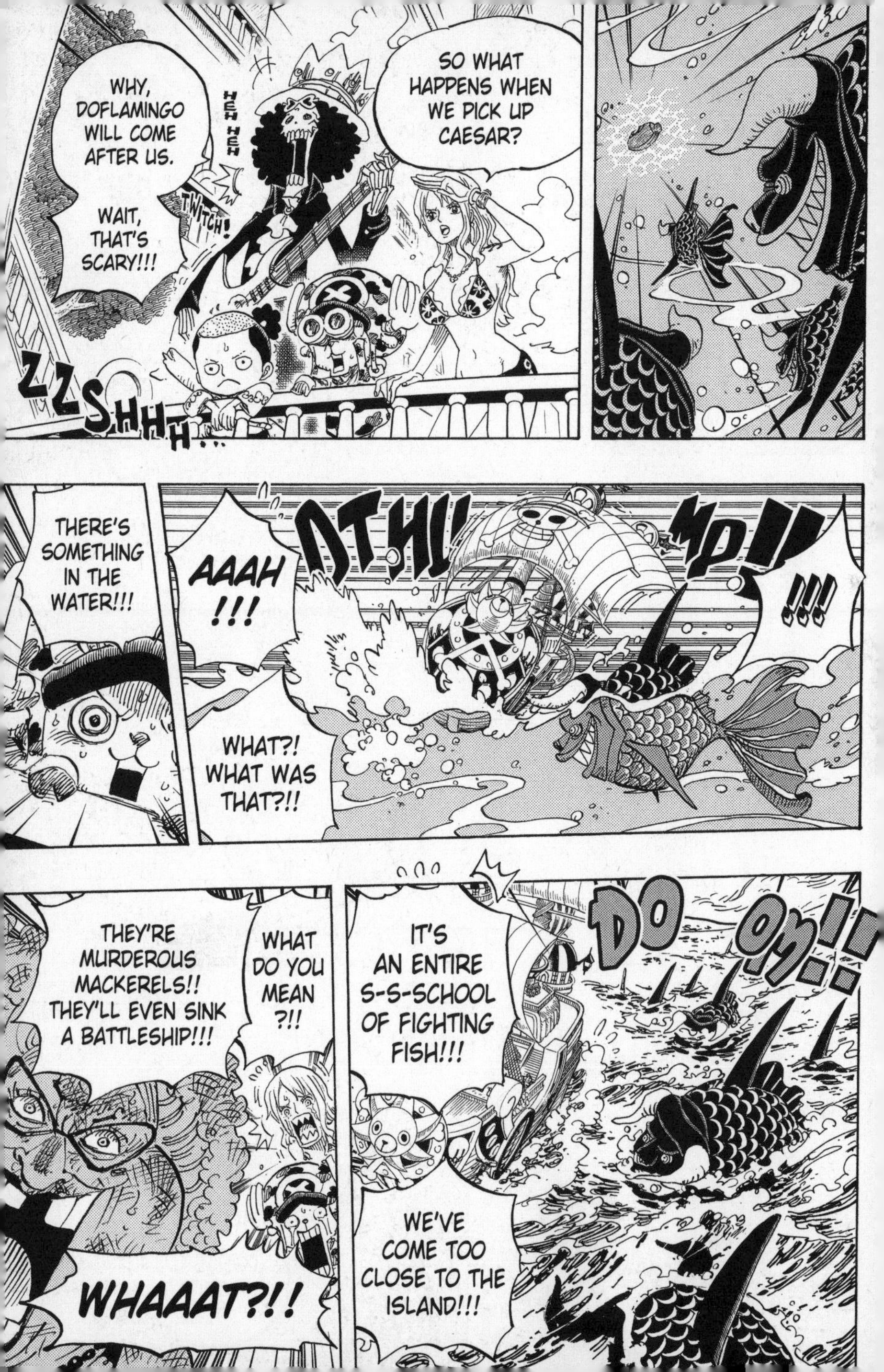
SO WHAT HAPPENS WHEN WE PICK UP CAESAR?
HEH HEH
WHY, DOFLAMINGO WILL COME AFTER US.
WAIT, THAT'S SCARY!!!
TWITCH!
ZZSHHHH...
AAAH !!!
WHAT?! WHAT WAS THAT?!!
!!!
THERE'S SOMETHING IN THE WATER!!!
IT'S AN ENTIRE S-S-SCHOOL OF FIGHTING FISH!!!
WE'VE COME TOO CLOSE TO THE ISLAND!!!
WHAT DO YOU MEAN ?!!
THEY'RE MURDEROUS MACKERELS!! THEY'LL EVEN SINK A BATTLESHIP!!!
WHAAAT?!!

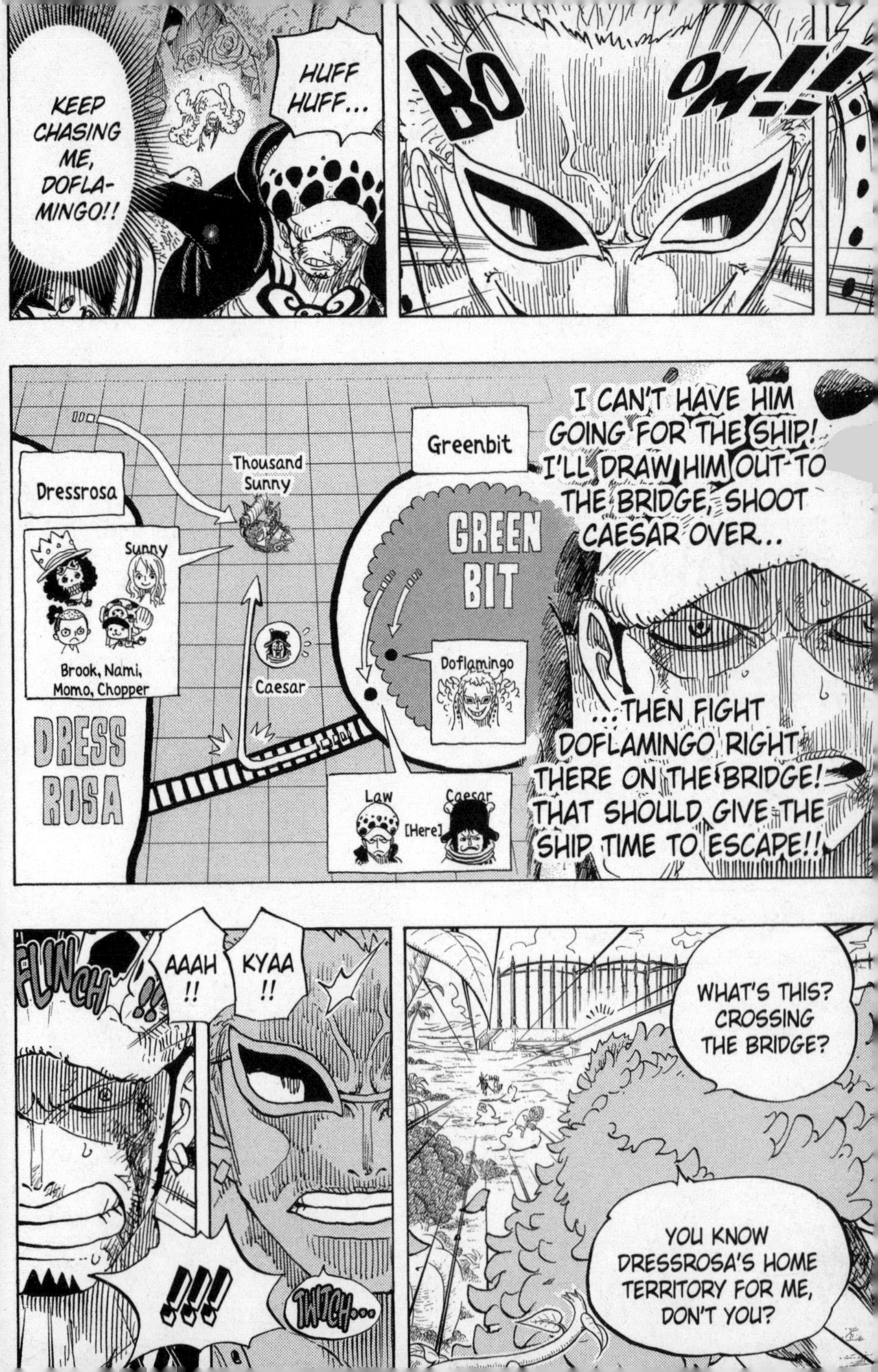
BOOM!!
HUFF HUFF...
KEEP CHASING ME, DOFLAMINGO!!
I CAN'T HAVE HIM GOING FOR THE SHIP! I'LL DRAW HIM OUT TO THE BRIDGE, SHOOT CAESAR OVER...
...THEN FIGHT DOFLAMINGO RIGHT THERE ON THE BRIDGE! THAT SHOULD GIVE THE SHIP TIME TO ESCAPE!!
Greenbit
GREEN BIT
Doflamingo
Law
[Here]
Caesar
Thousand Sunny
Caesar
Dressrosa
Sunny
Brook, Nami, Momo, Chopper
DRESS ROSA
WHAT'S THIS? CROSSING THE BRIDGE?
YOU KNOW DRESSROSA'S HOME TERRITORY FOR ME, DON'T YOU?
KYAA !!
AAAH !!
FLINCH
!!!
TWITCH...

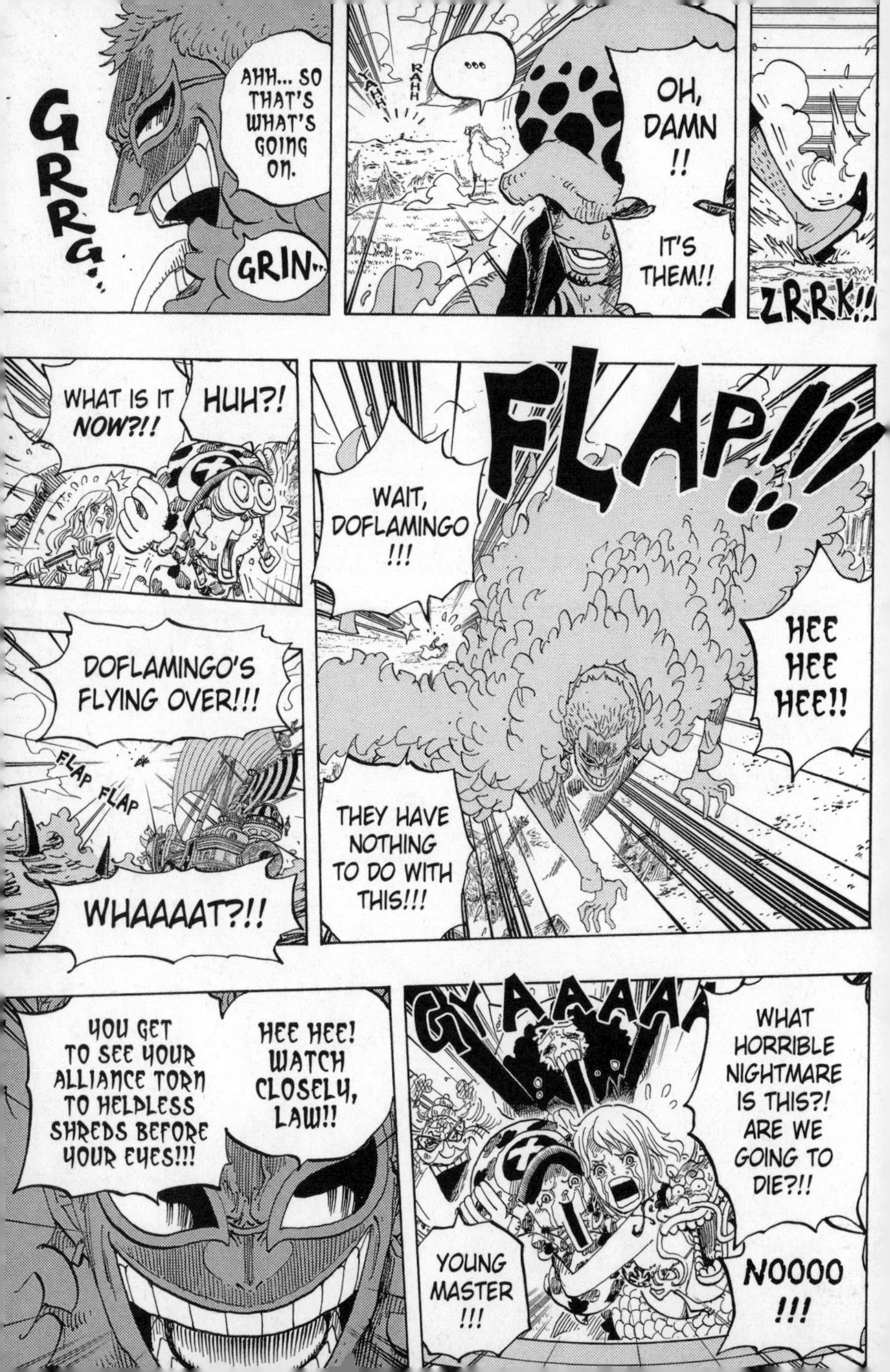
ZRRK!!
OH, DAMN!!
IT'S THEM!!
...
RAHH
YAHH
AHH... SO THAT'S WHAT'S GOING ON.
GRIN...
GRRRG...
FLAP!!!
WAIT, DOFLAMINGO!!!
HEE HEE HEE!!
THEY HAVE NOTHING TO DO WITH THIS!!!
HUH?!
WHAT IS IT NOW?!!
DOFLAMINGO'S FLYING OVER!!!
FLAP
FLAP
WHAAAAT?!!
GYAAAAA
WHAT HORRIBLE NIGHTMARE IS THIS?! ARE WE GOING TO DIE?!!
NOOOO!!!
YOUNG MASTER!!!
HEE HEE! WATCH CLOSELY, LAW!!
YOU GET TO SEE YOUR ALLIANCE TORN TO HELPLESS SHREDS BEFORE YOUR EYES!!!

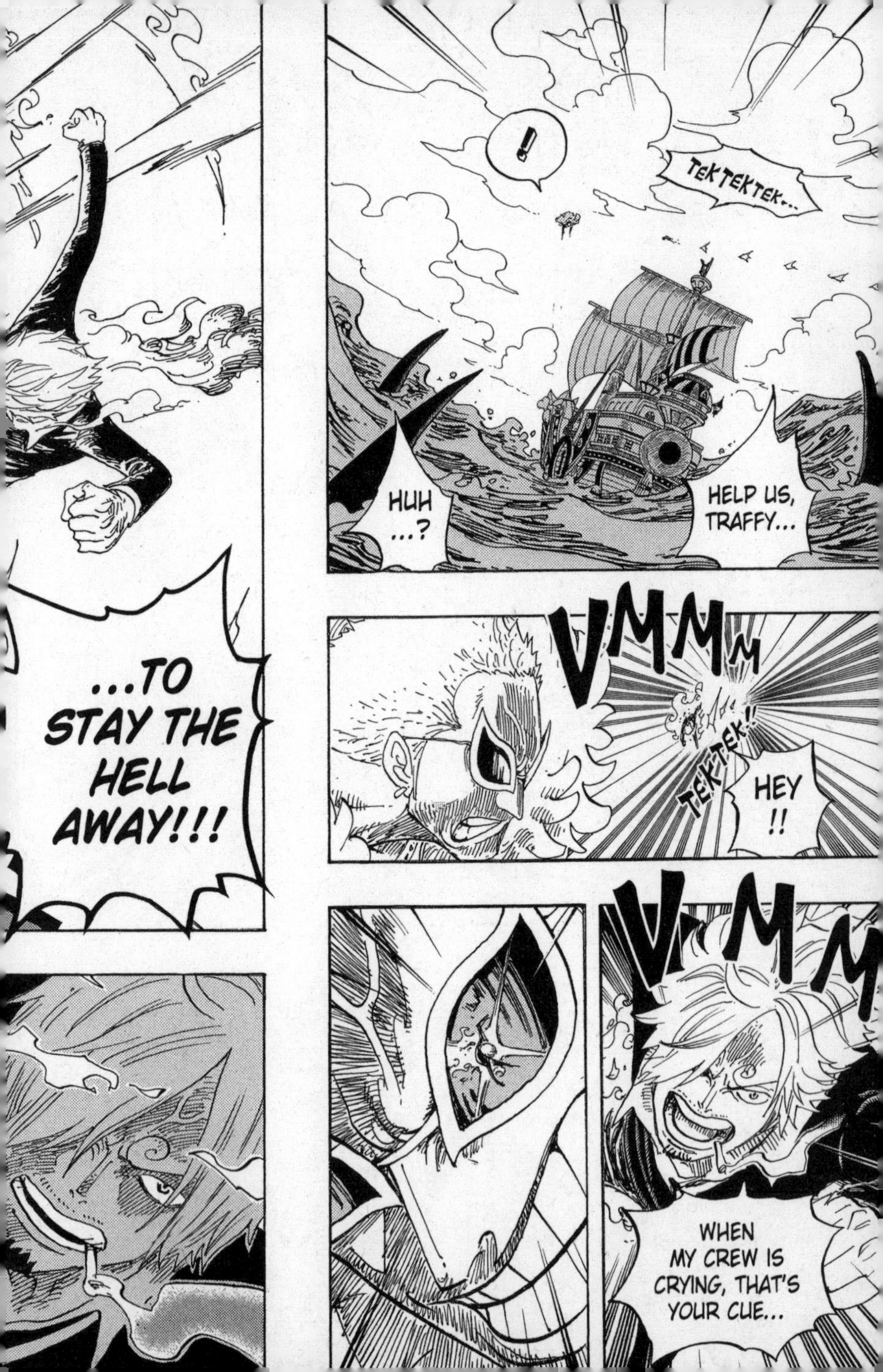
TEKTEKTEK...
!
HELP US, TRAFFY...
HUH ...?
VMMMM
TEKTEK!!
HEY !!
...TO STAY THE HELL AWAY!!!
VMMM
WHEN MY CREW IS CRYING, THAT'S YOUR CUE...

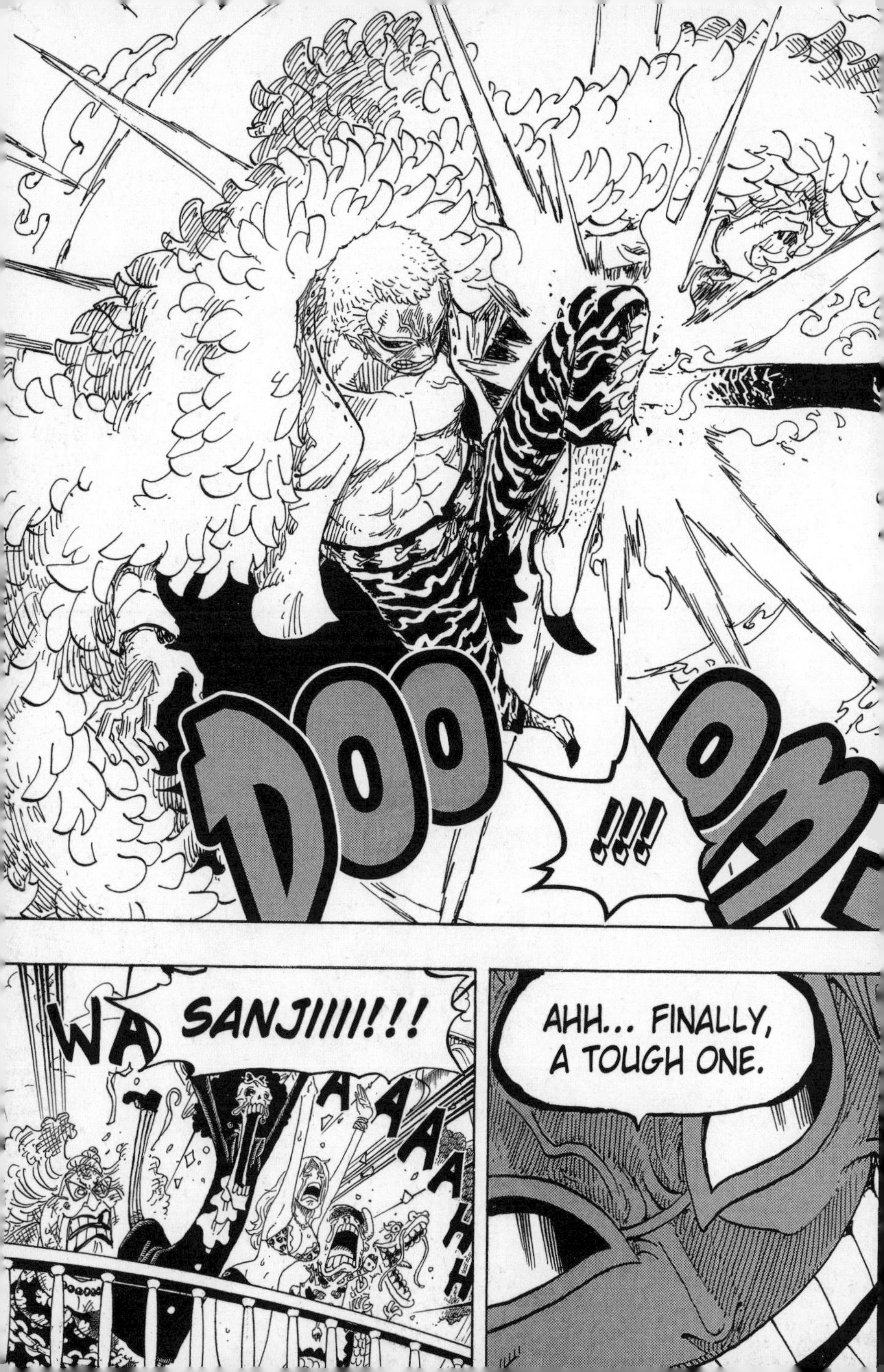
DOOOM!!!
AHH... FINALLY, A TOUGH ONE.
SANJIIIII!!!
WAAAAAAH

Chapter 724: LAW'S PLAN

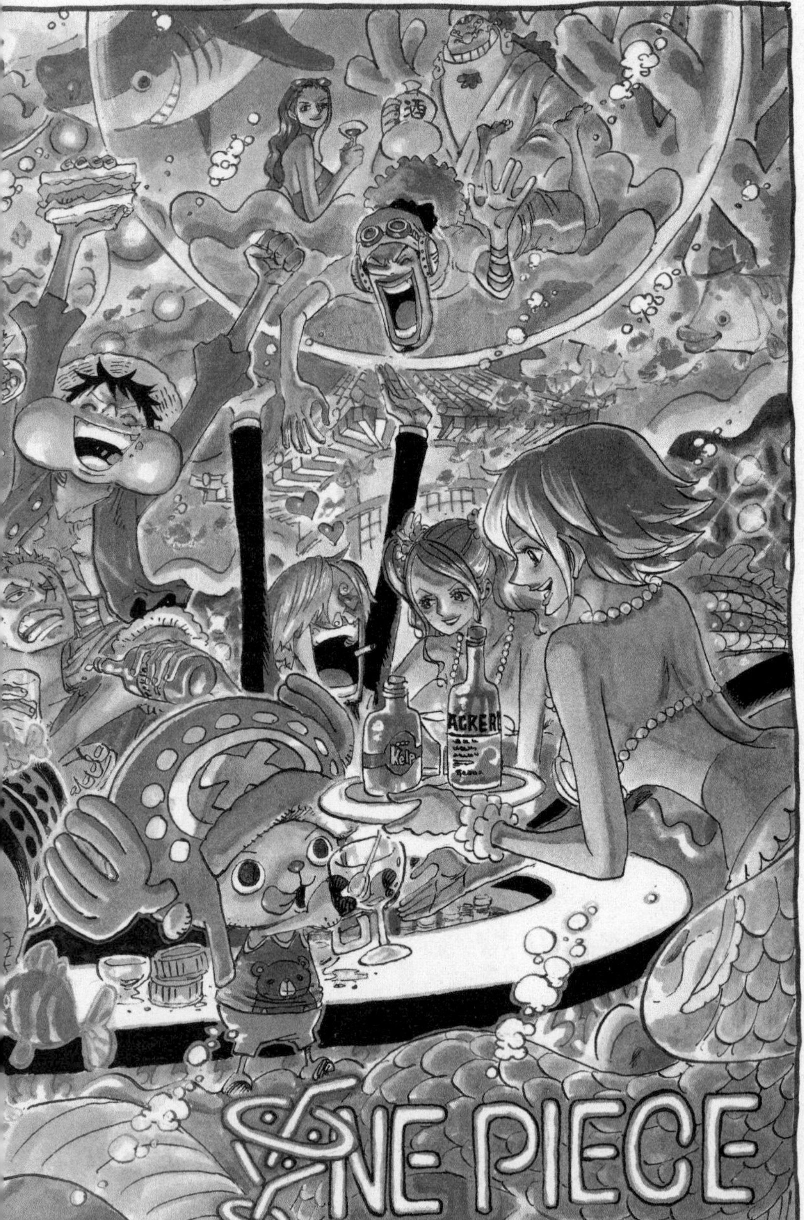
Kelp
ONE PIECE

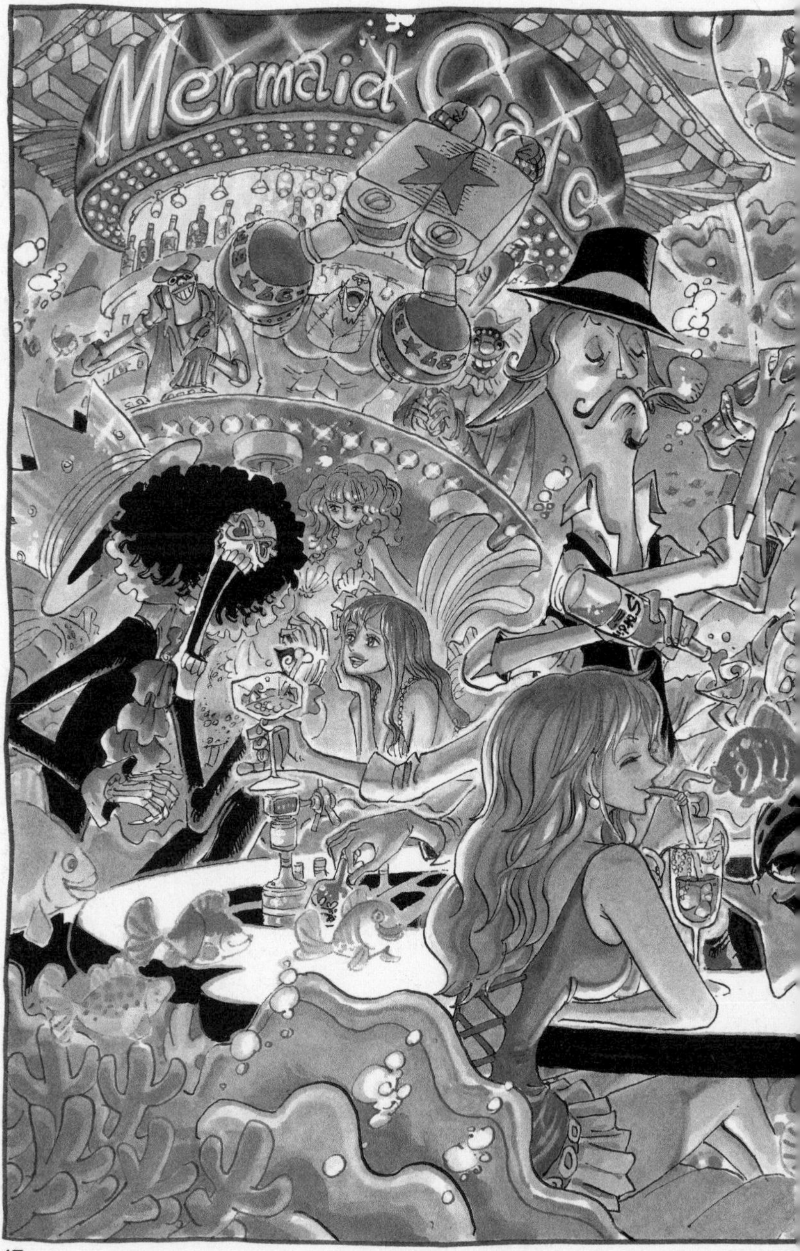
Mermaid

vol. 73
ONE PIECE

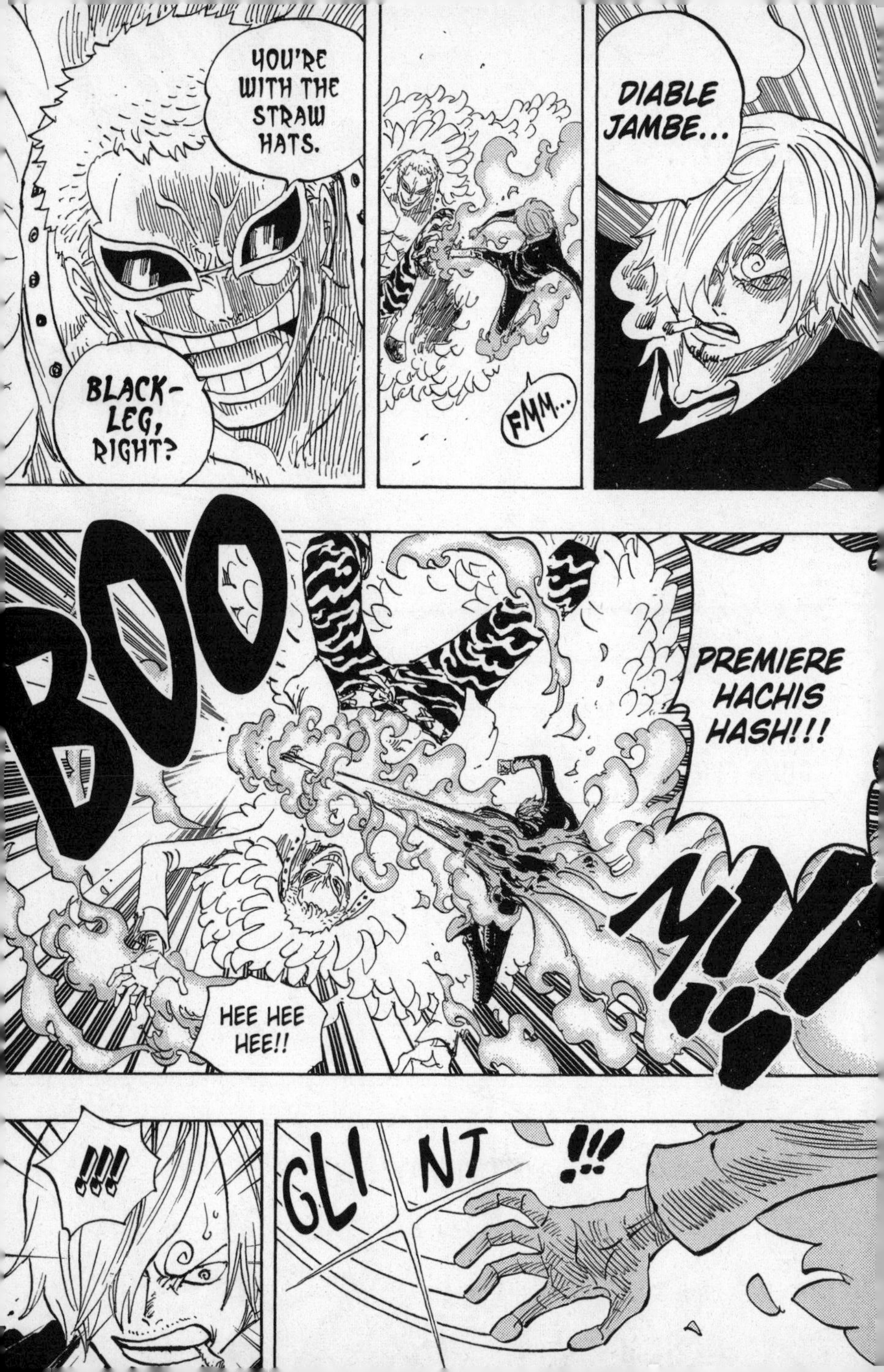
DIABLE JAMBE...
FMM...
YOU'RE WITH THE STRAW HATS.
BLACK-LEG, RIGHT?
PREMIERE HACHIS HASH!!!
BOOM!!
HEE HEE HEE!!
GLINT
!!!
!!!

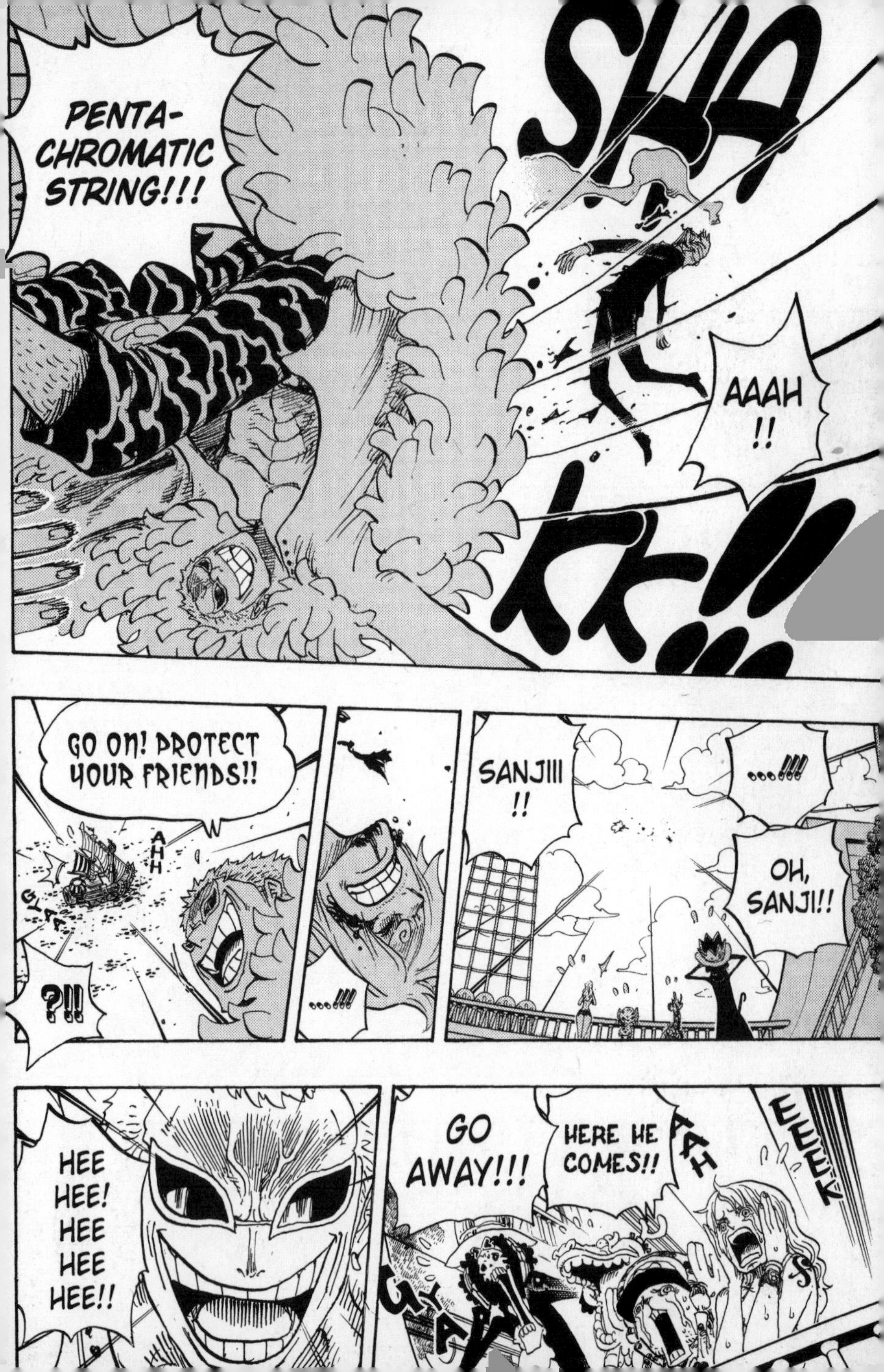
SHA
AAAH !!
KK!!
PENTA-CHROMATIC STRING!!!
...!!!
OH, SANJI!!
SANJIII !!
...!!!
GO ON! PROTECT YOUR FRIENDS!!
AHH
GYAA
?!!
EEEEK
AAH
HERE HE COMES!!
GO AWAY!!!
HEE HEE! HEE HEE HEE!!

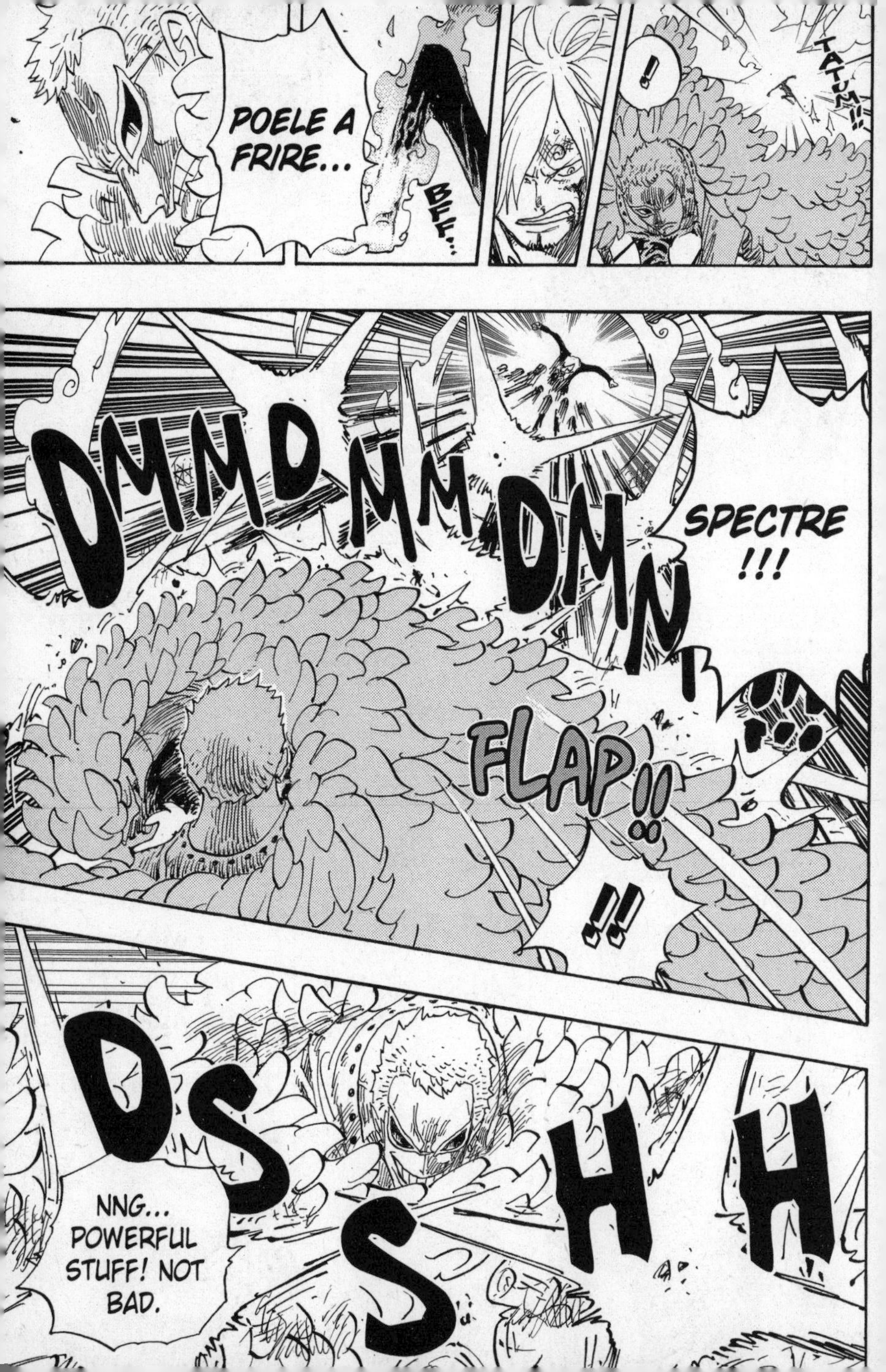
!
TATUM!!
BFF...
POELE A FRIRE...
SPECTRE !!!
DMMDMMDMN
FLAP!!
!!
DSSHH
NNG... POWERFUL STUFF! NOT BAD.

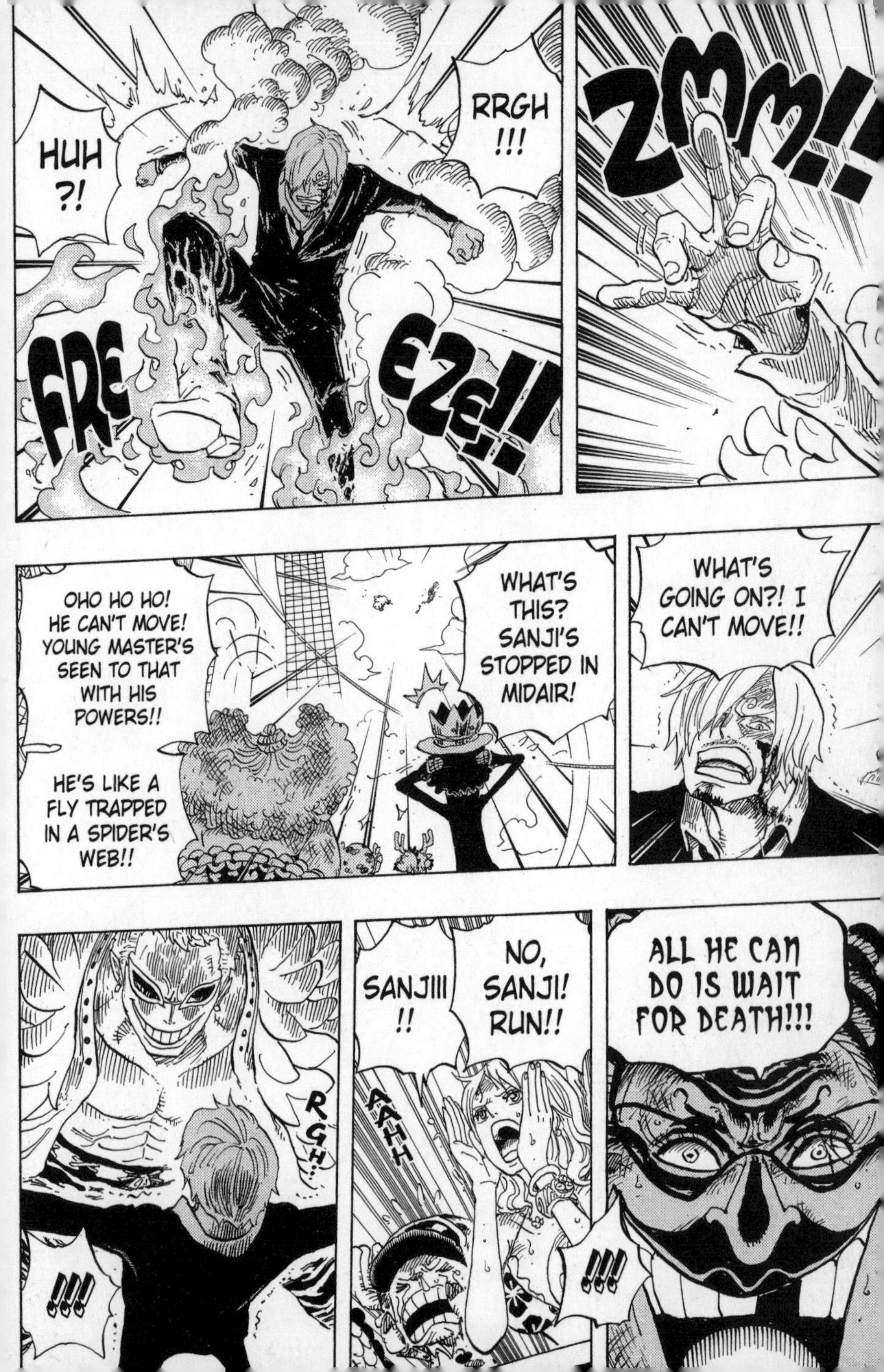
ZOOM!!
RRGH !!!
HUH ?!
FRE EZE!!
WHAT'S GOING ON?! I CAN'T MOVE!!
WHAT'S THIS? SANJI'S STOPPED IN MIDAIR!
OHO HO HO! HE CAN'T MOVE! YOUNG MASTER'S SEEN TO THAT WITH HIS POWERS!!
HE'S LIKE A FLY TRAPPED IN A SPIDER'S WEB!!
ALL HE CAN DO IS WAIT FOR DEATH!!!
!!!
NO, SANJI! RUN!!
SANJIII !!
AAHH
RGH..
!!!

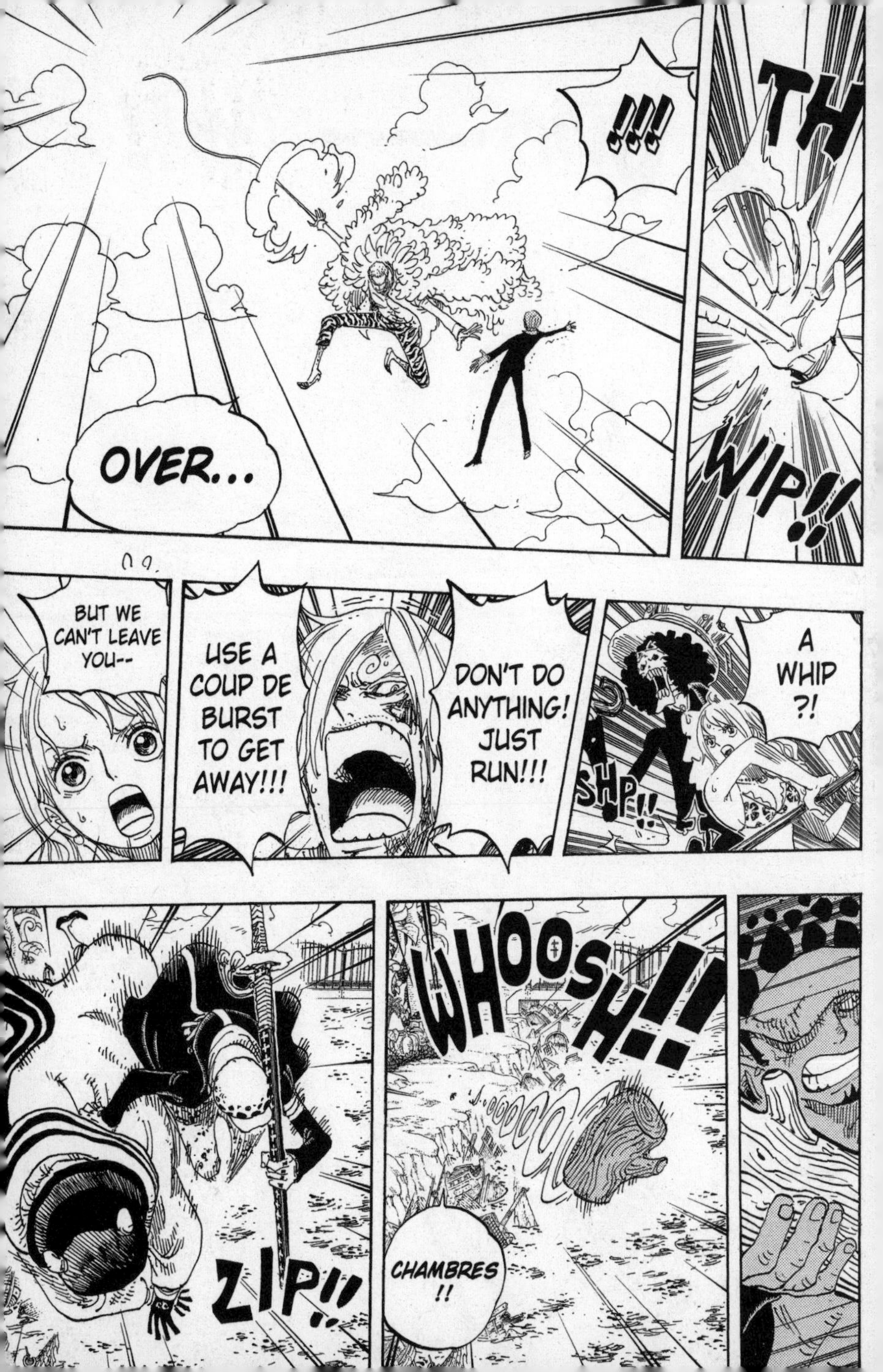
TH
WIP!!
!!!
OVER...
A WHIP ?!
SHP!!
DON'T DO ANYTHING! JUST RUN!!!
USE A COUP DE BURST TO GET AWAY!!!
BUT WE CAN'T LEAVE YOU--
WHOOSH!!
CHAMBRES !!
ZIP!!

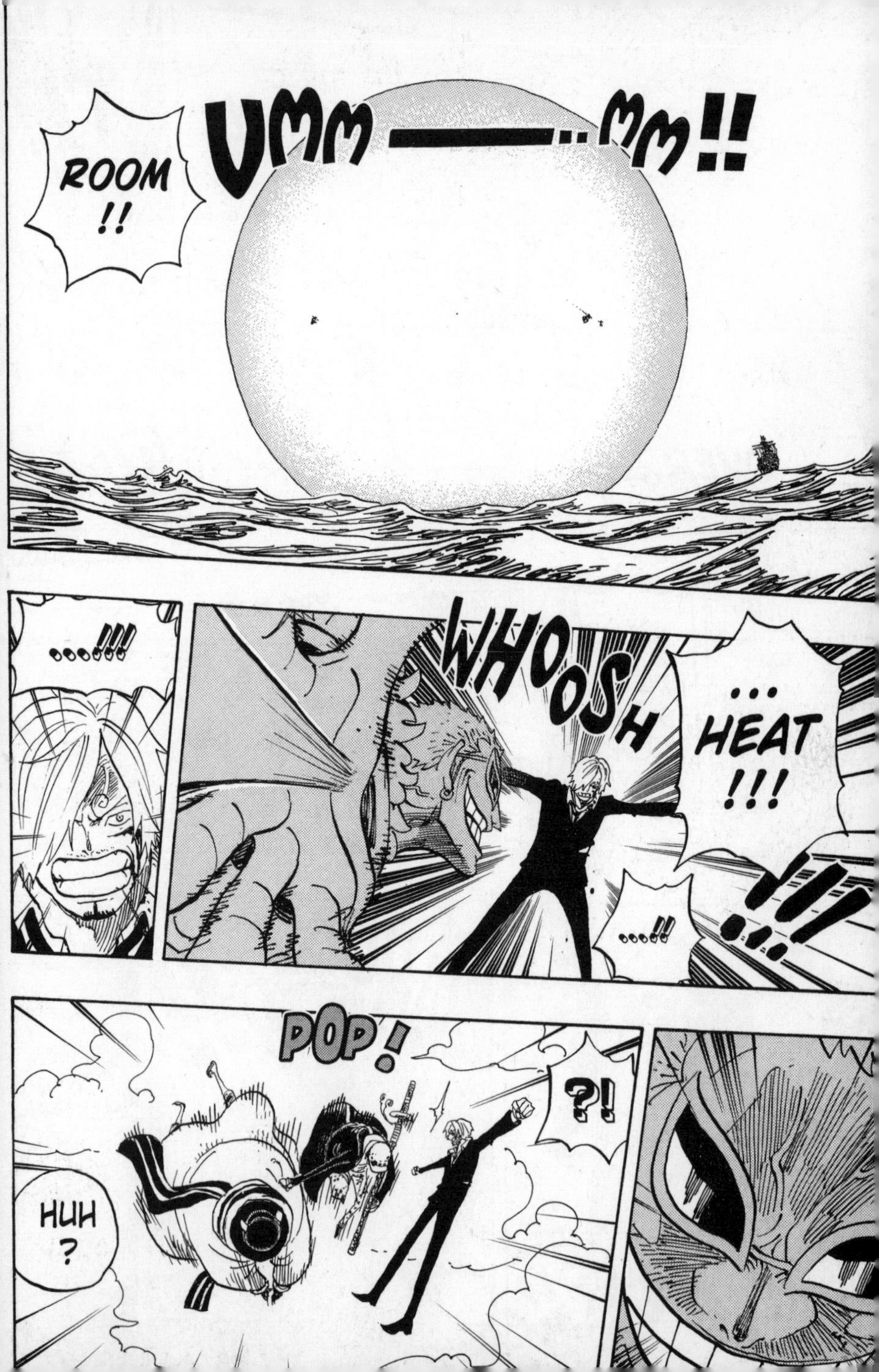
UMM——..MM!!
ROOM!!
WHOOSH
...HEAT!!!
...!!
...!!
...!!!
POP!
?!
HUH?

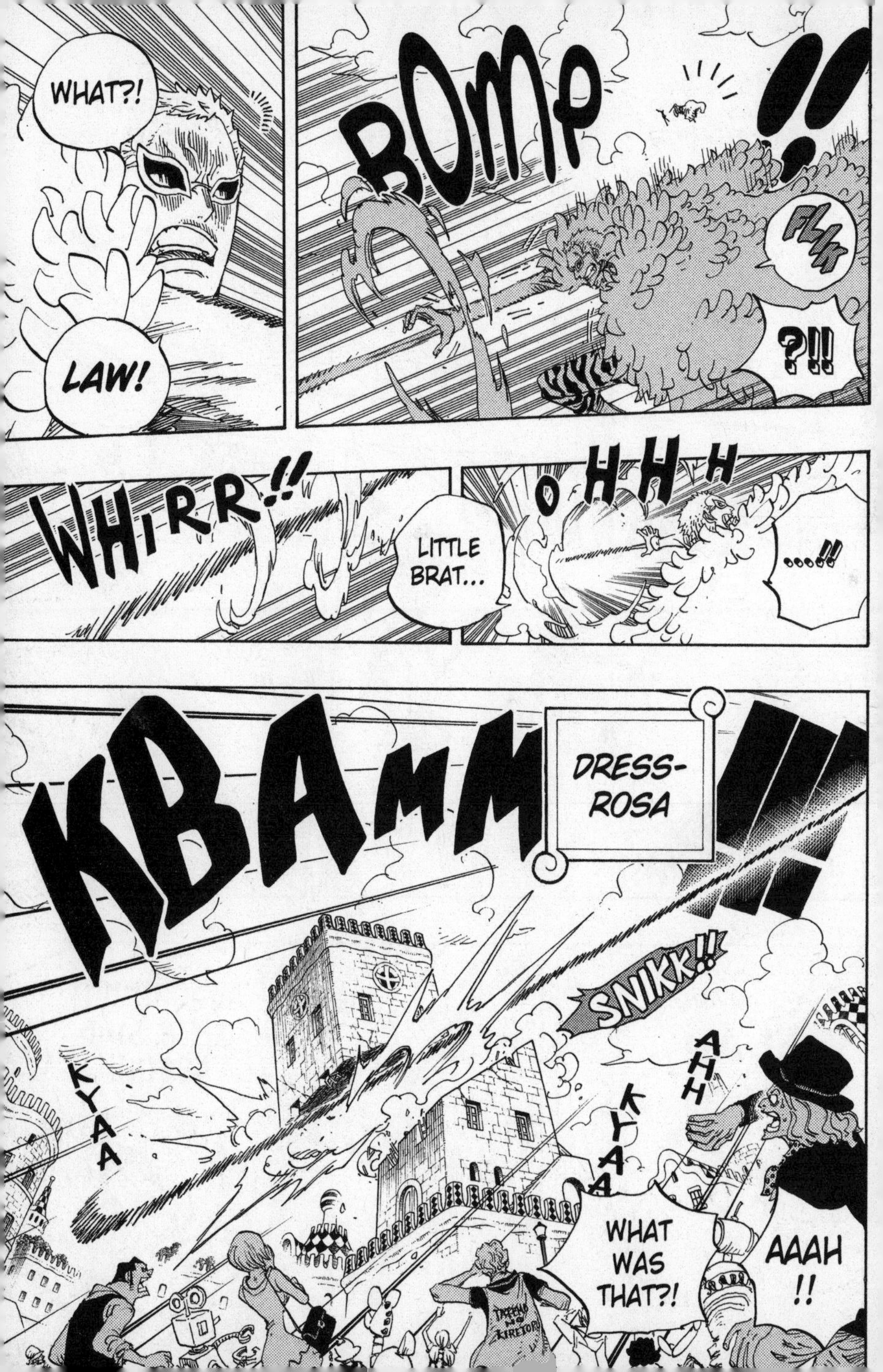
BOMP!!
FLIK
?!!
WHAT?!
LAW!
OHHHH
....!!
LITTLE BRAT...
WHIRR!!
KBAMM!!
DRESS-ROSA
SNIKK!!
AHH
KYAA
AAAH!!
WHAT WAS THAT?!
KYAA

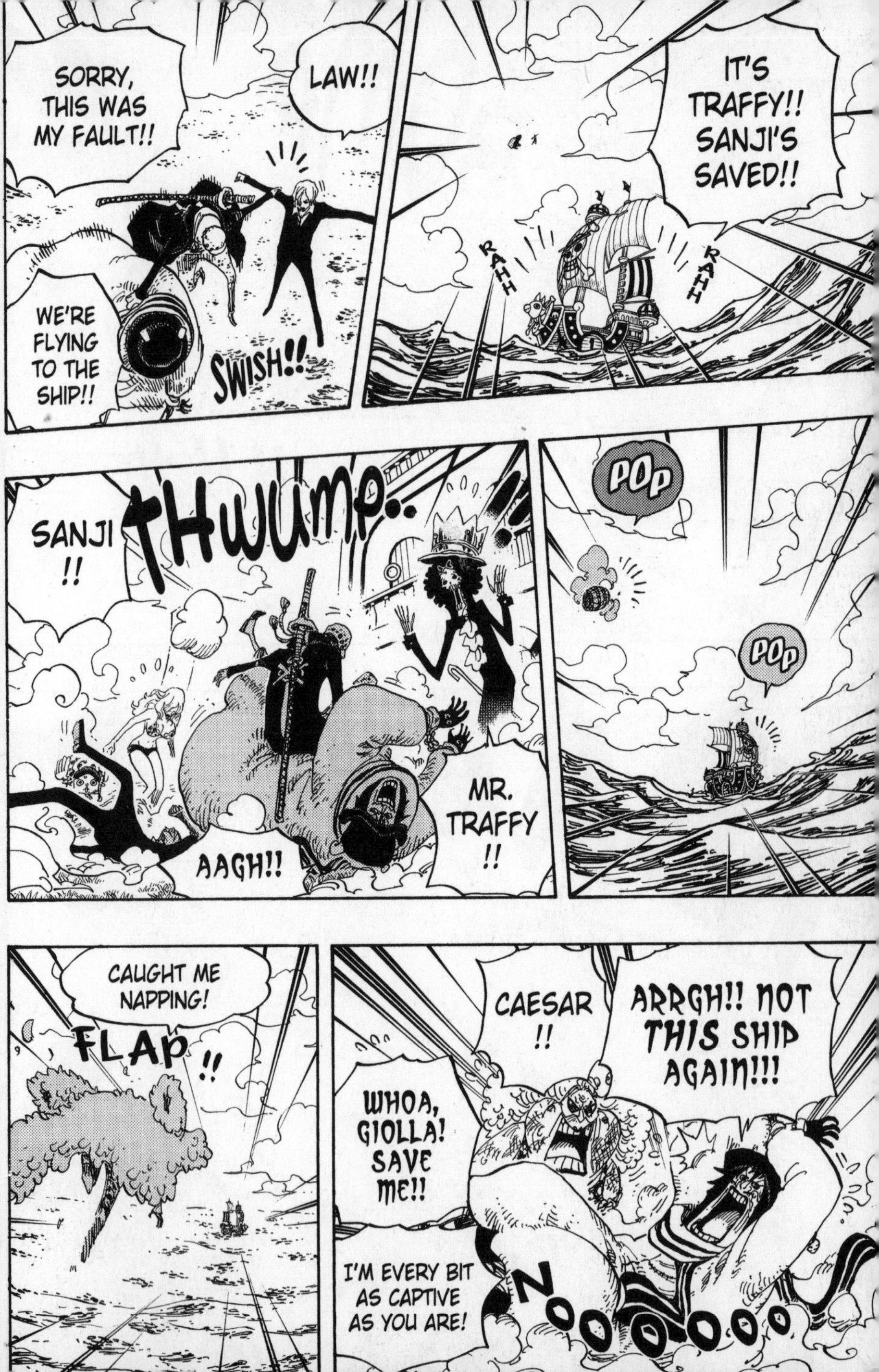
IT'S TRAFFY!! SANJI'S SAVED!!
RAHH
RAHH
LAW!!
SORRY, THIS WAS MY FAULT!!
WE'RE FLYING TO THE SHIP!!
SWISH!!
POP
POP
THWUMP..!!
MR. TRAFFY!!
AAGH!!
SANJI!!
ARRGH!! NOT THIS SHIP AGAIN!!!
CAESAR!!
WHOA, GIOLLA! SAVE ME!!
I'M EVERY BIT AS CAPTIVE AS YOU ARE!
NOOOOOO...
CAUGHT ME NAPPING!
FLAP!!

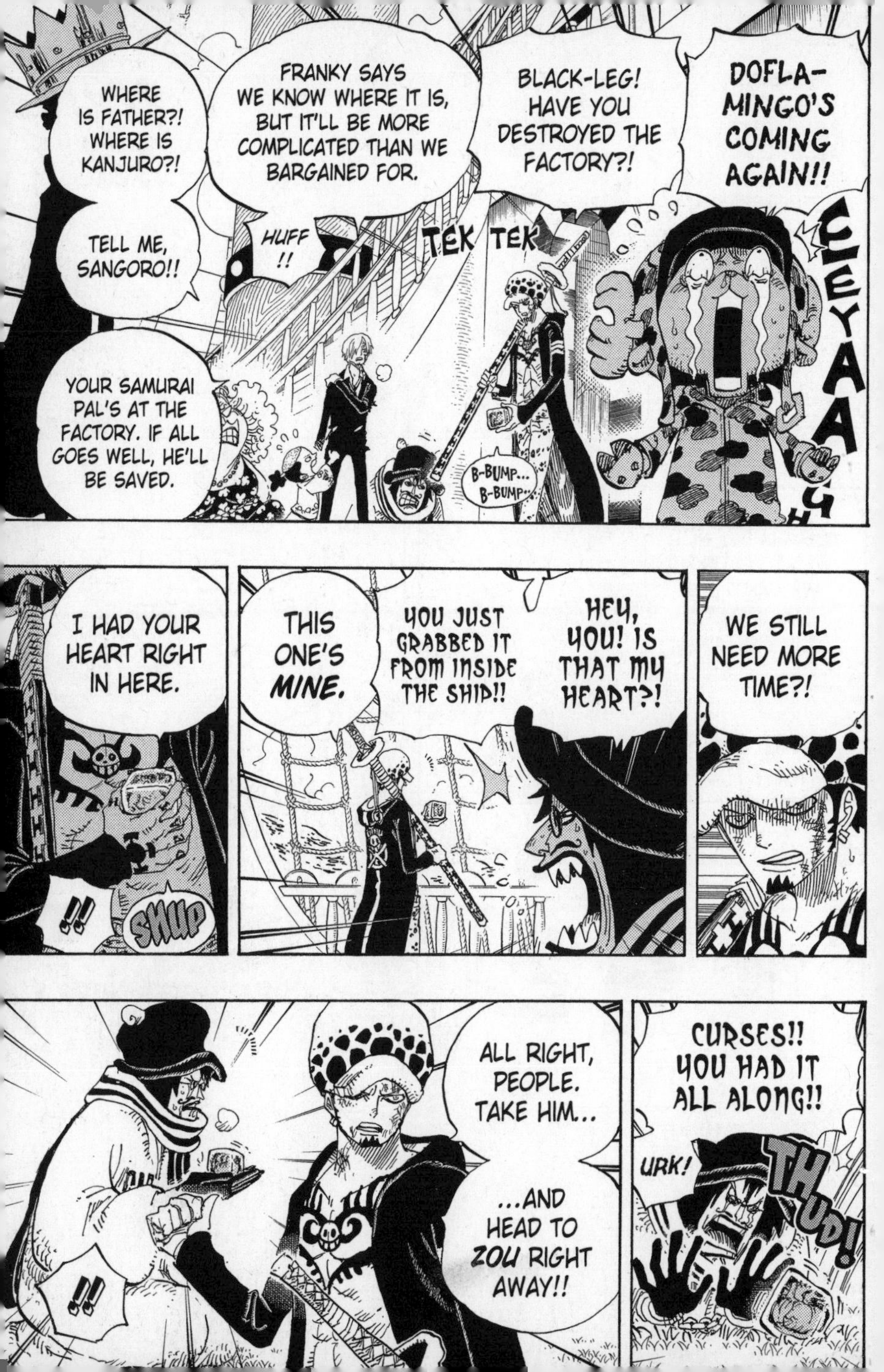
DOFLAMINGO'S COMING AGAIN!!
EEYAAAUGH
BLACK-LEG! HAVE YOU DESTROYED THE FACTORY?!
TEK TEK
FRANKY SAYS WE KNOW WHERE IT IS, BUT IT'LL BE MORE COMPLICATED THAN WE BARGAINED FOR.
HUFF !!
WHERE IS FATHER?! WHERE IS KANJURO?!
TELL ME, SANGORO!!
B-BUMP... B-BUMP...
YOUR SAMURAI PAL'S AT THE FACTORY. IF ALL GOES WELL, HE'LL BE SAVED.
WE STILL NEED MORE TIME?!
HEY, YOU! IS THAT MY HEART?!
YOU JUST GRABBED IT FROM INSIDE THE SHIP!!
THIS ONE'S *MINE.*
I HAD YOUR HEART RIGHT IN HERE.
!!
SHUP
CURSES!! YOU HAD IT ALL ALONG!!
THUD!
URK!
ALL RIGHT, PEOPLE. TAKE HIM...
...AND HEAD TO *ZOU* RIGHT AWAY!!
!!

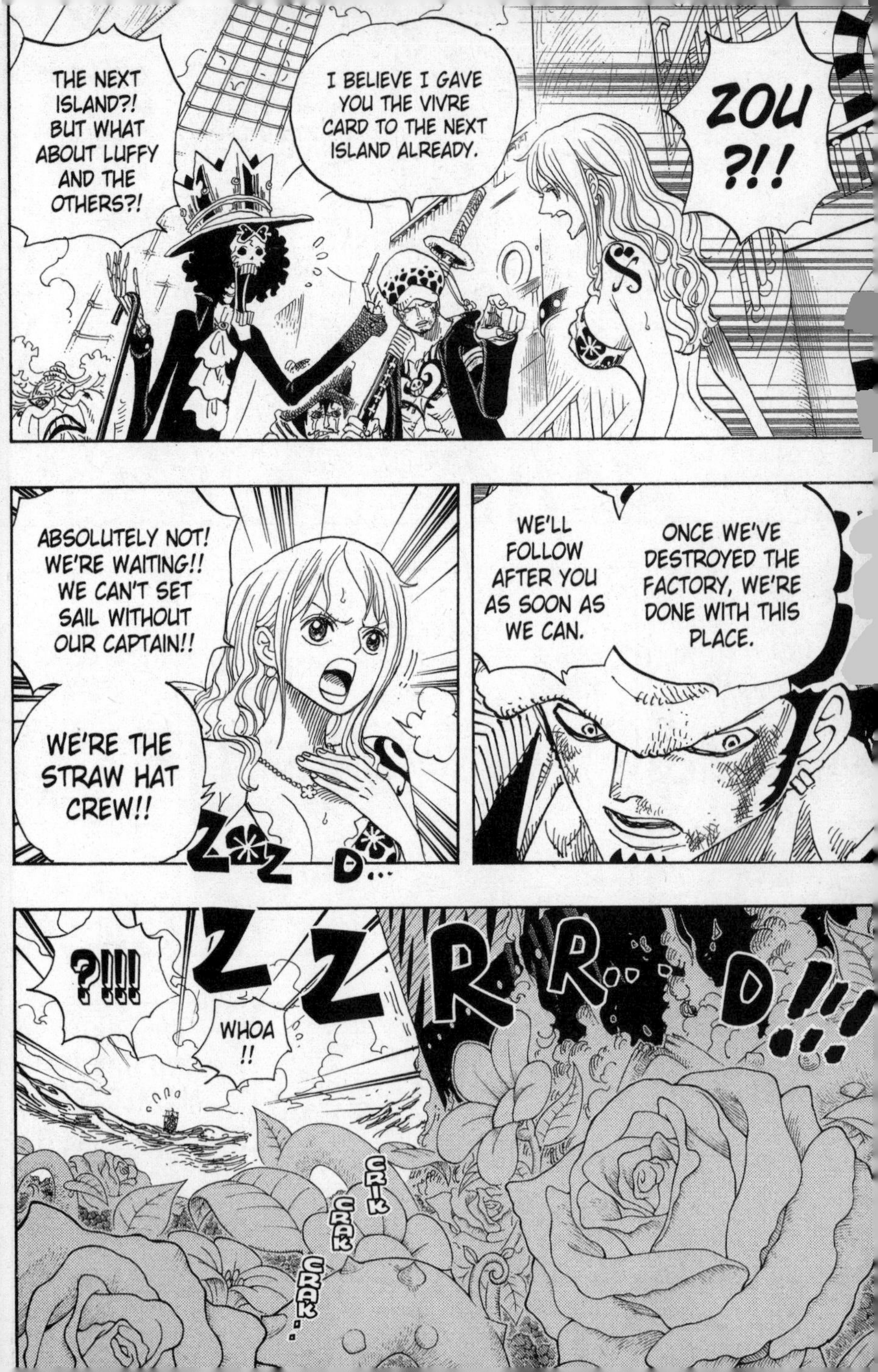
ZOU ?!!
I BELIEVE I GAVE YOU THE VIVRE CARD TO THE NEXT ISLAND ALREADY.
THE NEXT ISLAND?! BUT WHAT ABOUT LUFFY AND THE OTHERS?!
ONCE WE'VE DESTROYED THE FACTORY, WE'RE DONE WITH THIS PLACE.
WE'LL FOLLOW AFTER YOU AS SOON AS WE CAN.
ABSOLUTELY NOT! WE'RE WAITING!! WE CAN'T SET SAIL WITHOUT OUR CAPTAIN!!
WE'RE THE STRAW HAT CREW!!
ZZZ
D...
ZZRR..D!!!
?!!!
WHOA !!
CRIK
CRAK
CRAK..

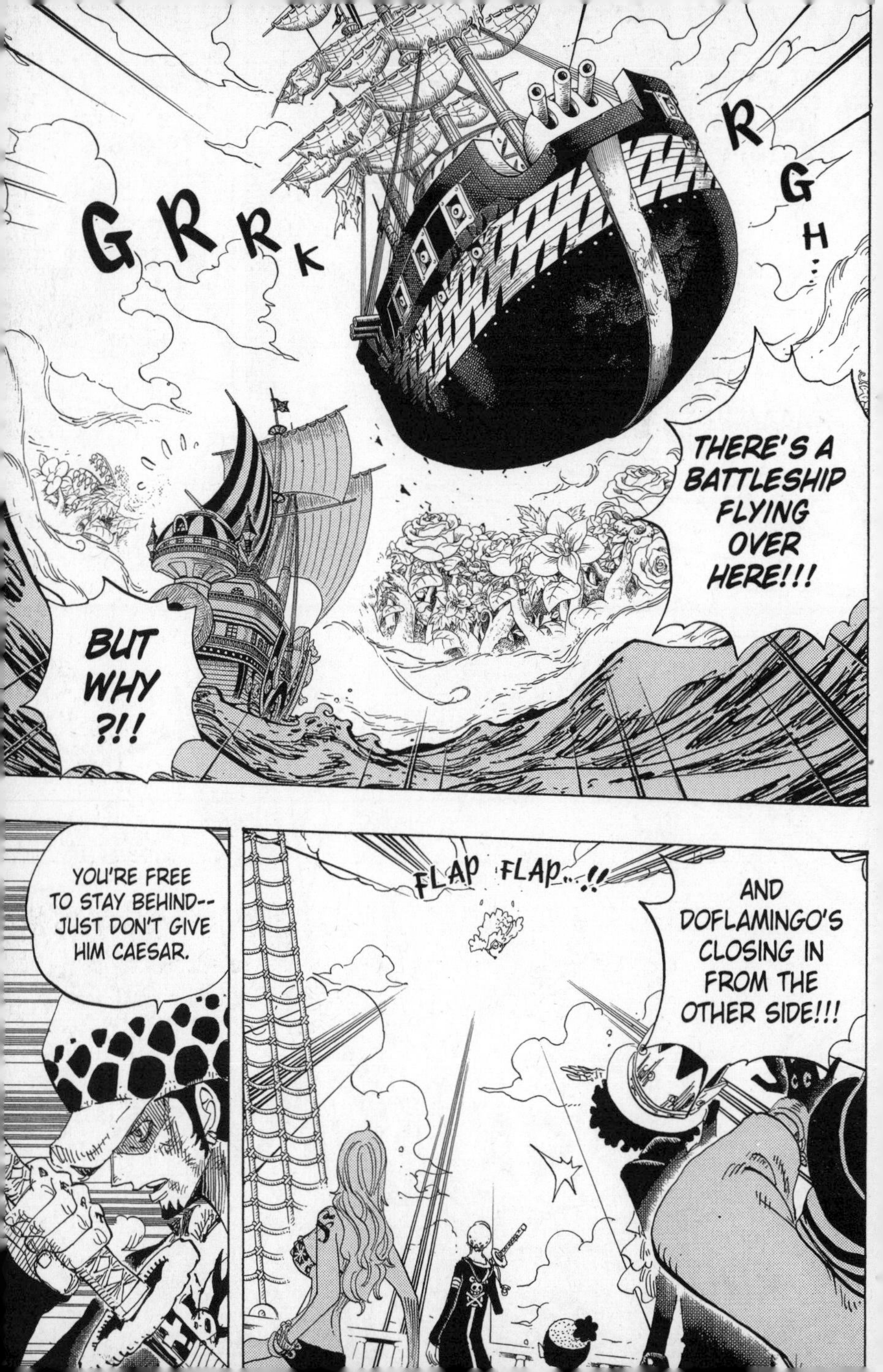
GRRK RGH...
THERE'S A BATTLESHIP FLYING OVER HERE!!!
BUT WHY?!!
FLAP FLAP...!!
AND DOFLAMINGO'S CLOSING IN FROM THE OTHER SIDE!!!
YOU'RE FREE TO STAY BEHIND-- JUST DON'T GIVE HIM CAESAR.

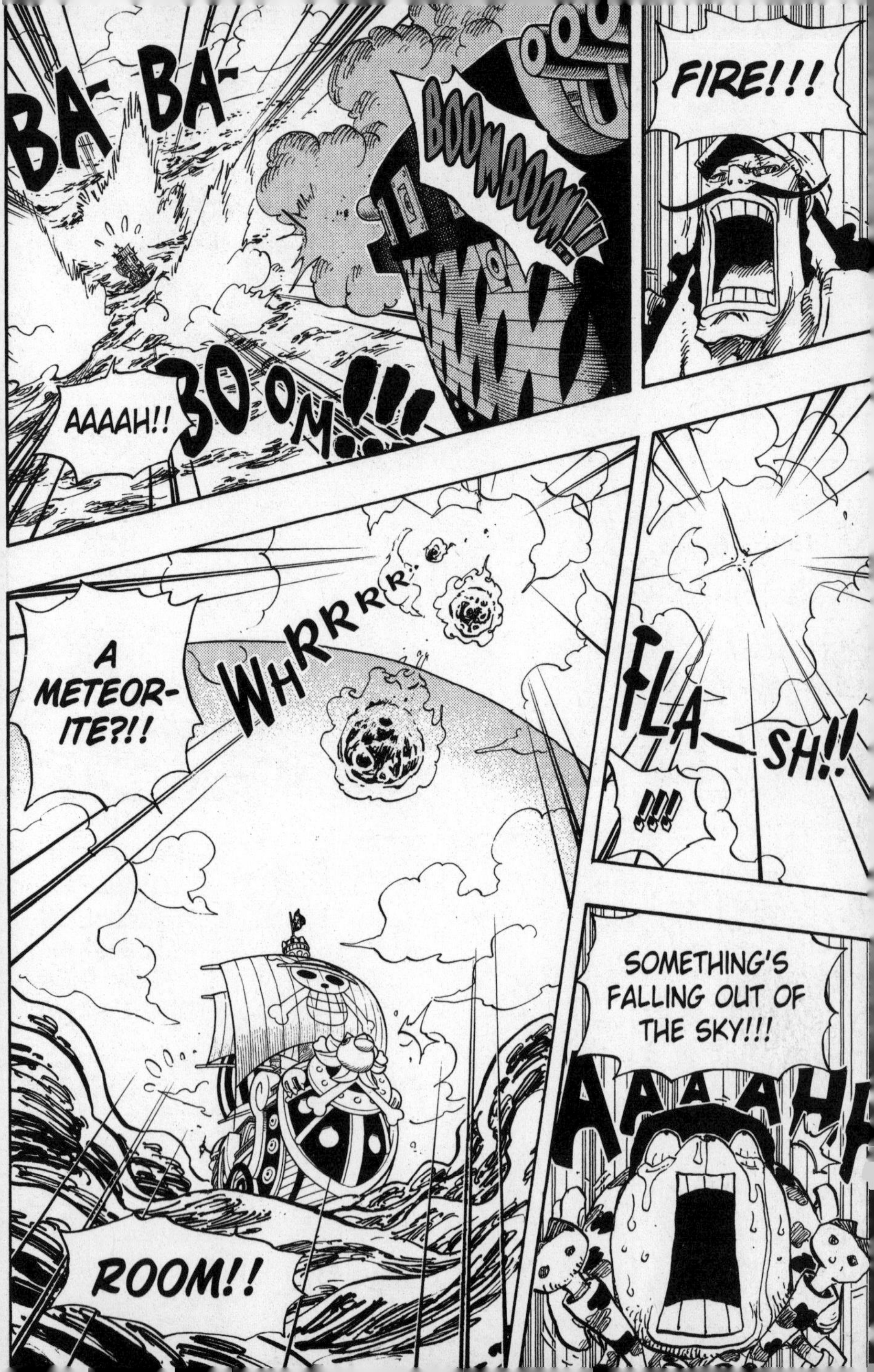
FIRE!!!
BOOMBOOM!!!
BA-BA-
AAAAH!!
BOOM!!!
FLA-SH!!
!!!
SOMETHING'S FALLING OUT OF THE SKY!!!
AAAAH!!
A METEORITE?!!
WHRRRRR
ROOM!!

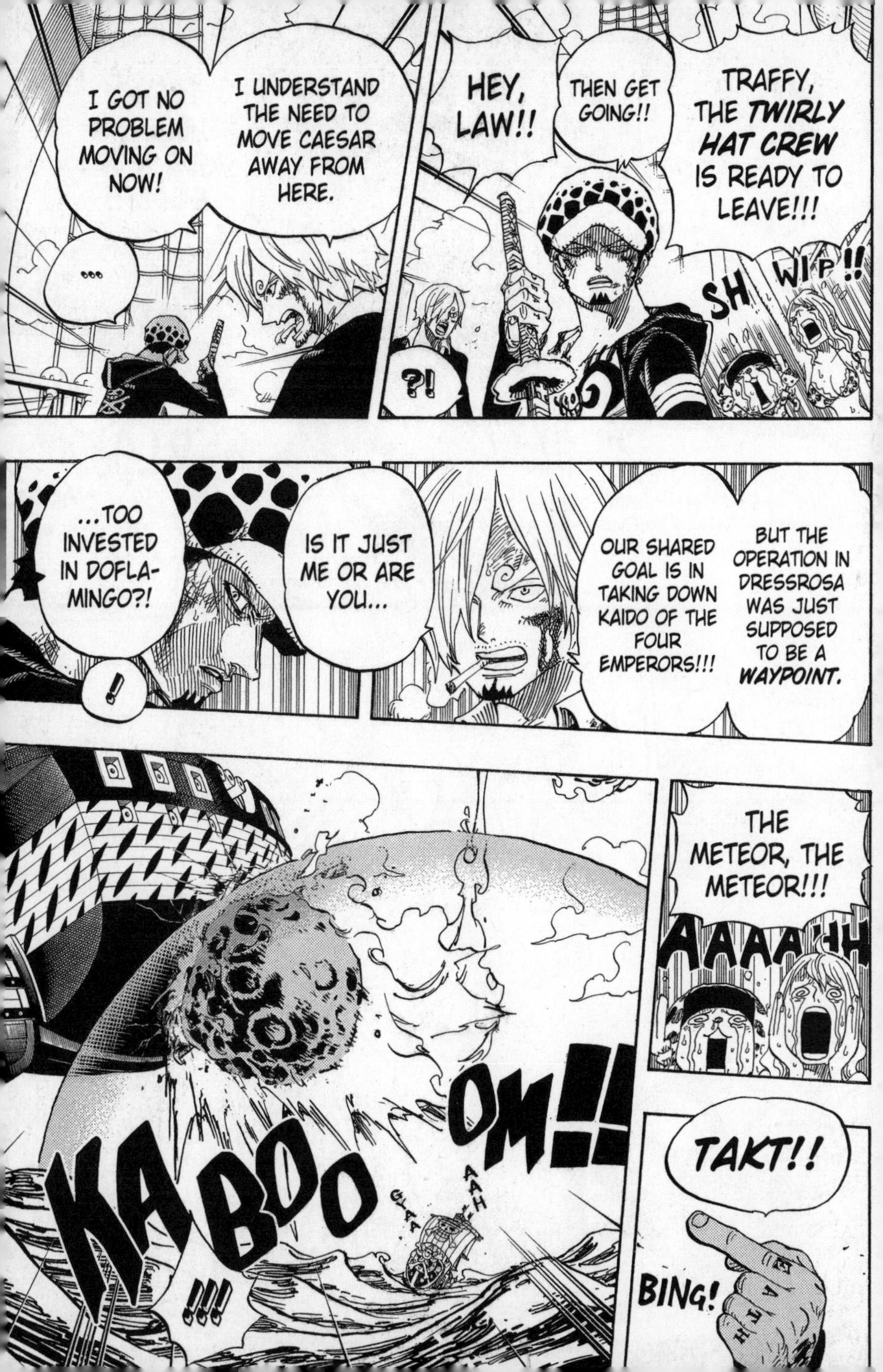
TRAFFY, THE TWIRLY HAT CREW IS READY TO LEAVE!!!
SHWIP!!
THEN GET GOING!!
HEY, LAW!!
?!
I UNDERSTAND THE NEED TO MOVE CAESAR AWAY FROM HERE.
I GOT NO PROBLEM MOVING ON NOW!
...
BUT THE OPERATION IN DRESSROSA WAS JUST SUPPOSED TO BE A WAYPOINT.
OUR SHARED GOAL IS IN TAKING DOWN KAIDO OF THE FOUR EMPERORS!!!
IS IT JUST ME OR ARE YOU...
...TOO INVESTED IN DOFLAMINGO?!
!
THE METEOR, THE METEOR!!!
AAAAHH
TAKT!!
BING!
KABOOOM!!!!!
GYAA
AAH

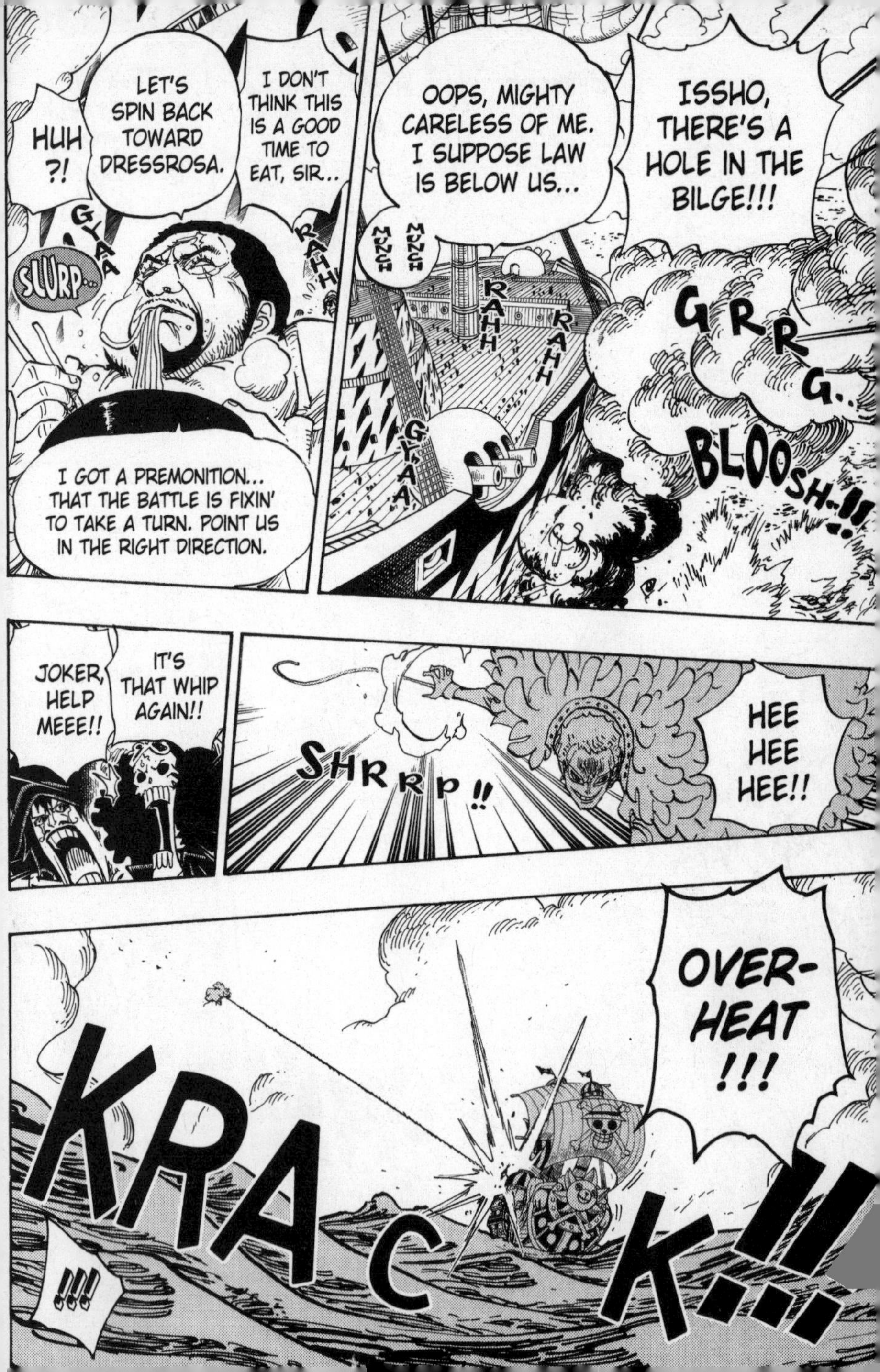
ISSHO, THERE'S A HOLE IN THE BILGE!!!
GRRRG..
BLOOSH..!!
OOPS, MIGHTY CARELESS OF ME. I SUPPOSE LAW IS BELOW US...
MUNCH MUNCH
RAHH
RAHH
GYAA
I DON'T THINK THIS IS A GOOD TIME TO EAT, SIR...
RAHH
LET'S SPIN BACK TOWARD DRESSROSA.
HUH ?!
GYAA
SLURP...
I GOT A PREMONITION... THAT THE BATTLE IS FIXIN' TO TAKE A TURN. POINT US IN THE RIGHT DIRECTION.
HEE HEE HEE!!
SHRRRP!!
IT'S THAT WHIP AGAIN!!
JOKER, HELP MEEE!!
OVER-HEAT!!!
KRACK...!!
!!!

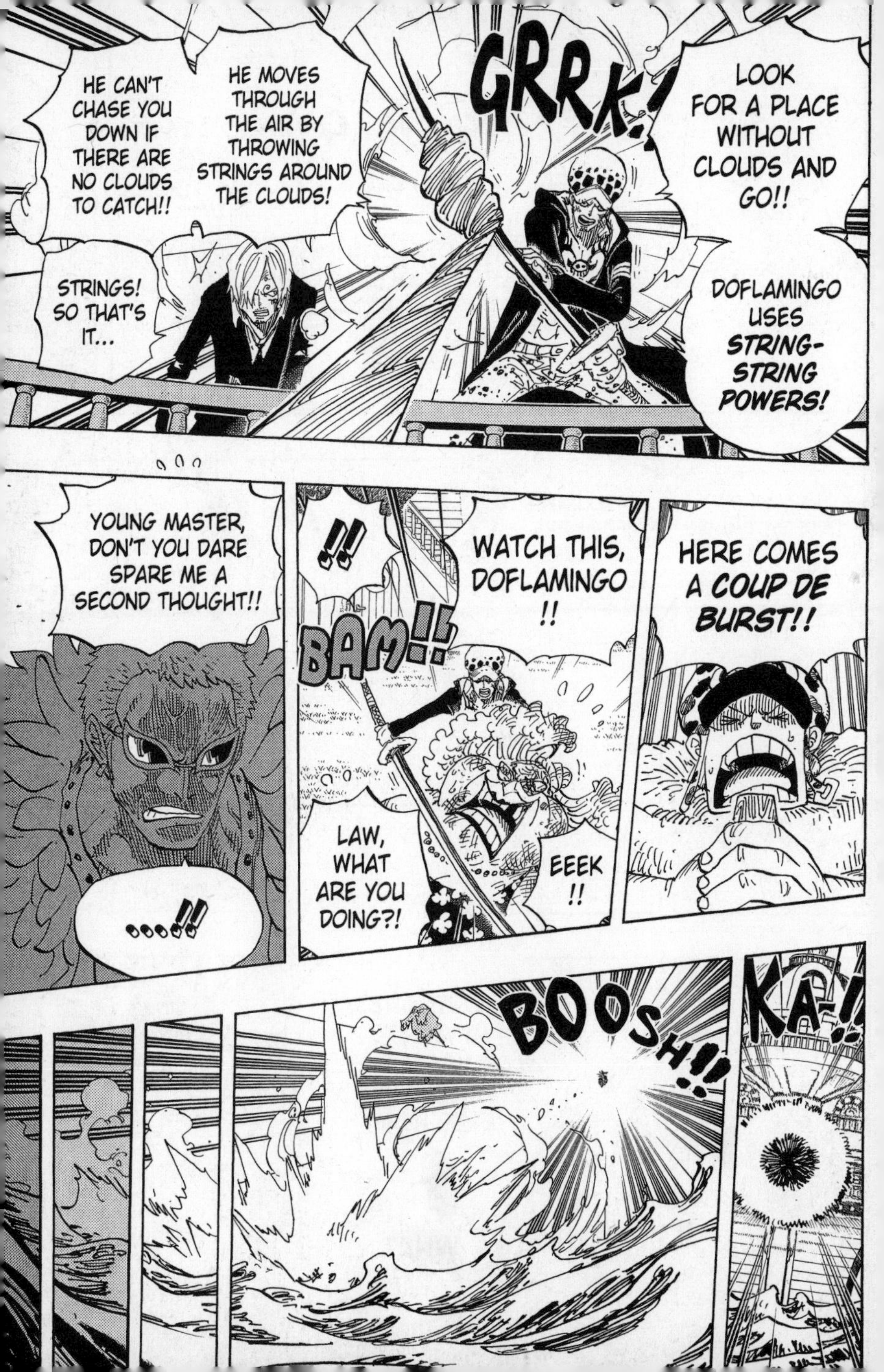
LOOK FOR A PLACE WITHOUT CLOUDS AND GO!!
GRRK!
DOFLAMINGO USES STRING-STRING POWERS!
HE MOVES THROUGH THE AIR BY THROWING STRINGS AROUND THE CLOUDS!
HE CAN'T CHASE YOU DOWN IF THERE ARE NO CLOUDS TO CATCH!!
STRINGS! SO THAT'S IT...
HERE COMES A COUP DE BURST!!
WATCH THIS, DOFLAMINGO !!
!!
BAM!!
LAW, WHAT ARE YOU DOING?!
EEEK !!
YOUNG MASTER, DON'T YOU DARE SPARE ME A SECOND THOUGHT!!
...!!
KA-!!
BOOSH!!!

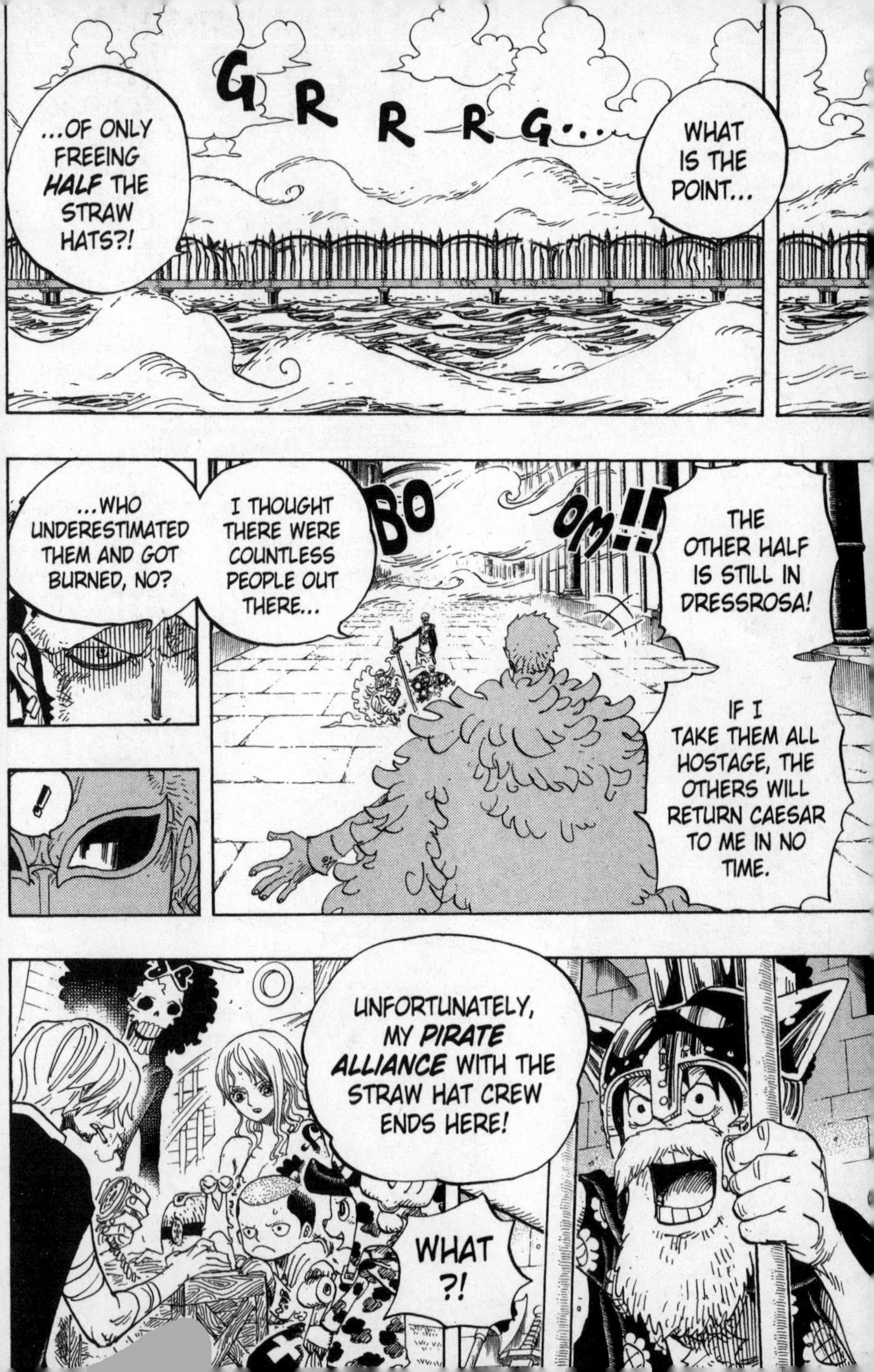
WHAT IS THE POINT...
GRRRG...
...OF ONLY FREEING HALF THE STRAW HATS?!
BOOM!!
THE OTHER HALF IS STILL IN DRESSROSA!
IF I TAKE THEM ALL HOSTAGE, THE OTHERS WILL RETURN CAESAR TO ME IN NO TIME.
I THOUGHT THERE WERE COUNTLESS PEOPLE OUT THERE...
...WHO UNDERESTIMATED THEM AND GOT BURNED, NO?
!
UNFORTUNATELY, MY PIRATE ALLIANCE WITH THE STRAW HAT CREW ENDS HERE!
WHAT ?!

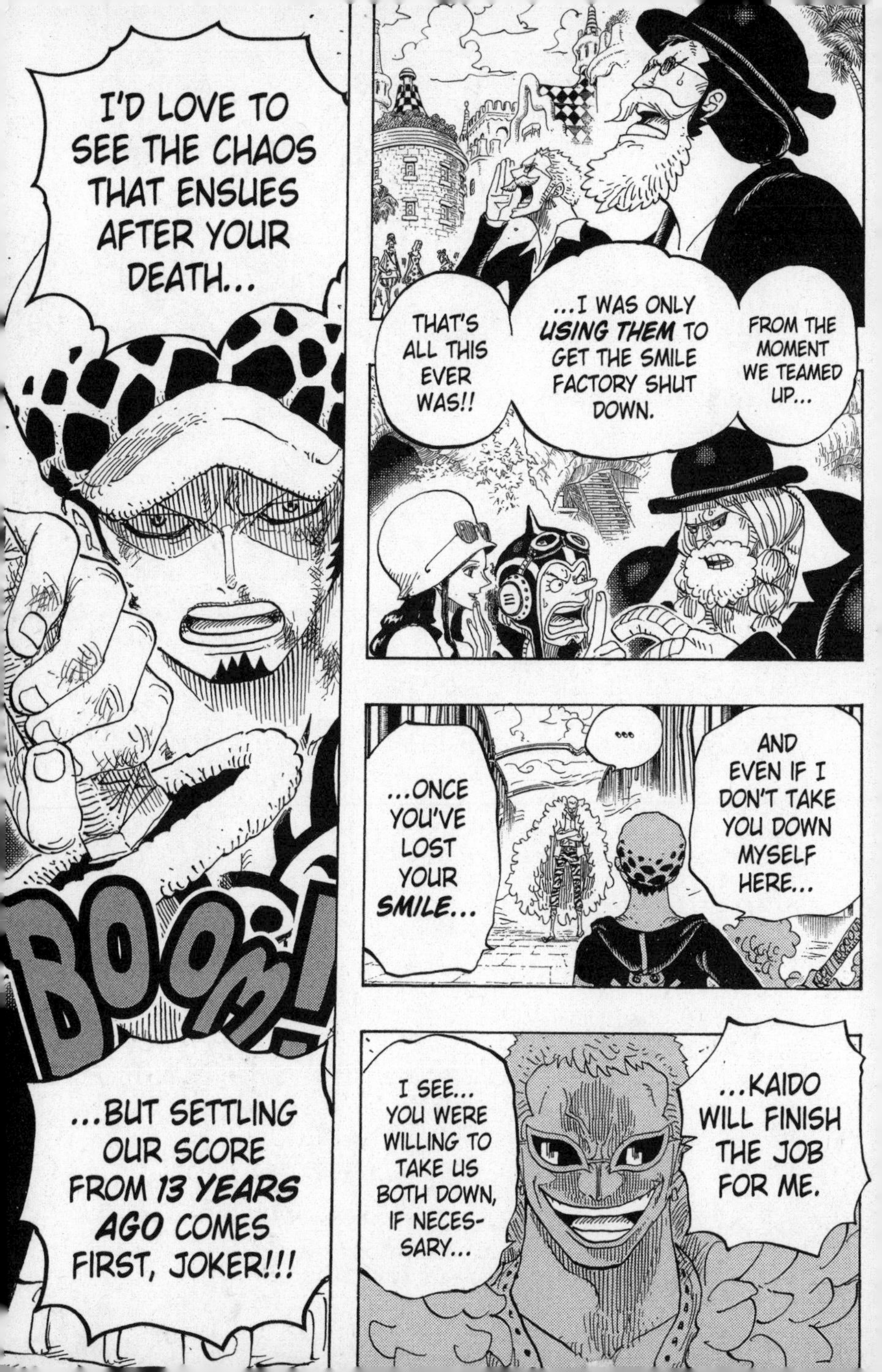
FROM THE MOMENT WE TEAMED UP...
...I WAS ONLY USING THEM TO GET THE SMILE FACTORY SHUT DOWN.
THAT'S ALL THIS EVER WAS!!
AND EVEN IF I DON'T TAKE YOU DOWN MYSELF HERE...
...
...ONCE YOU'VE LOST YOUR SMILE...
...KAIDO WILL FINISH THE JOB FOR ME.
I SEE... YOU WERE WILLING TO TAKE US BOTH DOWN, IF NECES-SARY...
I'D LOVE TO SEE THE CHAOS THAT ENSUES AFTER YOUR DEATH...
BOOM!
...BUT SETTLING OUR SCORE FROM 13 YEARS AGO COMES FIRST, JOKER!!!

(Yama, Nagano)

?!!
RAH

Q: Chapter 711 in Volume 71. The big panel. I see some candy falling out of Robin's bag. Was she going to give that to Chopper?

--Anmitsu Usagi

A: Yes! Robin loves Chopper, so she always keeps some of his favorite candy around to give to him at any time!!

Q: Hey, Odacchi!! On page 109 of Volume 71, was Luffy going to call Bellamy, "Mallony"?! Was he thinking of the snack food company Malony? If Luffy's head is full of nothing but food, then I'm more like Sanji--my head is full of girls. What's inside your head, Odacchi?

--Shin

OH! IT'S YOU!!
THE GUY WHO MESSED UP THE POOR DIAMOND-HEAD MAN...
MALLO ...?

A: I don't think about girls the way you do. It's nothing but serious bustiness--ahem, business--in there. And you're right about Luffy's train of thought! I guess he only remembered the rhythm of the name.

Q: Hello (^▼^) I have a question. You know how there's a woman in both Chapter 707 and 708 who's covering her face to avoid seeing Bartolomeo's "thing"? But…she's not covering her eyes. In fact, she's peeking right through her fingers. Who is she? Tell me her name!

--Rhett Butler

A: Oh, you mean "Peekatha Krotch"? She's a well-known young damsel from the town of Primula in the west of Dressrosa. She's very shy.

Chapter 725:
THE UNDEFEATED WOMAN

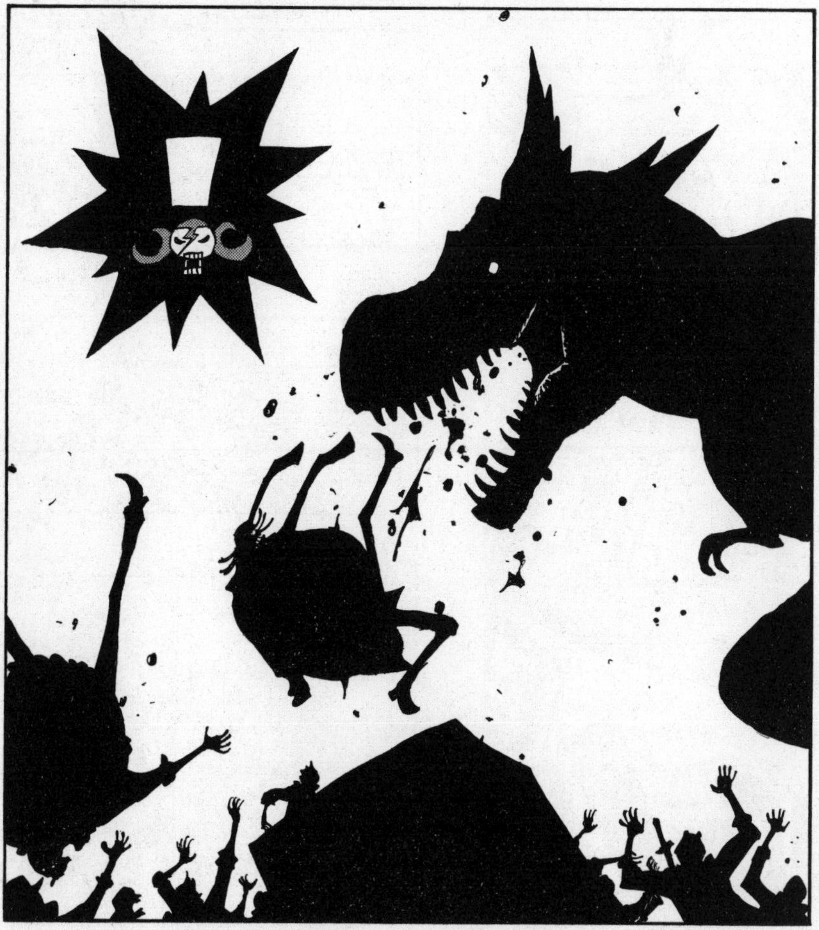

CARIBOU'S NEW WORLD KEE HEE HEE, VOL. 41:
"DINOSAUR ALERT"

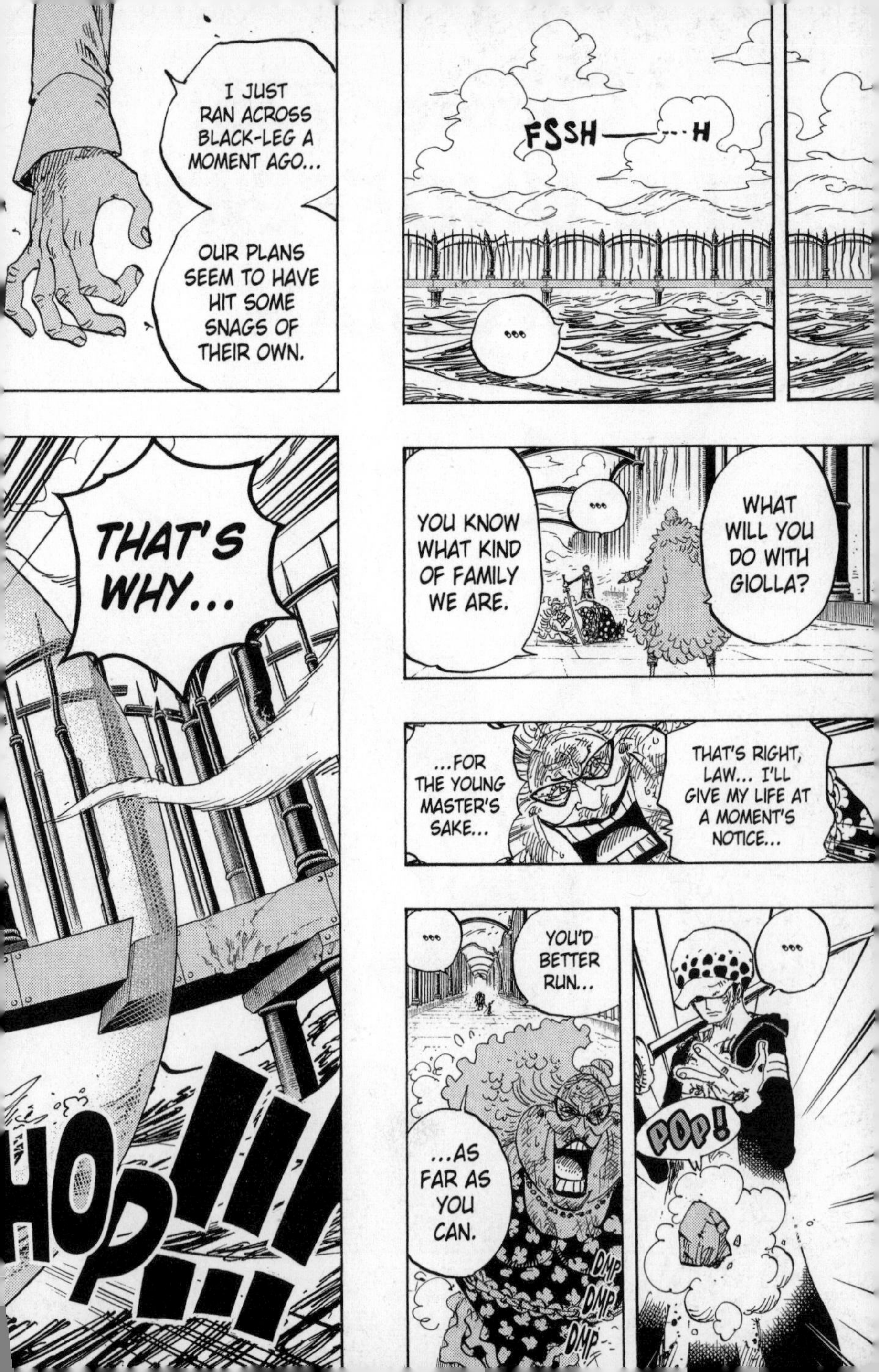
FSSH——···H
...
I JUST RAN ACROSS BLACK-LEG A MOMENT AGO...
OUR PLANS SEEM TO HAVE HIT SOME SNAGS OF THEIR OWN.
WHAT WILL YOU DO WITH GIOLLA?
...
YOU KNOW WHAT KIND OF FAMILY WE ARE.
THAT'S RIGHT, LAW... I'LL GIVE MY LIFE AT A MOMENT'S NOTICE...
...FOR THE YOUNG MASTER'S SAKE...
...
POP!
YOU'D BETTER RUN...
...
...AS FAR AS YOU CAN.
DMP DMP DMP
THAT'S WHY...
HOP!!...

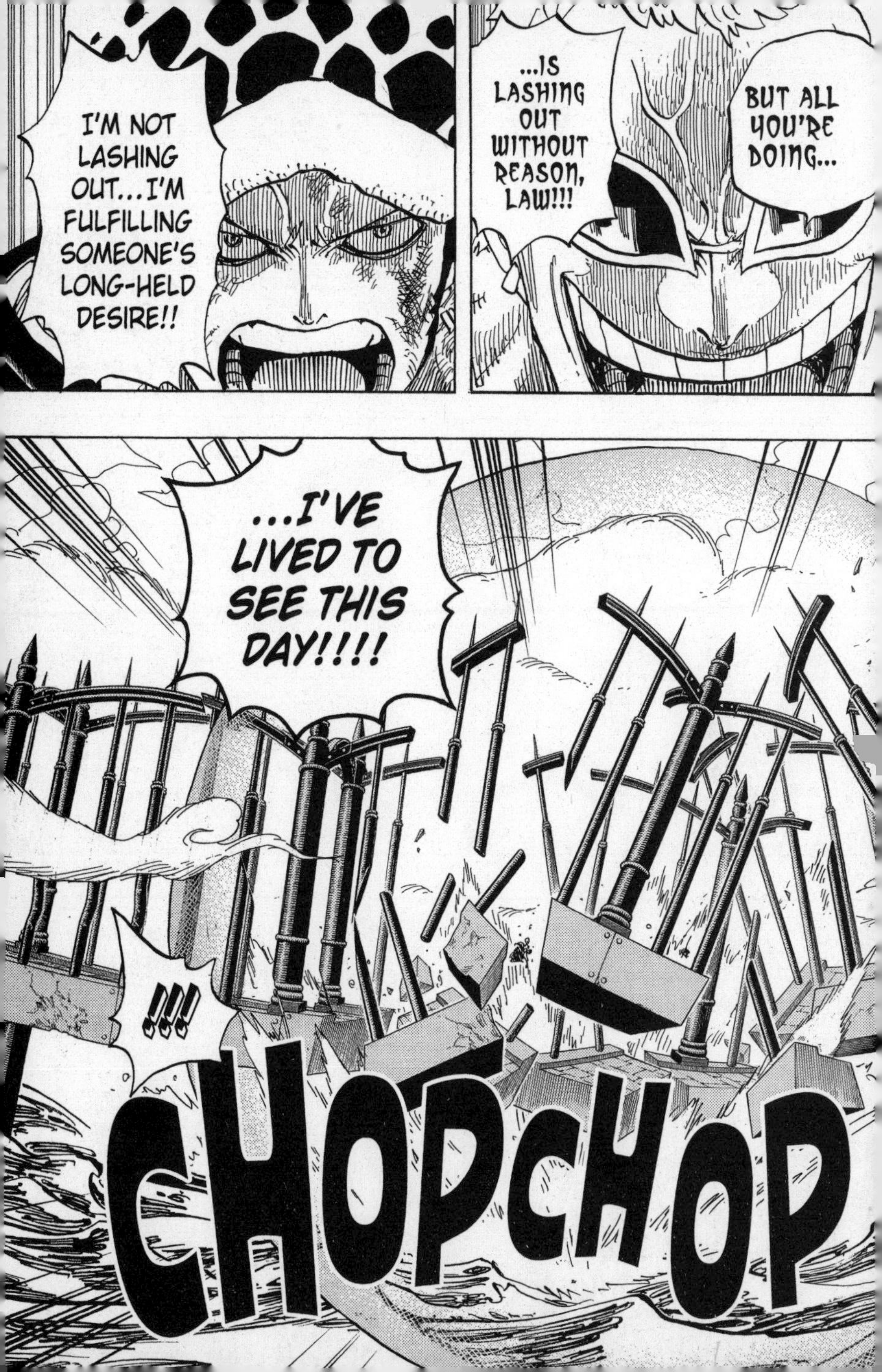
BUT ALL YOU'RE DOING...
...IS LASHING OUT WITHOUT REASON, LAW!!!
I'M NOT LASHING OUT...I'M FULFILLING SOMEONE'S LONG-HELD DESIRE!!
...I'VE LIVED TO SEE THIS DAY!!!!
!!!
CHOPCHOP

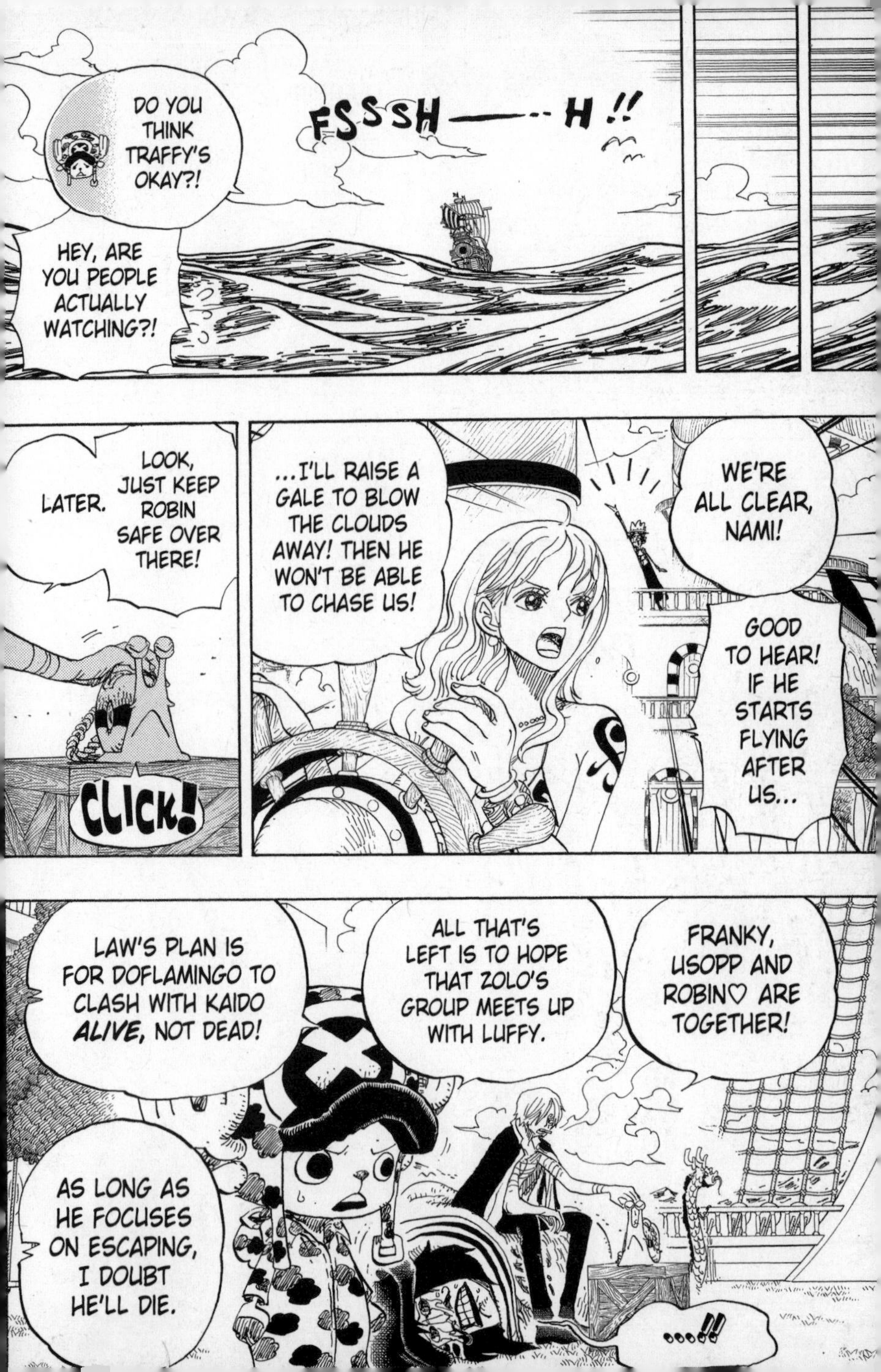
FSSSH——H!!
DO YOU THINK TRAFFY'S OKAY?!
HEY, ARE YOU PEOPLE ACTUALLY WATCHING?!
WE'RE ALL CLEAR, NAMI!
GOOD TO HEAR! IF HE STARTS FLYING AFTER US...
...I'LL RAISE A GALE TO BLOW THE CLOUDS AWAY! THEN HE WON'T BE ABLE TO CHASE US!
LOOK, JUST KEEP ROBIN SAFE OVER THERE!
LATER.
CLICK!
FRANKY, USOPP AND ROBIN♡ ARE TOGETHER!
ALL THAT'S LEFT IS TO HOPE THAT ZOLO'S GROUP MEETS UP WITH LUFFY.
LAW'S PLAN IS FOR DOFLAMINGO TO CLASH WITH KAIDO *ALIVE*, NOT DEAD!
AS LONG AS HE FOCUSES ON ESCAPING, I DOUBT HE'LL DIE.
....!!

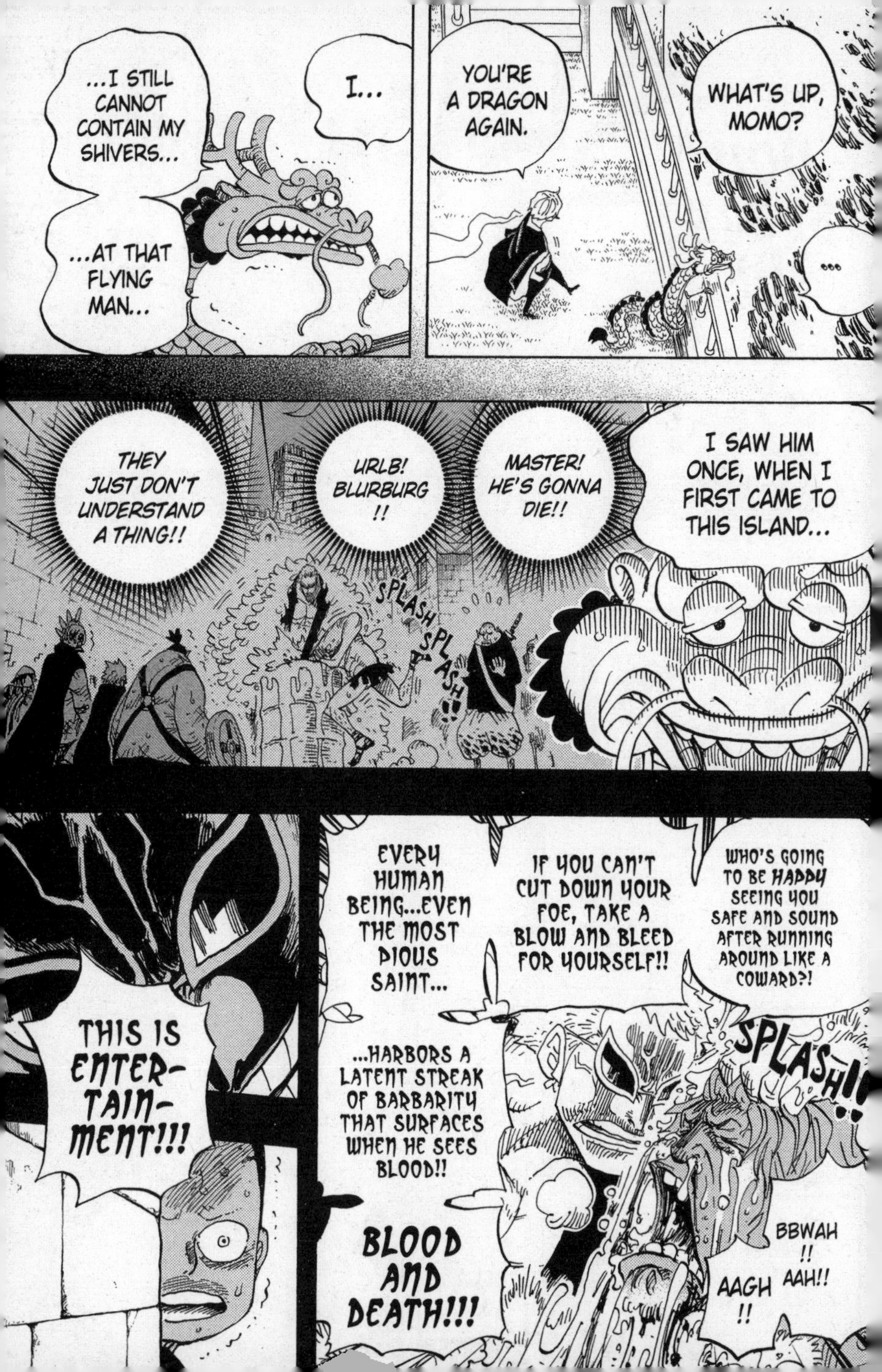
WHAT'S UP, MOMO?
YOU'RE A DRAGON AGAIN.
...
I...
...I STILL CANNOT CONTAIN MY SHIVERS...
...AT THAT FLYING MAN...
I SAW HIM ONCE, WHEN I FIRST CAME TO THIS ISLAND...
MASTER! HE'S GONNA DIE!!
URLB! BLURBURG !!
THEY JUST DON'T UNDERSTAND A THING!!
SPLASH
SPLASH!!
WHO'S GOING TO BE HAPPY SEEING YOU SAFE AND SOUND AFTER RUNNING AROUND LIKE A COWARD?!
IF YOU CAN'T CUT DOWN YOUR FOE, TAKE A BLOW AND BLEED FOR YOURSELF!!
EVERY HUMAN BEING...EVEN THE MOST PIOUS SAINT...
SPLASH!!
...HARBORS A LATENT STREAK OF BARBARITY THAT SURFACES WHEN HE SEES BLOOD!!
BBWAH !! AAH!!
AAGH !!
BLOOD AND DEATH!!!
THIS IS ENTERTAINMENT!!!

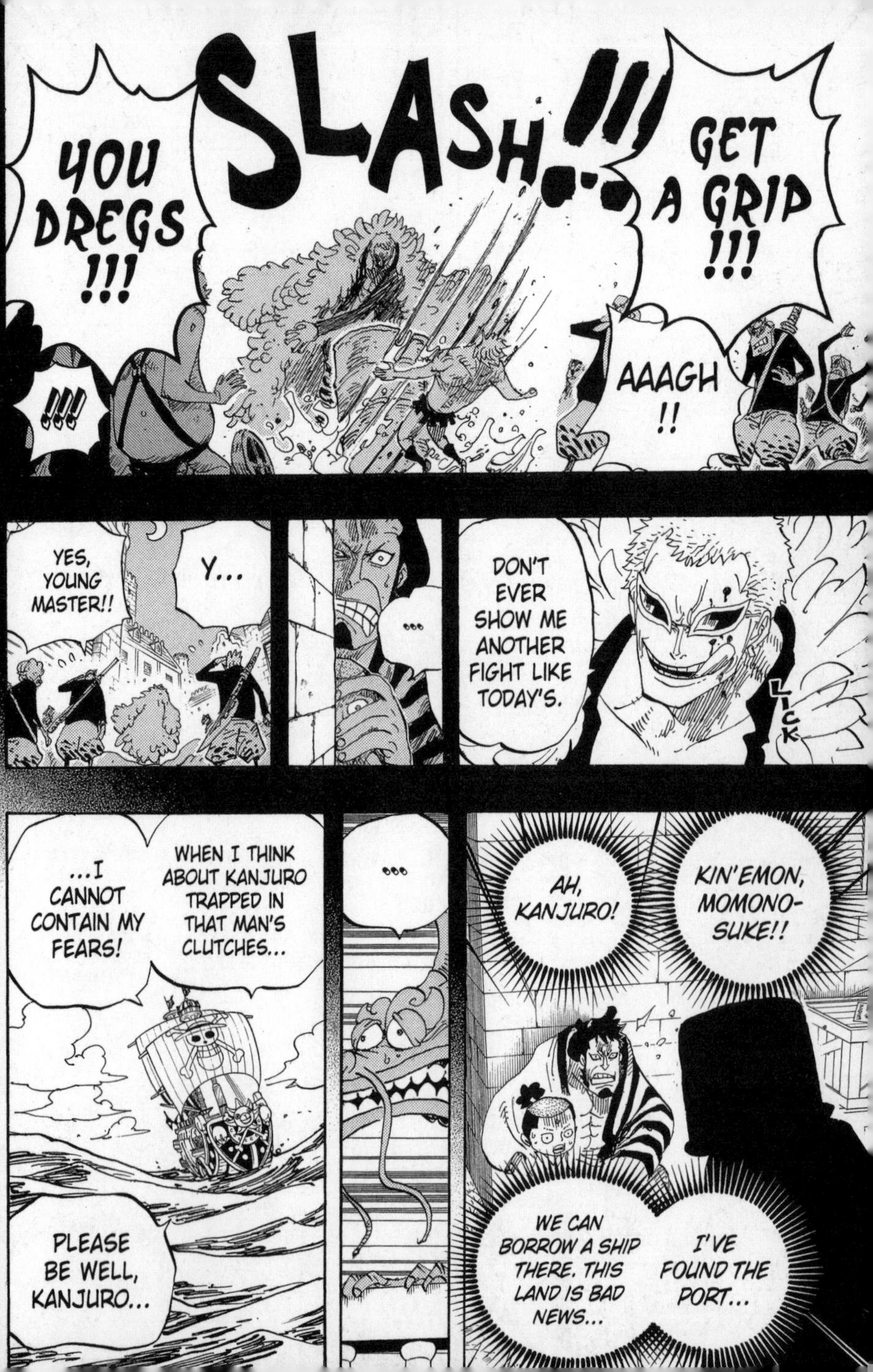
GET A GRIP!!!
SLASH...!!!
YOU DREGS!!!
AAAGH!!
!!!
DON'T EVER SHOW ME ANOTHER FIGHT LIKE TODAY'S.
LICK
...
Y...
YES, YOUNG MASTER!!
KIN'EMON, MOMONO-SUKE!!
AH, KANJURO!
I'VE FOUND THE PORT...
WE CAN BORROW A SHIP THERE. THIS LAND IS BAD NEWS...
...
WHEN I THINK ABOUT KANJURO TRAPPED IN THAT MAN'S CLUTCHES...
...I CANNOT CONTAIN MY FEARS!
PLEASE BE WELL, KANJURO...

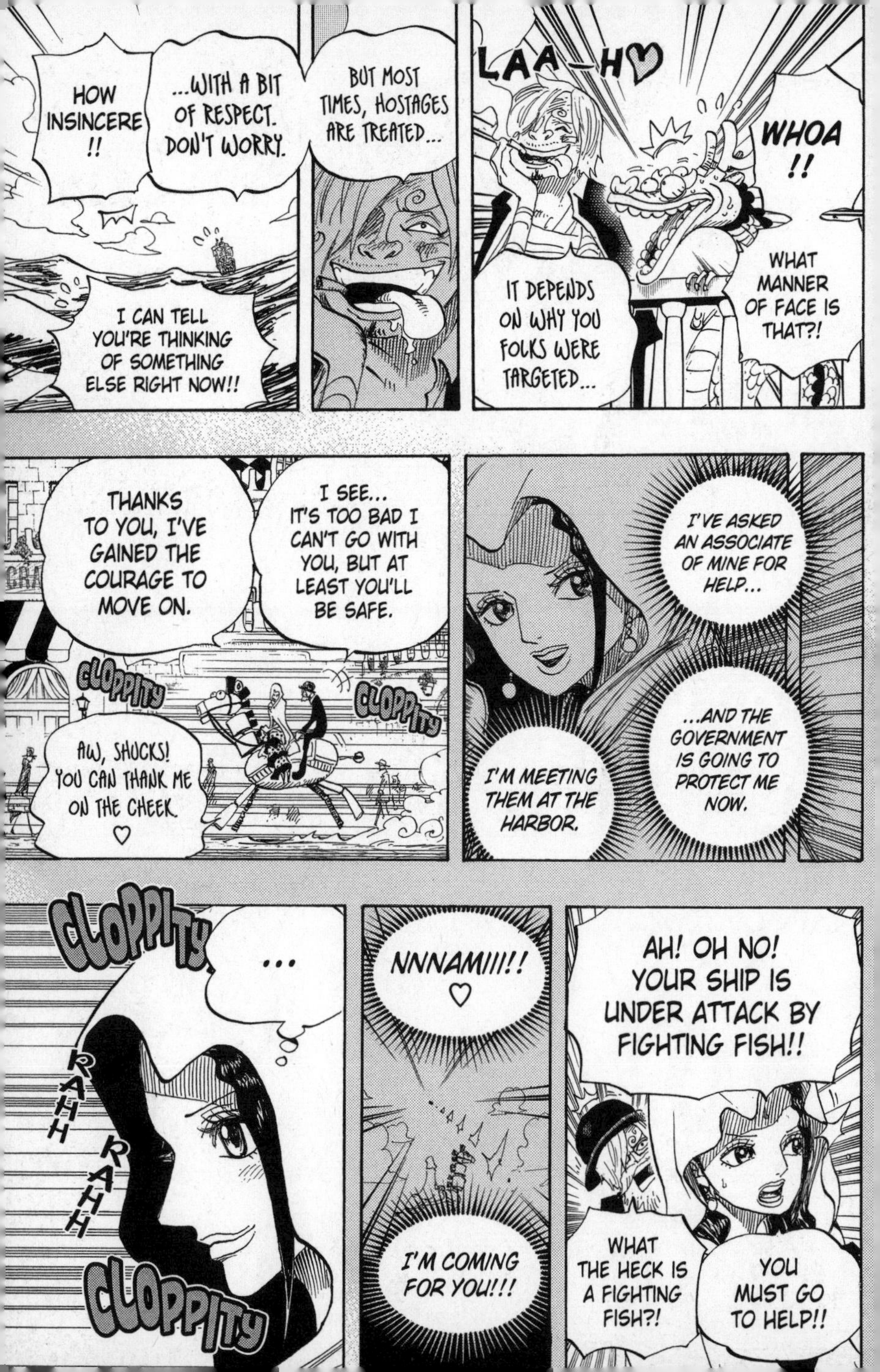
LAA-H♡
WHOA!!
WHAT MANNER OF FACE IS THAT?!
IT DEPENDS ON WHY YOU FOLKS WERE TARGETED...
BUT MOST TIMES, HOSTAGES ARE TREATED...
...WITH A BIT OF RESPECT. DON'T WORRY.
HOW INSINCERE!!
I CAN TELL YOU'RE THINKING OF SOMETHING ELSE RIGHT NOW!!
I'VE ASKED AN ASSOCIATE OF MINE FOR HELP...
...AND THE GOVERNMENT IS GOING TO PROTECT ME NOW.
I'M MEETING THEM AT THE HARBOR.
I SEE... IT'S TOO BAD I CAN'T GO WITH YOU, BUT AT LEAST YOU'LL BE SAFE.
THANKS TO YOU, I'VE GAINED THE COURAGE TO MOVE ON.
CLOPPITY
CLOPPITY
AW, SHUCKS! YOU CAN THANK ME ON THE CHEEK. ♡
AH! OH NO! YOUR SHIP IS UNDER ATTACK BY FIGHTING FISH!!
YOU MUST GO TO HELP!!
WHAT THE HECK IS A FIGHTING FISH?!
NNNAMI!!!! ♡
I'M COMING FOR YOU!!!
CLOPPITY
...
RAHH
RAHH
CLOPPITY

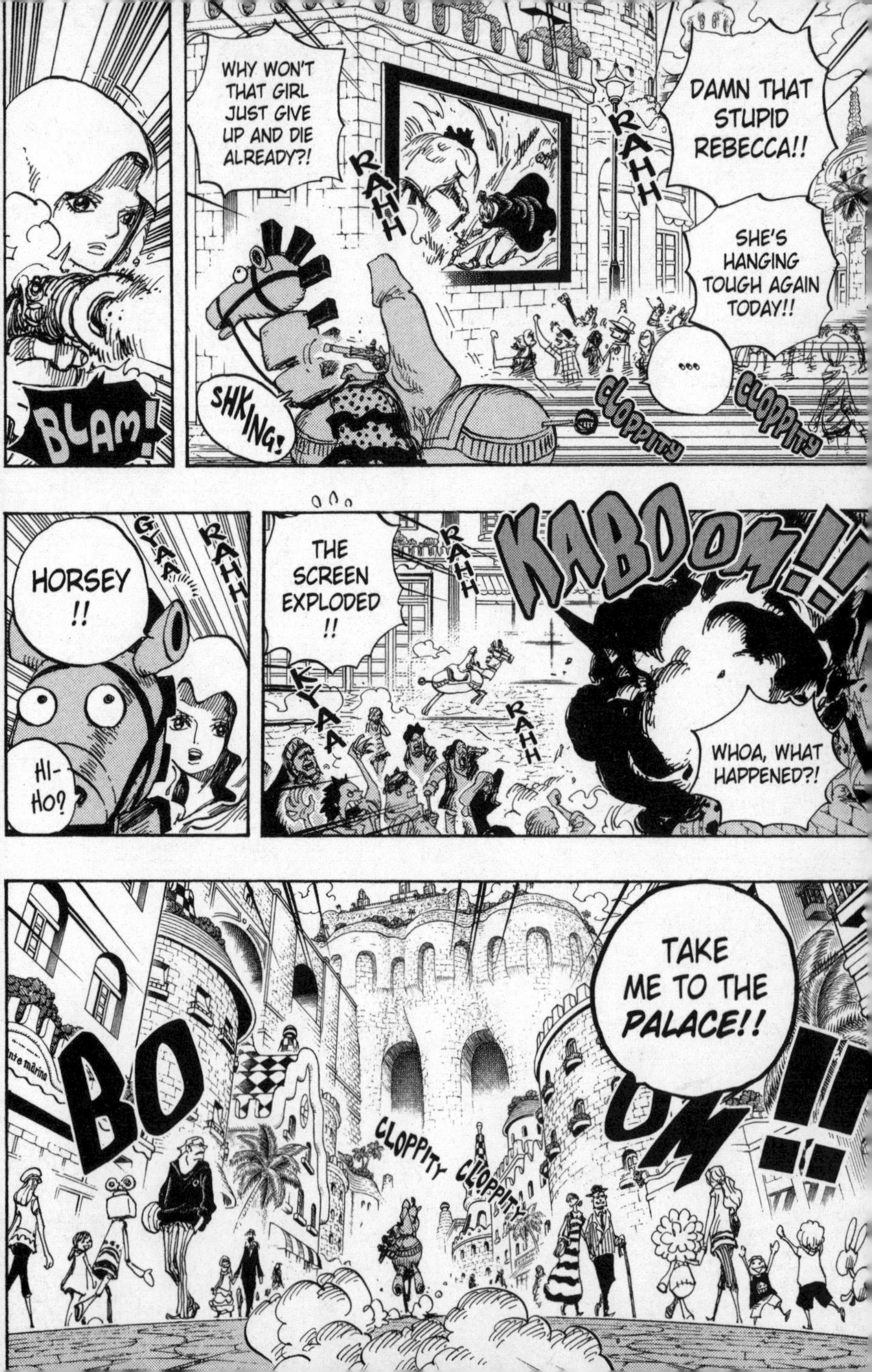
DAMN THAT STUPID REBECCA!!
RAHH
SHE'S HANGING TOUGH AGAIN TODAY!!
CLOPPITY
...
CLOPPITY
RAHH
WHY WON'T THAT GIRL JUST GIVE UP AND DIE ALREADY?!
SHKING!
BLAM!
KABOOM!!
WHOA, WHAT HAPPENED?!
RAHH
RAHH
THE SCREEN EXPLODED!!
KYAA
RAHH
GYAA
HORSEY!!
HI-HO?
TAKE ME TO THE PALACE!!
BOOM!!
CLOPPITY
CLOPPITY

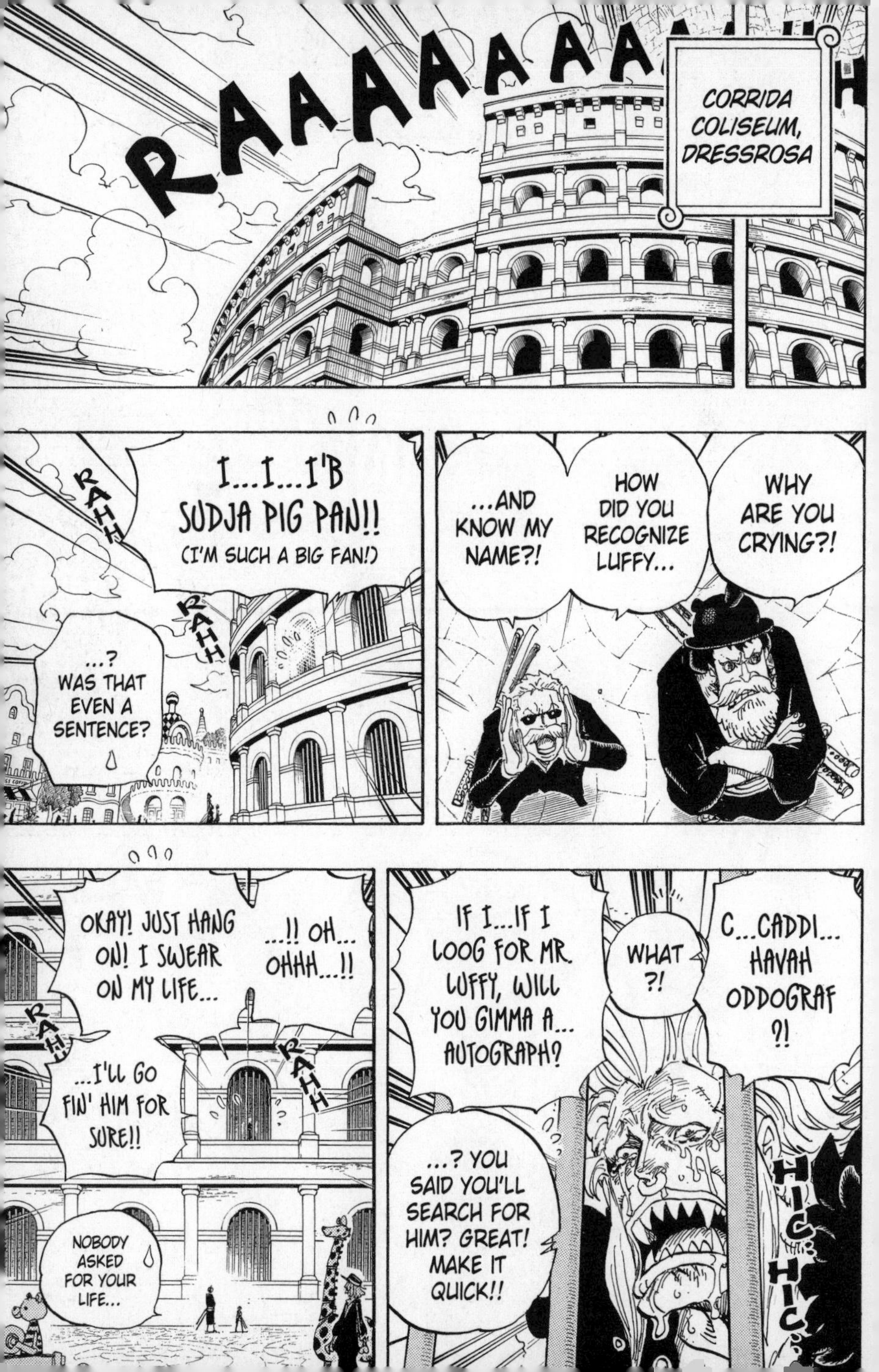

CORRIDA COLISEUM, DRESSROSA
RAAAAAAAAH
WHY ARE YOU CRYING?!
HOW DID YOU RECOGNIZE LUFFY...
...AND KNOW MY NAME?!
I...I...I'B SUDJA PIG PAN!!
(I'M SUCH A BIG FAN!)
RAHH
RAHH
...? WAS THAT EVEN A SENTENCE?
C...CADDI... HAVAH ODDOGRAF ?!
WHAT ?!
IF I...IF I LOOG FOR MR. LUFFY, WILL YOU GIMMA A... AUTOGRAPH?
HIC HIC HIC
...? YOU SAID YOU'LL SEARCH FOR HIM? GREAT! MAKE IT QUICK!!
...!! OH... OHHH...!!
OKAY! JUST HANG ON! I SWEAR ON MY LIFE...
RAHH
RAHH
...I'LL GO FIN' HIM FOR SURE!!
NOBODY ASKED FOR YOUR LIFE...

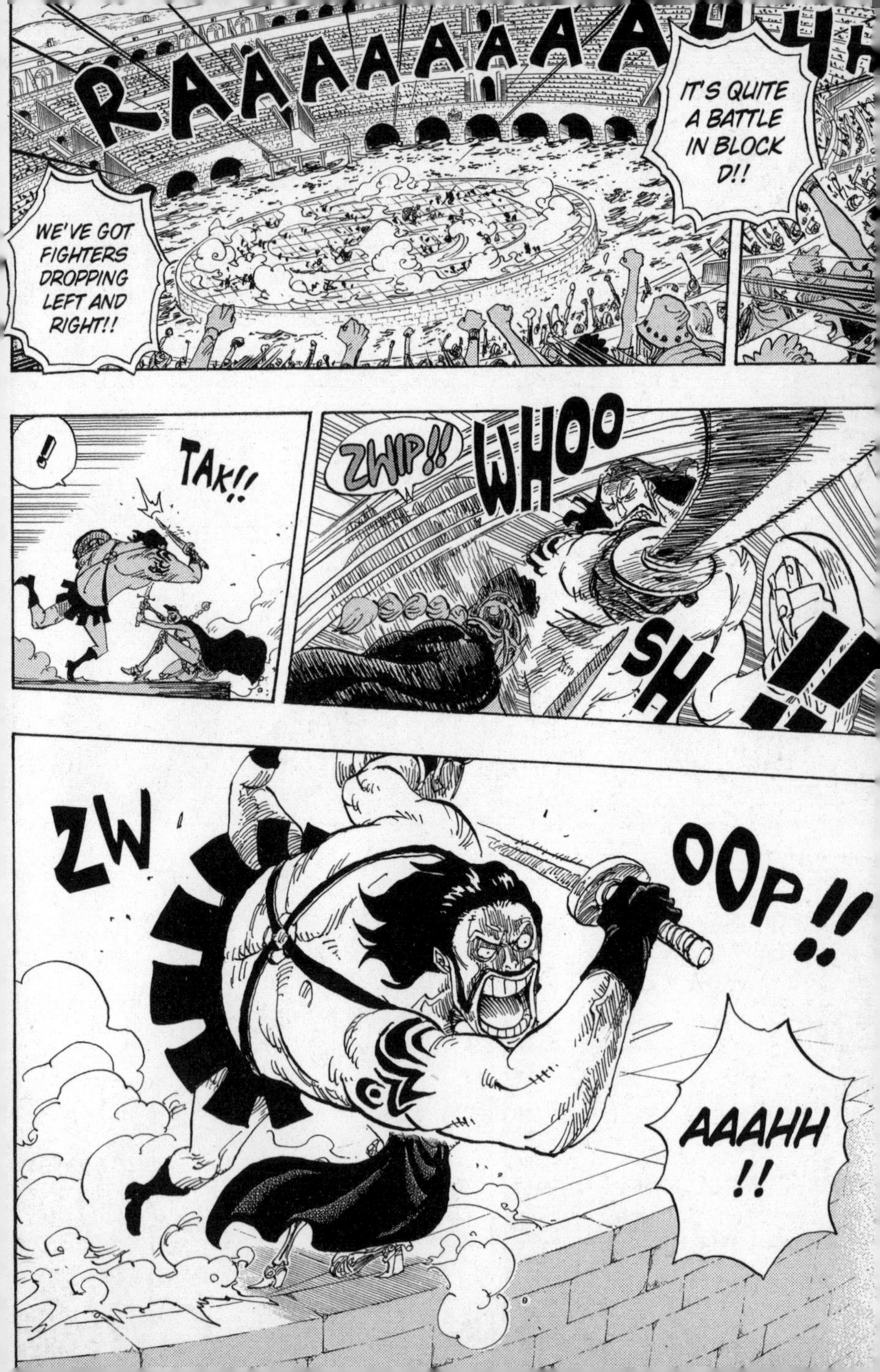
RAAAAAAAUHH
IT'S QUITE A BATTLE IN BLOCK D!!
WE'VE GOT FIGHTERS DROPPING LEFT AND RIGHT!!
ZWIP!!
WHOO
SH!!
!
TAK!!
ZW
OOP!!
AAAHH!!

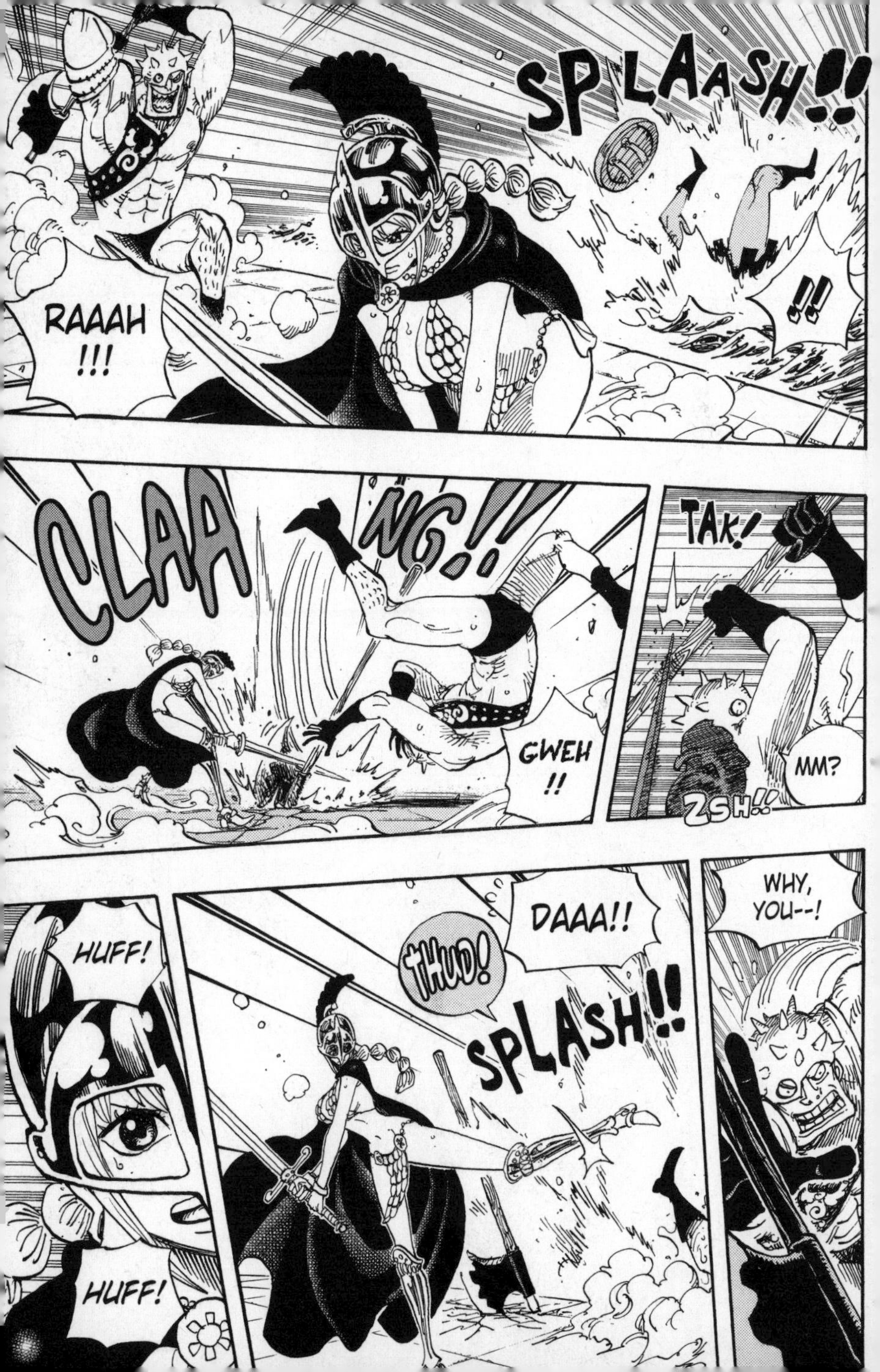
SPLAASH!!
!!
RAAAH !!!
TAK!
MM?
ZSH!!
CLAANG!!
GWEH !!
WHY, YOU--!
DAAA!!
THUD!
SPLASH!!
HUFF!
HUFF!

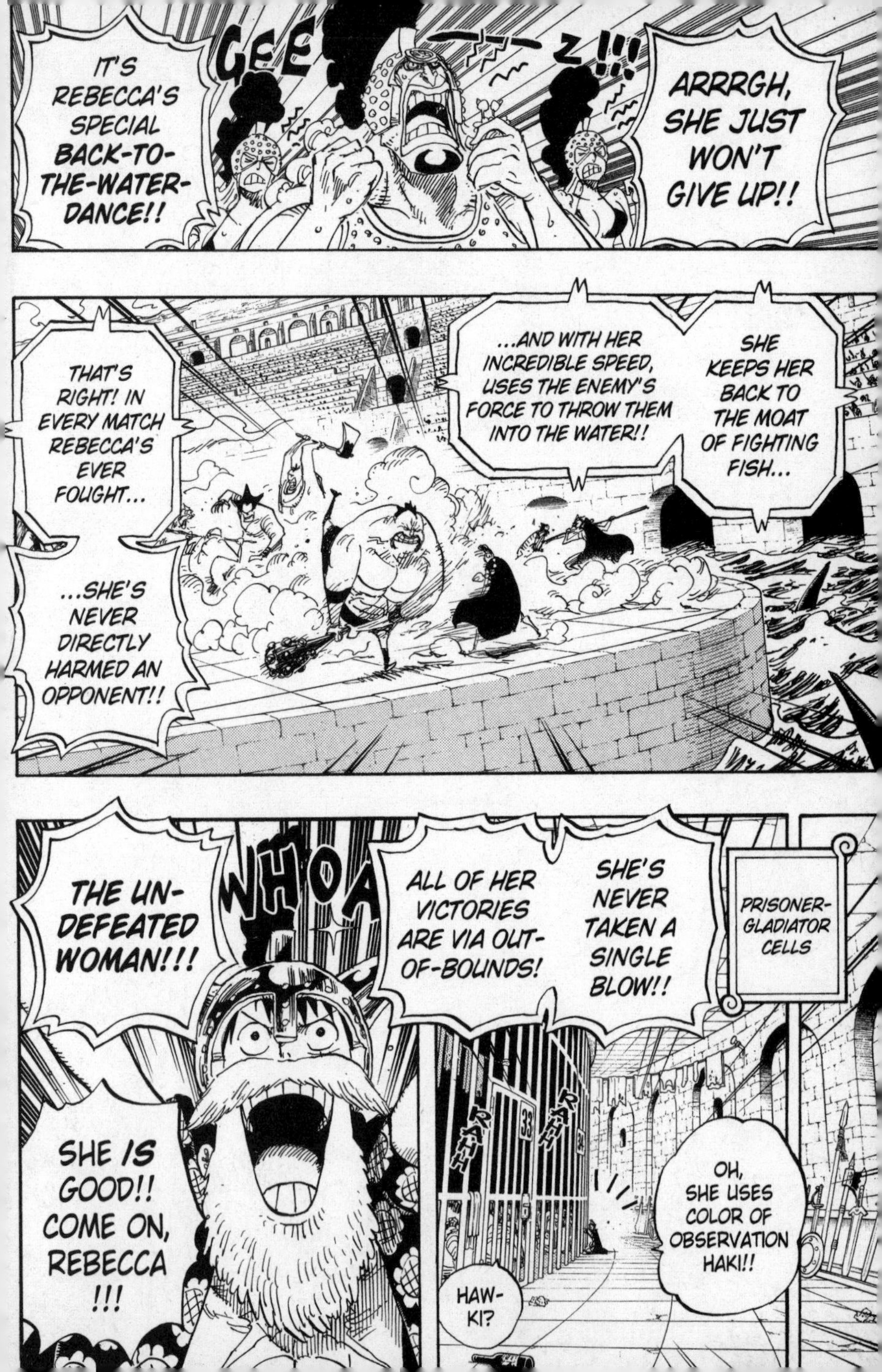
ARRRGH, SHE JUST WON'T GIVE UP!!
GEE———Z!!!
IT'S REBECCA'S SPECIAL BACK-TO-THE-WATER-DANCE!!
SHE KEEPS HER BACK TO THE MOAT OF FIGHTING FISH...
...AND WITH HER INCREDIBLE SPEED, USES THE ENEMY'S FORCE TO THROW THEM INTO THE WATER!!
THAT'S RIGHT! IN EVERY MATCH REBECCA'S EVER FOUGHT...
...SHE'S NEVER DIRECTLY HARMED AN OPPONENT!!
SHE'S NEVER TAKEN A SINGLE BLOW!!
ALL OF HER VICTORIES ARE VIA OUT-OF-BOUNDS!
WHOA
THE UN-DEFEATED WOMAN!!!
SHE IS GOOD!! COME ON, REBECCA!!!
PRISONER-GLADIATOR CELLS
OH, SHE USES COLOR OF OBSERVATION HAKI!!
HAW-KI?

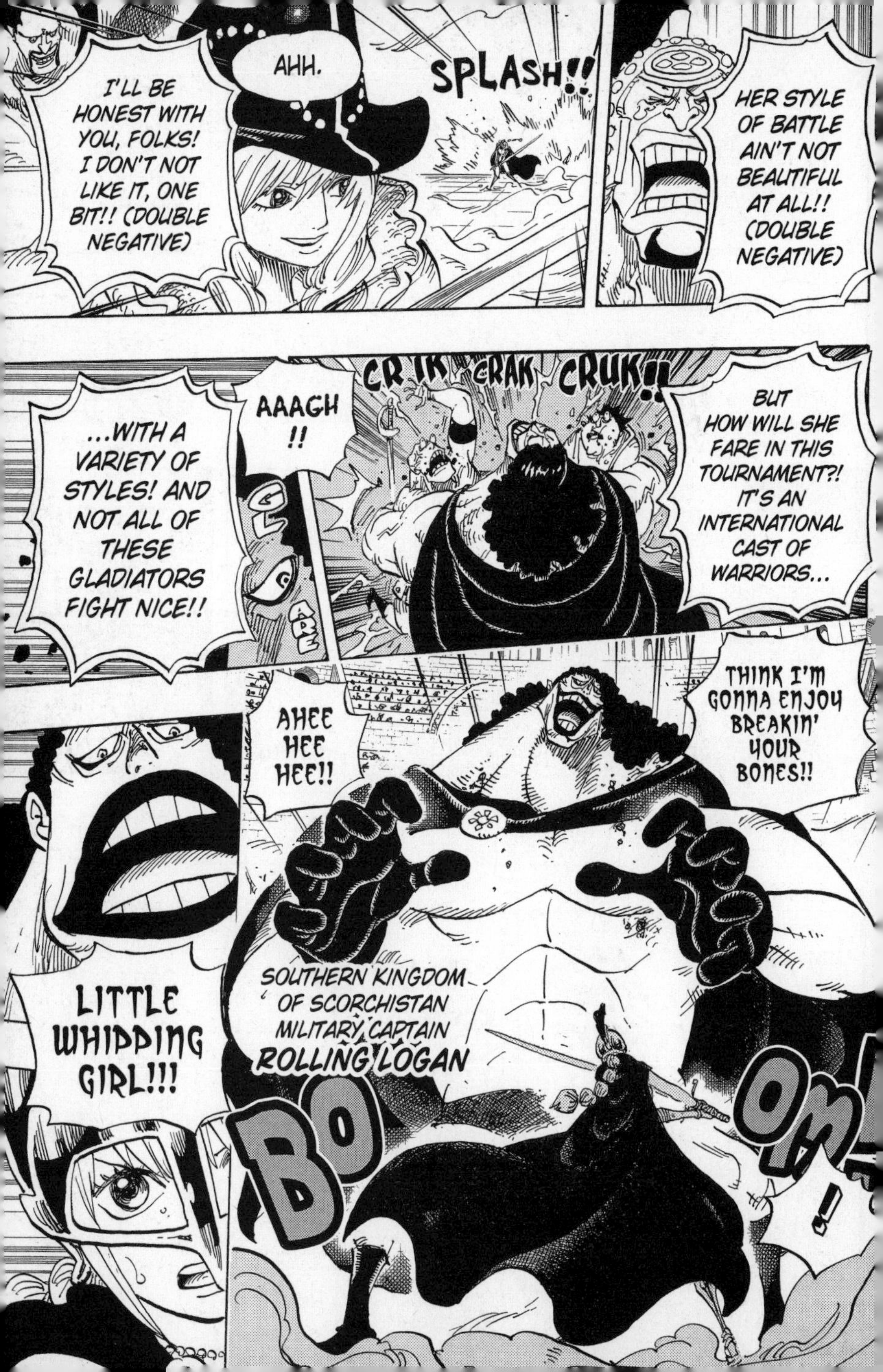
HER STYLE OF BATTLE AIN'T NOT BEAUTIFUL AT ALL!! (DOUBLE NEGATIVE)
SPLASH!!
AHH.
I'LL BE HONEST WITH YOU, FOLKS! I DON'T NOT LIKE IT, ONE BIT!! (DOUBLE NEGATIVE)
BUT HOW WILL SHE FARE IN THIS TOURNAMENT?! IT'S AN INTERNATIONAL CAST OF WARRIORS...
CRIK CRAK CRUK!!
AAAGH!!
...WITH A VARIETY OF STYLES! AND NOT ALL OF THESE GLADIATORS FIGHT NICE!!
THINK I'M GONNA ENJOY BREAKIN' YOUR BONES!!
AHEE HEE HEE!!
SOUTHERN KINGDOM OF SCORCHISTAN MILITARY CAPTAIN ROLLING LOGAN
BOOM!!
LITTLE WHIPPING GIRL!!!

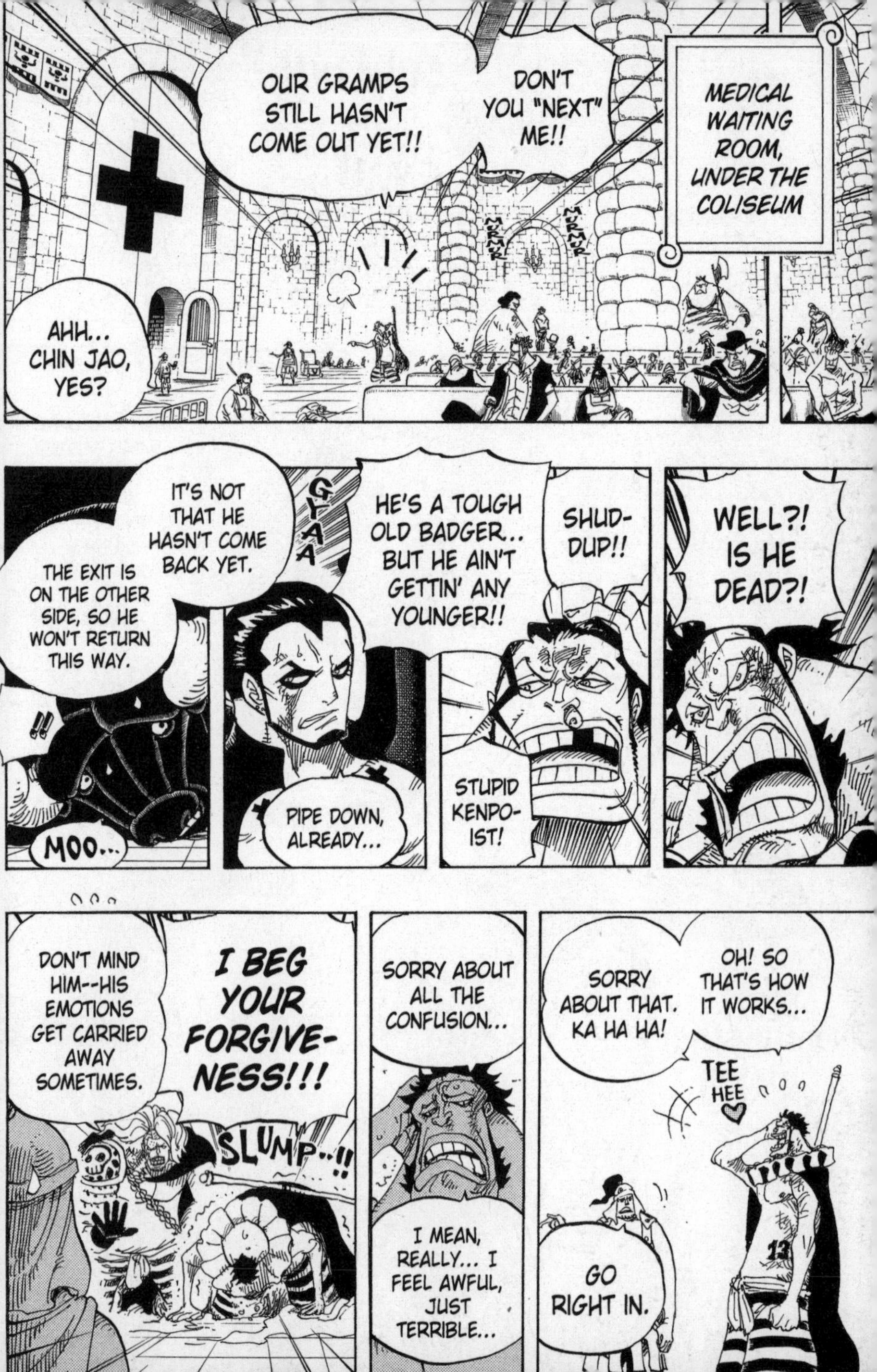
MEDICAL WAITING ROOM, UNDER THE COLISEUM
DON'T YOU "NEXT" ME!!
OUR GRAMPS STILL HASN'T COME OUT YET!!
MURMUR
MURMUR
AHH... CHIN JAO, YES?
WELL?! IS HE DEAD?!
SHUD-DUP!!
STUPID KENPO-IST!
HE'S A TOUGH OLD BADGER... BUT HE AIN'T GETTIN' ANY YOUNGER!!
GYAA
PIPE DOWN, ALREADY...
IT'S NOT THAT HE HASN'T COME BACK YET.
THE EXIT IS ON THE OTHER SIDE, SO HE WON'T RETURN THIS WAY.
!!
MOO...
OH! SO THAT'S HOW IT WORKS...
SORRY ABOUT THAT. KA HA HA!
TEE HEE
GO RIGHT IN.
SORRY ABOUT ALL THE CONFUSION...
I MEAN, REALLY... I FEEL AWFUL, JUST TERRIBLE...
I BEG YOUR FORGIVE-NESS!!!
DON'T MIND HIM--HIS EMOTIONS GET CARRIED AWAY SOMETIMES.
SLUMP..!!

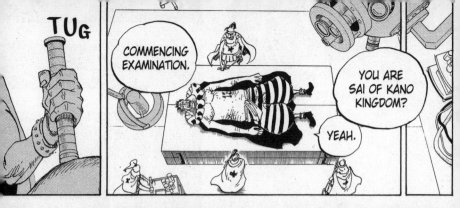

TUG

COMMENCING EXAMINATION.

YOU ARE SAI OF KANO KINGDOM?

YEAH.

WHA?

GCH

?!!

UNK!!!

HEY! WHAT THE--?!

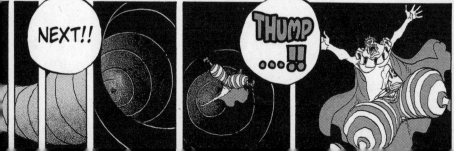

NEXT!!

THUMP
...!!

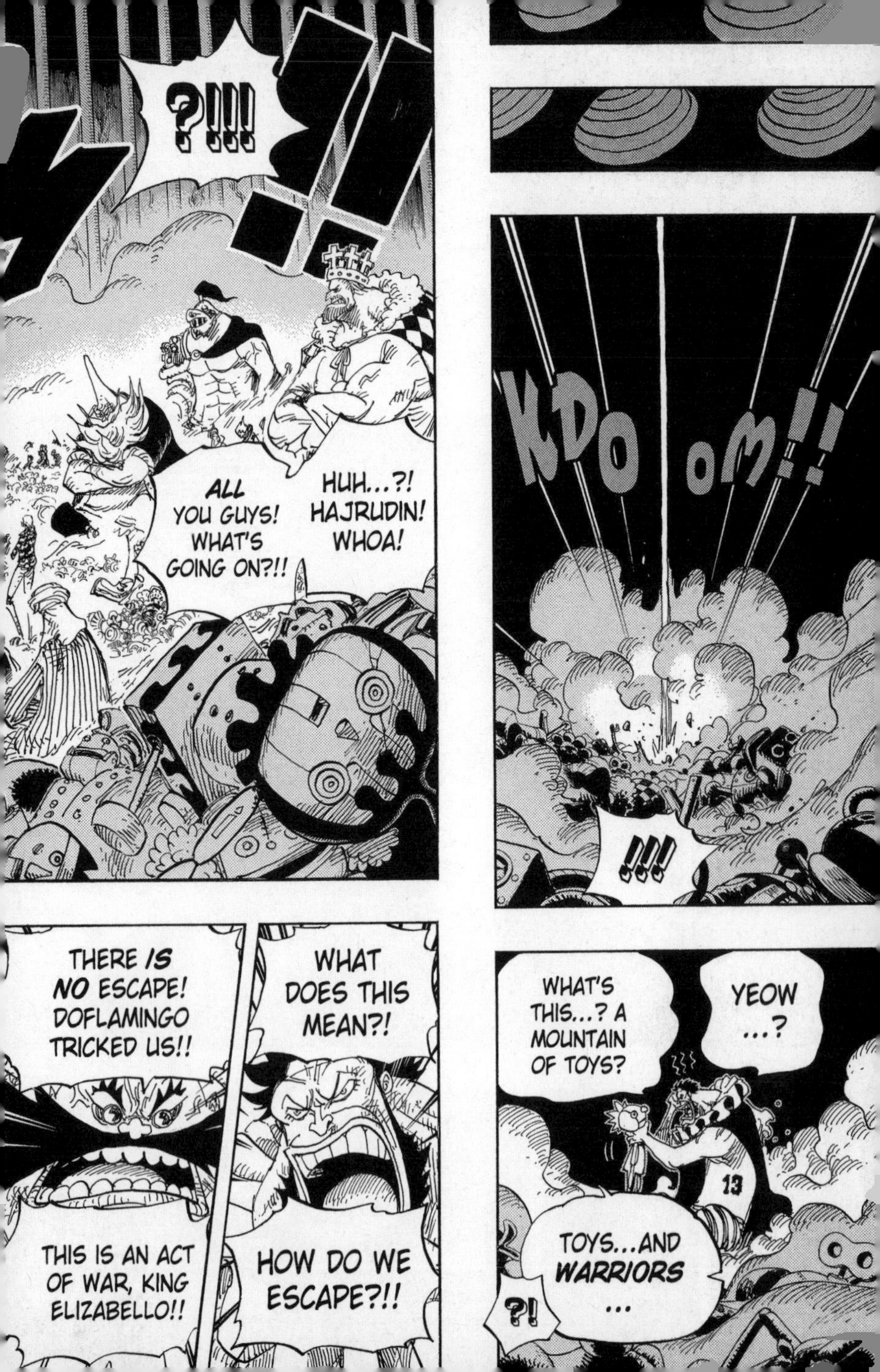
KDOOM!!
!!!
?!!!
HUH...?! HAJRUDIN! WHOA!
ALL YOU GUYS! WHAT'S GOING ON?!!
YEOW ...?
WHAT'S THIS...? A MOUNTAIN OF TOYS?
TOYS...AND *WARRIORS* ...
?!
WHAT DOES THIS MEAN?!
HOW DO WE ESCAPE?!!
THERE *IS NO* ESCAPE! DOFLAMINGO TRICKED US!!
THIS IS AN ACT OF WAR, KING ELIZABELLO!!

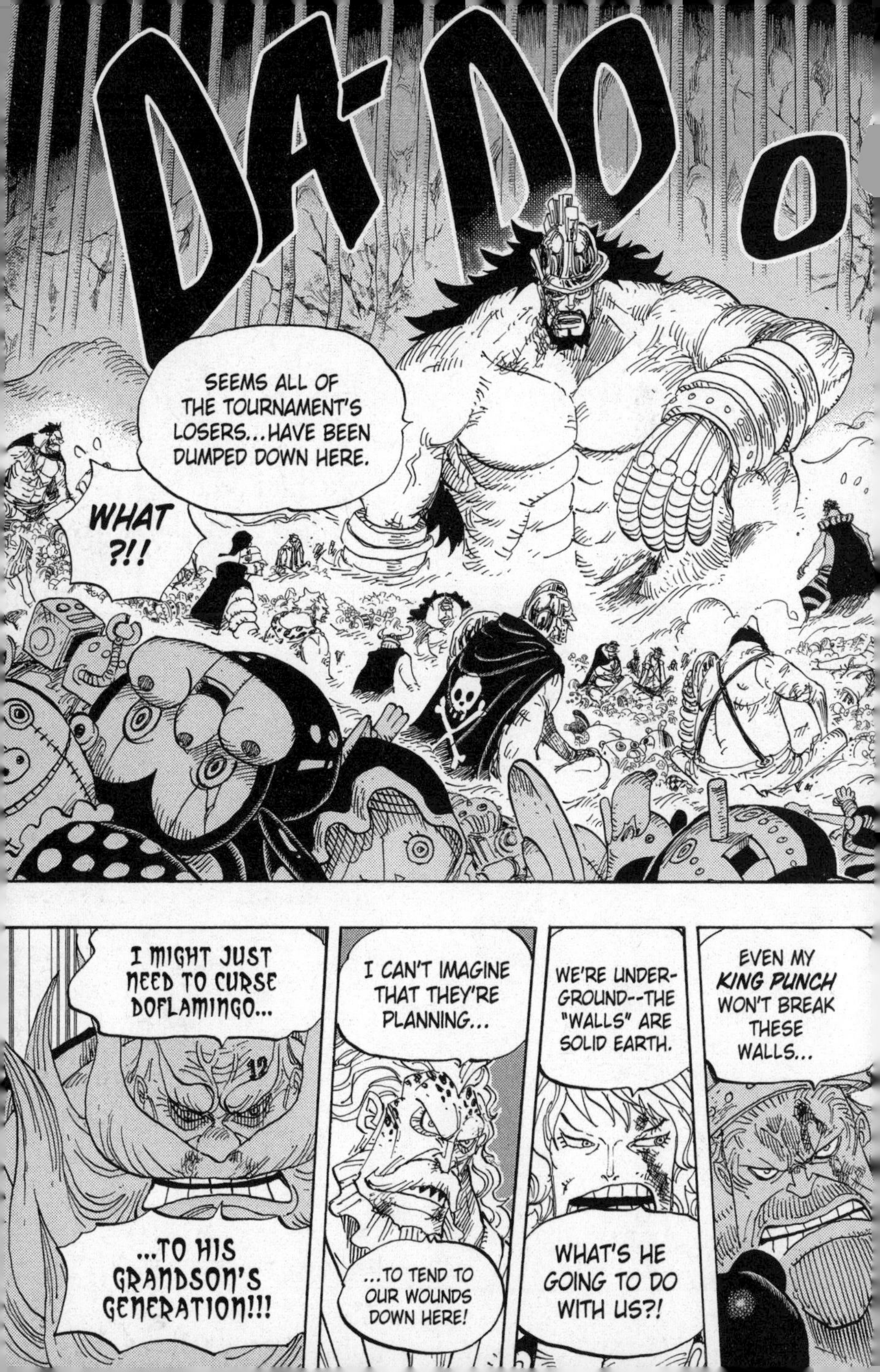
DA-DOO
SEEMS ALL OF THE TOURNAMENT'S LOSERS...HAVE BEEN DUMPED DOWN HERE.
WHAT ?!!
EVEN MY *KING PUNCH* WON'T BREAK THESE WALLS...
WE'RE UNDER-GROUND--THE "WALLS" ARE SOLID EARTH.
WHAT'S HE GOING TO DO WITH US?!
I CAN'T IMAGINE THAT THEY'RE PLANNING...
...TO TEND TO OUR WOUNDS DOWN HERE!
I MIGHT JUST NEED TO CURSE DOFLAMINGO...
...TO HIS GRANDSON'S GENERATION!!!

THE RIKU FAMILY

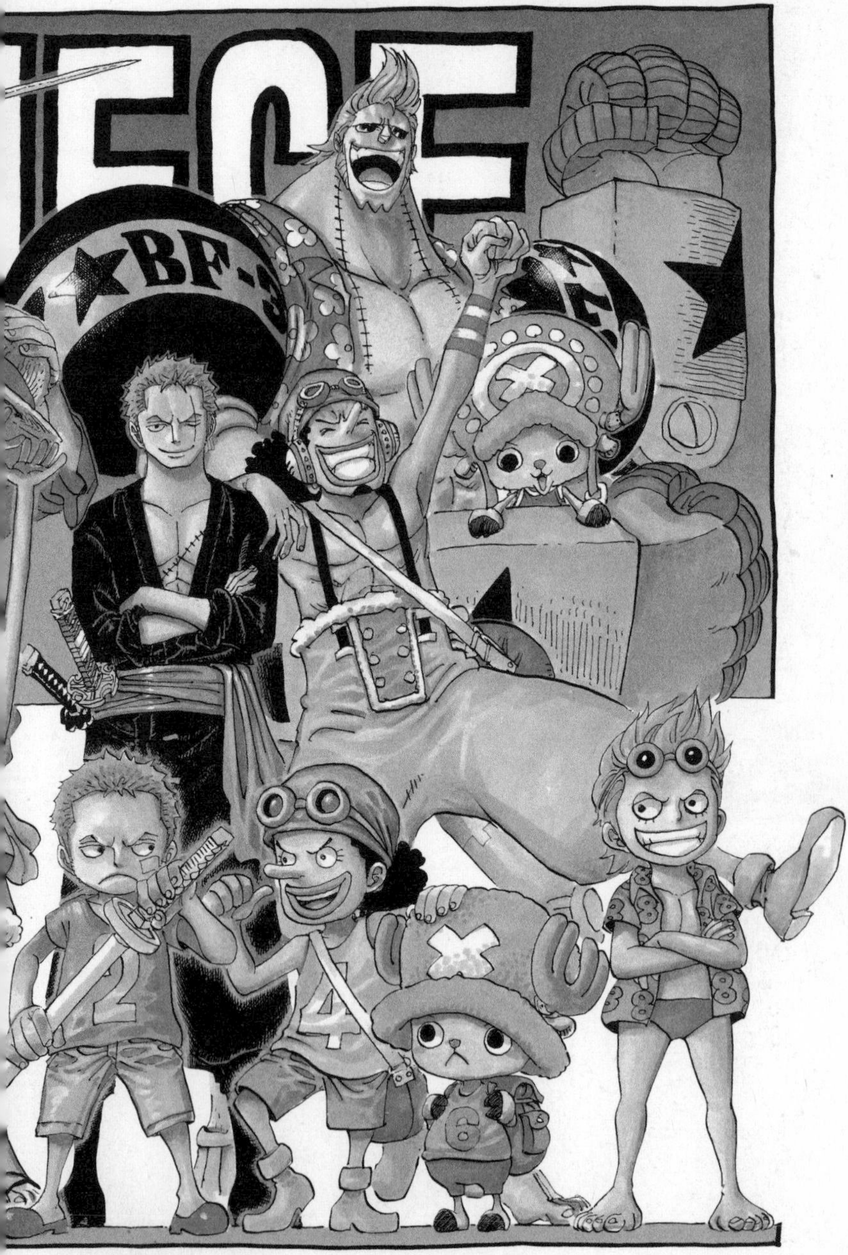

Chapter 726:

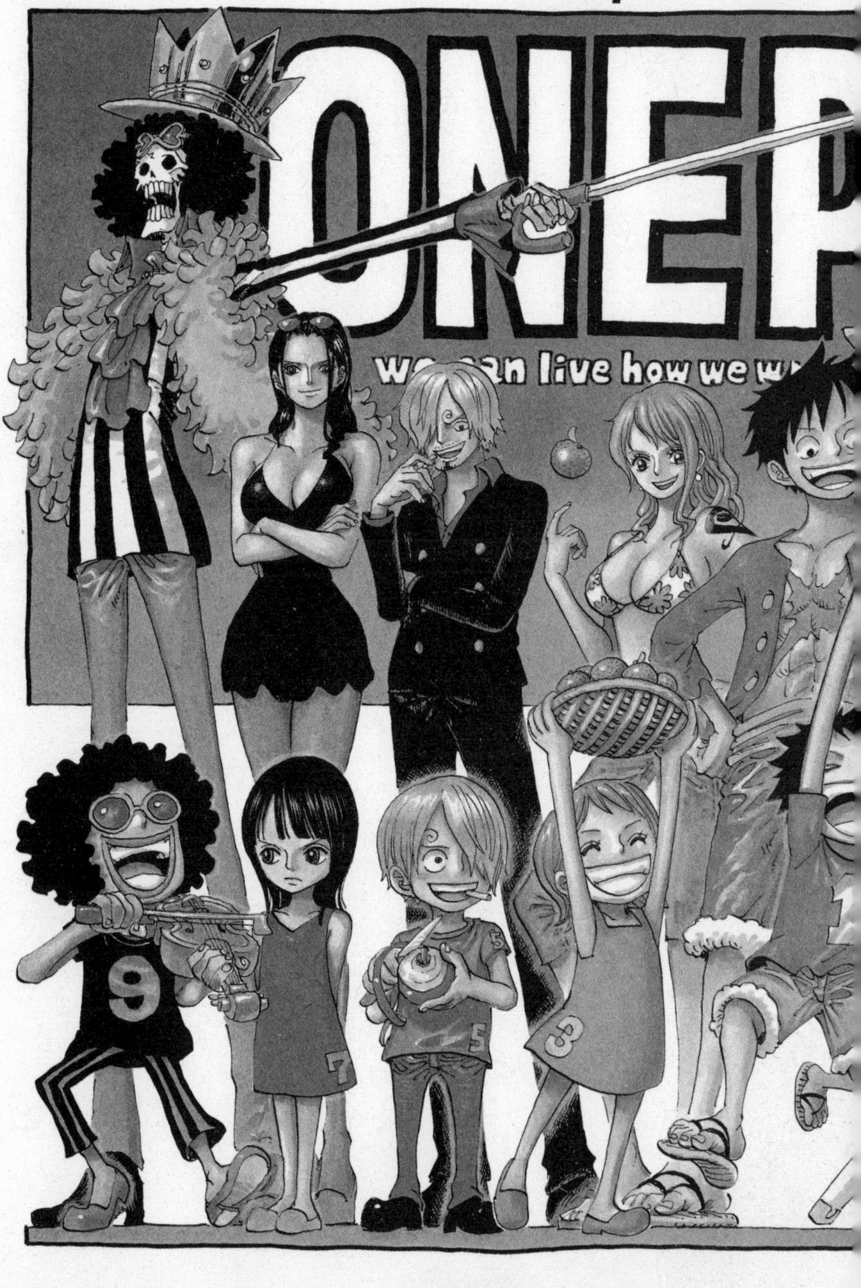

vol. 73

ONE PIECE

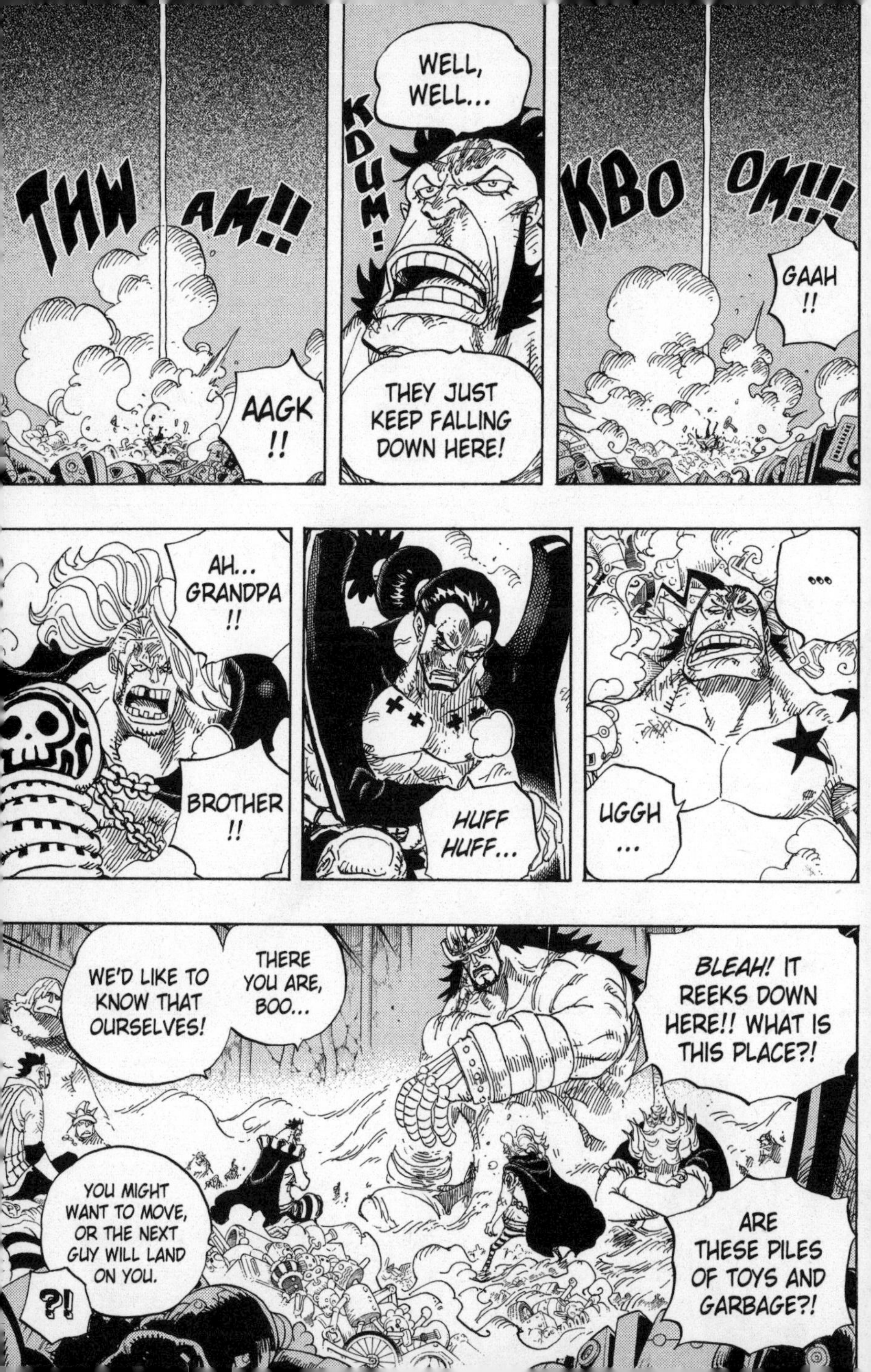
KBOOM!!!
GAAH !!
WELL, WELL...
KDUM!
THEY JUST KEEP FALLING DOWN HERE!
THWAM!!
AAGK !!
...
UGGH ...
HUFF HUFF...
AH... GRANDPA !!
BROTHER !!
BLEAH! IT REEKS DOWN HERE!! WHAT IS THIS PLACE?!
ARE THESE PILES OF TOYS AND GARBAGE?!
THERE YOU ARE, BOO...
WE'D LIKE TO KNOW THAT OURSELVES!
YOU MIGHT WANT TO MOVE, OR THE NEXT GUY WILL LAND ON YOU.
?!

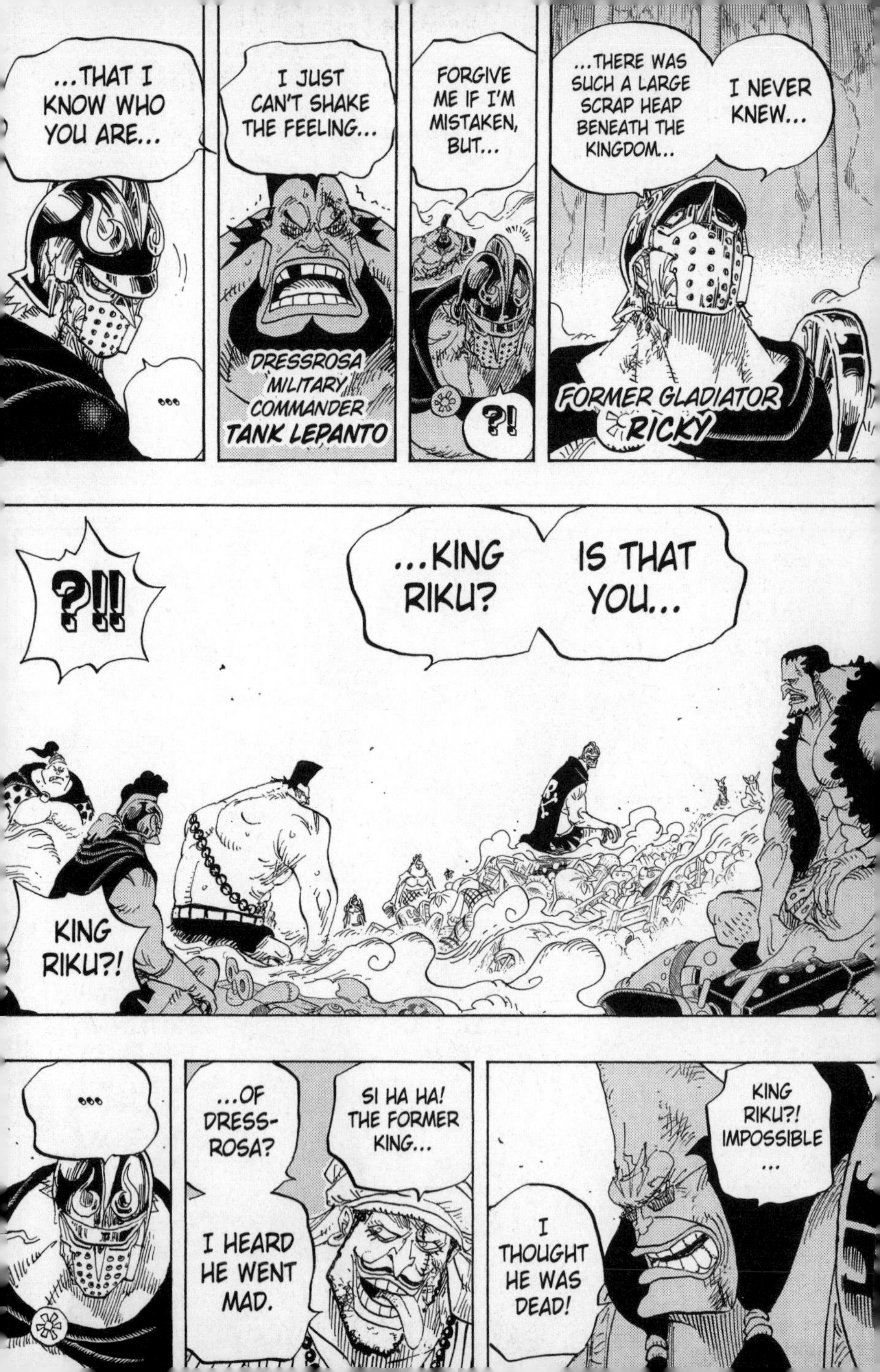
I NEVER KNEW...
...THERE WAS SUCH A LARGE SCRAP HEAP BENEATH THE KINGDOM...
FORMER GLADIATOR RICKY
FORGIVE ME IF I'M MISTAKEN, BUT...
?!
I JUST CAN'T SHAKE THE FEELING...
DRESSROSA MILITARY COMMANDER TANK LEPANTO
...THAT I KNOW WHO YOU ARE...
...
IS THAT YOU...
...KING RIKU?
?!!
KING RIKU?!
KING RIKU?! IMPOSSIBLE...
I THOUGHT HE WAS DEAD!
SI HA HA! THE FORMER KING...
...OF DRESS-ROSA?
I HEARD HE WENT MAD.
...

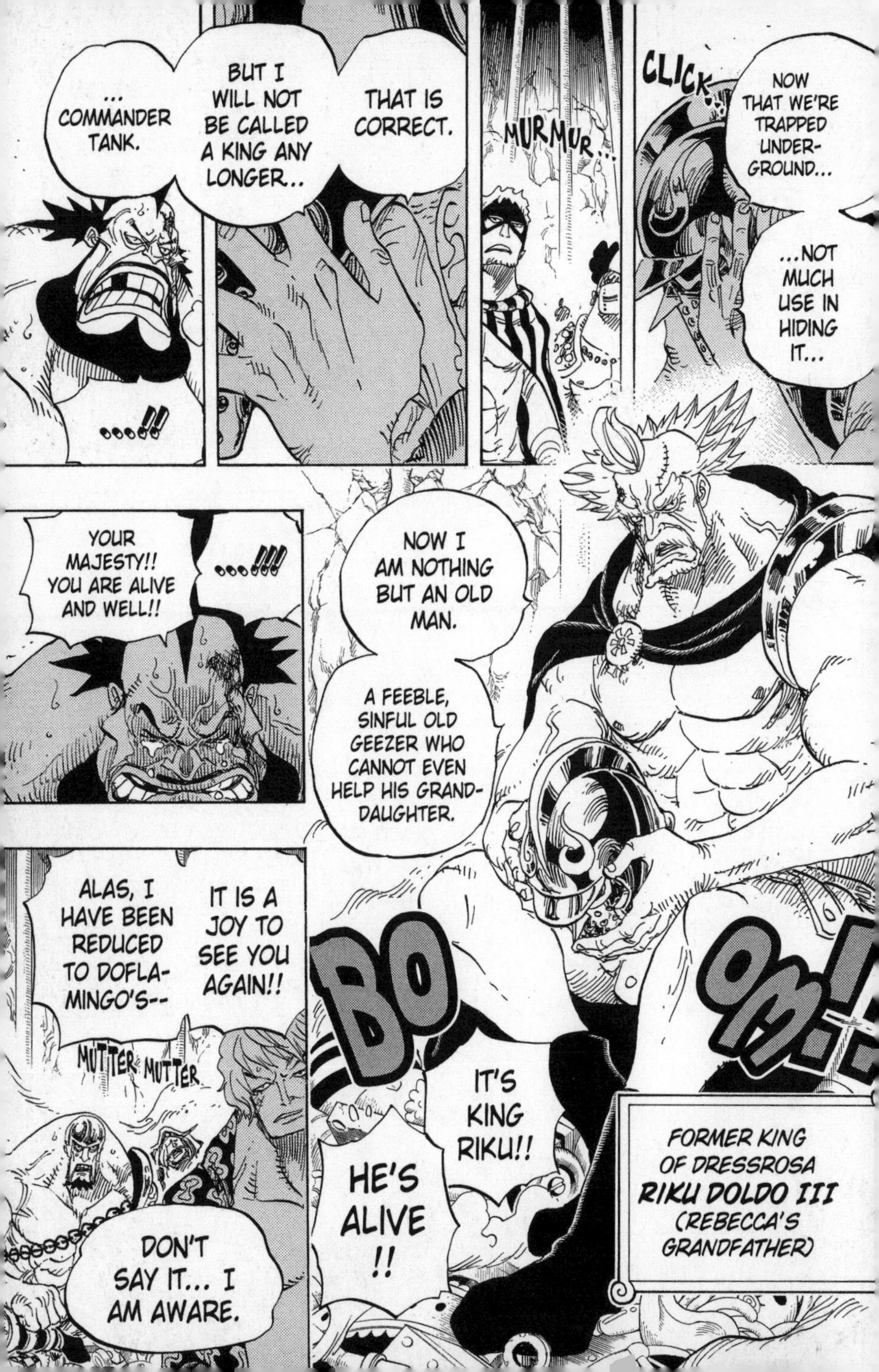
CLICK
NOW THAT WE'RE TRAPPED UNDER-GROUND...
...NOT MUCH USE IN HIDING IT...
MURMUR...
THAT IS CORRECT.
BUT I WILL NOT BE CALLED A KING ANY LONGER...
... COMMANDER TANK.
....!!
NOW I AM NOTHING BUT AN OLD MAN.
A FEEBLE, SINFUL OLD GEEZER WHO CANNOT EVEN HELP HIS GRAND-DAUGHTER.
BO
OM!!
IT'S KING RIKU!!
HE'S ALIVE !!
FORMER KING OF DRESSROSA
RIKU DOLDO III
(REBECCA'S GRANDFATHER)
....!!!
YOUR MAJESTY!! YOU ARE ALIVE AND WELL!!
IT IS A JOY TO SEE YOU AGAIN!!
ALAS, I HAVE BEEN REDUCED TO DOFLA-MINGO'S--
MUTTER MUTTER
DON'T SAY IT... I AM AWARE.

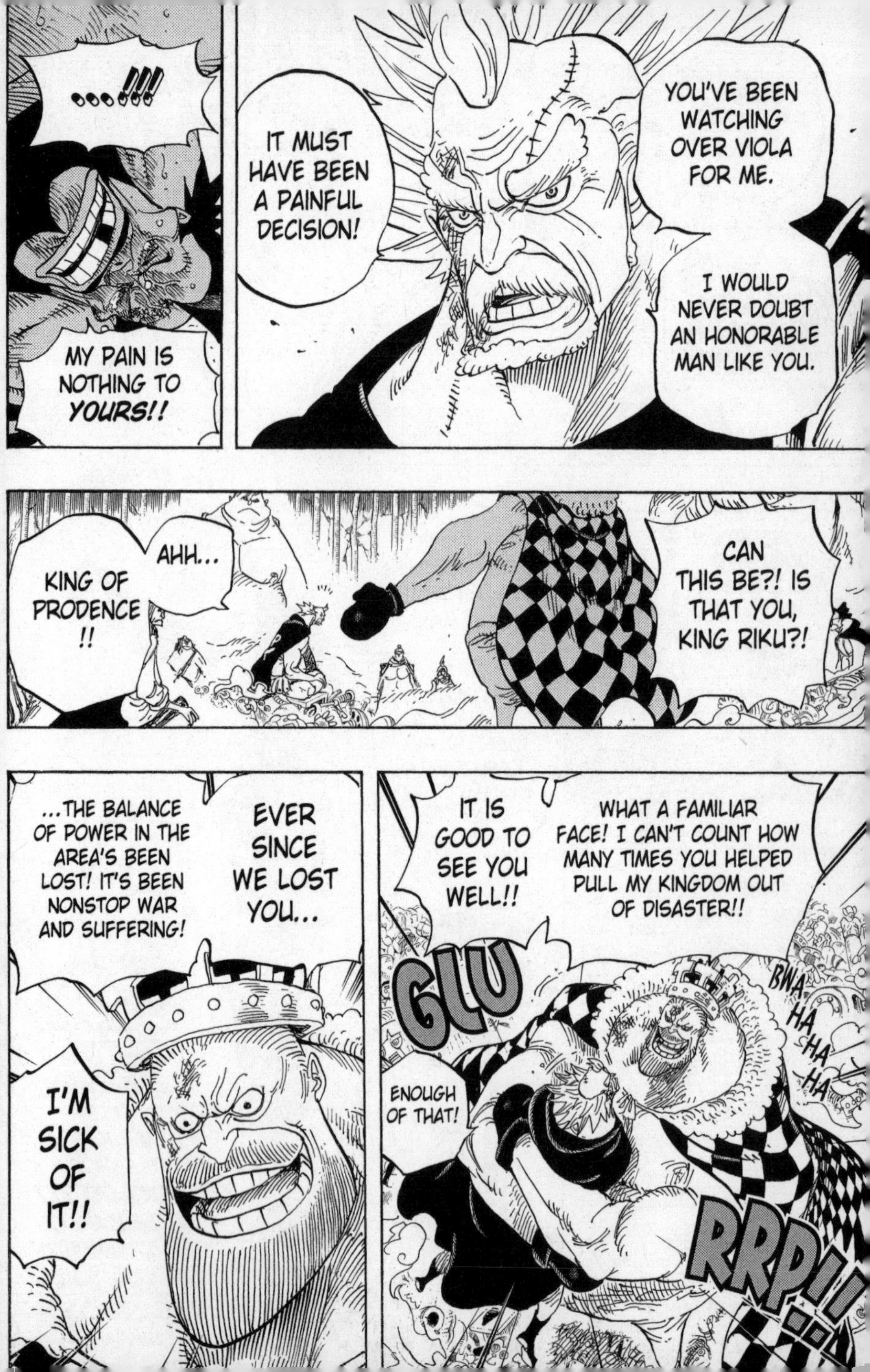
YOU'VE BEEN WATCHING OVER VIOLA FOR ME.
IT MUST HAVE BEEN A PAINFUL DECISION!
I WOULD NEVER DOUBT AN HONORABLE MAN LIKE YOU.
......!!!
MY PAIN IS NOTHING TO YOURS!!
CAN THIS BE?! IS THAT YOU, KING RIKU?!
AHH... KING OF PRODENCE!!
WHAT A FAMILIAR FACE! I CAN'T COUNT HOW MANY TIMES YOU HELPED PULL MY KINGDOM OUT OF DISASTER!!
IT IS GOOD TO SEE YOU WELL!!
BWA HA HA HA HA
GLU
ENOUGH OF THAT!
RRP!!
EVER SINCE WE LOST YOU...
...THE BALANCE OF POWER IN THE AREA'S BEEN LOST! IT'S BEEN NONSTOP WAR AND SUFFERING!
I'M SICK OF IT!!

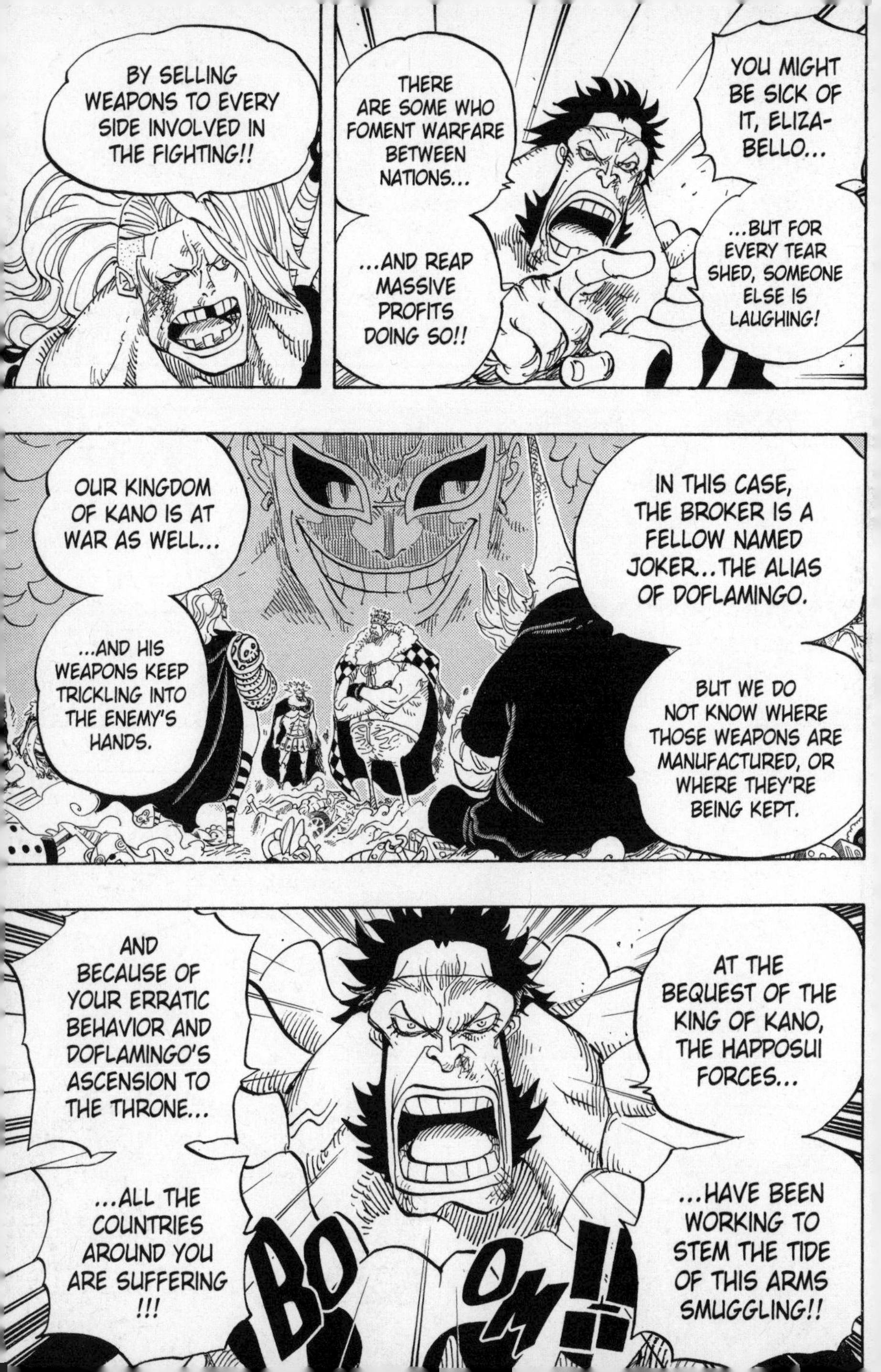
YOU MIGHT BE SICK OF IT, ELIZA-BELLO...
...BUT FOR EVERY TEAR SHED, SOMEONE ELSE IS LAUGHING!
THERE ARE SOME WHO FOMENT WARFARE BETWEEN NATIONS...
...AND REAP MASSIVE PROFITS DOING SO!!
BY SELLING WEAPONS TO EVERY SIDE INVOLVED IN THE FIGHTING!!
IN THIS CASE, THE BROKER IS A FELLOW NAMED JOKER...THE ALIAS OF DOFLAMINGO.
BUT WE DO NOT KNOW WHERE THOSE WEAPONS ARE MANUFACTURED, OR WHERE THEY'RE BEING KEPT.
OUR KINGDOM OF KANO IS AT WAR AS WELL...
...AND HIS WEAPONS KEEP TRICKLING INTO THE ENEMY'S HANDS.
AT THE BEQUEST OF THE KING OF KANO, THE HAPPOSUI FORCES...
...HAVE BEEN WORKING TO STEM THE TIDE OF THIS ARMS SMUGGLING!!
AND BECAUSE OF YOUR ERRATIC BEHAVIOR AND DOFLAMINGO'S ASCENSION TO THE THRONE...
...ALL THE COUNTRIES AROUND YOU ARE SUFFERING!!!
BOOM!!

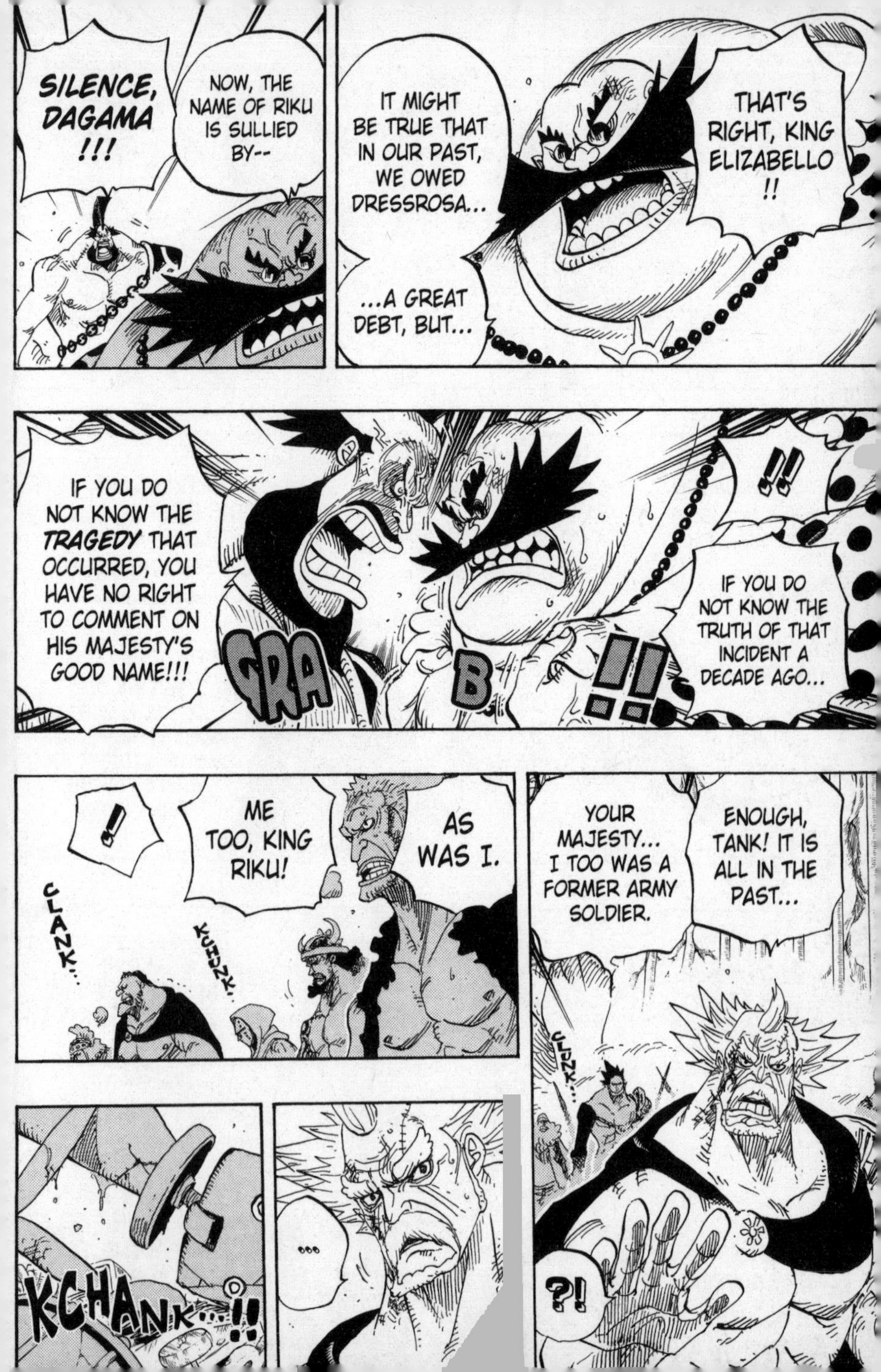
THAT'S RIGHT, KING ELIZABELLO !!
IT MIGHT BE TRUE THAT IN OUR PAST, WE OWED DRESSROSA...
...A GREAT DEBT, BUT...
NOW, THE NAME OF RIKU IS SULLIED BY--
SILENCE, DAGAMA !!!
!!
IF YOU DO NOT KNOW THE TRUTH OF THAT INCIDENT A DECADE AGO...
IF YOU DO NOT KNOW THE TRAGEDY THAT OCCURRED, YOU HAVE NO RIGHT TO COMMENT ON HIS MAJESTY'S GOOD NAME!!!
GRAB!!
ENOUGH, TANK! IT IS ALL IN THE PAST...
YOUR MAJESTY... I TOO WAS A FORMER ARMY SOLDIER.
CLUNK...
?!
AS WAS I.
ME TOO, KING RIKU!
!
KCHUNK...
CLANK...
...
K-CHANK...!!

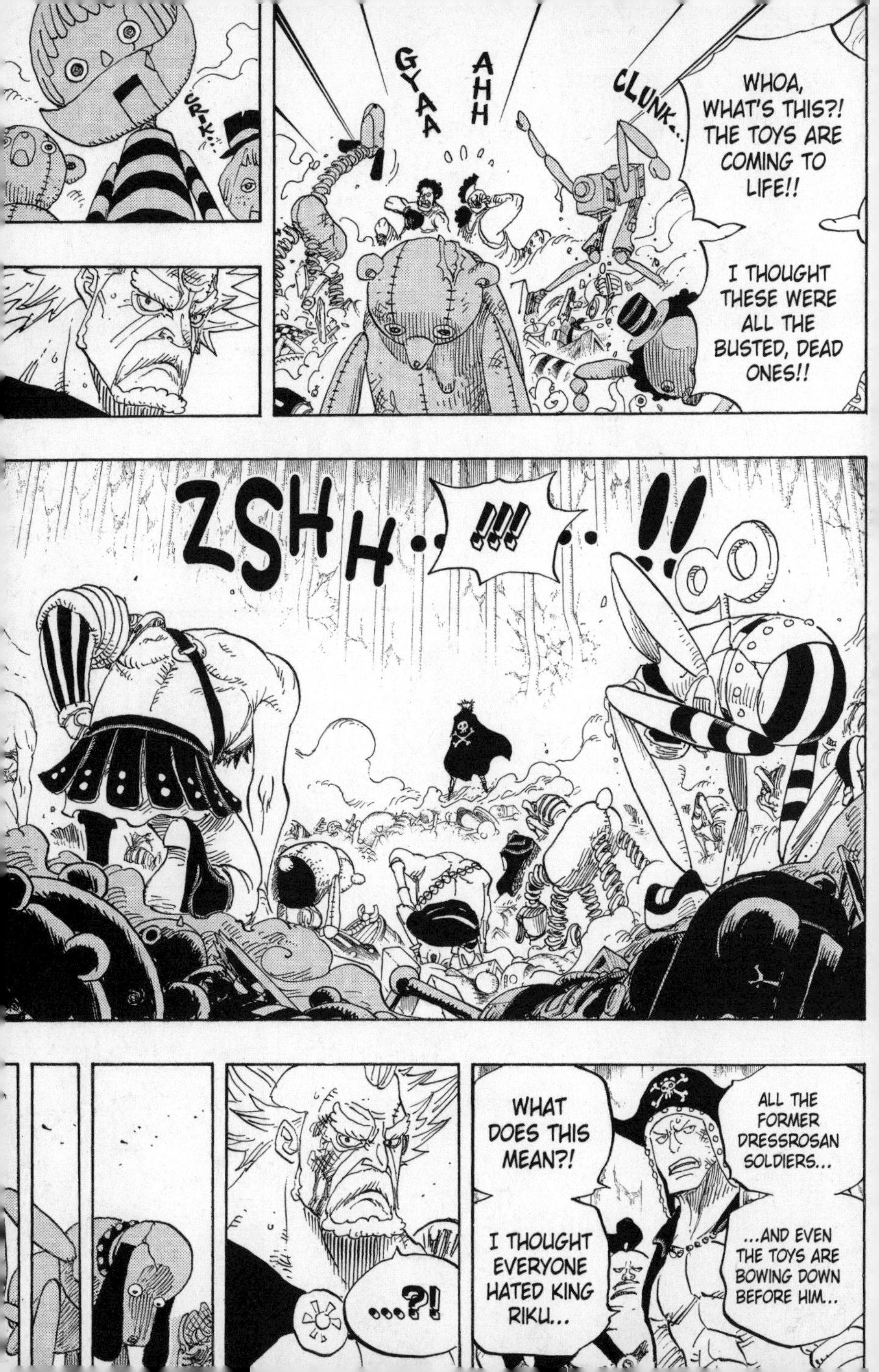
CLUNK...
WHOA, WHAT'S THIS?! THE TOYS ARE COMING TO LIFE!!
I THOUGHT THESE WERE ALL THE BUSTED, DEAD ONES!!
AHH
GYAA
CRIK...
ZSHH..!!!..!!
ALL THE FORMER DRESSROSAN SOLDIERS...
WHAT DOES THIS MEAN?!
...AND EVEN THE TOYS ARE BOWING DOWN BEFORE HIM...
I THOUGHT EVERYONE HATED KING RIKU...
...?!

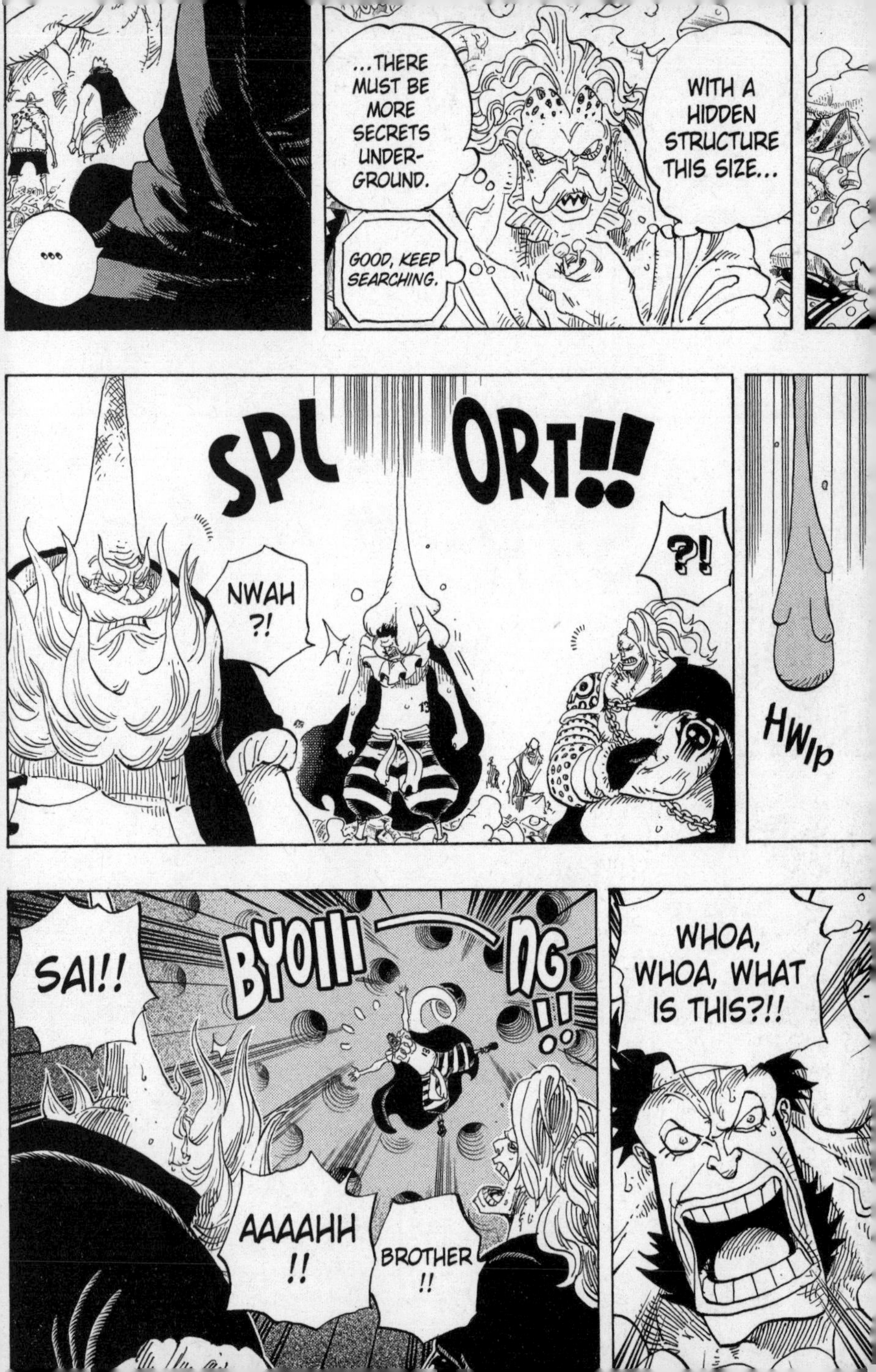
WITH A HIDDEN STRUCTURE THIS SIZE...
...THERE MUST BE MORE SECRETS UNDER-GROUND.
GOOD, KEEP SEARCHING.
...
HWIP
SPLORT!!
?!
NWAH ?!
WHOA, WHOA, WHAT IS THIS?!!
BYOIII-NG!!
SAI!!
BROTHER!!
AAAAHH!!

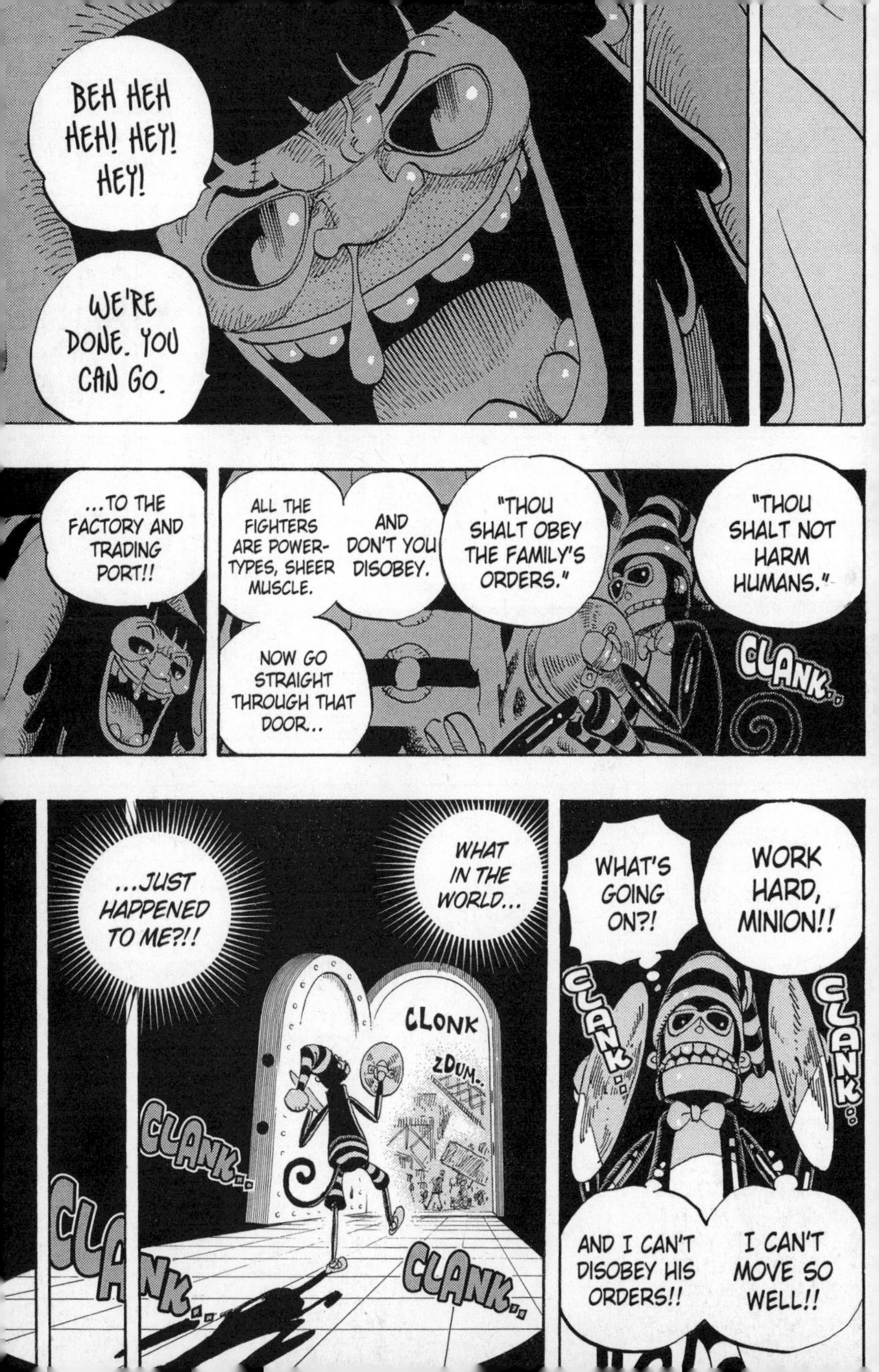
BEH HEH HEH! HEY! HEY!
WE'RE DONE. YOU CAN GO.
"THOU SHALT NOT HARM HUMANS."
CLANK..
"THOU SHALT OBEY THE FAMILY'S ORDERS."
AND DON'T YOU DISOBEY.
ALL THE FIGHTERS ARE POWER-TYPES, SHEER MUSCLE.
NOW GO STRAIGHT THROUGH THAT DOOR...
...TO THE FACTORY AND TRADING PORT!!
WORK HARD, MINION!!
WHAT'S GOING ON?!
CLANK..
CLANK..
I CAN'T MOVE SO WELL!!
AND I CAN'T DISOBEY HIS ORDERS!!
WHAT IN THE WORLD...
...JUST HAPPENED TO ME?!!
CLONK
ZDUM..
CLANK..
CLANK..
CLANK..

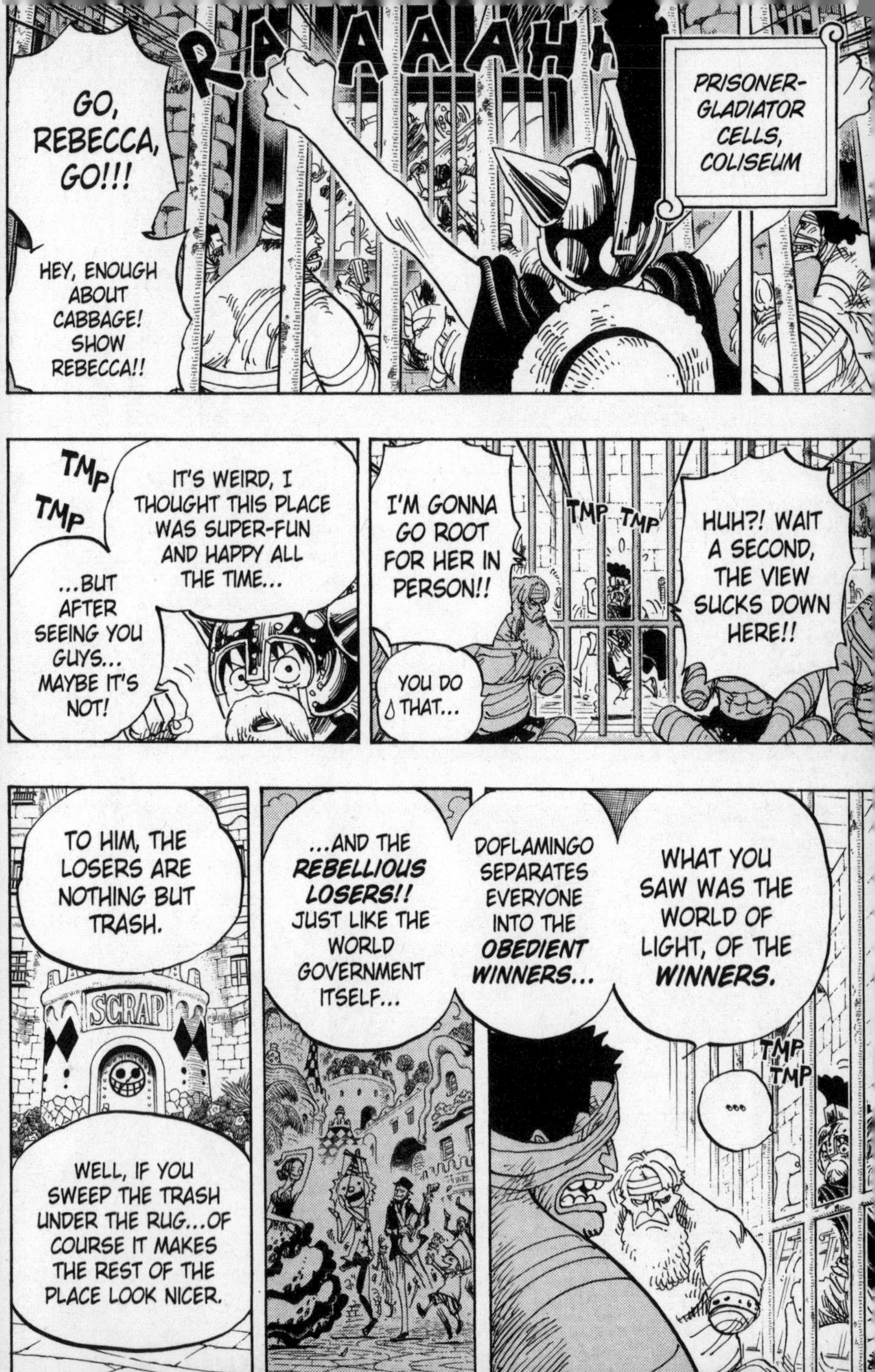
PRISONER-GLADIATOR CELLS, COLISEUM
RAAAAAH
GO, REBECCA, GO!!!
HEY, ENOUGH ABOUT CABBAGE! SHOW REBECCA!!
HUH?! WAIT A SECOND, THE VIEW SUCKS DOWN HERE!!
TMP TMP
I'M GONNA GO ROOT FOR HER IN PERSON!!
YOU DO THAT...
TMP TMP
IT'S WEIRD, I THOUGHT THIS PLACE WAS SUPER-FUN AND HAPPY ALL THE TIME...
...BUT AFTER SEEING YOU GUYS... MAYBE IT'S NOT!
WHAT YOU SAW WAS THE WORLD OF LIGHT, OF THE WINNERS.
DOFLAMINGO SEPARATES EVERYONE INTO THE OBEDIENT WINNERS...
...AND THE REBELLIOUS LOSERS!! JUST LIKE THE WORLD GOVERNMENT ITSELF...
TMP TMP
...
TO HIM, THE LOSERS ARE NOTHING BUT TRASH.
SCRAP
WELL, IF YOU SWEEP THE TRASH UNDER THE RUG...OF COURSE IT MAKES THE REST OF THE PLACE LOOK NICER.

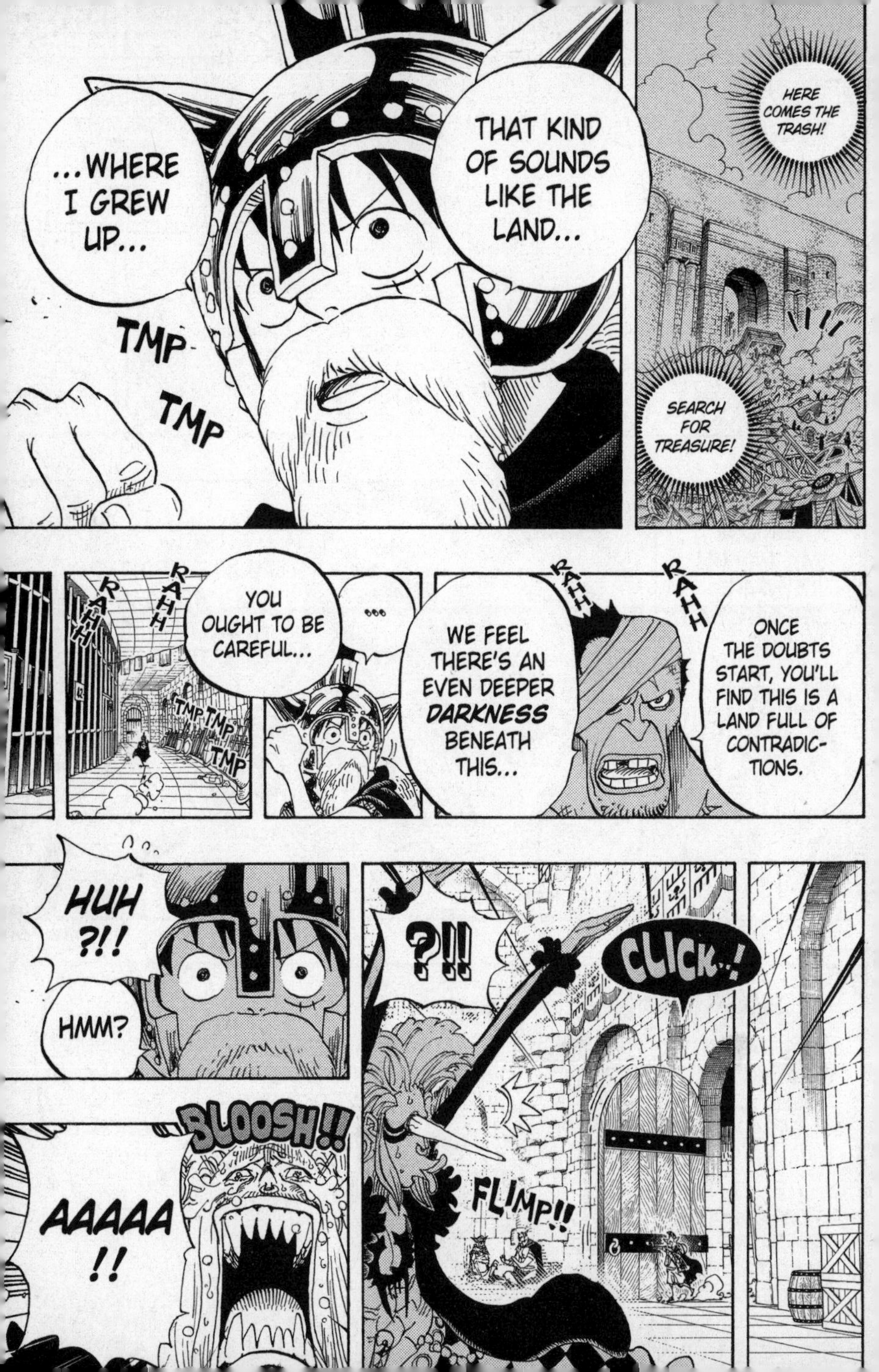
HERE COMES THE TRASH!
SEARCH FOR TREASURE!
THAT KIND OF SOUNDS LIKE THE LAND...
...WHERE I GREW UP...
TMP
TMP
ONCE THE DOUBTS START, YOU'LL FIND THIS IS A LAND FULL OF CONTRADIC-TIONS.
RAHH
RAHH
WE FEEL THERE'S AN EVEN DEEPER ***DARKNESS*** BENEATH THIS...
...
YOU OUGHT TO BE CAREFUL...
RAHH
RAHH
TMP TMP TMP
CLICK..!
?!!
FLIMP!!
HUH ?!!
HMM?
BLOOSH!!
AAAAA !!

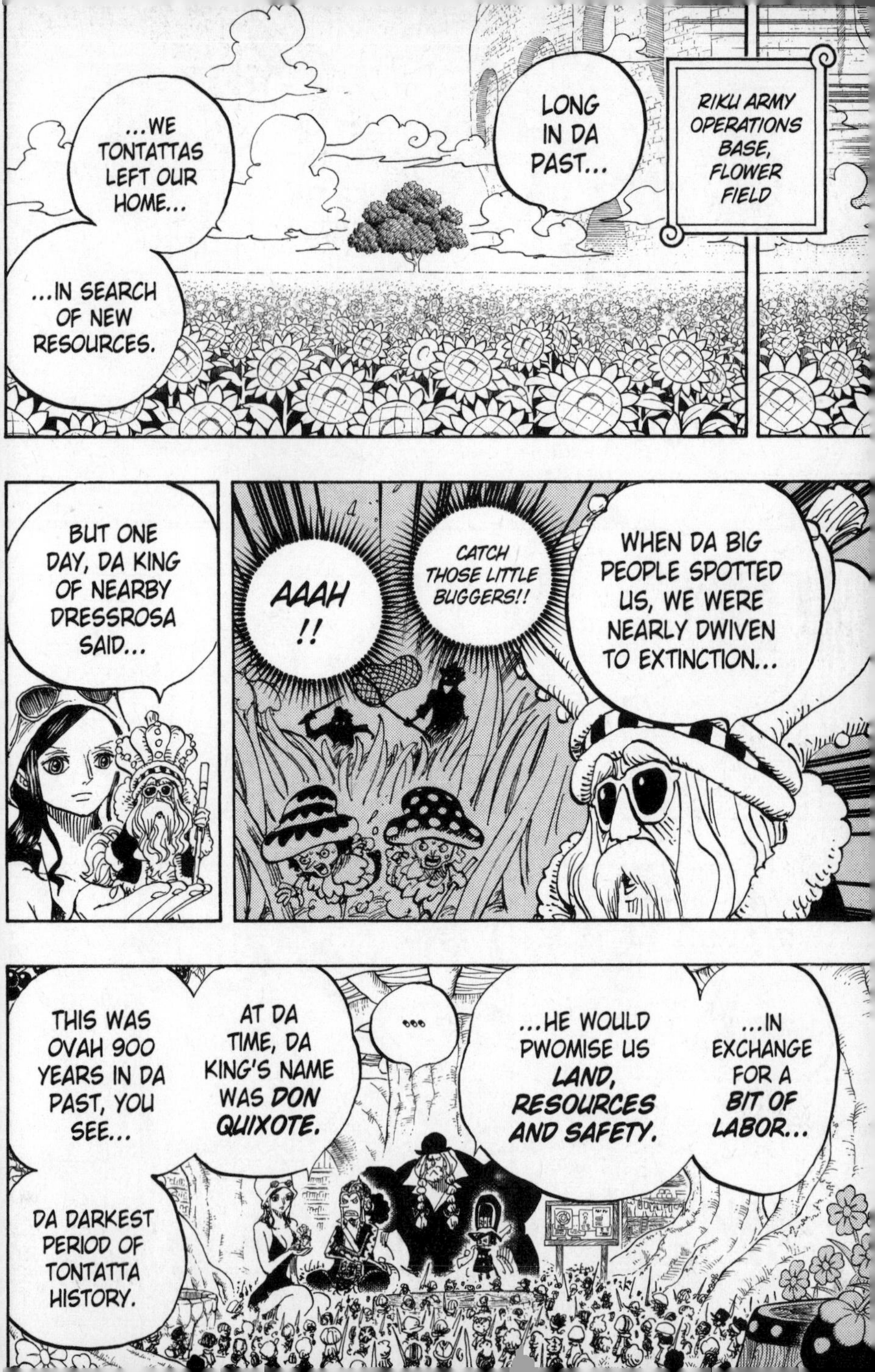
RIKU ARMY OPERATIONS BASE, FLOWER FIELD
LONG IN DA PAST...
...WE TONTATTAS LEFT OUR HOME...
...IN SEARCH OF NEW RESOURCES.
WHEN DA BIG PEOPLE SPOTTED US, WE WERE NEARLY DWIVEN TO EXTINCTION...
CATCH THOSE LITTLE BUGGERS!!
AAAH!!
BUT ONE DAY, DA KING OF NEARBY DRESSROSA SAID...
...HE WOULD PWOMISE US LAND, RESOURCES AND SAFETY.
...IN EXCHANGE FOR A BIT OF LABOR...
...
AT DA TIME, DA KING'S NAME WAS DON QUIXOTE.
THIS WAS OVAH 900 YEARS IN DA PAST, YOU SEE...
DA DARKEST PERIOD OF TONTATTA HISTORY.

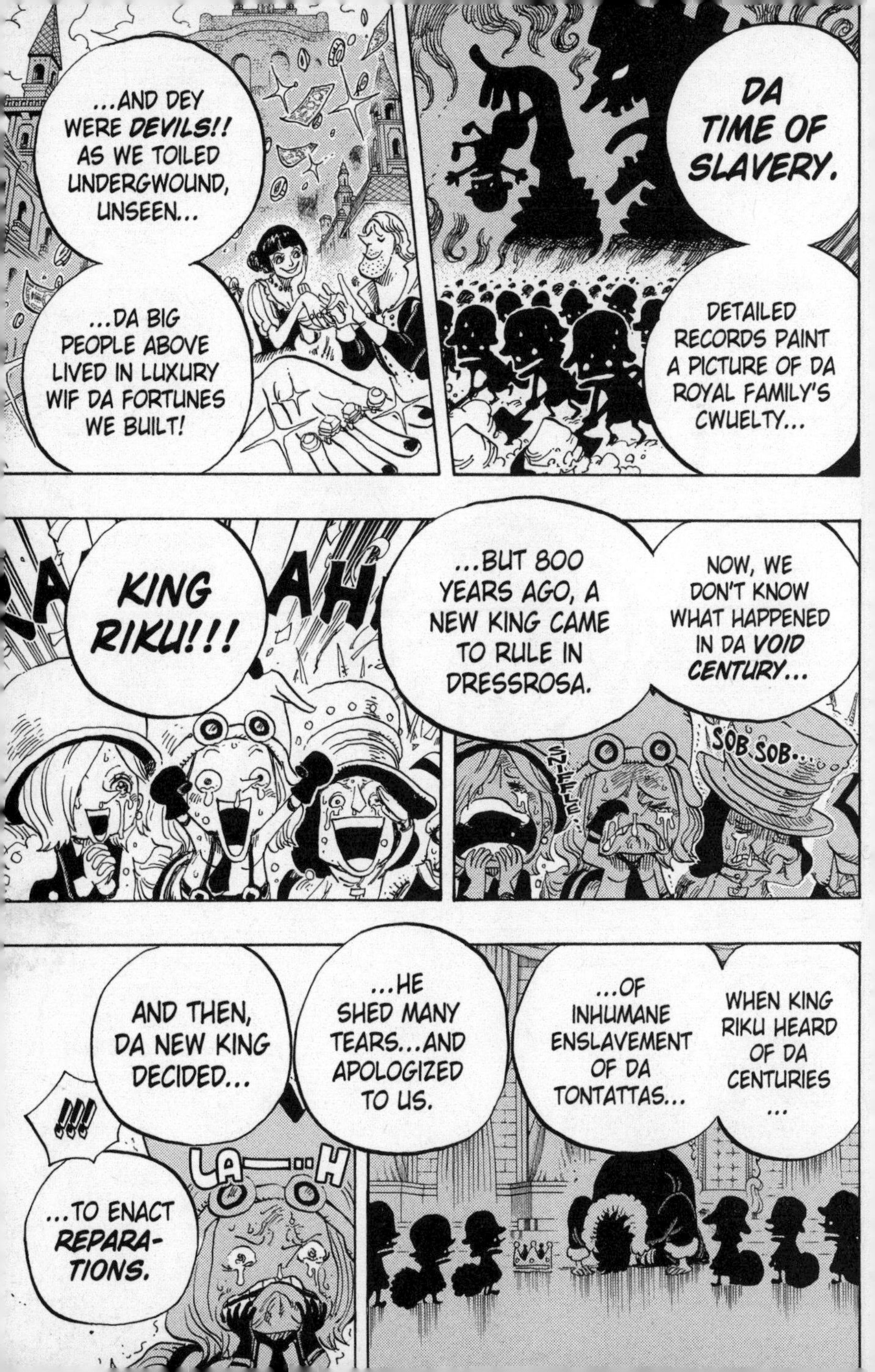
DA TIME OF SLAVERY.
DETAILED RECORDS PAINT A PICTURE OF DA ROYAL FAMILY'S CWUELTY...
...AND DEY WERE DEVILS!! AS WE TOILED UNDERGWOUND, UNSEEN...
...DA BIG PEOPLE ABOVE LIVED IN LUXURY WIF DA FORTUNES WE BUILT!
NOW, WE DON'T KNOW WHAT HAPPENED IN DA VOID CENTURY...
...BUT 800 YEARS AGO, A NEW KING CAME TO RULE IN DRESSROSA.
SNIFFLE...
SOB SOB...
AH
KING RIKU!!!
WHEN KING RIKU HEARD OF DA CENTURIES...
...OF INHUMANE ENSLAVEMENT OF DA TONTATTAS...
...HE SHED MANY TEARS...AND APOLOGIZED TO US.
AND THEN, DA NEW KING DECIDED...
!!!
LA—H
...TO ENACT REPARATIONS.

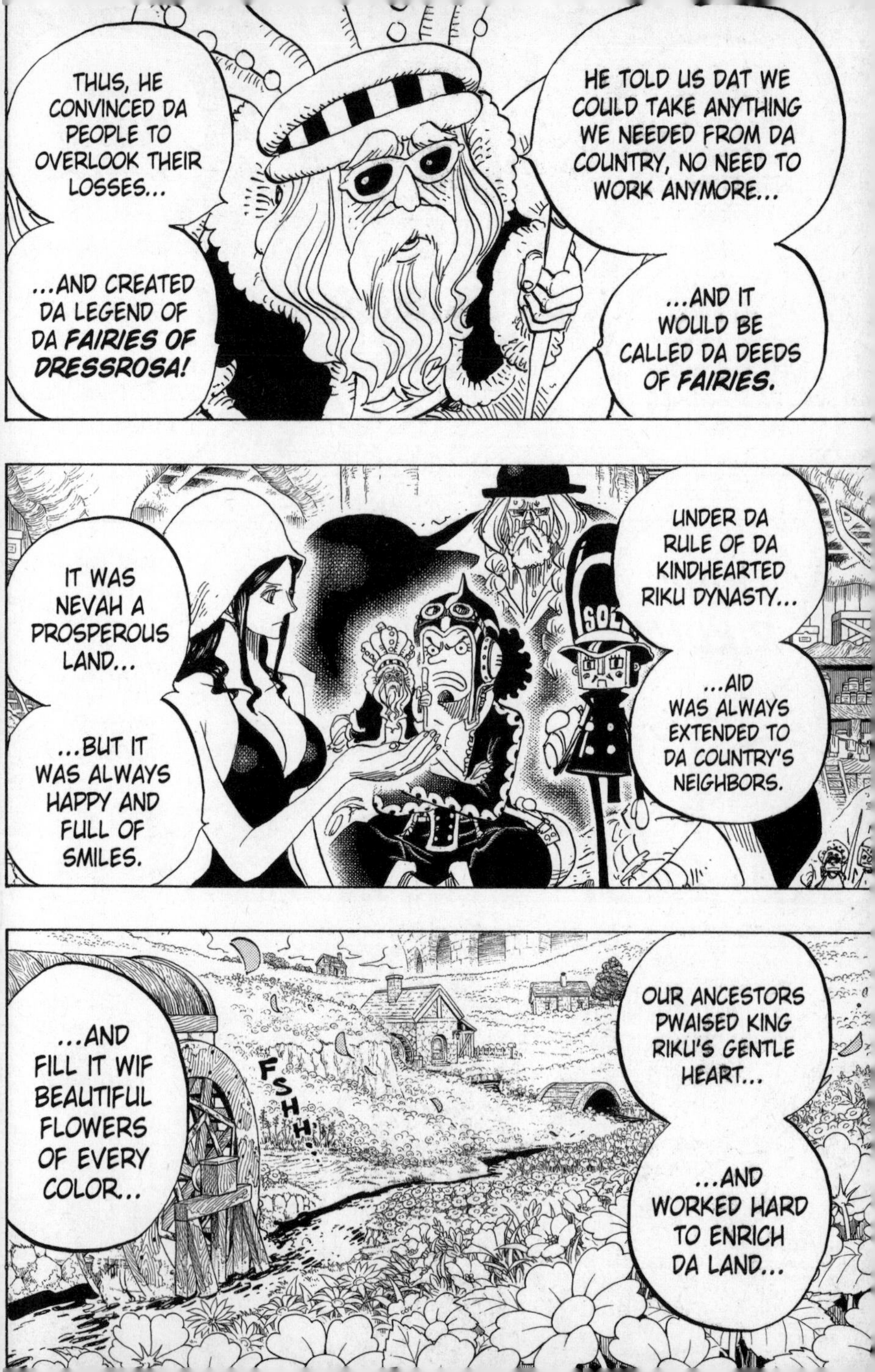
HE TOLD US DAT WE COULD TAKE ANYTHING WE NEEDED FROM DA COUNTRY, NO NEED TO WORK ANYMORE...
...AND IT WOULD BE CALLED DA DEEDS OF **FAIRIES.**
THUS, HE CONVINCED DA PEOPLE TO OVERLOOK THEIR LOSSES...
...AND CREATED DA LEGEND OF DA ***FAIRIES OF DRESSROSA!***
UNDER DA RULE OF DA KINDHEARTED RIKU DYNASTY...
...AID WAS ALWAYS EXTENDED TO DA COUNTRY'S NEIGHBORS.
IT WAS NEVAH A PROSPEROUS LAND...
...BUT IT WAS ALWAYS HAPPY AND FULL OF SMILES.
OUR ANCESTORS PWAISED KING RIKU'S GENTLE HEART...
...AND WORKED HARD TO ENRICH DA LAND...
...AND FILL IT WIF BEAUTIFUL FLOWERS OF EVERY COLOR...
FSHH

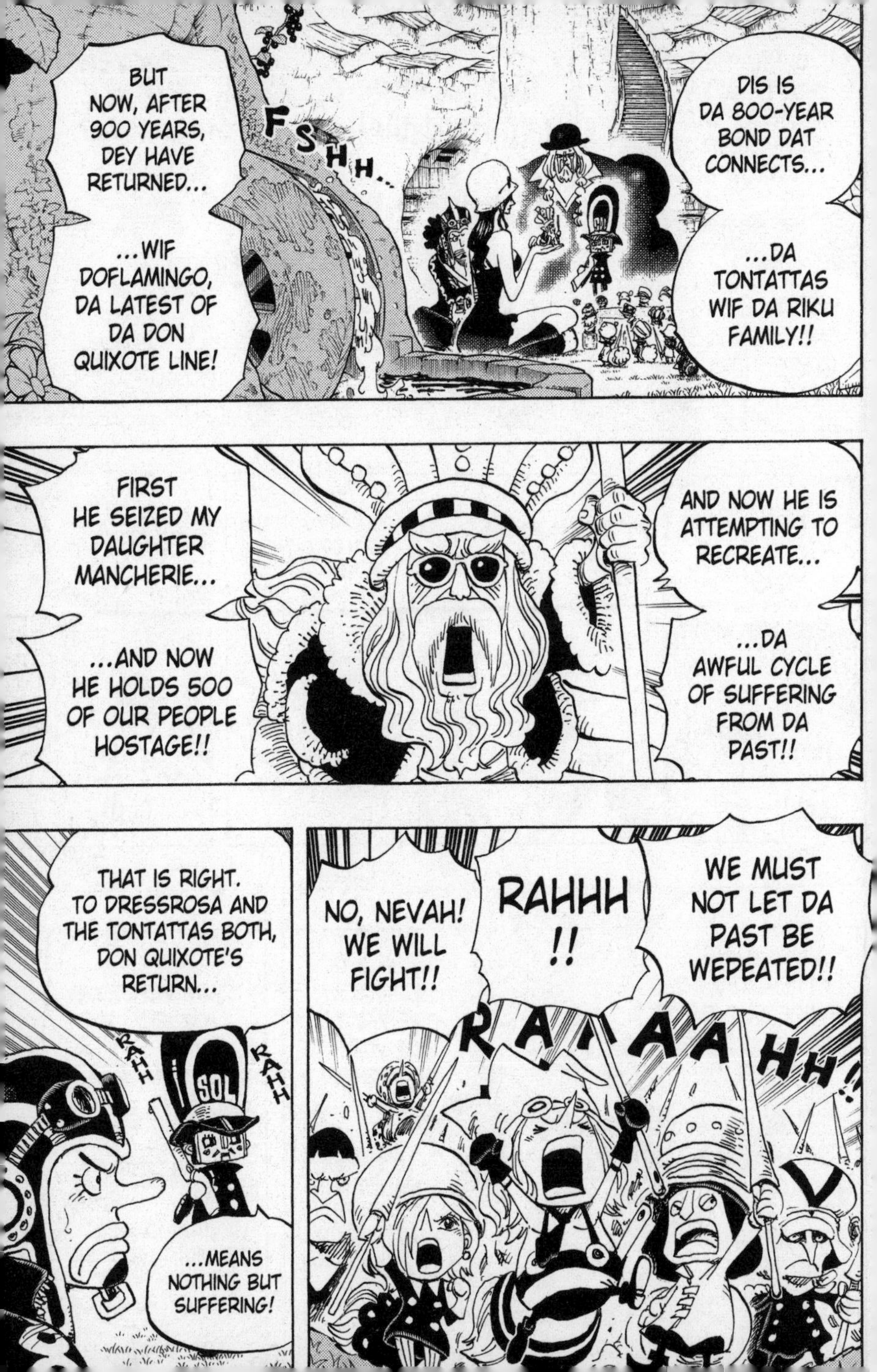
DIS IS DA 800-YEAR BOND DAT CONNECTS...
...DA TONTATTAS WIF DA RIKU FAMILY!!
FSHH...
BUT NOW, AFTER 900 YEARS, DEY HAVE RETURNED...
...WIF DOFLAMINGO, DA LATEST OF DA DON QUIXOTE LINE!
AND NOW HE IS ATTEMPTING TO RECREATE...
...DA AWFUL CYCLE OF SUFFERING FROM DA PAST!!
FIRST HE SEIZED MY DAUGHTER MANCHERIE...
...AND NOW HE HOLDS 500 OF OUR PEOPLE HOSTAGE!!
WE MUST NOT LET DA PAST BE WEPEATED!!
RAHHH !!
NO, NEVAH! WE WILL FIGHT!!
RAAAAHH!!
THAT IS RIGHT. TO DRESSROSA AND THE TONTATTAS BOTH, DON QUIXOTE'S RETURN...
RAHH
RAHH
SOL
...MEANS NOTHING BUT SUFFERING!

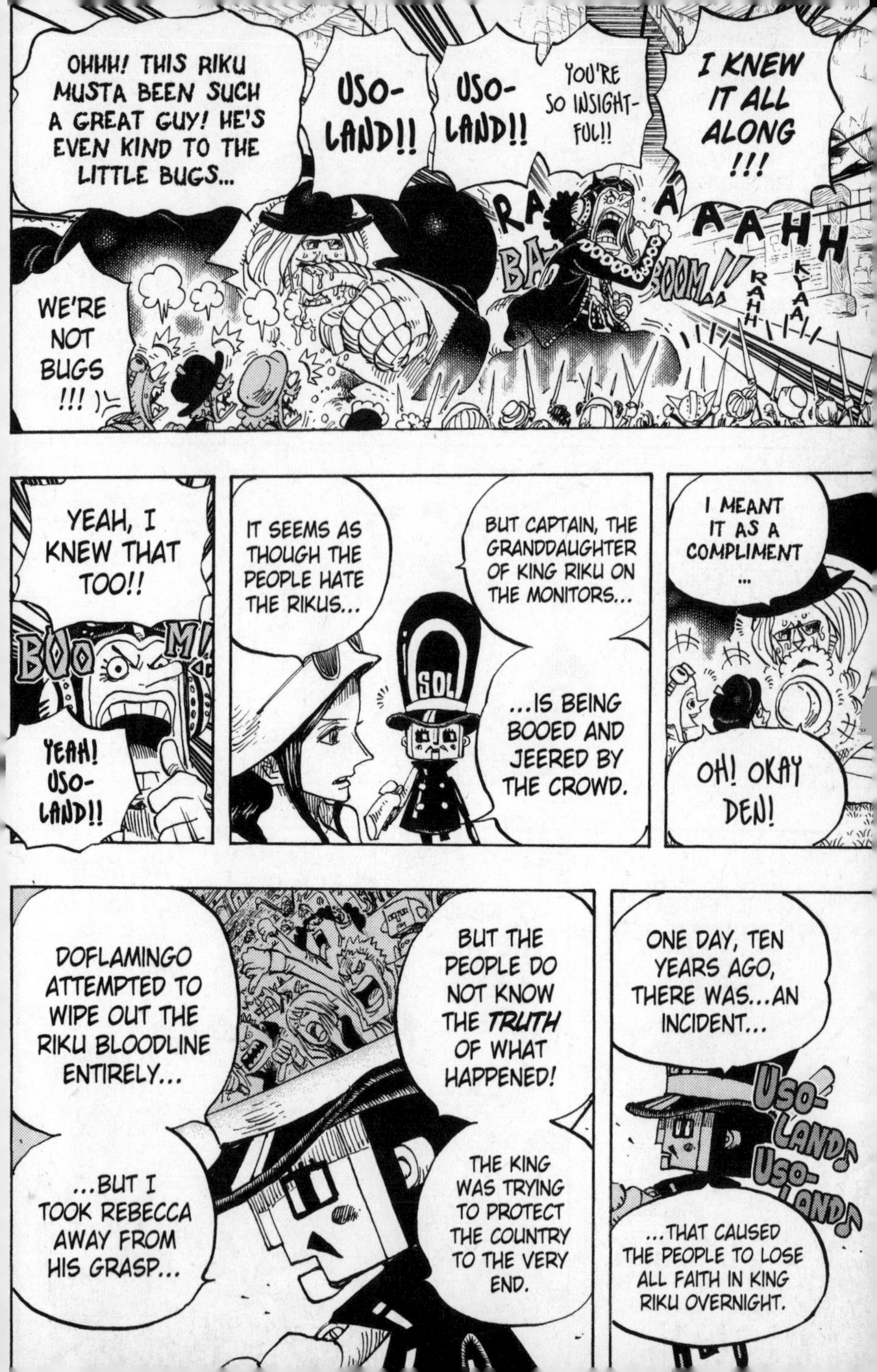
I KNEW IT ALL ALONG!!!
YOU'RE SO INSIGHT-FUL!!
USO-LAND!!
USO-LAND!!
OHHH! THIS RIKU MUSTA BEEN SUCH A GREAT GUY! HE'S EVEN KIND TO THE LITTLE BUGS...
RAAAAHH
BA-BOOM!!
RAHH
KYAA
WE'RE NOT BUGS!!!
I MEANT IT AS A COMPLIMENT...
OH! OKAY DEN!
BUT CAPTAIN, THE GRANDDAUGHTER OF KING RIKU ON THE MONITORS...
...IS BEING BOOED AND JEERED BY THE CROWD.
IT SEEMS AS THOUGH THE PEOPLE HATE THE RIKUS...
SOL
YEAH, I KNEW THAT TOO!!
BOOM!
YEAH! USO-LAND!!
ONE DAY, TEN YEARS AGO, THERE WAS...AN INCIDENT...
USO-LAND♪ USO-LAND♪
...THAT CAUSED THE PEOPLE TO LOSE ALL FAITH IN KING RIKU OVERNIGHT.
BUT THE PEOPLE DO NOT KNOW THE *TRUTH* OF WHAT HAPPENED!
THE KING WAS TRYING TO PROTECT THE COUNTRY TO THE VERY END.
DOFLAMINGO ATTEMPTED TO WIPE OUT THE RIKU BLOODLINE ENTIRELY...
...BUT I TOOK REBECCA AWAY FROM HIS GRASP...

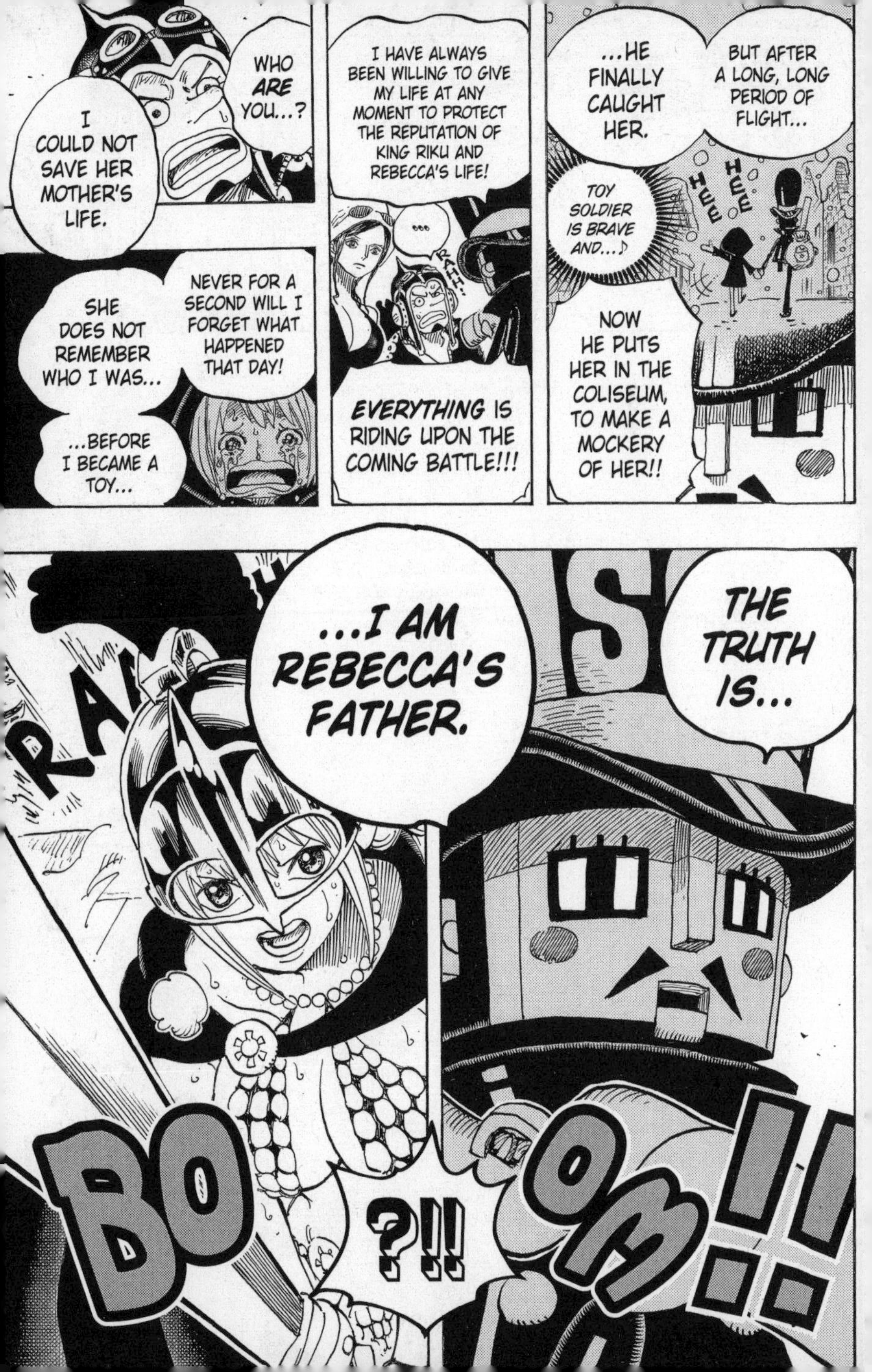
BUT AFTER A LONG, LONG PERIOD OF FLIGHT...
...HE FINALLY CAUGHT HER.
TOY SOLDIER IS BRAVE AND...♪
HEE HEE
NOW HE PUTS HER IN THE COLISEUM, TO MAKE A MOCKERY OF HER!!
I HAVE ALWAYS BEEN WILLING TO GIVE MY LIFE AT ANY MOMENT TO PROTECT THE REPUTATION OF KING RIKU AND REBECCA'S LIFE!
...
RAHH!
EVERYTHING IS RIDING UPON THE COMING BATTLE!!!
WHO ARE YOU...?
I COULD NOT SAVE HER MOTHER'S LIFE.
NEVER FOR A SECOND WILL I FORGET WHAT HAPPENED THAT DAY!
SHE DOES NOT REMEMBER WHO I WAS...
...BEFORE I BECAME A TOY...
THE TRUTH IS...
...I AM REBECCA'S FATHER.
?!!
BOOM!!

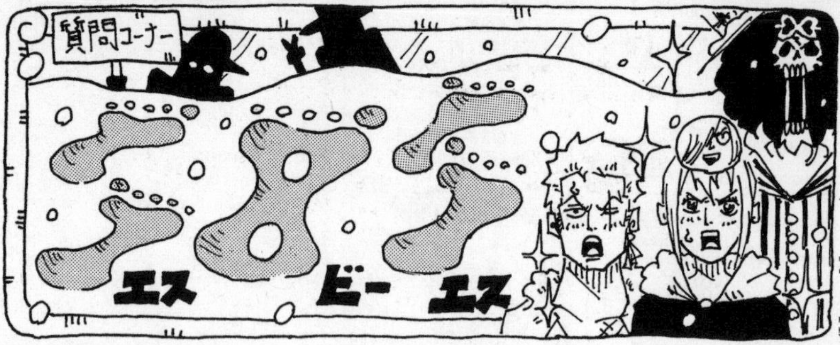
質問コーナー
エス ビー エス

(Haru, Nagano)

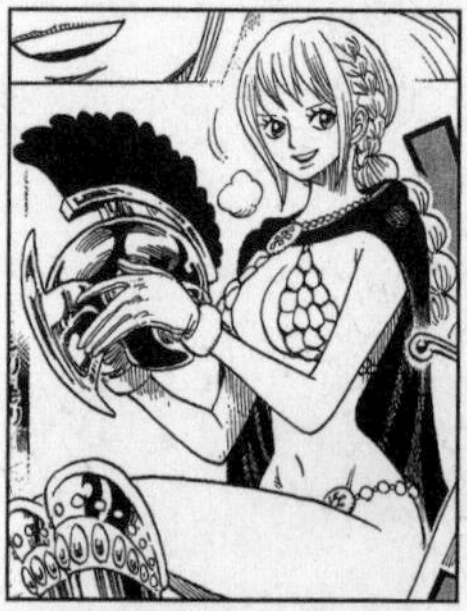

Q: Are you and I the only ones hoping for a nip-slip from Rebecca? Are you and I the only ones who turn each page during the coliseum scenes thinking, "Come on! Come on!!"

--Mojaman (16)

A: I hear you! It sets my heart racing. You think, "When is the wardrobe malfunction?!" You might wonder why she'd wear such a skimpy outfit, but there's that pesky weight limit. I don't want to draw her that way, I swear. Come on! Come on!!

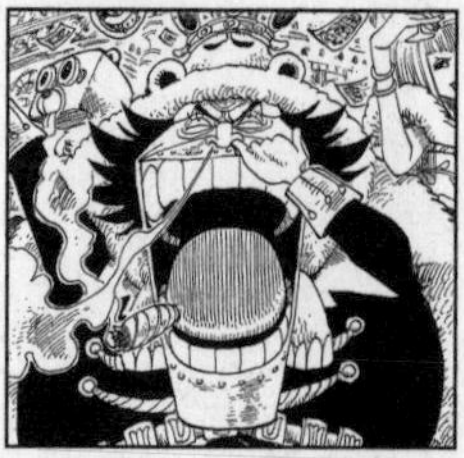

Q: I hear I look like Wapol.

--Kozuetty

A: It gets better.

Q: Hey, Oda! In all of these fight scenes, why doesn't anyone go for the men's groins? Doesn't that seem like the quickest path to victory?

--Eldest of the Asada Siblings

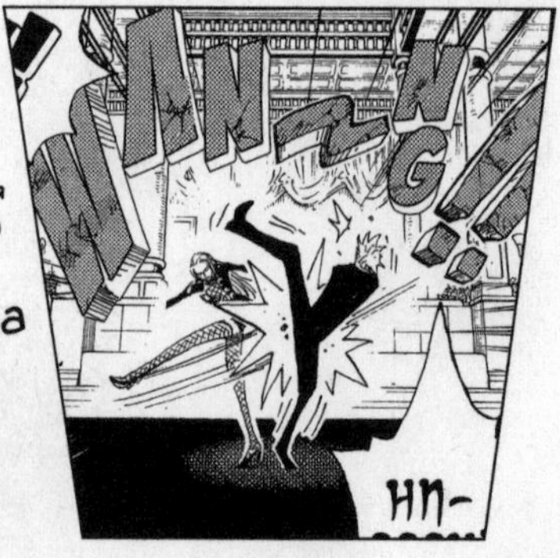
WHNNNG!!
HN-

A: True, that is a vital area. Just imagine legends among men--Whitebeard, Shanks, Mihawk--staring each other down, bearing their weighty ideals...and trying to whack each other in the balls!
Is that the kind of manga you want to read?!

Chapter 727:
THE HERO'S AMBUSH

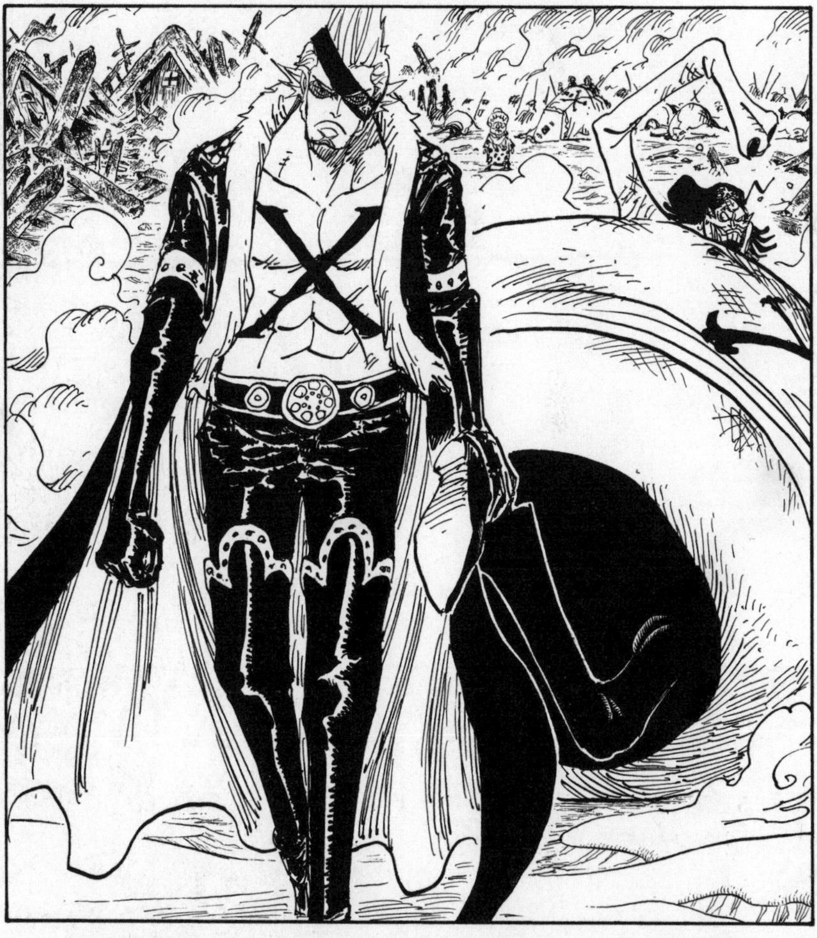

CARIBOU'S NEW WORLD KEE HEE HEE, VOL. 42:
"CRUSH ALL WHO RESIST! THE CAPTAIN IS ARRESTED"

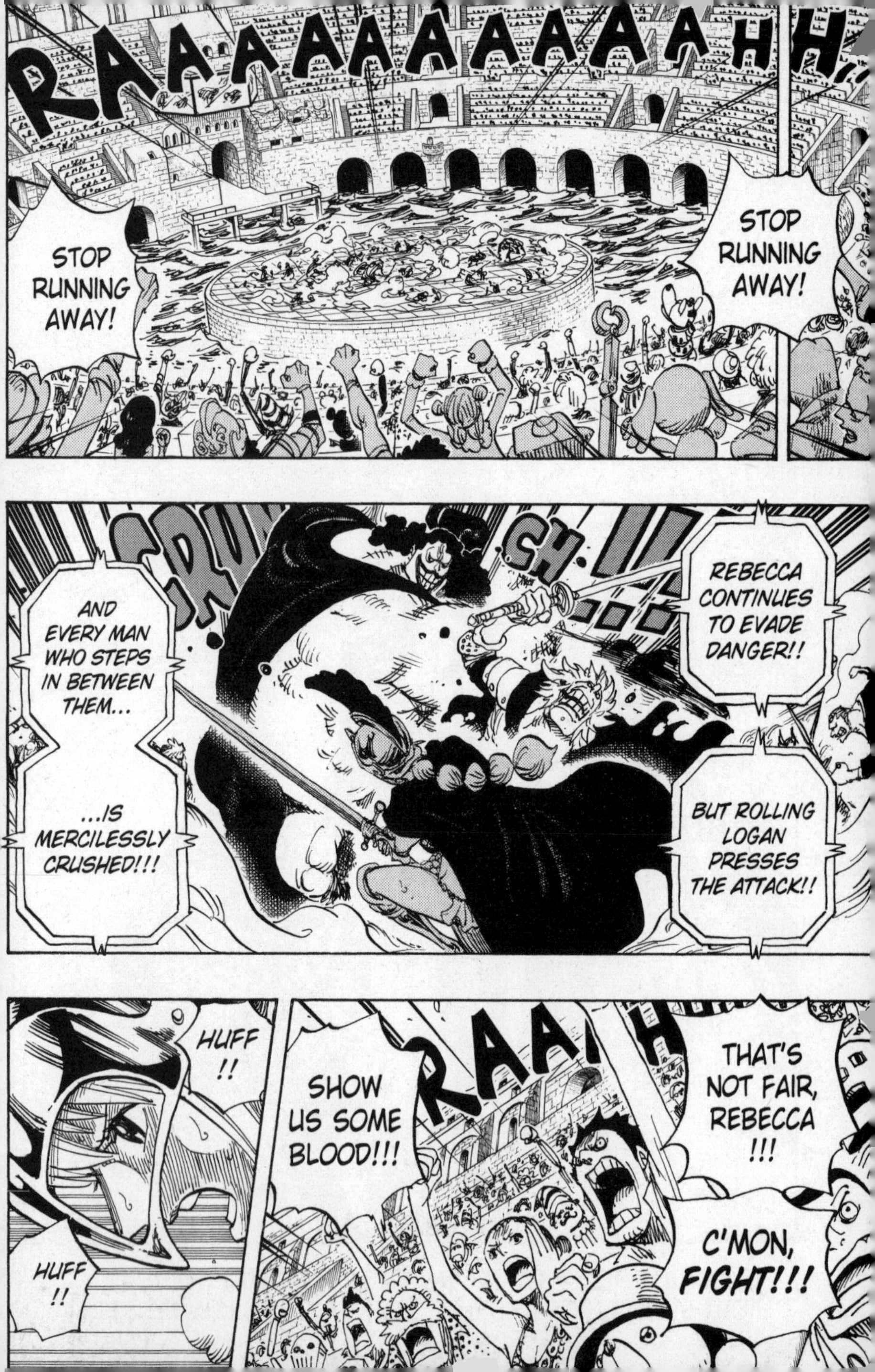
RAAAAAAAAAAHH!!
STOP RUNNING AWAY!
STOP RUNNING AWAY!
REBECCA CONTINUES TO EVADE DANGER!!
BUT ROLLING LOGAN PRESSES THE ATTACK!!
AND EVERY MAN WHO STEPS IN BETWEEN THEM...
...IS MERCILESSLY CRUSHED!!!
RAAH
THAT'S NOT FAIR, REBECCA!!!
C'MON, FIGHT!!!
SHOW US SOME BLOOD!!!
HUFF!!
HUFF!!

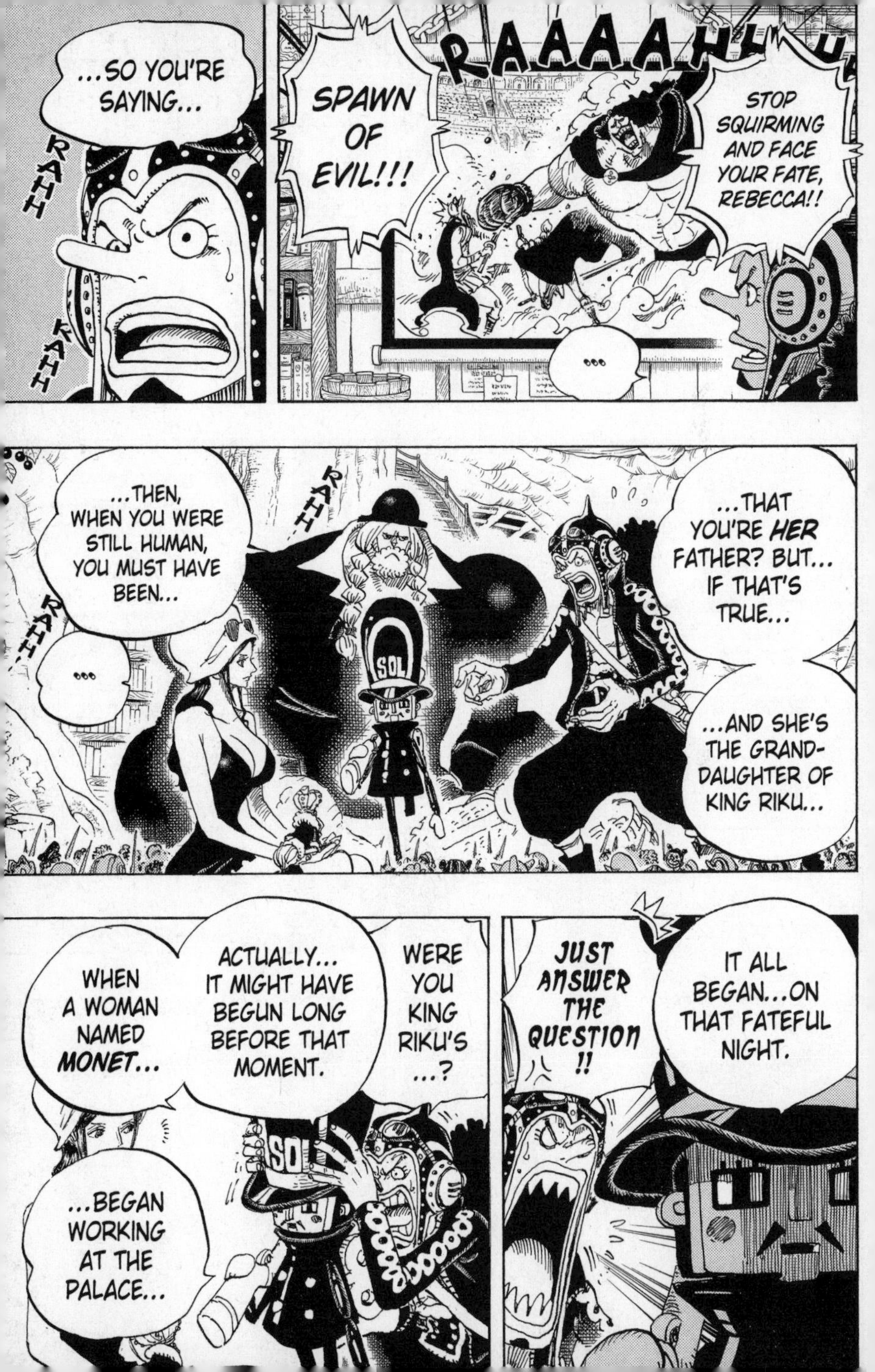
RAAAAHUU
STOP SQUIRMING AND FACE YOUR FATE, REBECCA!!
SPAWN OF EVIL!!!
...
...SO YOU'RE SAYING...
RAHH
RAHH
...THAT YOU'RE HER FATHER? BUT... IF THAT'S TRUE...
...AND SHE'S THE GRAND-DAUGHTER OF KING RIKU...
RAHH
...THEN, WHEN YOU WERE STILL HUMAN, YOU MUST HAVE BEEN...
RAHH
...
IT ALL BEGAN...ON THAT FATEFUL NIGHT.
JUST ANSWER THE QUESTION!!
WERE YOU KING RIKU'S ...?
ACTUALLY... IT MIGHT HAVE BEGUN LONG BEFORE THAT MOMENT.
WHEN A WOMAN NAMED MONET...
...BEGAN WORKING AT THE PALACE...
SOL
SOL

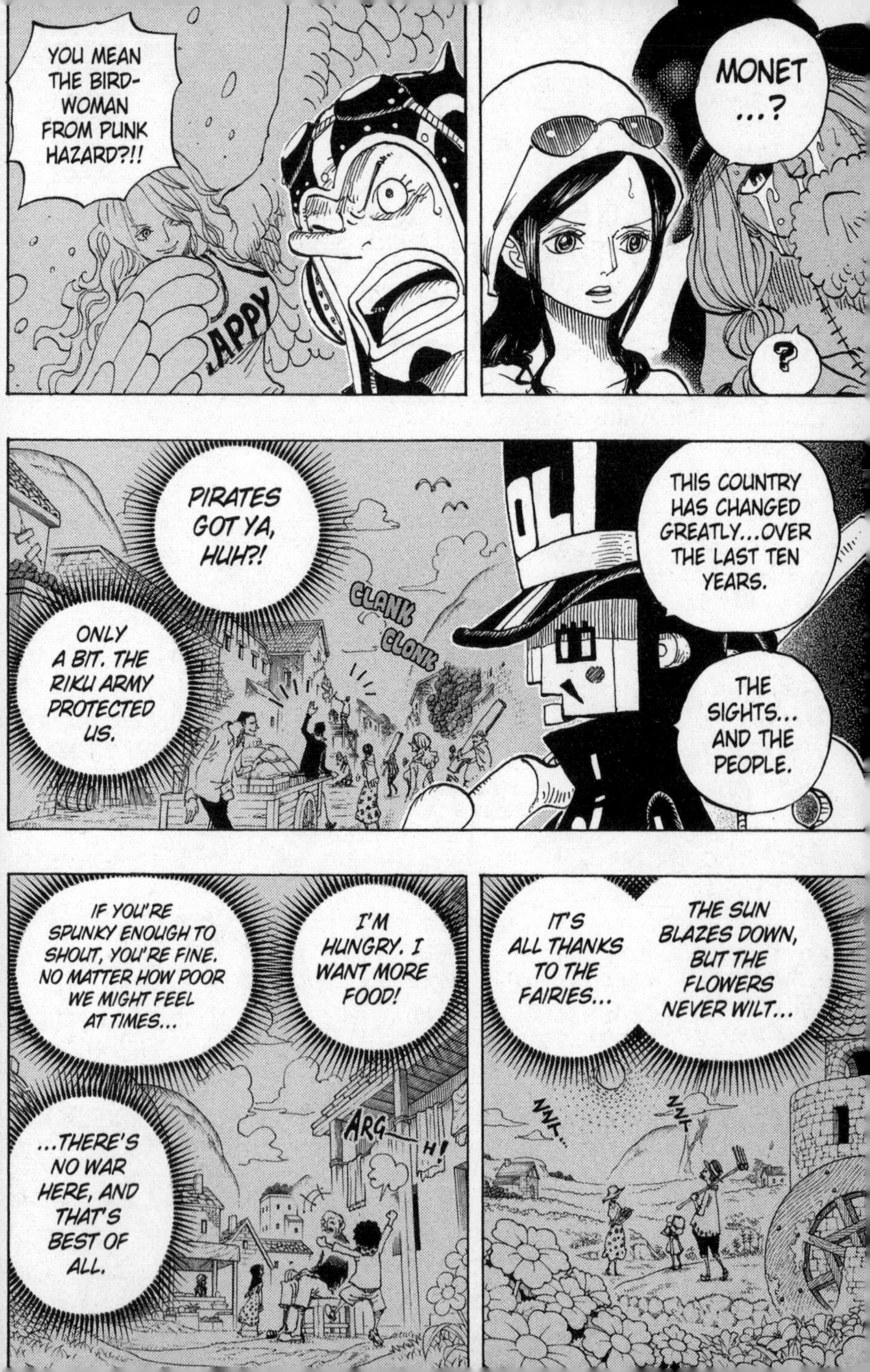
MONET ...?
?
YOU MEAN THE BIRD-WOMAN FROM PUNK HAZARD?!!
APPY
THIS COUNTRY HAS CHANGED GREATLY...OVER THE LAST TEN YEARS.
THE SIGHTS... AND THE PEOPLE.
CLANK
CLONK
PIRATES GOT YA, HUH?!
ONLY A BIT. THE RIKU ARMY PROTECTED US.
THE SUN BLAZES DOWN, BUT THE FLOWERS NEVER WILT...
IT'S ALL THANKS TO THE FAIRIES...
I'M HUNGRY. I WANT MORE FOOD!
IF YOU'RE SPUNKY ENOUGH TO SHOUT, YOU'RE FINE. NO MATTER HOW POOR WE MIGHT FEEL AT TIMES...
ARGH!
...THERE'S NO WAR HERE, AND THAT'S BEST OF ALL.

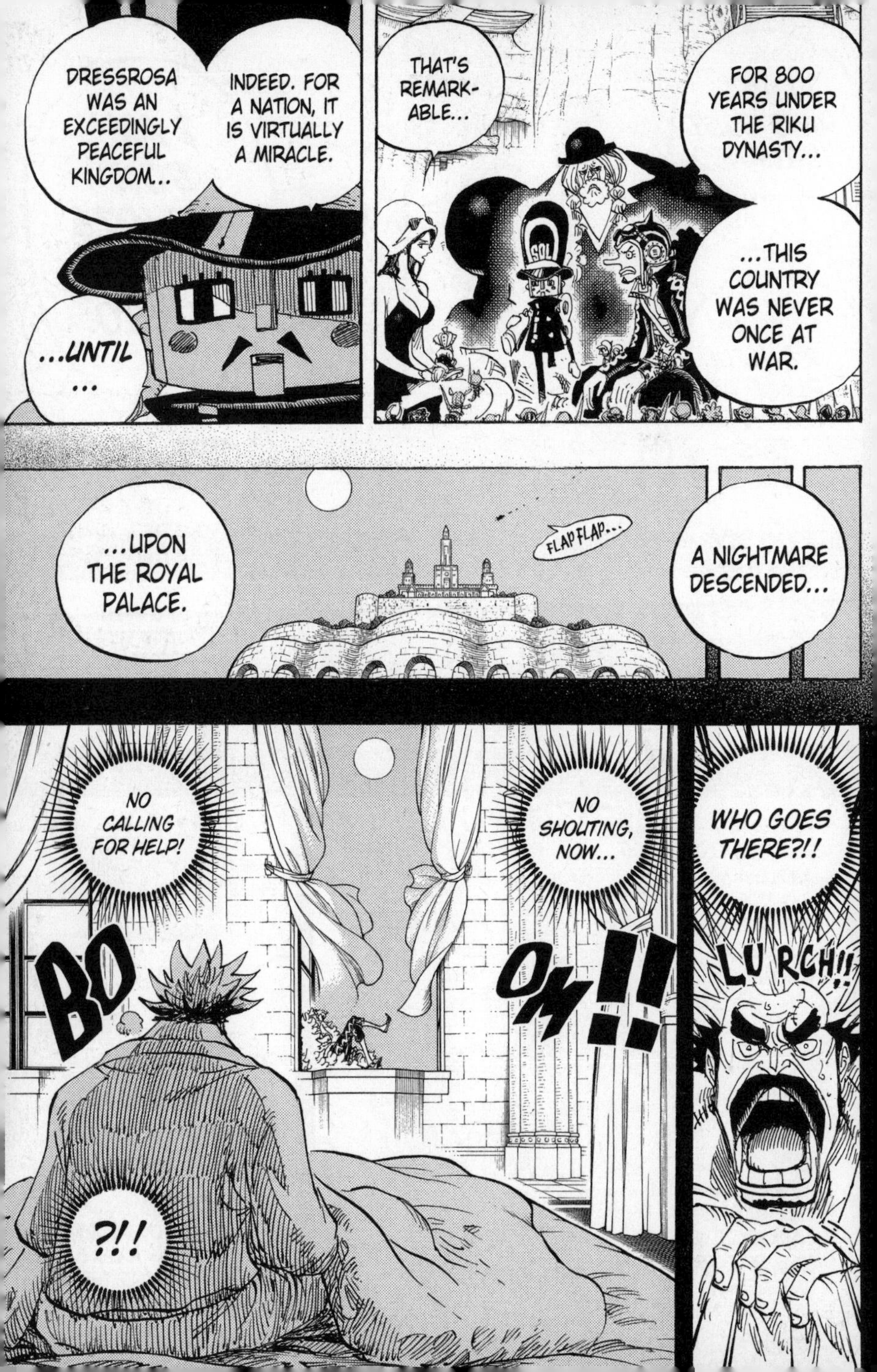
FOR 800 YEARS UNDER THE RIKU DYNASTY...
...THIS COUNTRY WAS NEVER ONCE AT WAR.
THAT'S REMARKABLE...
INDEED. FOR A NATION, IT IS VIRTUALLY A MIRACLE.
DRESSROSA WAS AN EXCEEDINGLY PEACEFUL KINGDOM...
...UNTIL...
A NIGHTMARE DESCENDED...
FLAP FLAP...
...UPON THE ROYAL PALACE.
LURCH!!
WHO GOES THERE?!!
NO SHOUTING, NOW...
NO CALLING FOR HELP!
BOOM!!
?!!

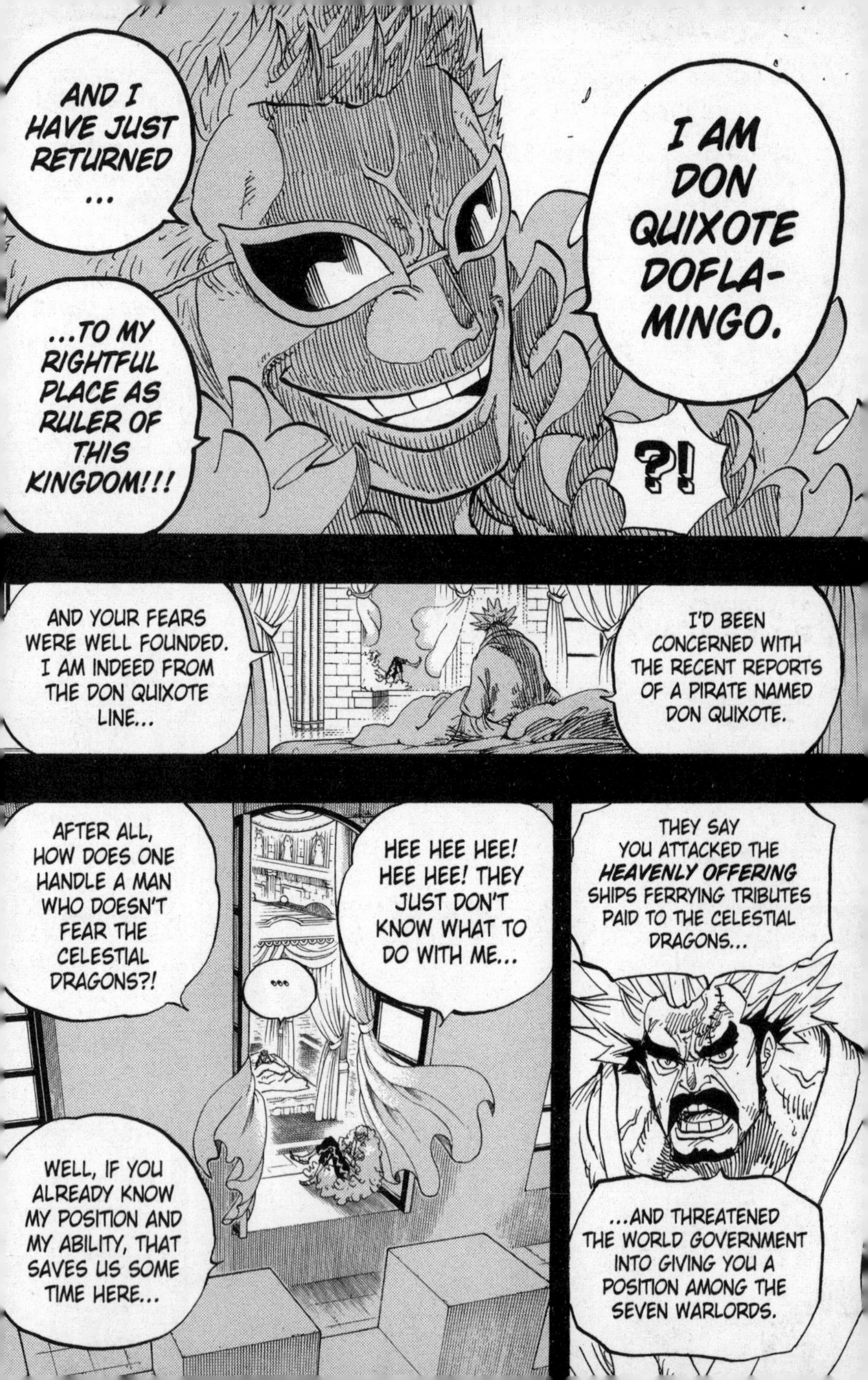
I AM DON QUIXOTE DOFLA-MINGO.
?!
AND I HAVE JUST RETURNED ...
...TO MY RIGHTFUL PLACE AS RULER OF THIS KINGDOM!!!
I'D BEEN CONCERNED WITH THE RECENT REPORTS OF A PIRATE NAMED DON QUIXOTE.
AND YOUR FEARS WERE WELL FOUNDED. I AM INDEED FROM THE DON QUIXOTE LINE...
THEY SAY YOU ATTACKED THE HEAVENLY OFFERING SHIPS FERRYING TRIBUTES PAID TO THE CELESTIAL DRAGONS...
...AND THREATENED THE WORLD GOVERNMENT INTO GIVING YOU A POSITION AMONG THE SEVEN WARLORDS.
HEE HEE HEE! HEE HEE! THEY JUST DON'T KNOW WHAT TO DO WITH ME...
AFTER ALL, HOW DOES ONE HANDLE A MAN WHO DOESN'T FEAR THE CELESTIAL DRAGONS?!
...
WELL, IF YOU ALREADY KNOW MY POSITION AND MY ABILITY, THAT SAVES US SOME TIME HERE...

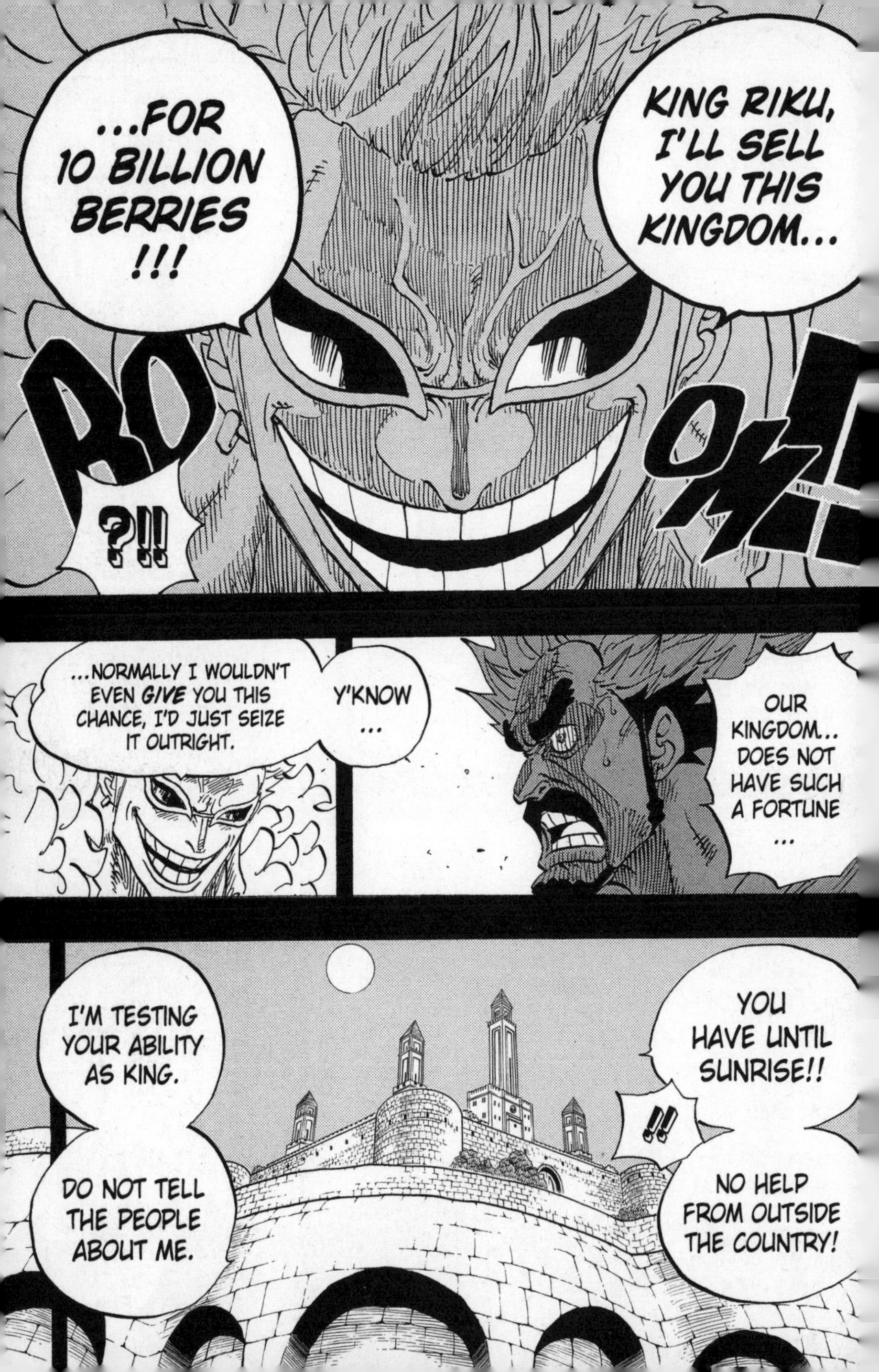
KING RIKU, I'LL SELL YOU THIS KINGDOM...
...FOR 10 BILLION BERRIES!!!
RO
OH!!
?!!
OUR KINGDOM... DOES NOT HAVE SUCH A FORTUNE ...
Y'KNOW ...
...NORMALLY I WOULDN'T EVEN *GIVE* YOU THIS CHANCE, I'D JUST SEIZE IT OUTRIGHT.
YOU HAVE UNTIL SUNRISE!!
!!
NO HELP FROM OUTSIDE THE COUNTRY!
I'M TESTING YOUR ABILITY AS KING.
DO NOT TELL THE PEOPLE ABOUT ME.

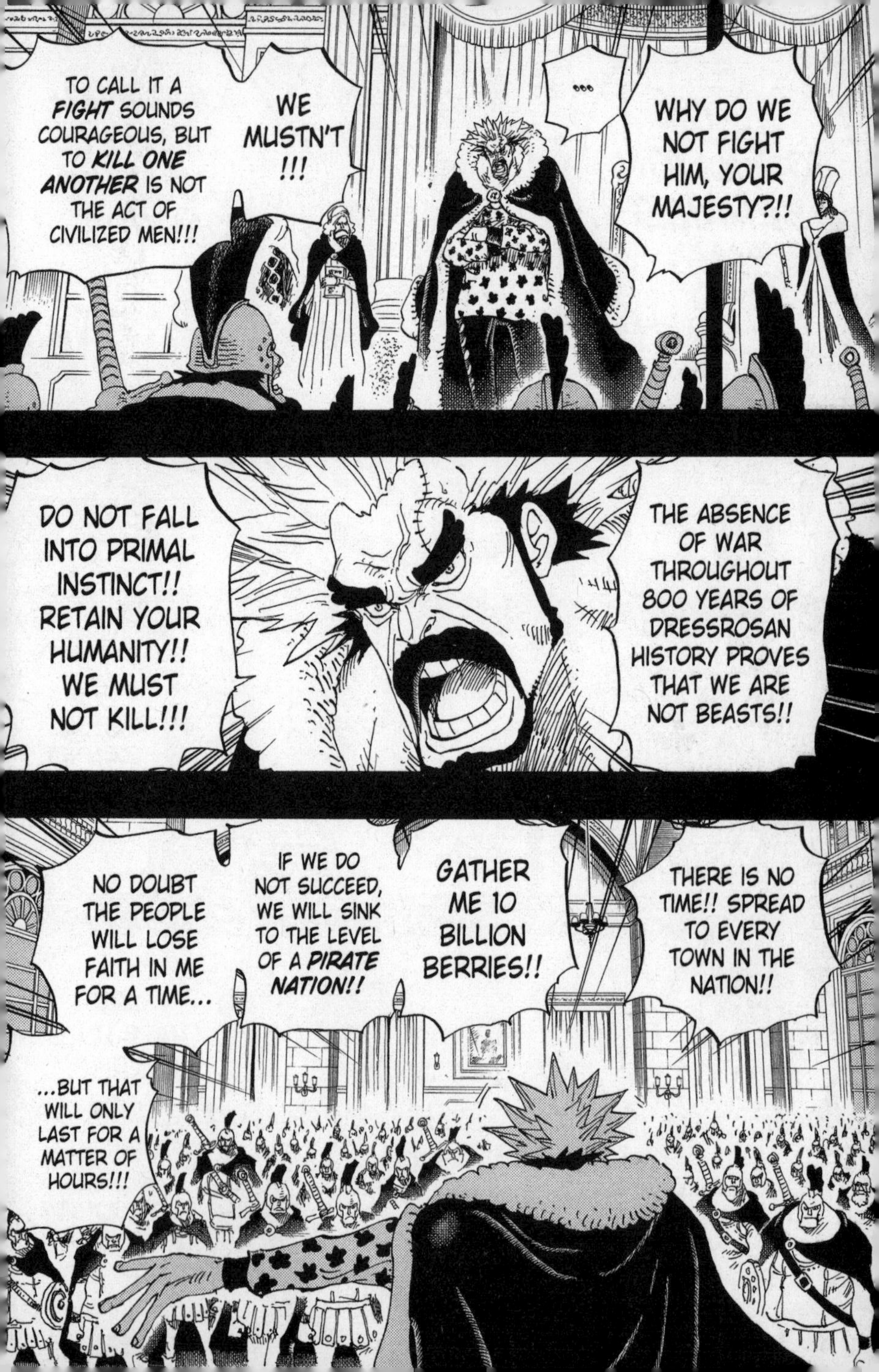
WHY DO WE NOT FIGHT HIM, YOUR MAJESTY?!!
...
WE MUSTN'T!!!
TO CALL IT A FIGHT SOUNDS COURAGEOUS, BUT TO KILL ONE ANOTHER IS NOT THE ACT OF CIVILIZED MEN!!!
THE ABSENCE OF WAR THROUGHOUT 800 YEARS OF DRESSROSAN HISTORY PROVES THAT WE ARE NOT BEASTS!!
DO NOT FALL INTO PRIMAL INSTINCT!! RETAIN YOUR HUMANITY!! WE MUST NOT KILL!!!
THERE IS NO TIME!! SPREAD TO EVERY TOWN IN THE NATION!!
GATHER ME 10 BILLION BERRIES!!
IF WE DO NOT SUCCEED, WE WILL SINK TO THE LEVEL OF A PIRATE NATION!!
NO DOUBT THE PEOPLE WILL LOSE FAITH IN ME FOR A TIME...
...BUT THAT WILL ONLY LAST FOR A MATTER OF HOURS!!!

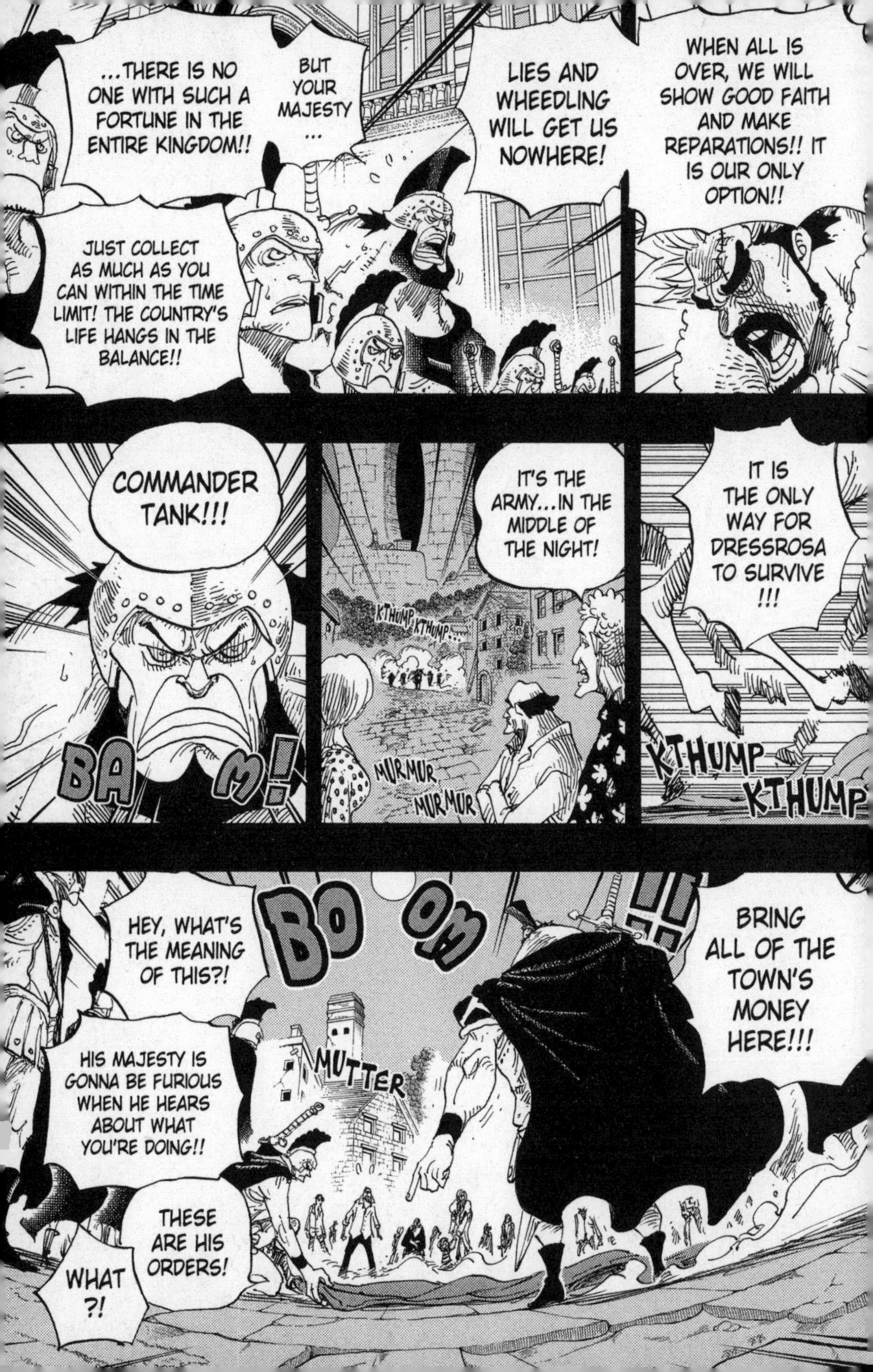
WHEN ALL IS OVER, WE WILL SHOW GOOD FAITH AND MAKE REPARATIONS!! IT IS OUR ONLY OPTION!!
LIES AND WHEEDLING WILL GET US NOWHERE!
BUT YOUR MAJESTY ...
...THERE IS NO ONE WITH SUCH A FORTUNE IN THE ENTIRE KINGDOM!!
JUST COLLECT AS MUCH AS YOU CAN WITHIN THE TIME LIMIT! THE COUNTRY'S LIFE HANGS IN THE BALANCE!!
IT IS THE ONLY WAY FOR DRESSROSA TO SURVIVE !!!
KTHUMP KTHUMP
IT'S THE ARMY...IN THE MIDDLE OF THE NIGHT!
KTHUMP KTHUMP...
MURMUR MURMUR
COMMANDER TANK!!!
BAM!
BRING ALL OF THE TOWN'S MONEY HERE!!!
BOOM
HEY, WHAT'S THE MEANING OF THIS?!
HIS MAJESTY IS GONNA BE FURIOUS WHEN HE HEARS ABOUT WHAT YOU'RE DOING!!
MUTTER
THESE ARE HIS ORDERS!
WHAT ?!

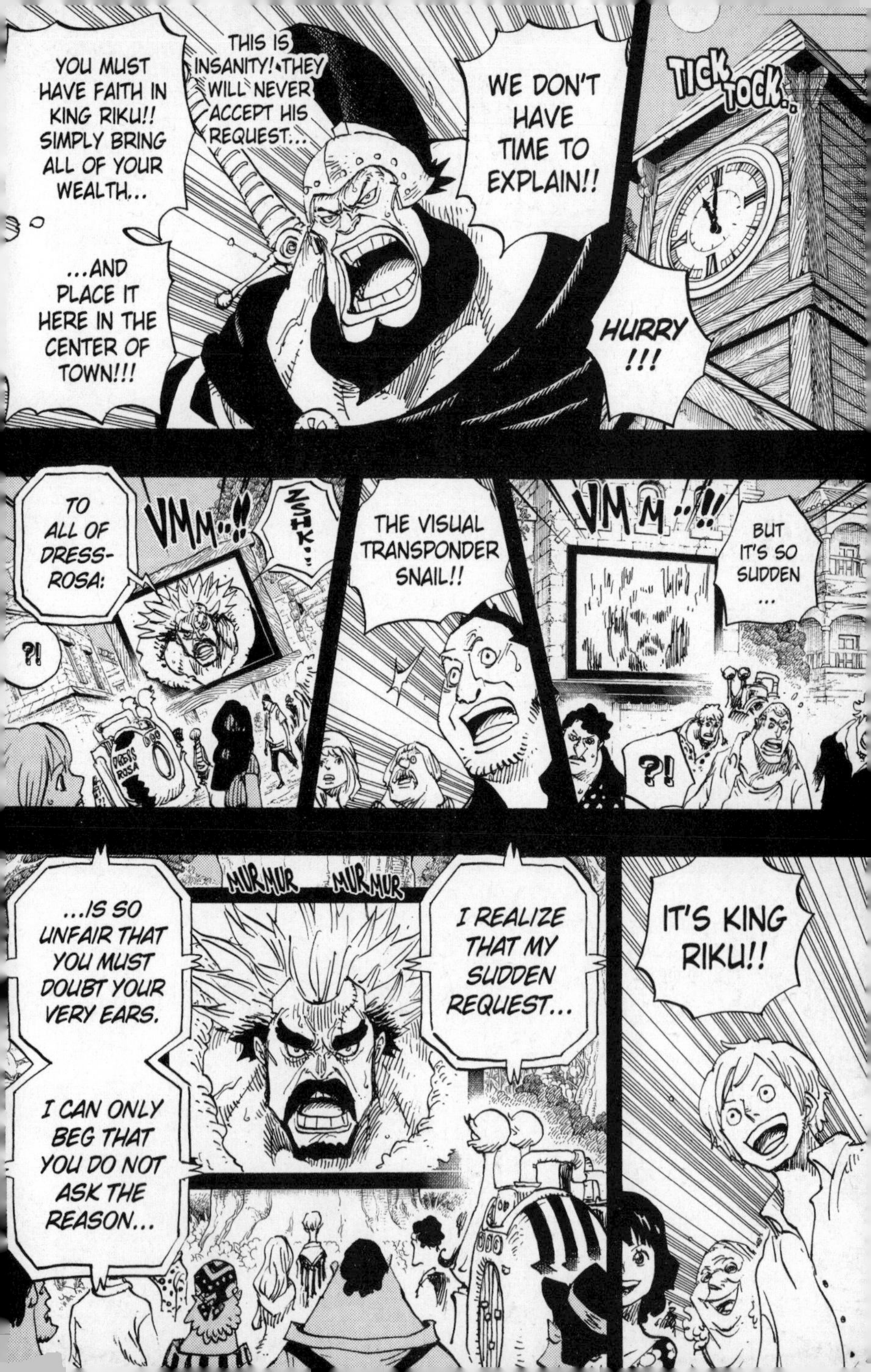
TICK TOCK..
HURRY!!!
WE DON'T HAVE TIME TO EXPLAIN!!
THIS IS INSANITY! THEY WILL NEVER ACCEPT HIS REQUEST...
YOU MUST HAVE FAITH IN KING RIKU!! SIMPLY BRING ALL OF YOUR WEALTH...
...AND PLACE IT HERE IN THE CENTER OF TOWN!!!
VMM..!!
BUT IT'S SO SUDDEN...
?!
THE VISUAL TRANSPONDER SNAIL!!
ZSHK..
VMM..!!
TO ALL OF DRESS-ROSA:
?!
DRESS ROSA
IT'S KING RIKU!!
MURMUR
MURMUR
I REALIZE THAT MY SUDDEN REQUEST...
...IS SO UNFAIR THAT YOU MUST DOUBT YOUR VERY EARS.
I CAN ONLY BEG THAT YOU DO NOT ASK THE REASON...

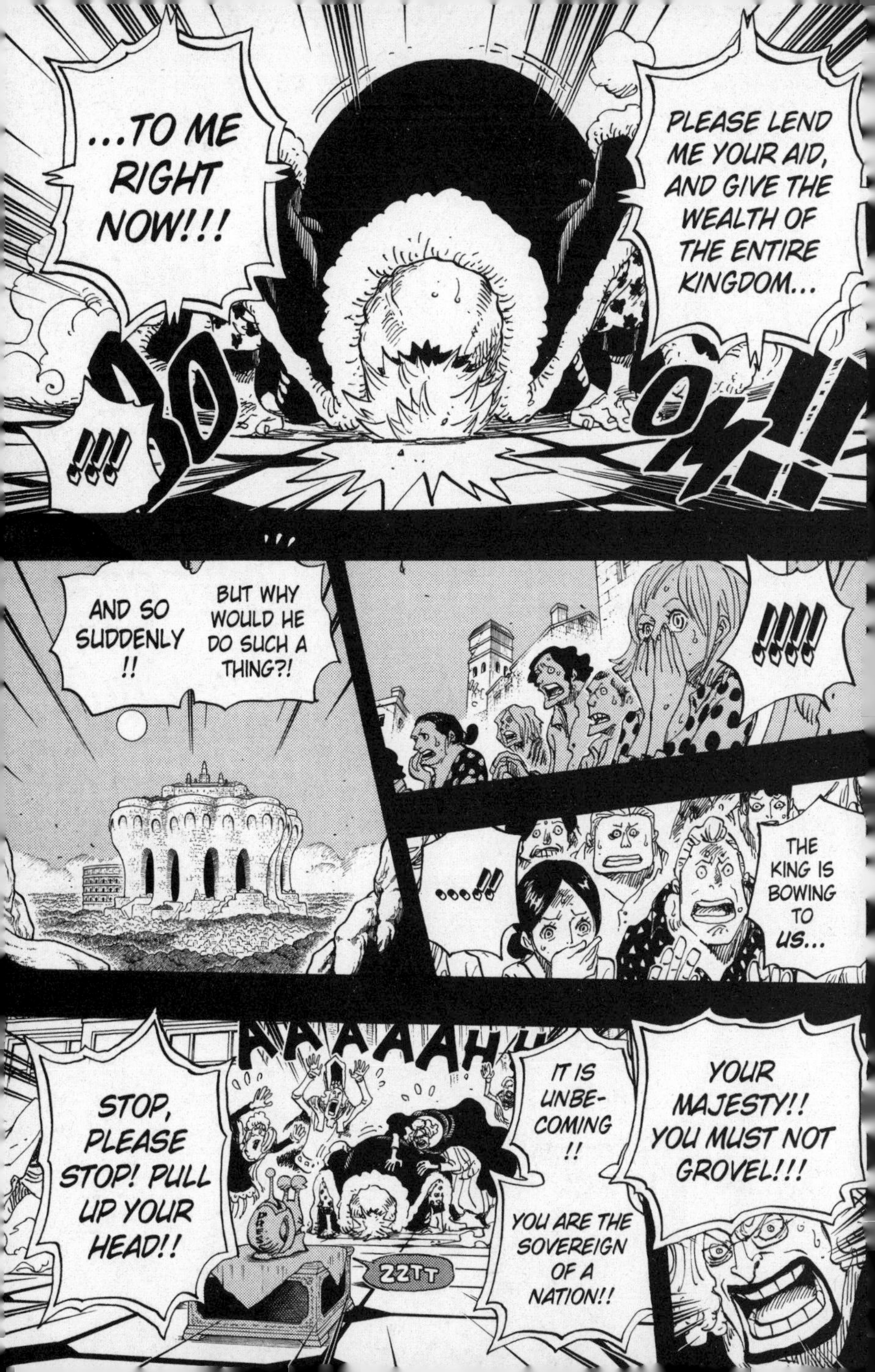
PLEASE LEND ME YOUR AID, AND GIVE THE WEALTH OF THE ENTIRE KINGDOM...
...TO ME RIGHT NOW!!!
ON!!
DO!!!
!!!!!
THE KING IS BOWING TO US...
....!!
BUT WHY WOULD HE DO SUCH A THING?!
AND SO SUDDENLY !!
YOUR MAJESTY!! YOU MUST NOT GROVEL!!!
IT IS UNBE-COMING !!
YOU ARE THE SOVEREIGN OF A NATION!!
AAAAAH!!
STOP, PLEASE STOP! PULL UP YOUR HEAD!!
ZZTT

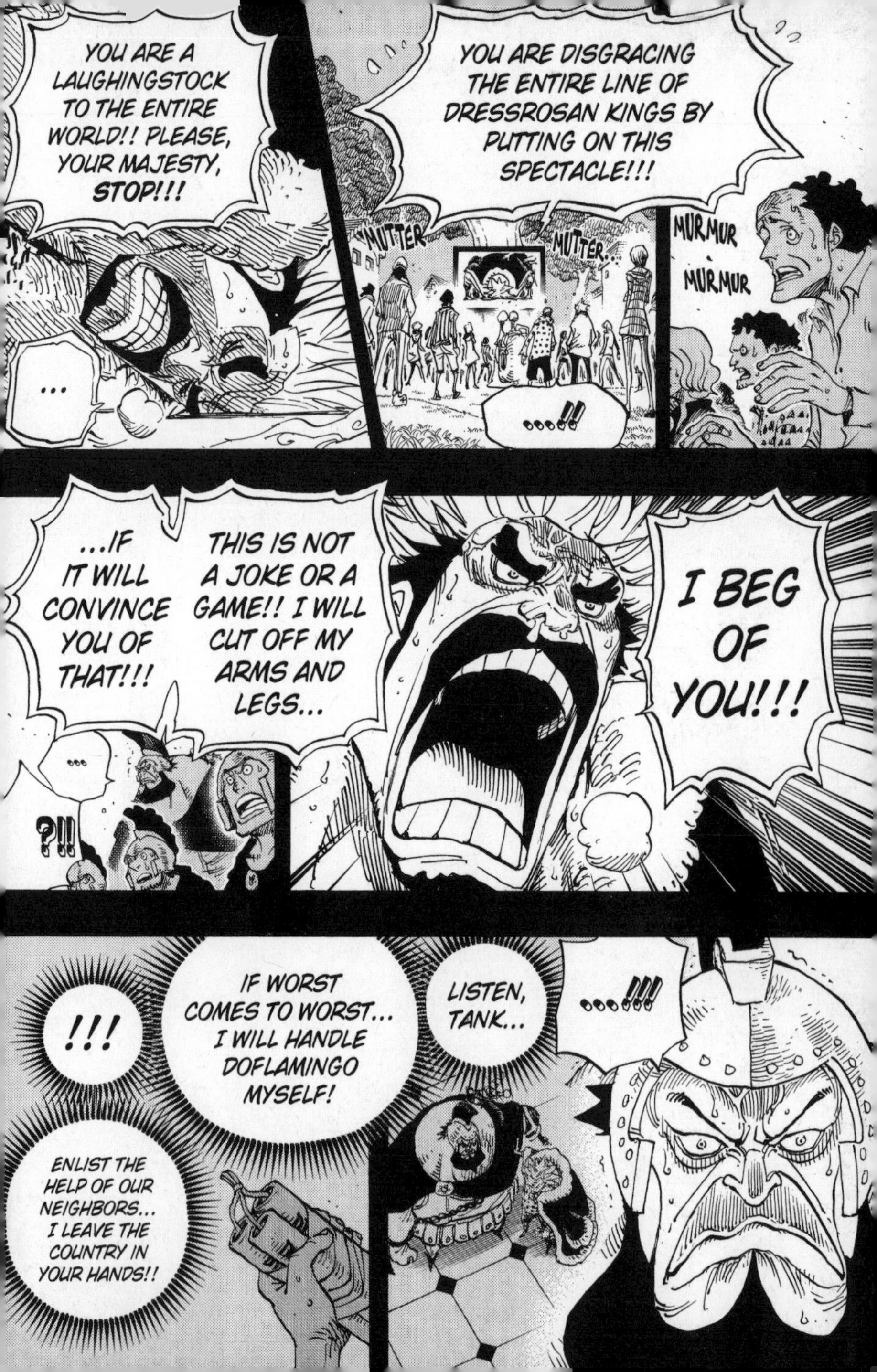
YOU ARE DISGRACING THE ENTIRE LINE OF DRESSROSAN KINGS BY PUTTING ON THIS SPECTACLE!!!
MURMUR
MURMUR
MUTTER...
MUTTER
....!!
YOU ARE A LAUGHINGSTOCK TO THE ENTIRE WORLD!! PLEASE, YOUR MAJESTY, STOP!!!
...
I BEG OF YOU!!!
THIS IS NOT A JOKE OR A GAME!! I WILL CUT OFF MY ARMS AND LEGS...
...IF IT WILL CONVINCE YOU OF THAT!!!
...
?!!
...!!!
LISTEN, TANK...
IF WORST COMES TO WORST... I WILL HANDLE DOFLAMINGO MYSELF!
!!!
ENLIST THE HELP OF OUR NEIGHBORS... I LEAVE THE COUNTRY IN YOUR HANDS!!

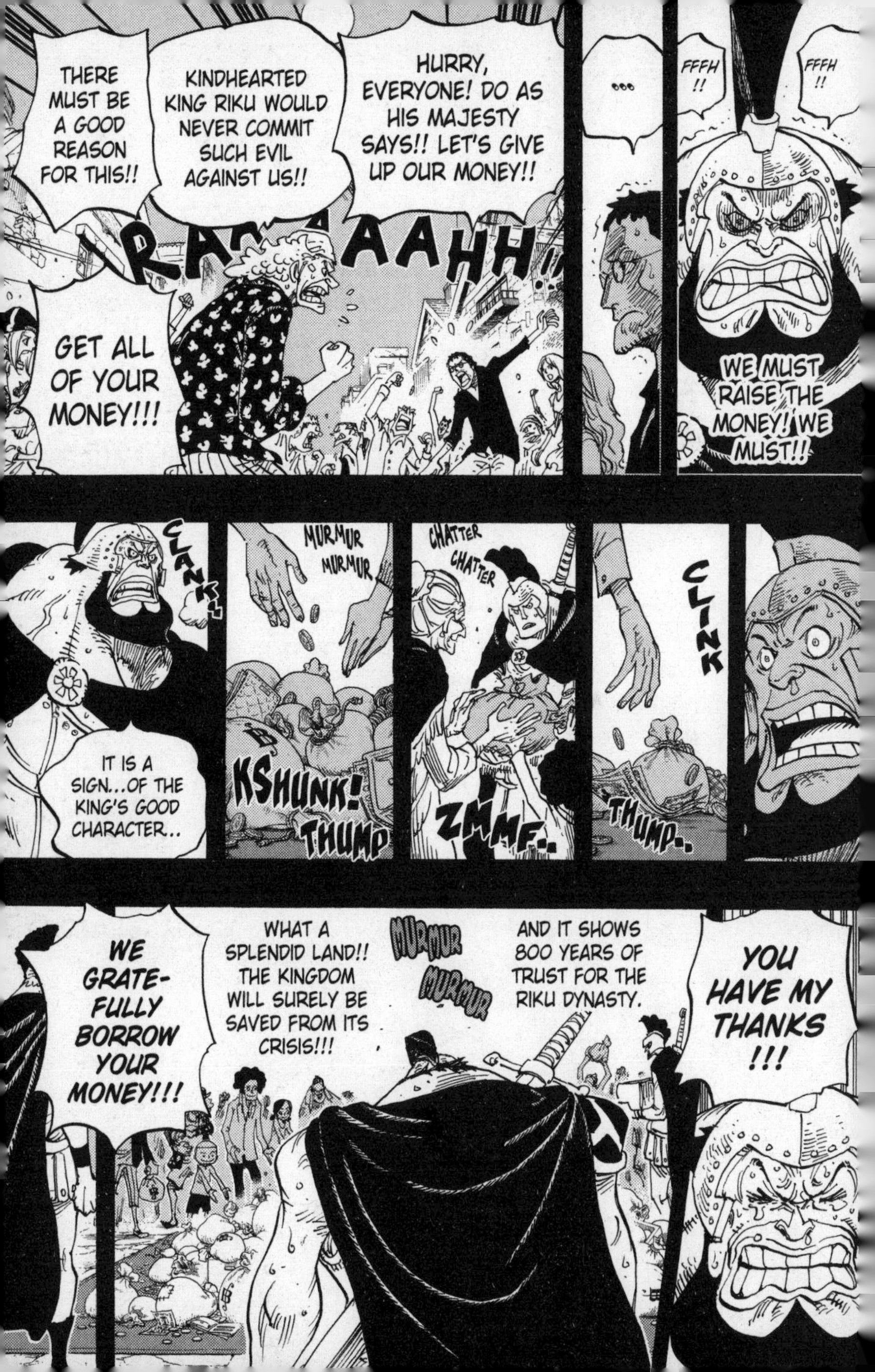
FFFH !!
FFFH !!
WE MUST RAISE THE MONEY!! WE MUST!!
...
HURRY, EVERYONE! DO AS HIS MAJESTY SAYS!! LET'S GIVE UP OUR MONEY!!
KINDHEARTED KING RIKU WOULD NEVER COMMIT SUCH EVIL AGAINST US!!
THERE MUST BE A GOOD REASON FOR THIS!!
AAHH!!
GET ALL OF YOUR MONEY!!!
CLINK
THUMP..
CHATTER
CHATTER
ZMMF..
MURMUR
MURMUR
KSHUNK!
THUMP
CLANK
IT IS A SIGN...OF THE KING'S GOOD CHARACTER...
YOU HAVE MY THANKS!!!
AND IT SHOWS 800 YEARS OF TRUST FOR THE RIKU DYNASTY.
MURMUR
MURMUR
WHAT A SPLENDID LAND!! THE KINGDOM WILL SURELY BE SAVED FROM ITS CRISIS!!!
WE GRATEFULLY BORROW YOUR MONEY!!!

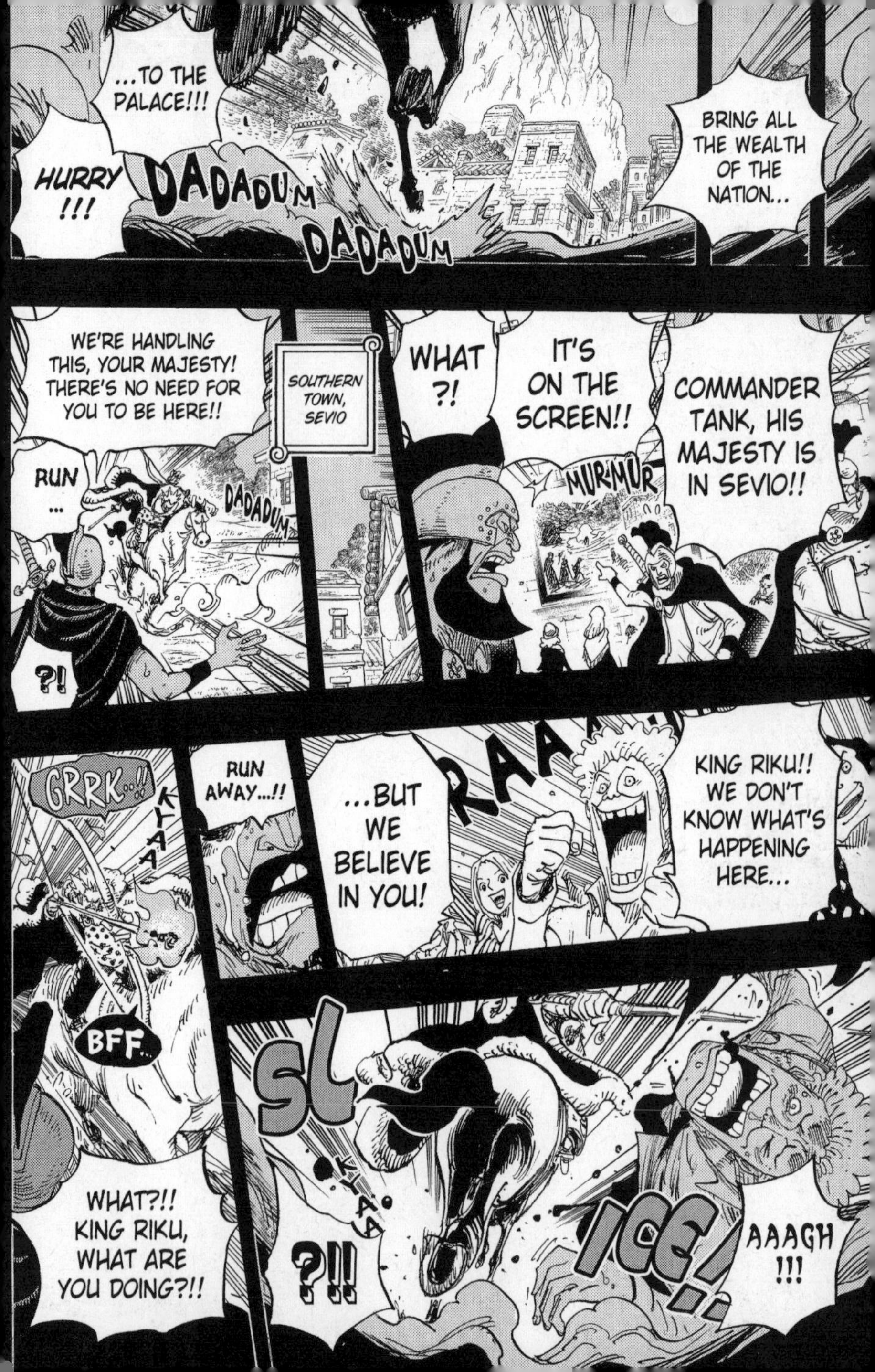
BRING ALL THE WEALTH OF THE NATION...
...TO THE PALACE!!!
HURRY!!!
DADADUM
DADADUM
COMMANDER TANK, HIS MAJESTY IS IN SEVIO!!
MUR MUR
IT'S ON THE SCREEN!!
WHAT?!
SOUTHERN TOWN, SEVIO
WE'RE HANDLING THIS, YOUR MAJESTY! THERE'S NO NEED FOR YOU TO BE HERE!!
DADADUM
RUN...
?!
KING RIKU!! WE DON'T KNOW WHAT'S HAPPENING HERE...
RAAA
...BUT WE BELIEVE IN YOU!
RUN AWAY...!!
GRRK..!!
KYAAA
BFF...
AAAGH!!!
ICE..
SL
KYAA
?!!
WHAT?!! KING RIKU, WHAT ARE YOU DOING?!!

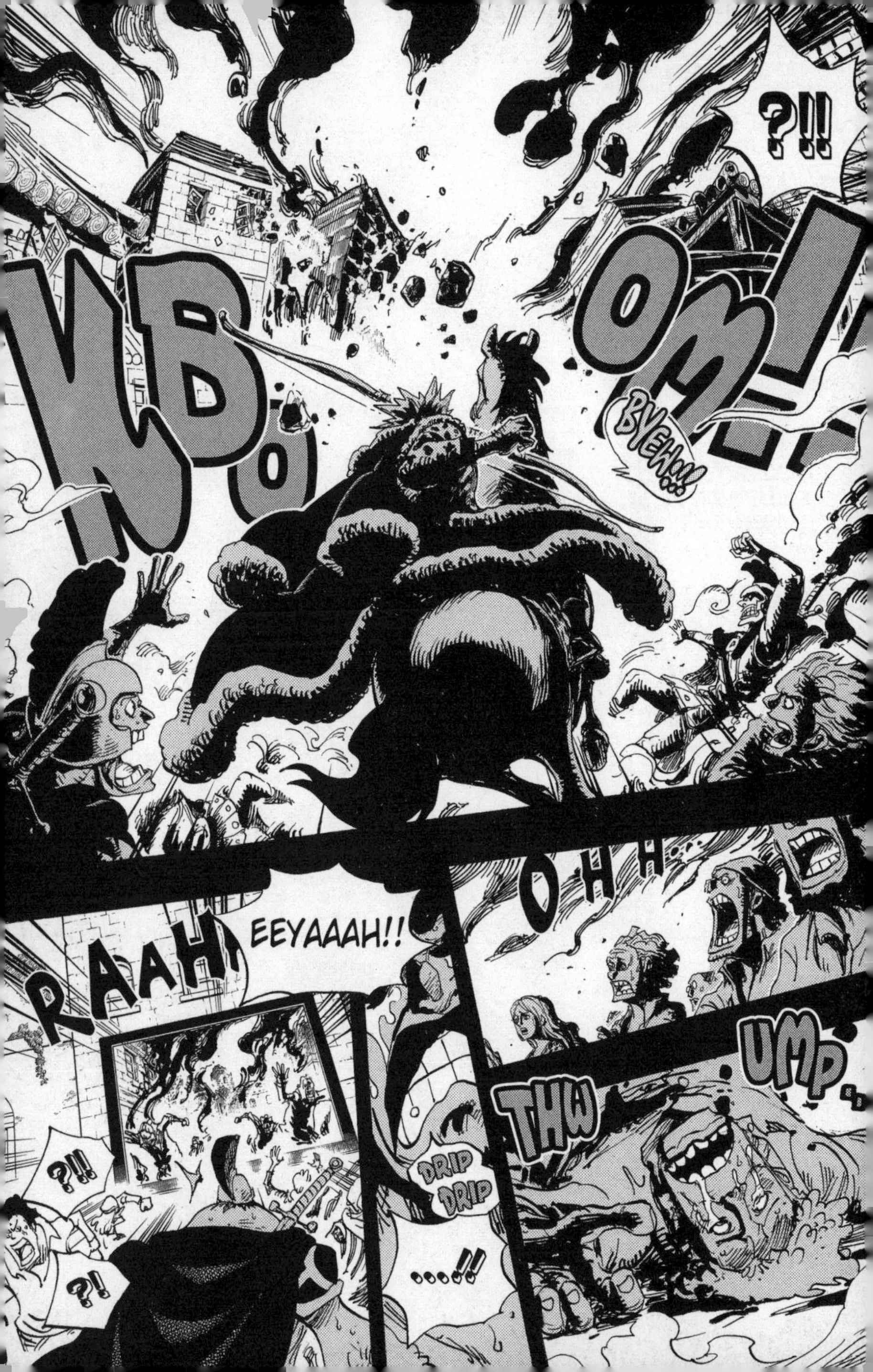
?!!
KBOOOM!!
BYEH...!!
OHH...
THWUMP..
DRIP DRIP
....!!
RAAH!
EEYAAAH!!
?!!
?!

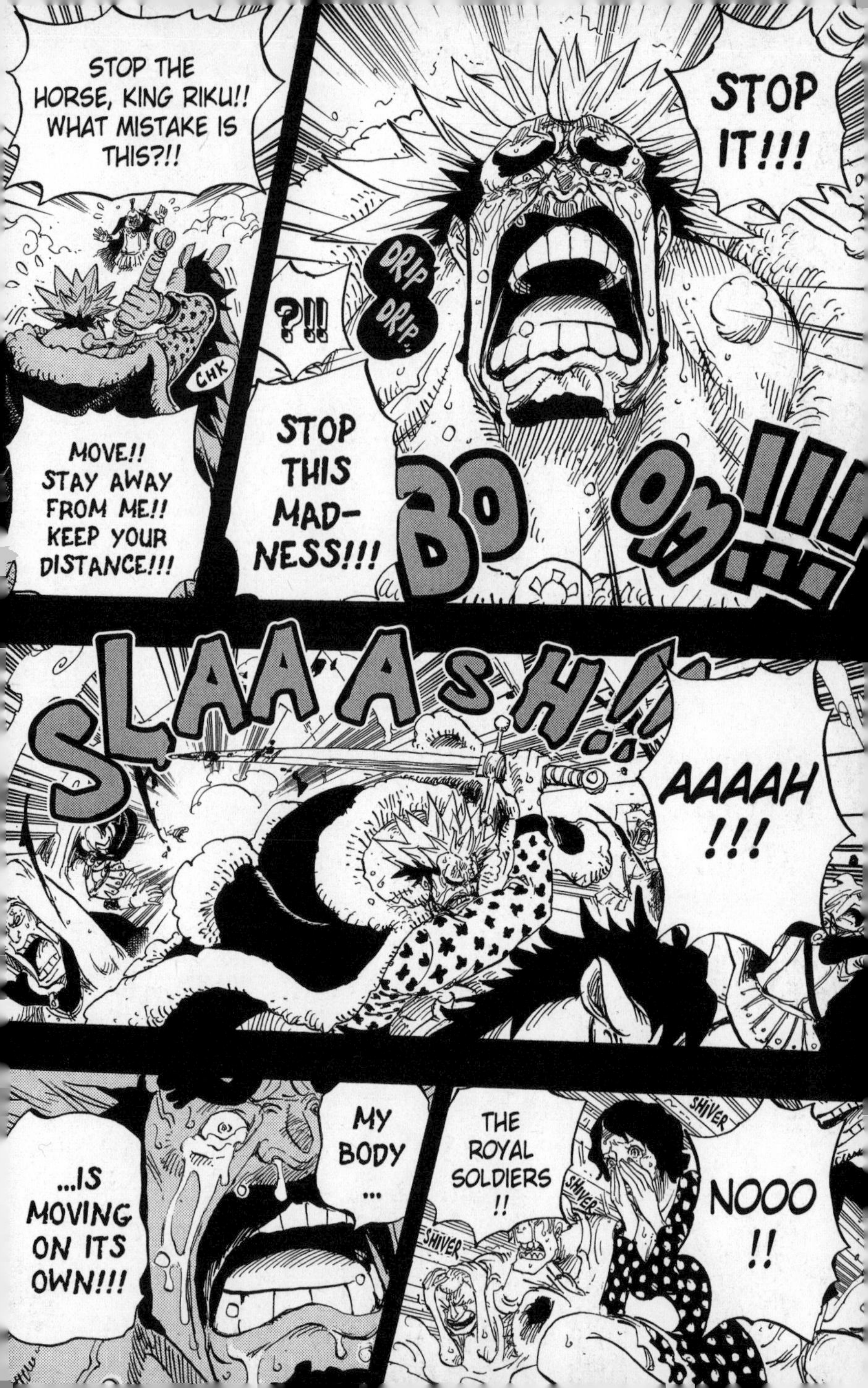
STOP IT!!!
?!!
DRIP DRIP
STOP THIS MAD-NESS!!!
BOOM!!!
STOP THE HORSE, KING RIKU!! WHAT MISTAKE IS THIS?!!
CHK
MOVE!! STAY AWAY FROM ME!! KEEP YOUR DISTANCE!!!
SLAAASH!!
AAAAH!!!
SHIVER
NOOO!!
THE ROYAL SOLDIERS!!
SHIVER
SHIVER
MY BODY...
...IS MOVING ON ITS OWN!!!

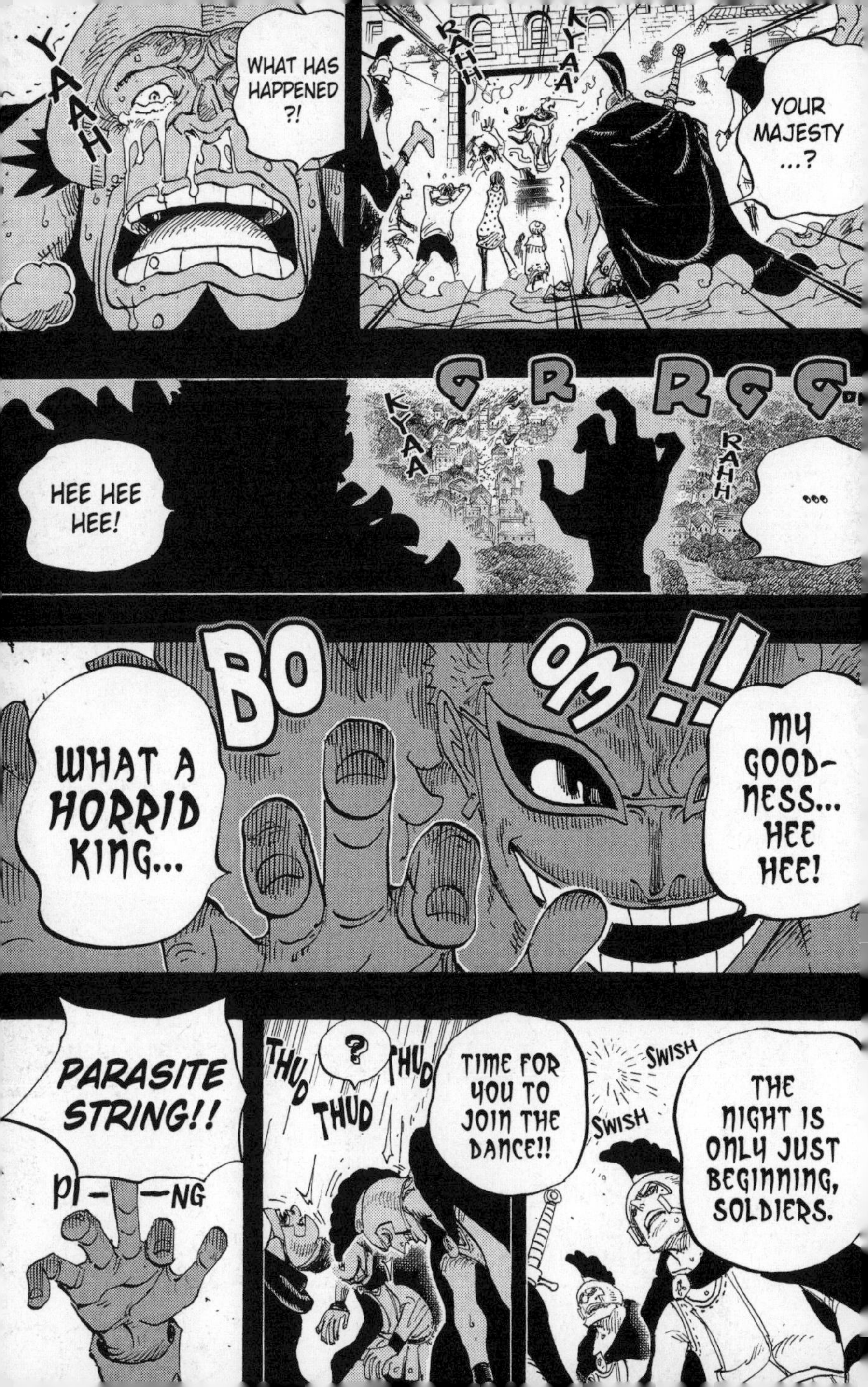
YOUR MAJESTY ...?
KYAA
RAHH
WHAT HAS HAPPENED ?!
YAAAH
GRRGG..
RAHH
...
KYAA
HEE HEE HEE!
BOOM!!
MY GOODNESS... HEE HEE!
WHAT A HORRID KING...
SWISH
THE NIGHT IS ONLY JUST BEGINNING, SOLDIERS.
SWISH
TIME FOR YOU TO JOIN THE DANCE!!
THUD
?
THUD
THUD
PARASITE STRING!!
PI— —NG

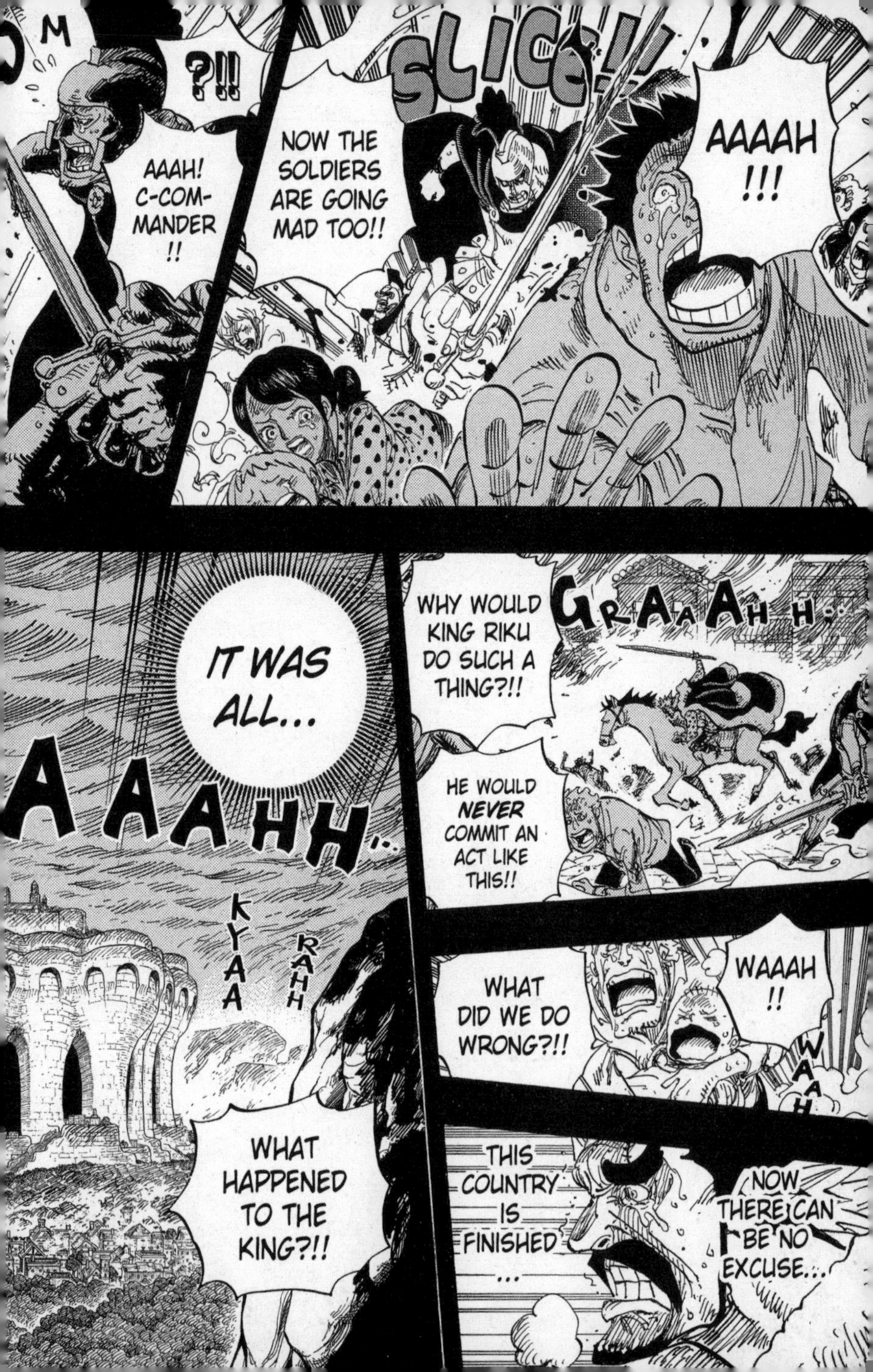
AAAAH!!!
SLICE!!
NOW THE SOLDIERS ARE GOING MAD TOO!!
?!!
AAAH! C-COMMANDER!!
WHY WOULD KING RIKU DO SUCH A THING?!!
GRAAAHH...
HE WOULD **NEVER** COMMIT AN ACT LIKE THIS!!
WAAAH!!
WAAAH
WHAT DID WE DO WRONG?!!
NOW THERE CAN BE NO EXCUSE...
THIS COUNTRY IS FINISHED...
IT WAS ALL...
AAAAHH...
KYAAA
RAHH
WHAT HAPPENED TO THE KING?!!

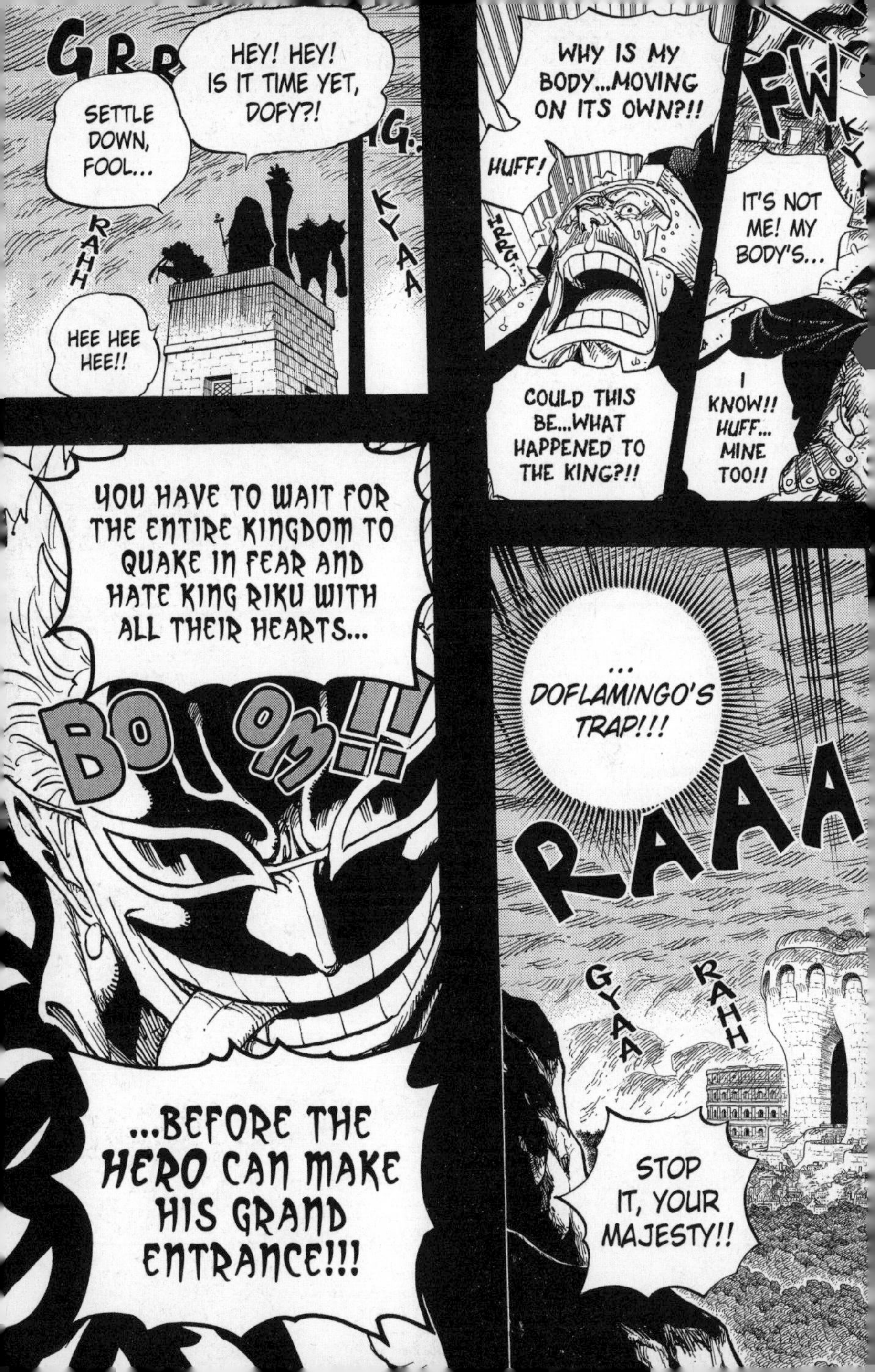
FWKY
IT'S NOT ME! MY BODY'S...
I KNOW!! HUFF... MINE TOO!!
WHY IS MY BODY...MOVING ON ITS OWN?!!
HUFF!
HRRG...
COULD THIS BE...WHAT HAPPENED TO THE KING?!!
HEY! HEY! IS IT TIME YET, DOFY?!
GRR
SETTLE DOWN, FOOL...
RAHH
KYAA
HEE HEE HEE!!
...DOFLAMINGO'S TRAP!!!
RAAA
RAHH
GYAA
STOP IT, YOUR MAJESTY!!
YOU HAVE TO WAIT FOR THE ENTIRE KINGDOM TO QUAKE IN FEAR AND HATE KING RIKU WITH ALL THEIR HEARTS...
BOOOM!!
...BEFORE THE HERO CAN MAKE HIS GRAND ENTRANCE!!!

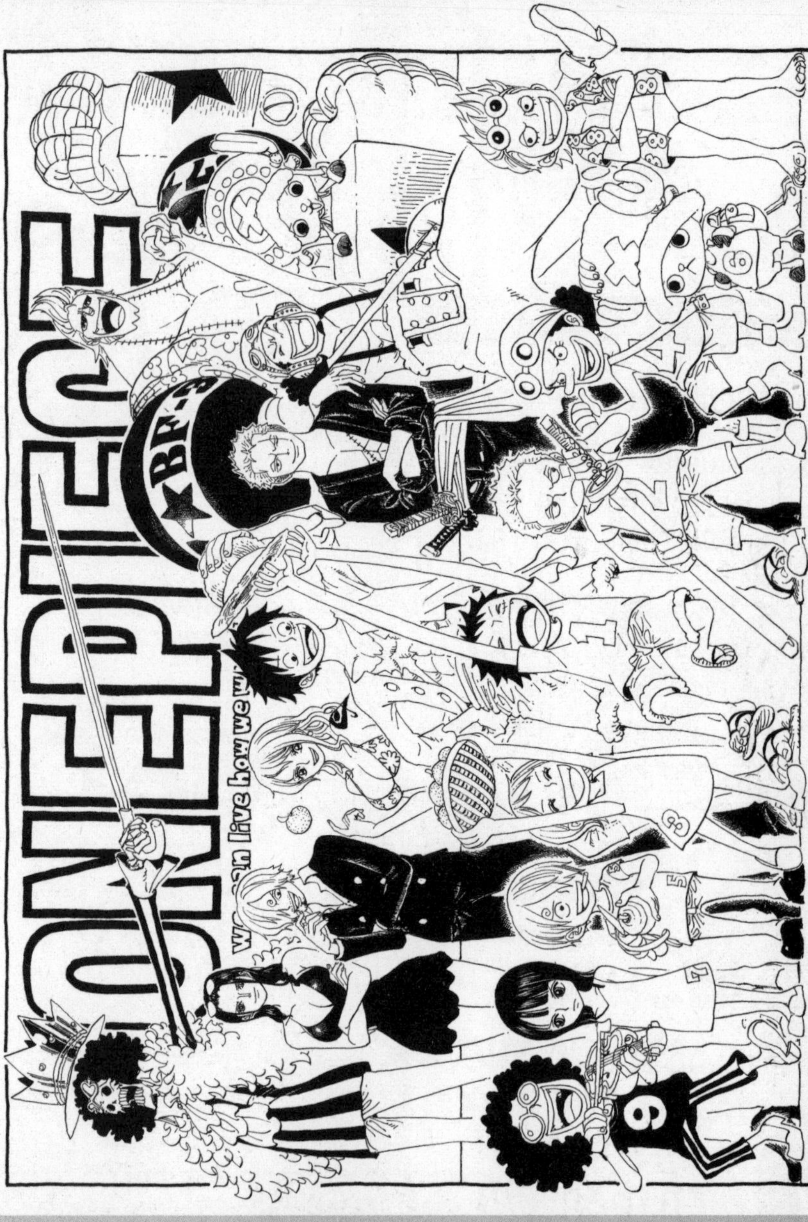
ONE PIECE

Chapter 728:

THE NUMBER OF TRAGEDIES

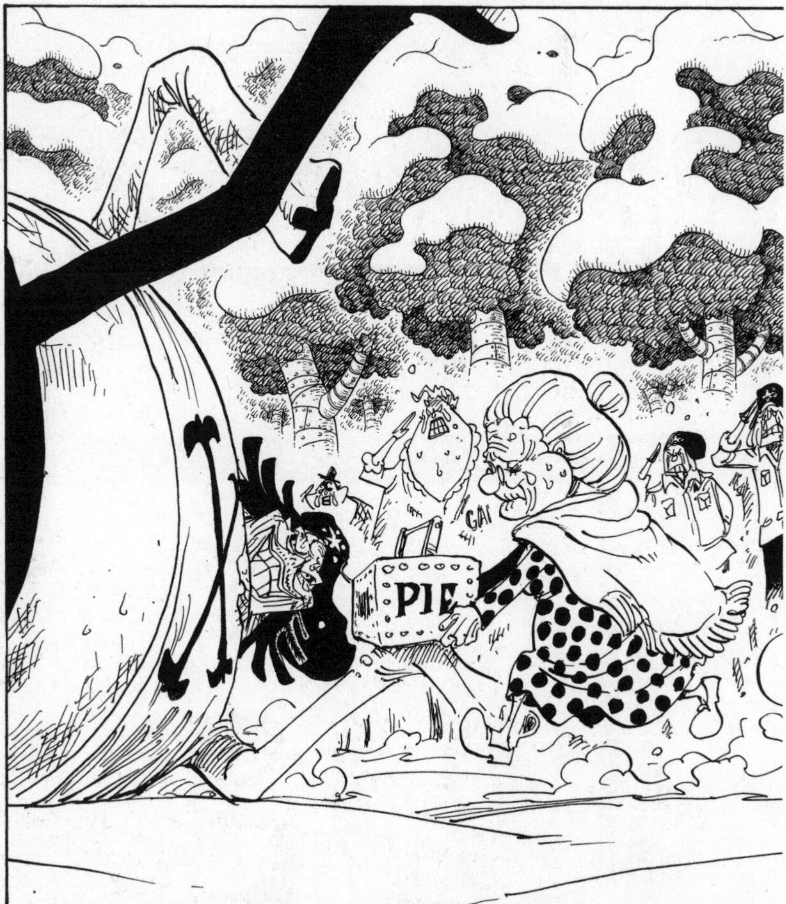
PIE

CARIBOU'S NEW WORLD KEE HEE HEE, VOL. 43:
"THE LAST MEAT PIE FOR MY GRANDSON, WHO SACRIFICED HIMSELF TO THE UNSTOPPABLE WARRIOR"

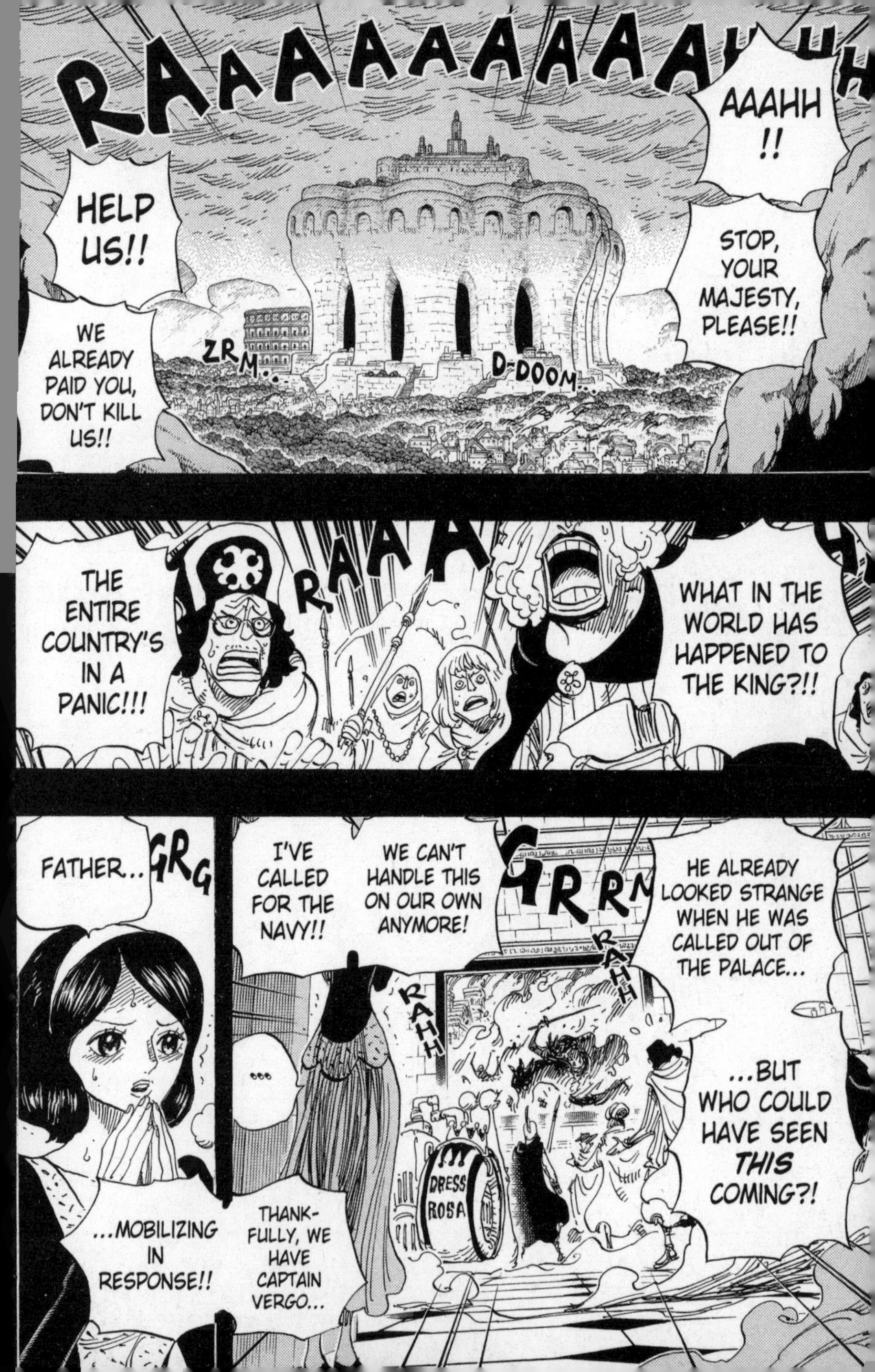
RAAAAAAAAAHH
AAAHH!!
STOP, YOUR MAJESTY, PLEASE!!
HELP US!!
D-DOOM...
WE ALREADY PAID YOU, DON'T KILL US!!
ZRM..
WHAT IN THE WORLD HAS HAPPENED TO THE KING?!!
RAAA
THE ENTIRE COUNTRY'S IN A PANIC!!!
HE ALREADY LOOKED STRANGE WHEN HE WAS CALLED OUT OF THE PALACE...
...BUT WHO COULD HAVE SEEN THIS COMING?!
GRRRN
RAHH
WE CAN'T HANDLE THIS ON OUR OWN ANYMORE!
I'VE CALLED FOR THE NAVY!!
RAHH
...
THANKFULLY, WE HAVE CAPTAIN VERGO...
...MOBILIZING IN RESPONSE!!
DRESS ROSA
GRG
FATHER...

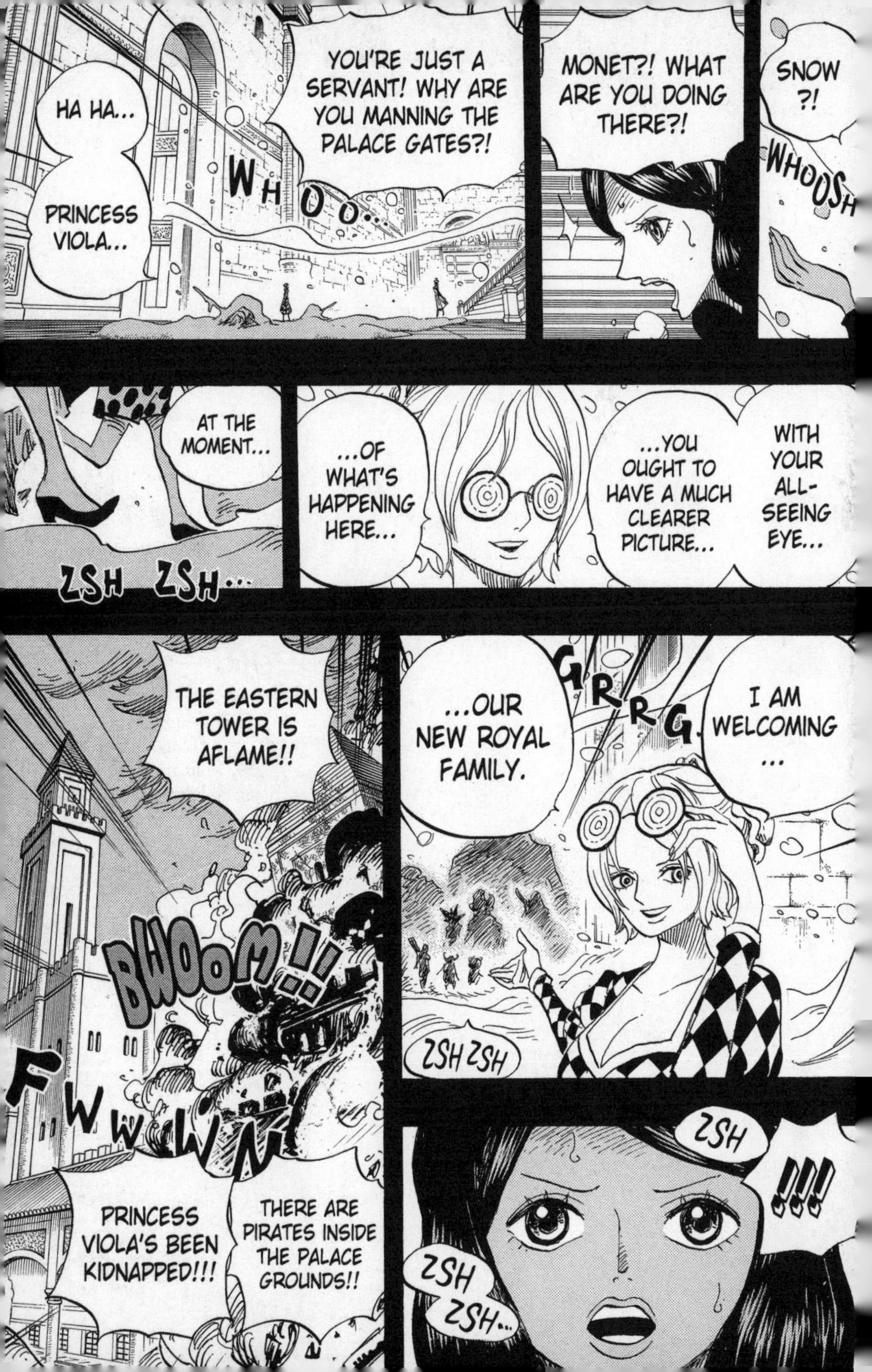
SNOW ?!
WHOOSH
MONET?! WHAT ARE YOU DOING THERE?!
YOU'RE JUST A SERVANT! WHY ARE YOU MANNING THE PALACE GATES?!
WHOO...
HA HA...
PRINCESS VIOLA...
WITH YOUR ALL-SEEING EYE...
...YOU OUGHT TO HAVE A MUCH CLEARER PICTURE...
...OF WHAT'S HAPPENING HERE...
AT THE MOMENT...
ZSH ZSH...
I AM WELCOMING ...
GRRG
...OUR NEW ROYAL FAMILY.
ZSH ZSH
ZSH
!!!
ZSH ZSH...
THE EASTERN TOWER IS AFLAME!!
BWOOM!!
FWWWN
THERE ARE PIRATES INSIDE THE PALACE GROUNDS!!
PRINCESS VIOLA'S BEEN KIDNAPPED!!!

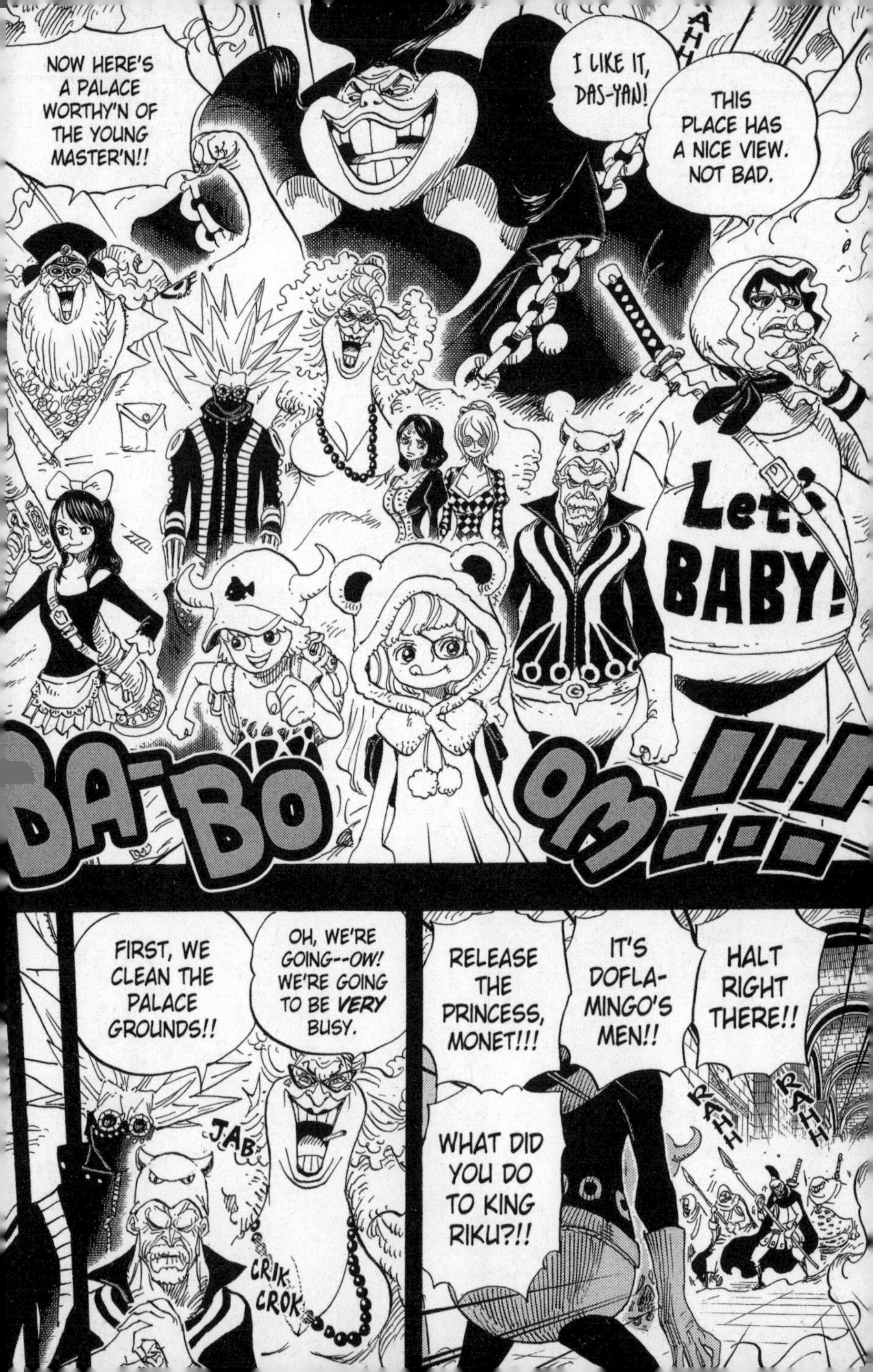
THIS PLACE HAS A NICE VIEW. NOT BAD.
I LIKE IT, DAS-YAN!
NOW HERE'S A PALACE WORTHY'N OF THE YOUNG MASTER'N!!
Let's BABY!
DA-BOOM...!!!
HALT RIGHT THERE!!
RAHH
RAHH
IT'S DOFLAMINGO'S MEN!!
RELEASE THE PRINCESS, MONET!!!
WHAT DID YOU DO TO KING RIKU?!!
OH, WE'RE GOING--OW! WE'RE GOING TO BE VERY BUSY.
FIRST, WE CLEAN THE PALACE GROUNDS!!
JAB
CRIK CROK

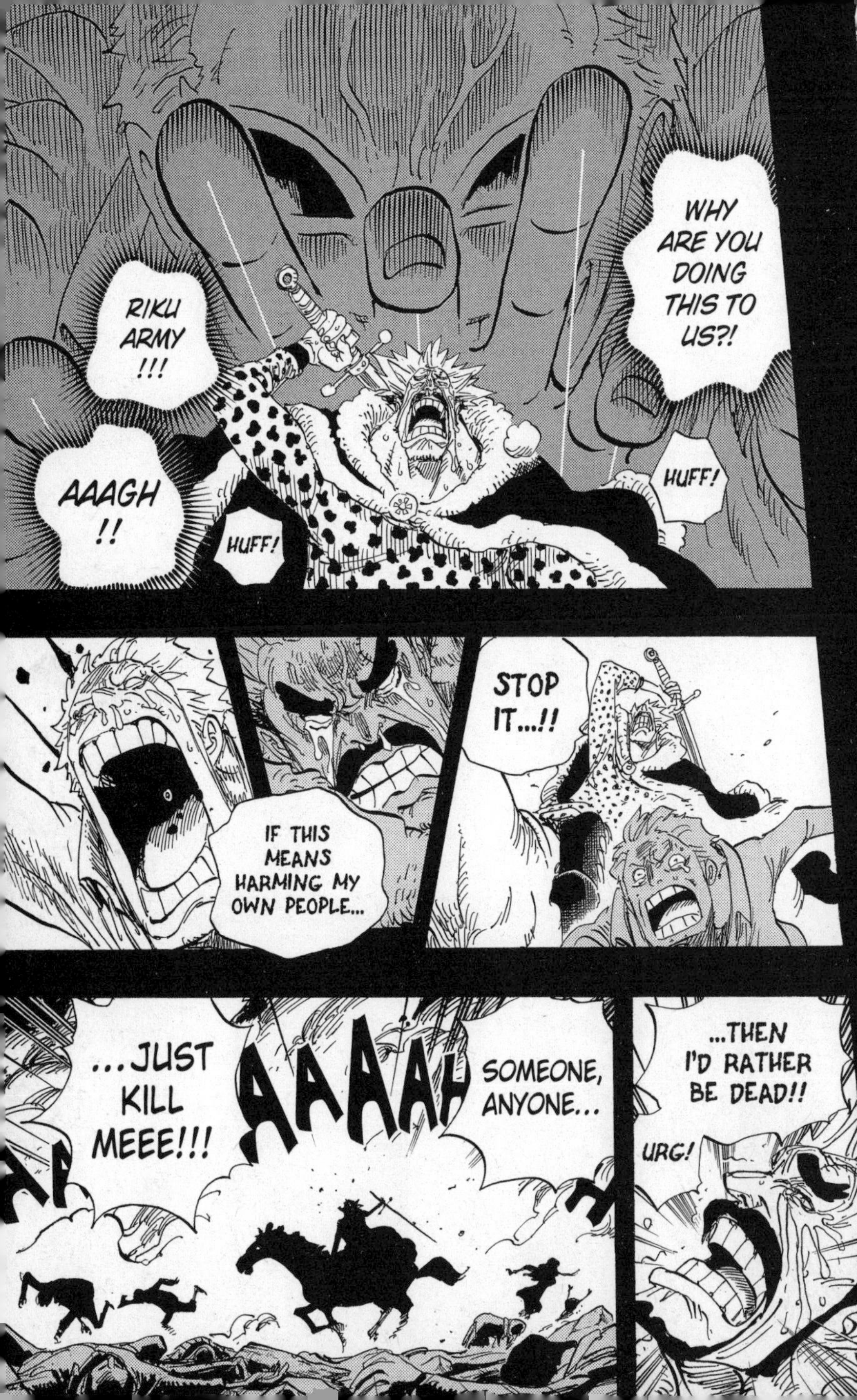
WHY ARE YOU DOING THIS TO US?!
HUFF!
RIKU ARMY!!!
AAAGH!!
HUFF!
STOP IT...!!
IF THIS MEANS HARMING MY OWN PEOPLE...
...THEN I'D RATHER BE DEAD!!
URG!
SOMEONE, ANYONE...
AAAAH
...JUST KILL MEEE!!!

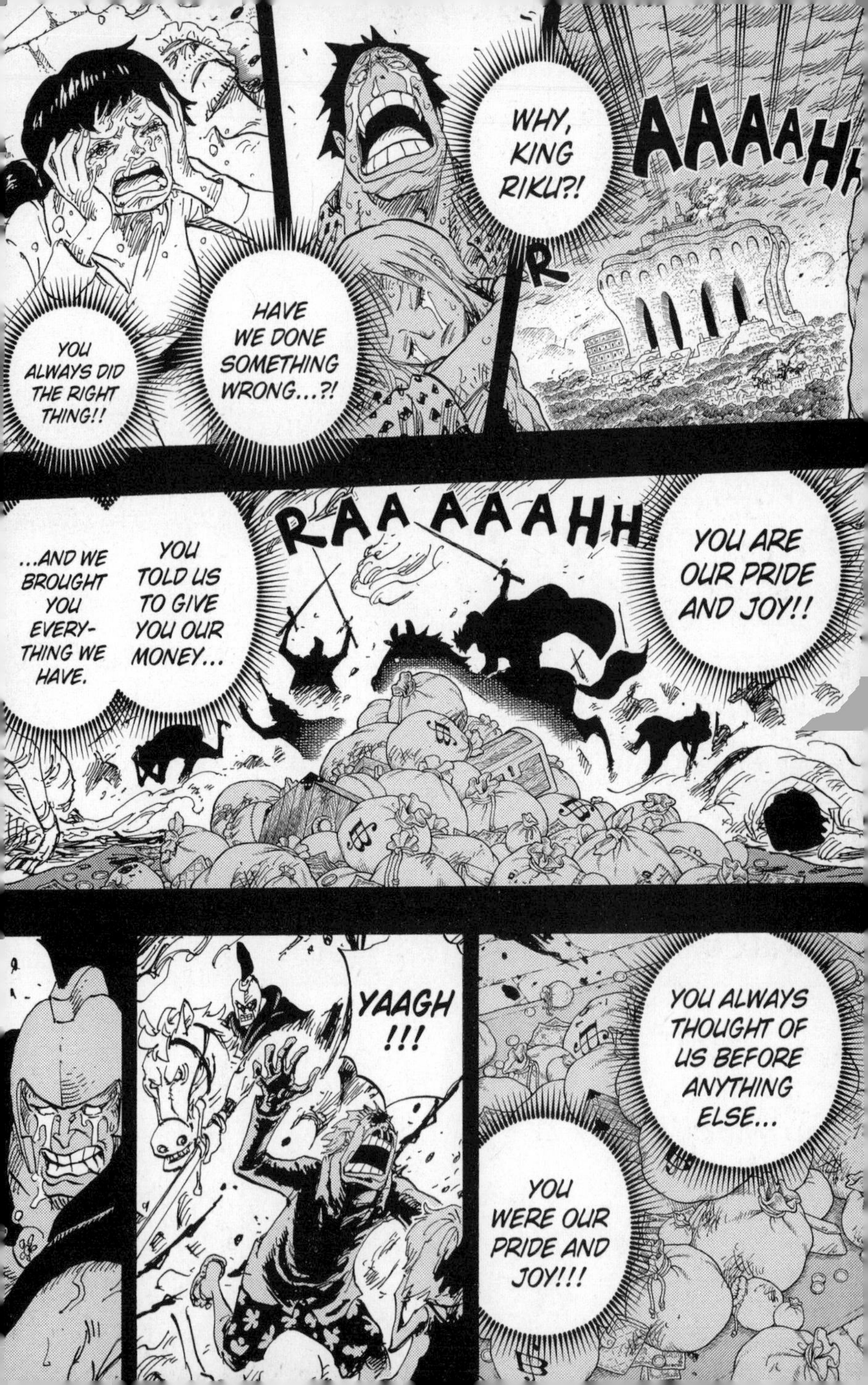
AAAAHH
R
WHY, KING RIKU?!
HAVE WE DONE SOMETHING WRONG...?!
YOU ALWAYS DID THE RIGHT THING!!
YOU ARE OUR PRIDE AND JOY!!
RAAAAAHH
YOU TOLD US TO GIVE YOU OUR MONEY...
...AND WE BROUGHT YOU EVERYTHING WE HAVE.
YOU ALWAYS THOUGHT OF US BEFORE ANYTHING ELSE...
YOU WERE OUR PRIDE AND JOY!!!
YAAGH!!!

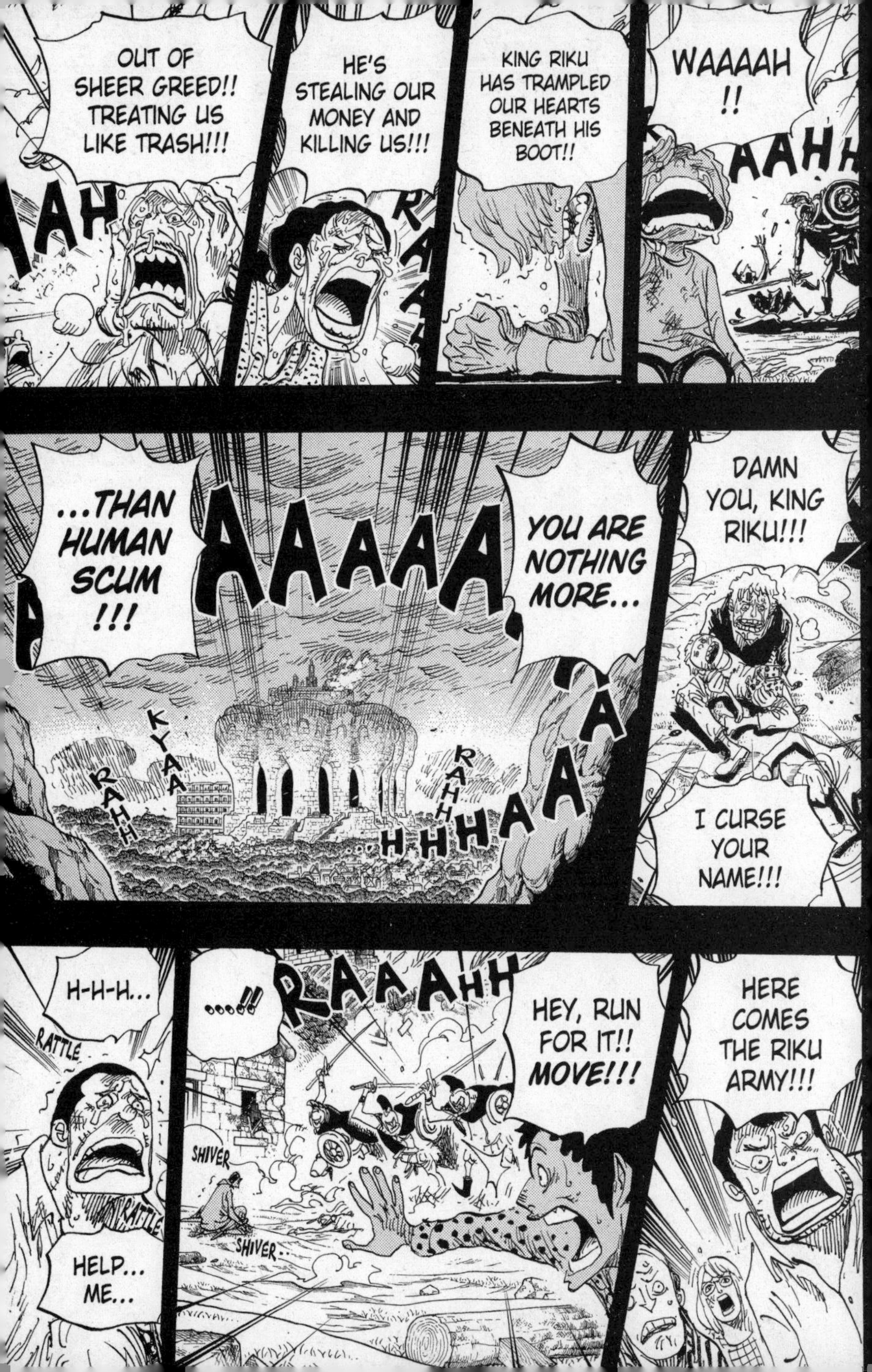
WAAAAH !!
AAHH
KING RIKU HAS TRAMPLED OUR HEARTS BENEATH HIS BOOT!!
HE'S STEALING OUR MONEY AND KILLING US!!!
OUT OF SHEER GREED!! TREATING US LIKE TRASH!!!
AH
DAMN YOU, KING RIKU!!!
I CURSE YOUR NAME!!!
YOU ARE NOTHING MORE...
AAAAA
...THAN HUMAN SCUM!!!
RAHHHHHH
KYAA
RAHH
HERE COMES THE RIKU ARMY!!!
HEY, RUN FOR IT!! MOVE!!!
RAAAHH
...!!
SHIVER
SHIVER...
H-H-H...
RATTLE
RATTLE
HELP... ME...

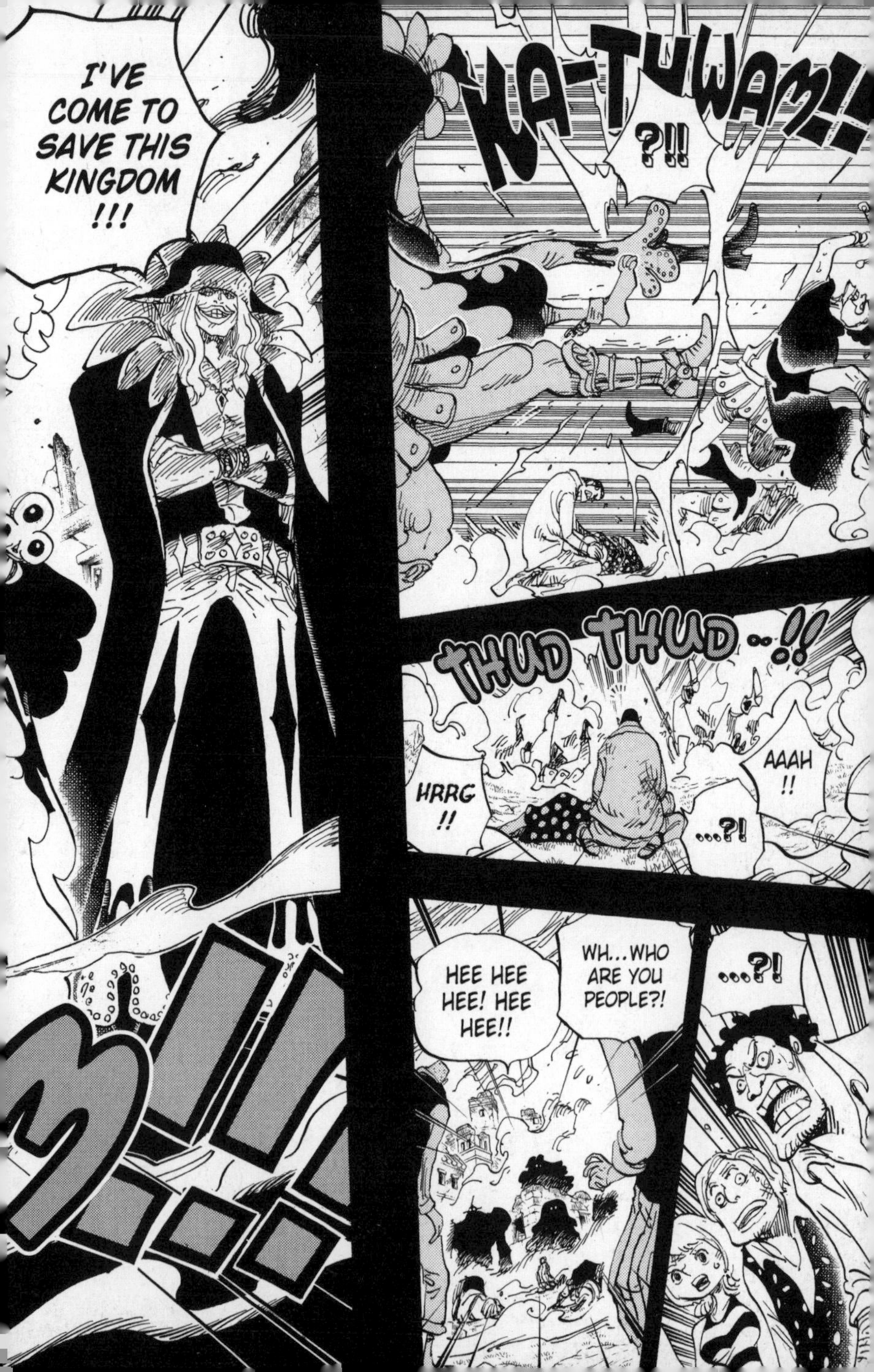
KA-TWAM!!
?!!
THUD THUD..!!
AAAH!!
...?!
HRRG!!
...?!
WH...WHO ARE YOU PEOPLE?!
HEE HEE HEE! HEE HEE!!
I'VE COME TO SAVE THIS KINGDOM!!!

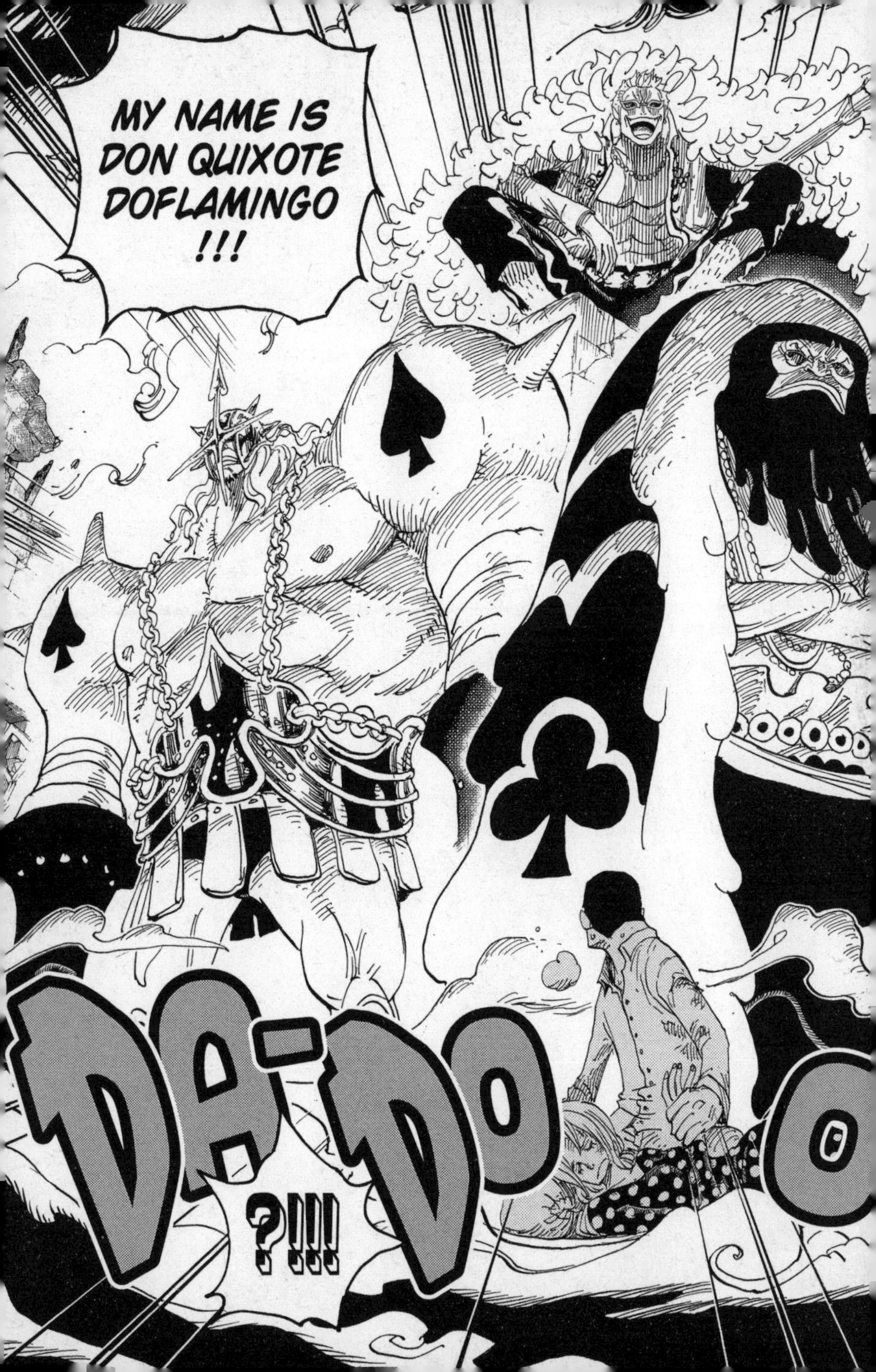
MY NAME IS DON QUIXOTE DOFLAMINGO !!!
DA-DO-O
?!!!

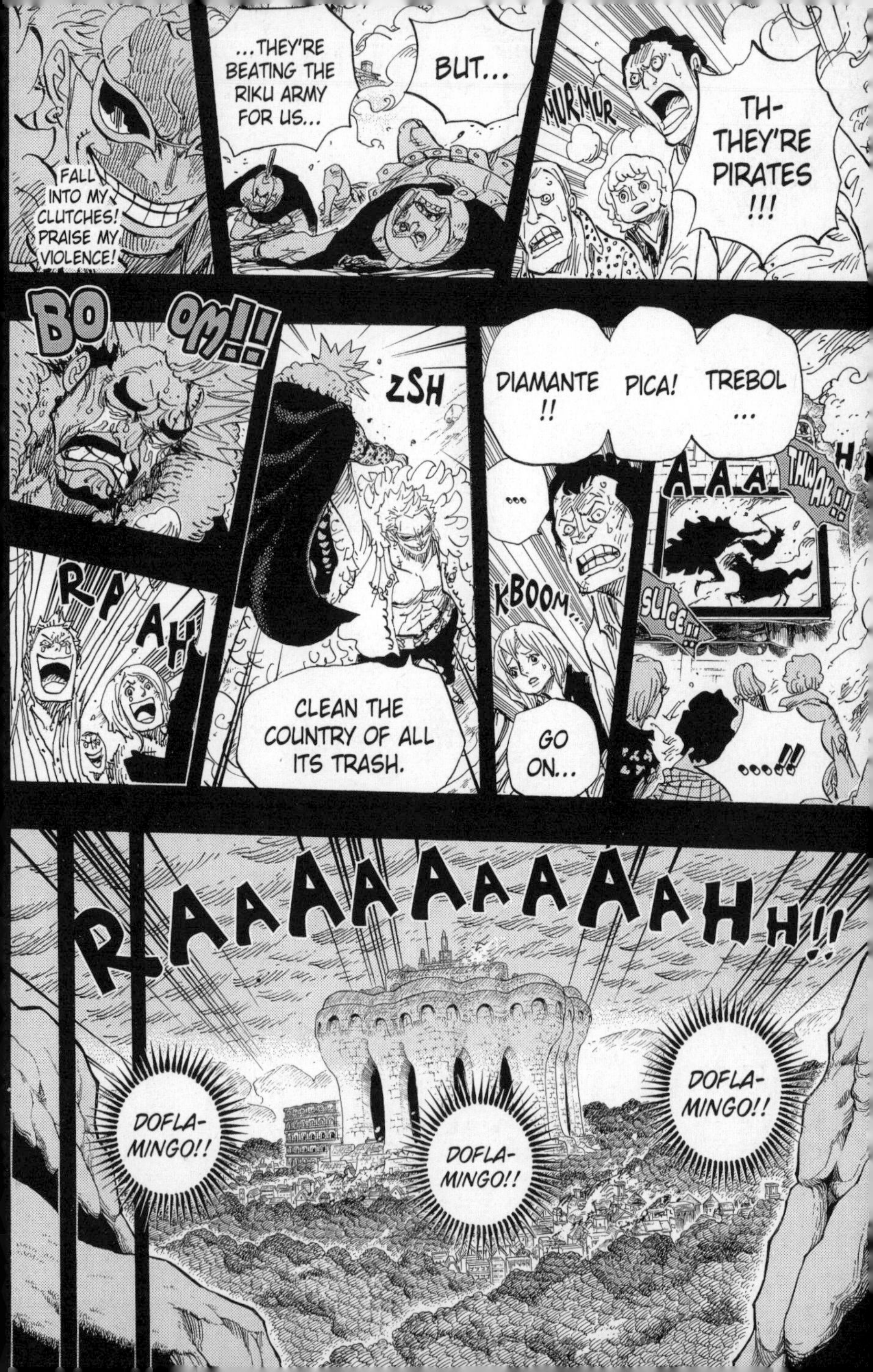
TH- THEY'RE PIRATES!!!
MURMUR
...THEY'RE BEATING THE RIKU ARMY FOR US...
BUT...
FALL INTO MY CLUTCHES! PRAISE MY VIOLENCE!
TREBOL...
PICA!
DIAMANTE!!
THWAK!!
AAA
SLICE!!
...
KBOOM
GO ON...
....!!
ZSH
CLEAN THE COUNTRY OF ALL ITS TRASH.
BOOM!!
RAAH
RAAAAAAAAAAHH!!
DOFLAMINGO!!
DOFLAMINGO!!
DOFLAMINGO!!

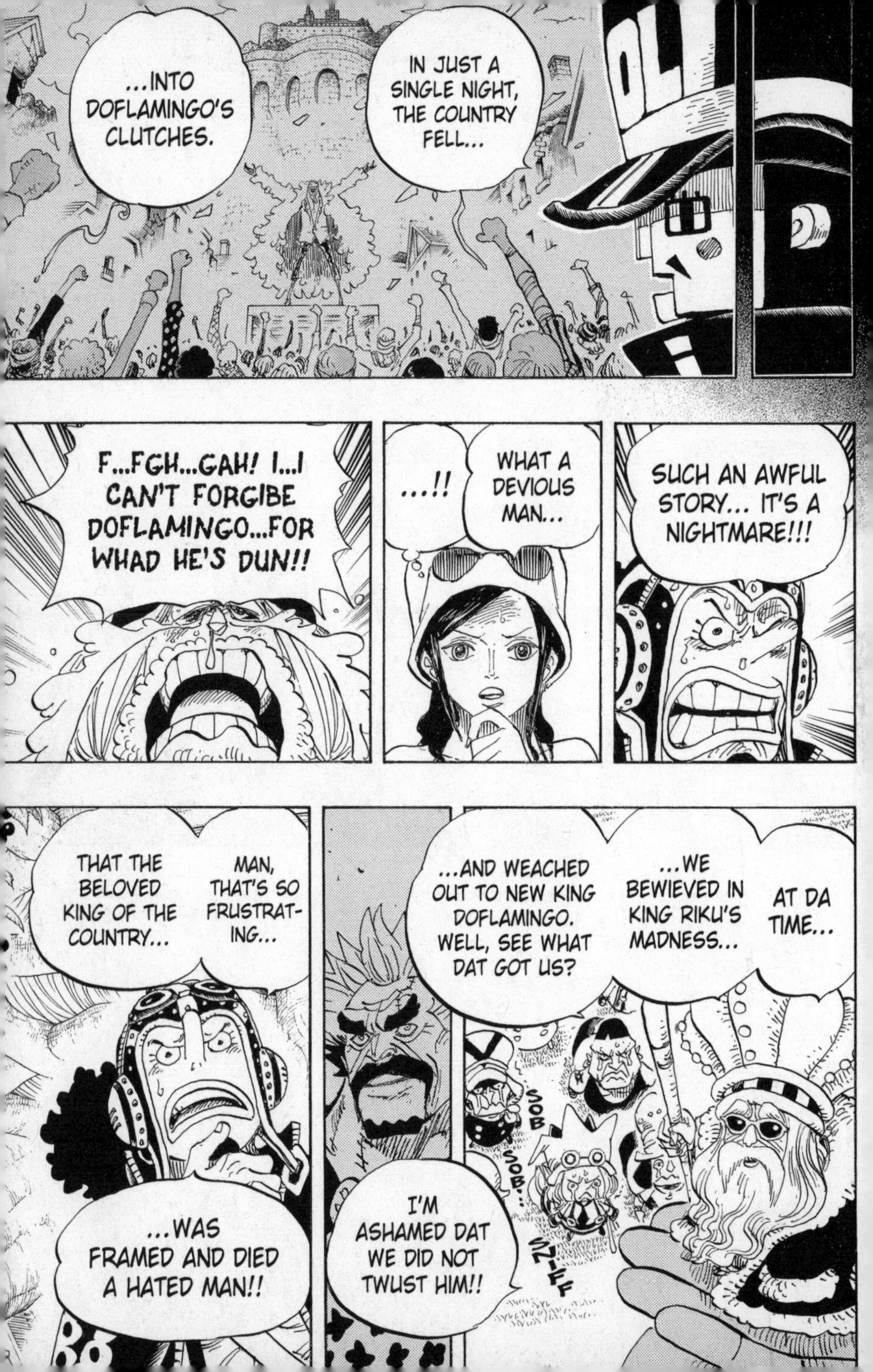
IN JUST A SINGLE NIGHT, THE COUNTRY FELL...
...INTO DOFLAMINGO'S CLUTCHES.
SUCH AN AWFUL STORY... IT'S A NIGHTMARE!!!
WHAT A DEVIOUS MAN...
...!!
F...FGH...GAH! I...I CAN'T FORGIBE DOFLAMINGO...FOR WHAD HE'S DUN!!
AT DA TIME...
...WE BEWIEVED IN KING RIKU'S MADNESS...
...AND WEACHED OUT TO NEW KING DOFLAMINGO. WELL, SEE WHAT DAT GOT US?
SOB
SOB...
SNIFF
I'M ASHAMED DAT WE DID NOT TWUST HIM!!
MAN, THAT'S SO FRUSTRATING...
THAT THE BELOVED KING OF THE COUNTRY...
...WAS FRAMED AND DIED A HATED MAN!!

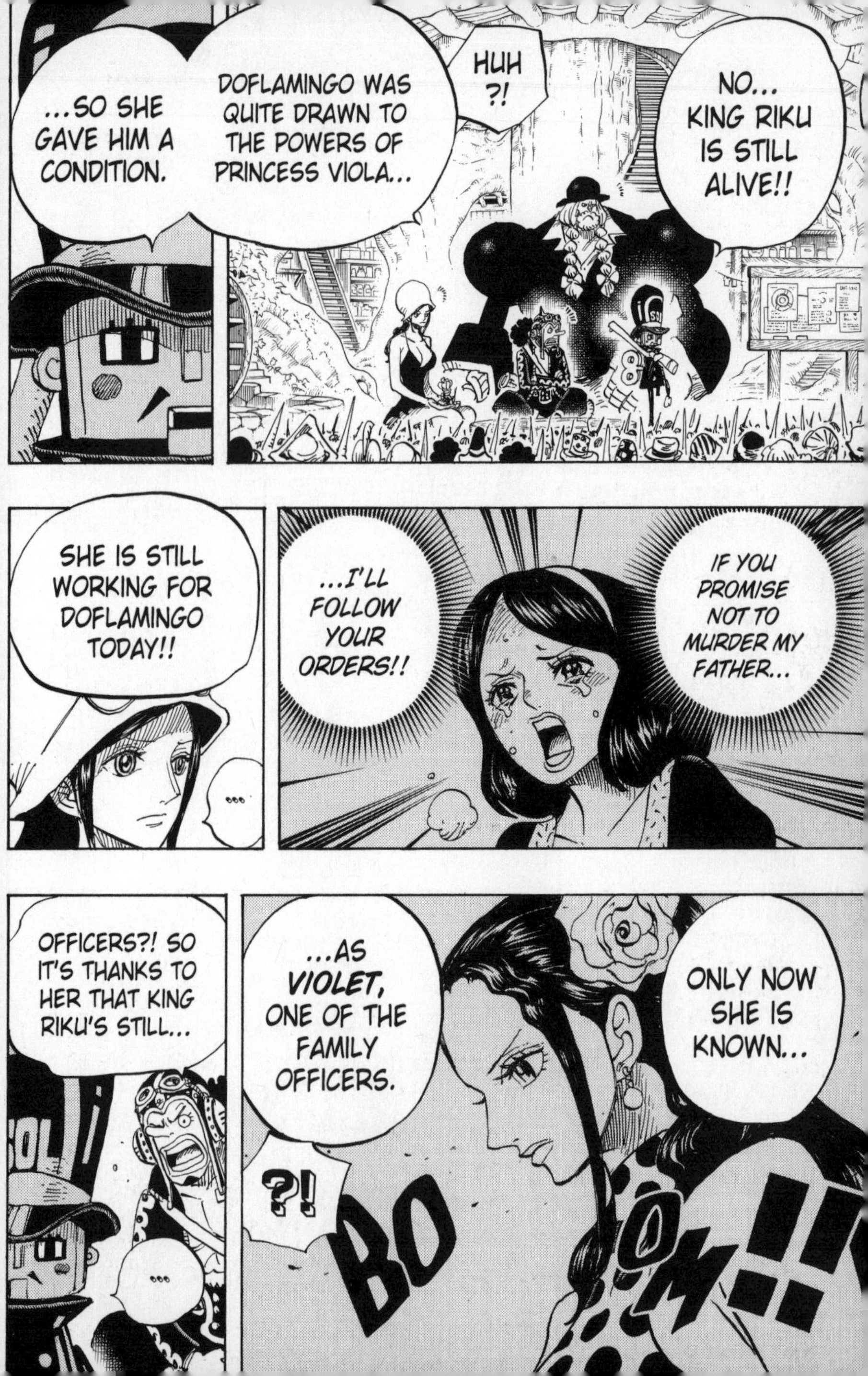
NO... KING RIKU IS STILL ALIVE!!
HUH ?!
DOFLAMINGO WAS QUITE DRAWN TO THE POWERS OF PRINCESS VIOLA...
...SO SHE GAVE HIM A CONDITION.
IF YOU PROMISE NOT TO MURDER MY FATHER...
...I'LL FOLLOW YOUR ORDERS!!
SHE IS STILL WORKING FOR DOFLAMINGO TODAY!!
...
ONLY NOW SHE IS KNOWN...
...AS *VIOLET*, ONE OF THE FAMILY OFFICERS.
?!
BOOM!!
OFFICERS?! SO IT'S THANKS TO HER THAT KING RIKU'S STILL...
...

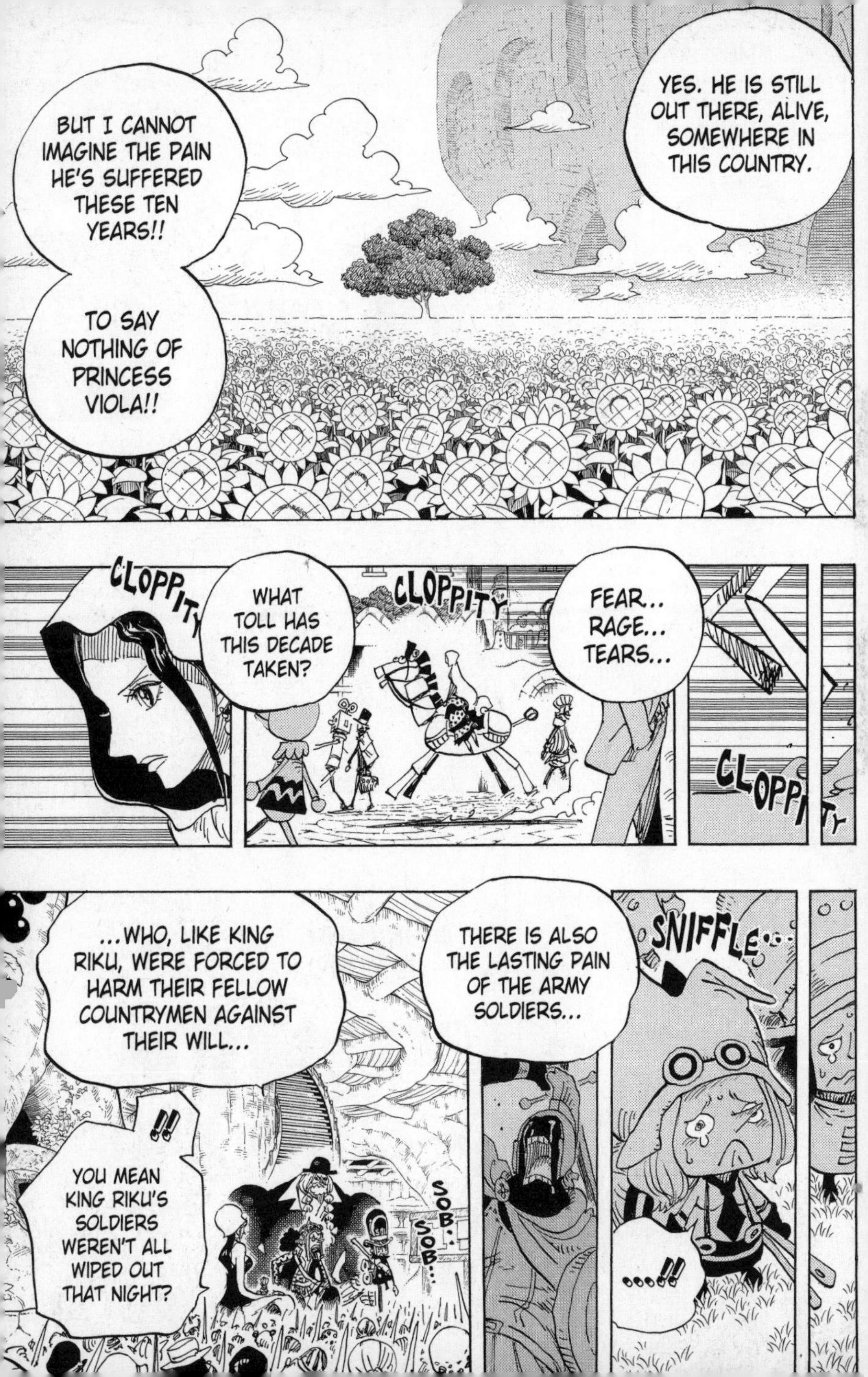
YES. HE IS STILL OUT THERE, ALIVE, SOMEWHERE IN THIS COUNTRY.
BUT I CANNOT IMAGINE THE PAIN HE'S SUFFERED THESE TEN YEARS!!
TO SAY NOTHING OF PRINCESS VIOLA!!
CLOPPITY
FEAR... RAGE... TEARS...
CLOPPITY
WHAT TOLL HAS THIS DECADE TAKEN?
CLOPPITY
SNIFFLE...
...!!
THERE IS ALSO THE LASTING PAIN OF THE ARMY SOLDIERS...
...WHO, LIKE KING RIKU, WERE FORCED TO HARM THEIR FELLOW COUNTRYMEN AGAINST THEIR WILL...
!!
YOU MEAN KING RIKU'S SOLDIERS WEREN'T ALL WIPED OUT THAT NIGHT?
SOB... SOB...

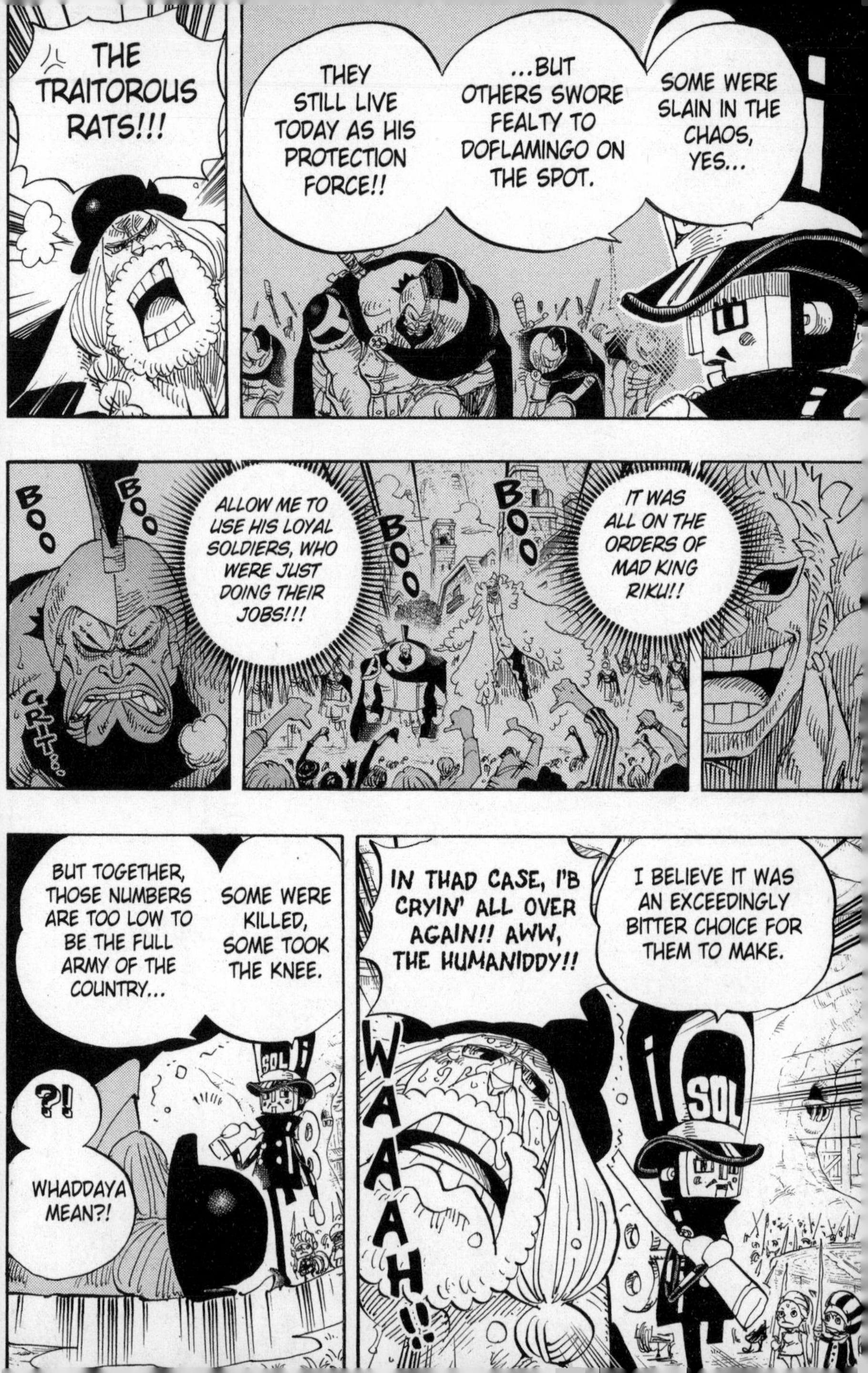
SOME WERE SLAIN IN THE CHAOS, YES...
...BUT OTHERS SWORE FEALTY TO DOFLAMINGO ON THE SPOT.
THEY STILL LIVE TODAY AS HIS PROTECTION FORCE!!
THE TRAITOROUS RATS!!!
IT WAS ALL ON THE ORDERS OF MAD KING RIKU!!
BOO
ALLOW ME TO USE HIS LOYAL SOLDIERS, WHO WERE JUST DOING THEIR JOBS!!!
BOO
BOO
BOO
I BELIEVE IT WAS AN EXCEEDINGLY BITTER CHOICE FOR THEM TO MAKE.
IN THAD CASE, I'B CRYIN' ALL OVER AGAIN!! AWW, THE HUMANIDDY!!
WAAAH!!
SOME WERE KILLED, SOME TOOK THE KNEE.
BUT TOGETHER, THOSE NUMBERS ARE TOO LOW TO BE THE FULL ARMY OF THE COUNTRY...
?!
WHADDAYA MEAN?!

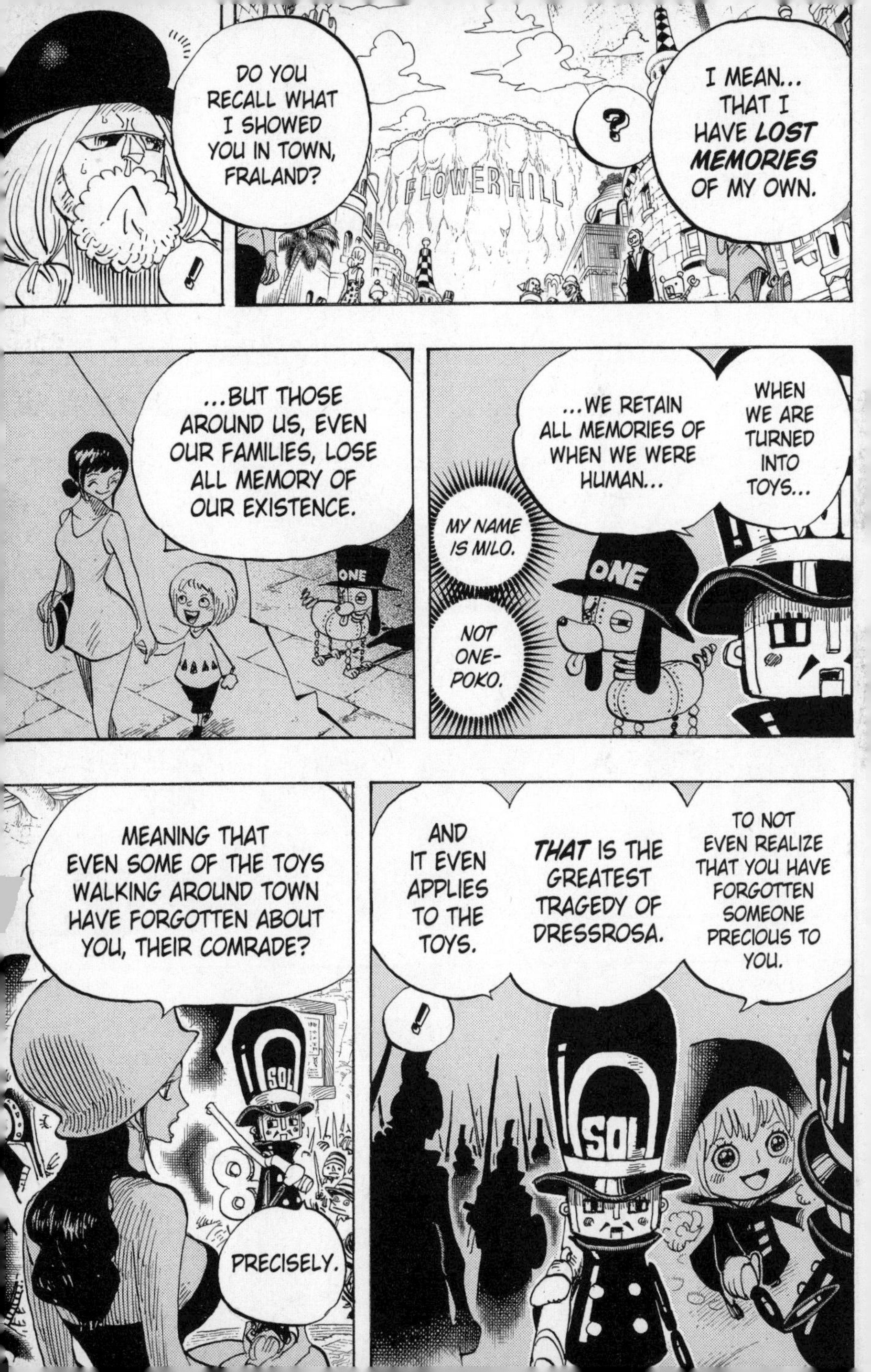
I MEAN... THAT I HAVE **LOST MEMORIES** OF MY OWN.
?
FLOWER HILL
DO YOU RECALL WHAT I SHOWED YOU IN TOWN, FRALAND?
!
WHEN WE ARE TURNED INTO TOYS...
...WE RETAIN ALL MEMORIES OF WHEN WE WERE HUMAN...
MY NAME IS MILO.
NOT ONE-POKO.
ONE
...BUT THOSE AROUND US, EVEN OUR FAMILIES, LOSE ALL MEMORY OF OUR EXISTENCE.
ONE
TO NOT EVEN REALIZE THAT YOU HAVE FORGOTTEN SOMEONE PRECIOUS TO YOU.
THAT IS THE GREATEST TRAGEDY OF DRESSROSA.
AND IT EVEN APPLIES TO THE TOYS.
!
SOL
MEANING THAT EVEN SOME OF THE TOYS WALKING AROUND TOWN HAVE FORGOTTEN ABOUT YOU, THEIR COMRADE?
SOL
PRECISELY.

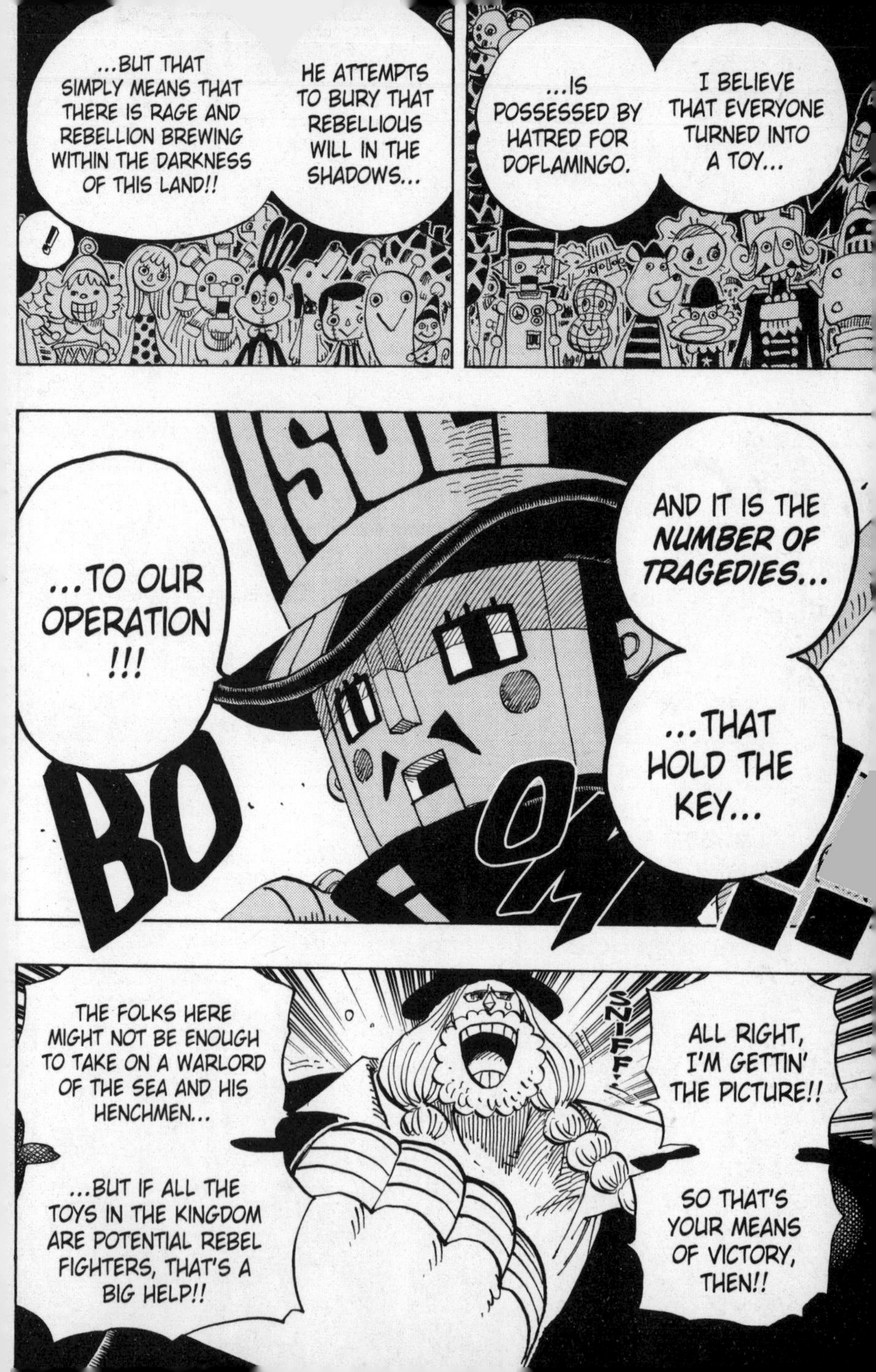
I BELIEVE THAT EVERYONE TURNED INTO A TOY...
...IS POSSESSED BY HATRED FOR DOFLAMINGO.
HE ATTEMPTS TO BURY THAT REBELLIOUS WILL IN THE SHADOWS...
...BUT THAT SIMPLY MEANS THAT THERE IS RAGE AND REBELLION BREWING WITHIN THE DARKNESS OF THIS LAND!!
!
AND IT IS THE *NUMBER OF TRAGEDIES...*
...THAT HOLD THE KEY...
...TO OUR OPERATION !!!
BOOM
ALL RIGHT, I'M GETTIN' THE PICTURE!!
SO THAT'S YOUR MEANS OF VICTORY, THEN!!
SNIFF
THE FOLKS HERE MIGHT NOT BE ENOUGH TO TAKE ON A WARLORD OF THE SEA AND HIS HENCHMEN...
...BUT IF ALL THE TOYS IN THE KINGDOM ARE POTENTIAL REBEL FIGHTERS, THAT'S A BIG HELP!!

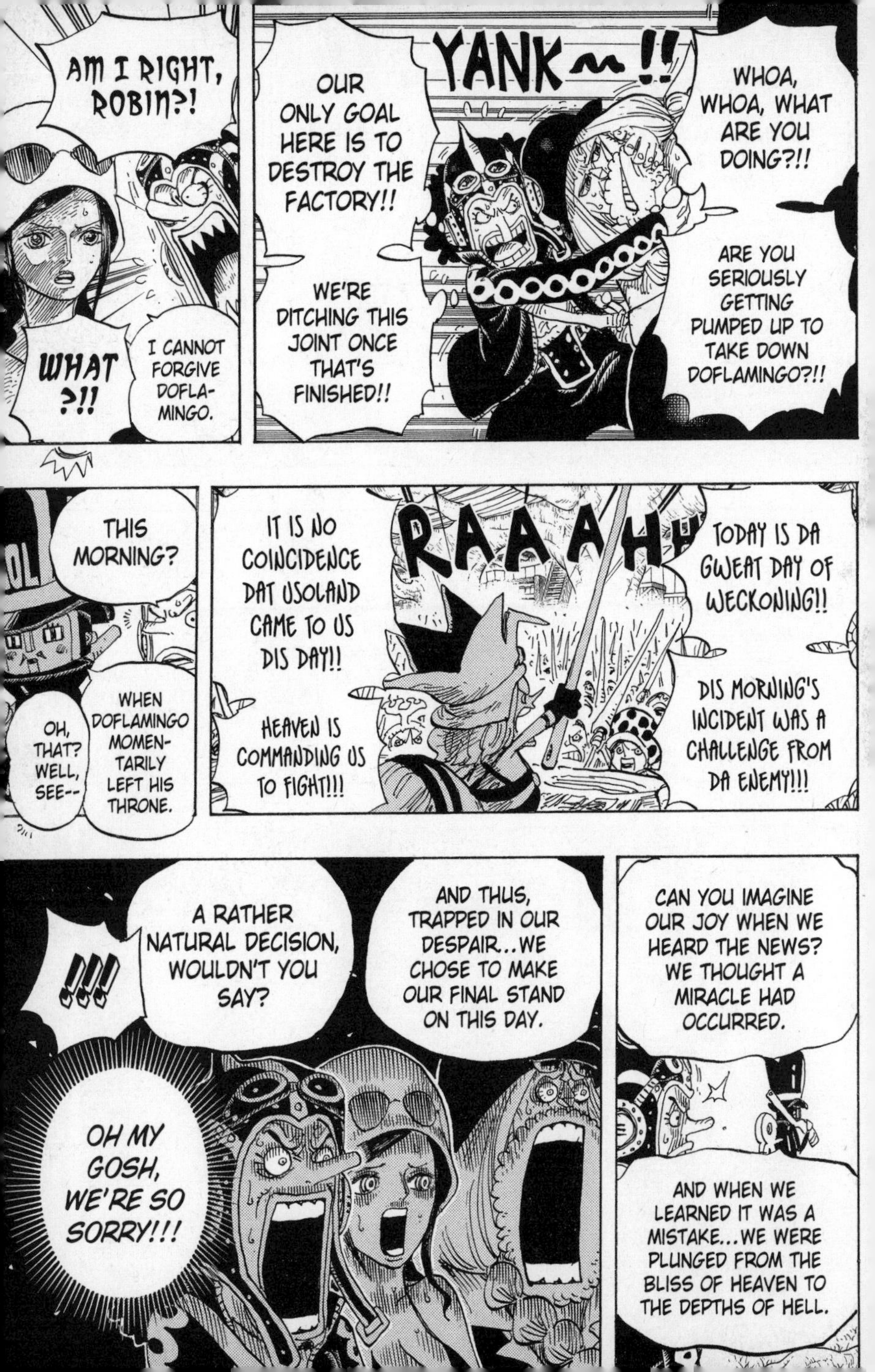
WHOA, WHOA, WHAT ARE YOU DOING?!!
ARE YOU SERIOUSLY GETTING PUMPED UP TO TAKE DOWN DOFLAMINGO?!!
YANK~!!
OUR ONLY GOAL HERE IS TO DESTROY THE FACTORY!!
WE'RE DITCHING THIS JOINT ONCE THAT'S FINISHED!!
AM I RIGHT, ROBIN?!
I CANNOT FORGIVE DOFLA-MINGO.
WHAT ?!!
TODAY IS DA GWEAT DAY OF WECKONING!!
DIS MORNING'S INCIDENT WAS A CHALLENGE FROM DA ENEMY!!!
RAAAH
IT IS NO COINCIDENCE DAT USOLAND CAME TO US DIS DAY!!
HEAVEN IS COMMANDING US TO FIGHT!!!
THIS MORNING?
WHEN DOFLAMINGO MOMEN-TARILY LEFT HIS THRONE.
OH, THAT? WELL, SEE--
CAN YOU IMAGINE OUR JOY WHEN WE HEARD THE NEWS? WE THOUGHT A MIRACLE HAD OCCURRED.
AND WHEN WE LEARNED IT WAS A MISTAKE...WE WERE PLUNGED FROM THE BLISS OF HEAVEN TO THE DEPTHS OF HELL.
AND THUS, TRAPPED IN OUR DESPAIR...WE CHOSE TO MAKE OUR FINAL STAND ON THIS DAY.
A RATHER NATURAL DECISION, WOULDN'T YOU SAY?
!!!
OH MY GOSH, WE'RE SO SORRY!!!

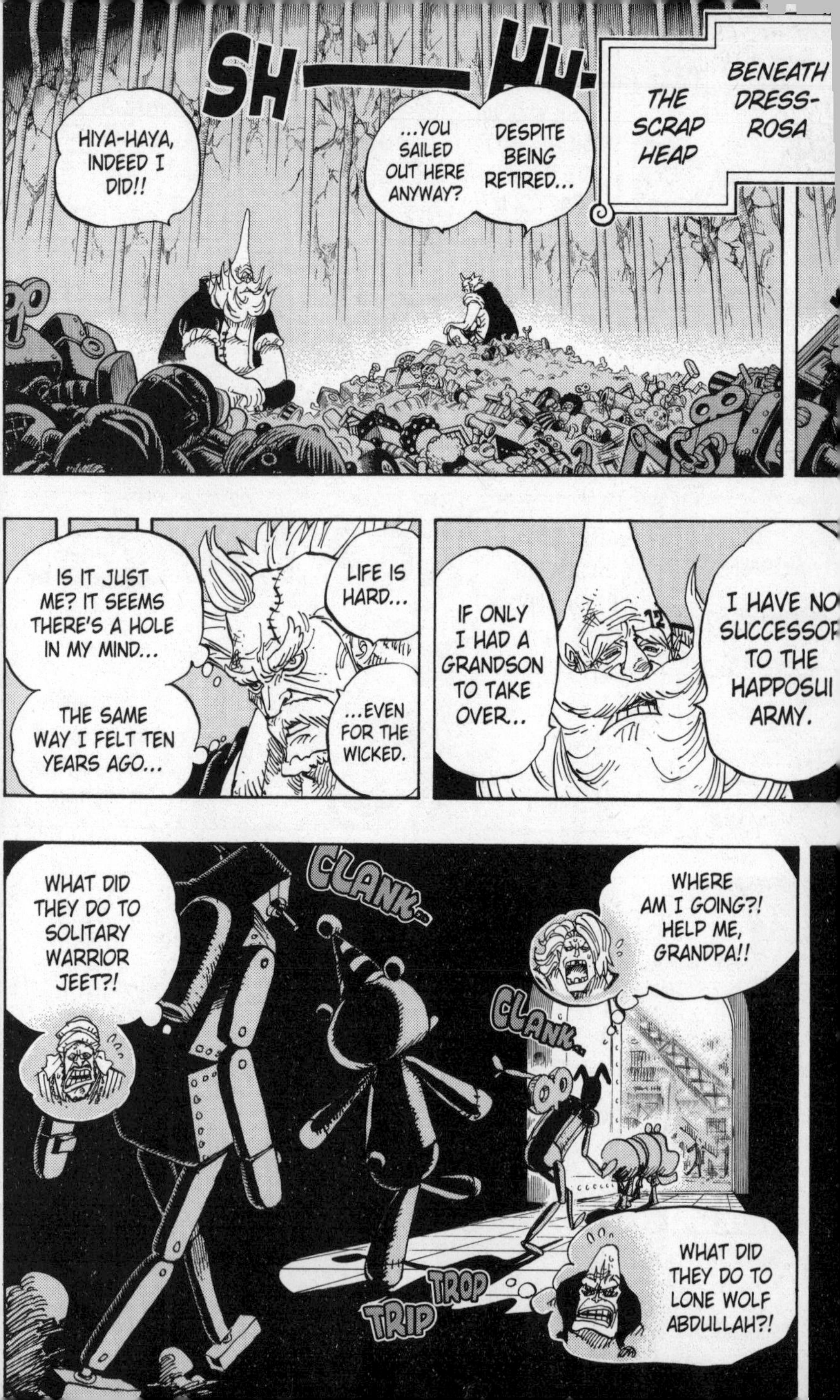
BENEATH DRESS-ROSA
THE SCRAP HEAP
SH—HU-
DESPITE BEING RETIRED...
...YOU SAILED OUT HERE ANYWAY?
HIYA-HAYA, INDEED I DID!!
I HAVE NO SUCCESSOR TO THE HAPPOSUI ARMY.
IF ONLY I HAD A GRANDSON TO TAKE OVER...
LIFE IS HARD...
...EVEN FOR THE WICKED.
IS IT JUST ME? IT SEEMS THERE'S A HOLE IN MY MIND...
THE SAME WAY I FELT TEN YEARS AGO...
WHERE AM I GOING?! HELP ME, GRANDPA!!
CLANK
CLANK
WHAT DID THEY DO TO LONE WOLF ABDULLAH?!
TROP
TRIP
CLANK
WHAT DID THEY DO TO SOLITARY WARRIOR JEET?!

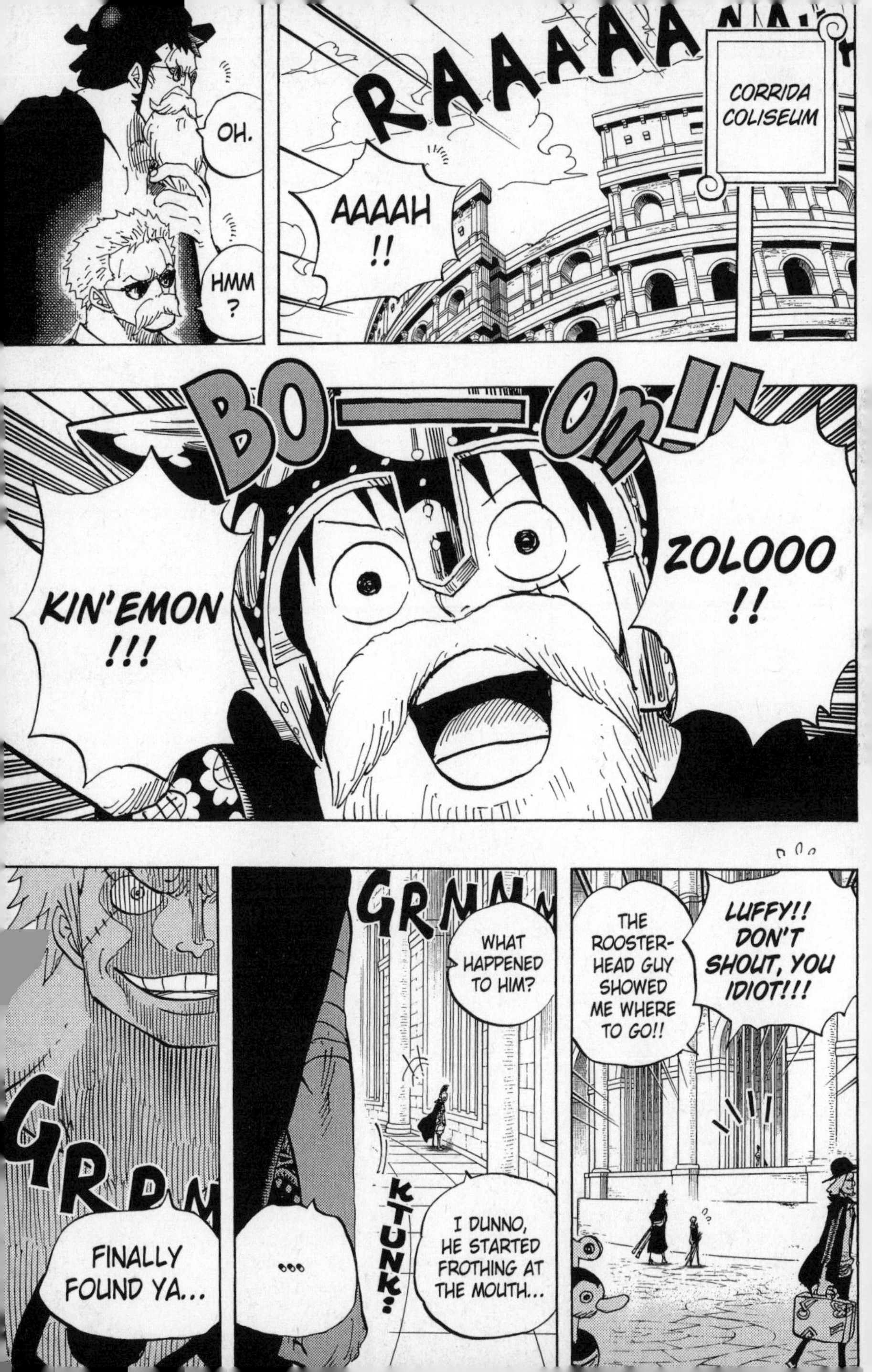
RAAAAA
CORRIDA COLISEUM
AAAAH !!
OH.
HMM ?
BO—OM!!
ZOLOOO !!
KIN'EMON !!!
LUFFY!! DON'T SHOUT, YOU IDIOT!!!
THE ROOSTER-HEAD GUY SHOWED ME WHERE TO GO!!
GRMM
WHAT HAPPENED TO HIM?
KTUNK
I DUNNO, HE STARTED FROTHING AT THE MOUTH...
...
GRDM
FINALLY FOUND YA...

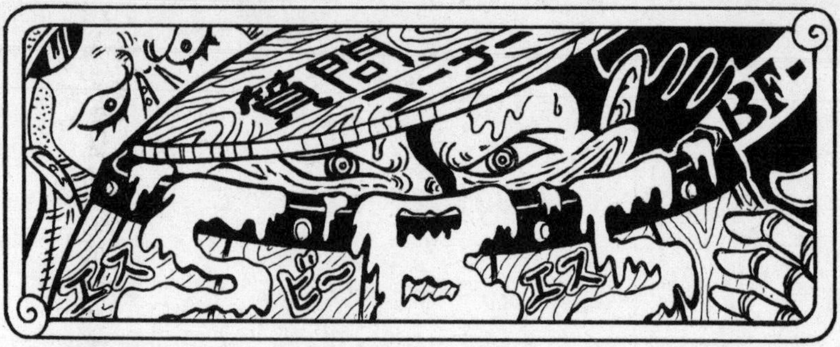
質問コーナー
エス
ビ～
エス

(Sashinji, Chiba)

Q: I was looking up trivia on the Straw Hats, and I found that although they've all been given a favorite food, I can't find anything about their least favorite. So what are each of the Straw Hat Pirates' least favorite foods?!

--Ice Cream Nyangoro

A: Here you go. The reasons are inside the parentheses.

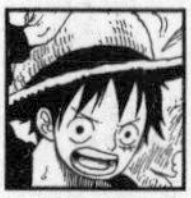
A certain establishment's cherry pie (No reason)

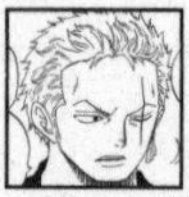
Chocolate (Too sweet)

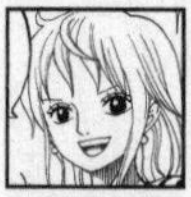
Chocolate-covered orange slices (If she wants fruit, she'll eat regular fruit)

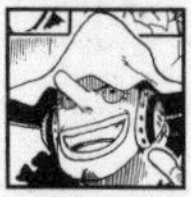
All fungi (Got sick once)

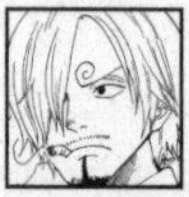
Konnyaku (No nutritional value)

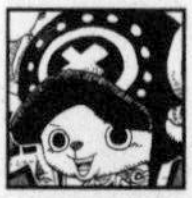
Anything spicy (Not sweet enough)

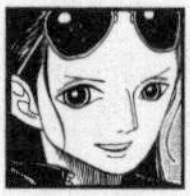
Gum (Can't swallow it)

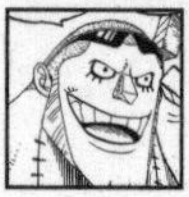
Marshmallows (Not hard enough)

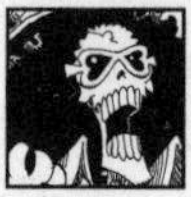
Lemons (No cheeks to make a sour face)

Q: We've learned about two new Naval admirals: Fujitora and Ryokugyu. I wondered why you went with "fuji" (for "light purple" or "lilac") instead of regular "purple"?

--Aye-Aye Planet

A: Good question. I've made red, blue, yellow and green, so it seems natural to go with "purple" next. But when I started trying to turn that into a Japanese name, I had "Murasakitora" and "Shitora"... Hmm...

They don't roll off the tongue. Not catchy enough.

Well, how about Fujitora?

Now that's cool!!

RYOKUGYU (Imagined)

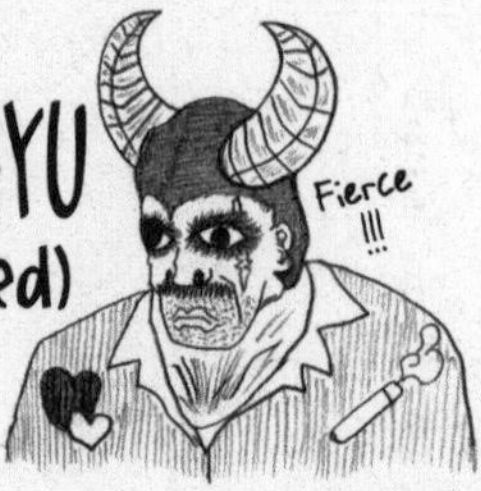
Fierce !!!

That's all there is to it. More importantly, what is wrong with your Ryokugyu?! As it happens, I've already designed his character, and he's super-duper cool! I can't wait to draw him.

Chapter 729: WARLORD DOFLAMINGO VS. WARLORD LAW

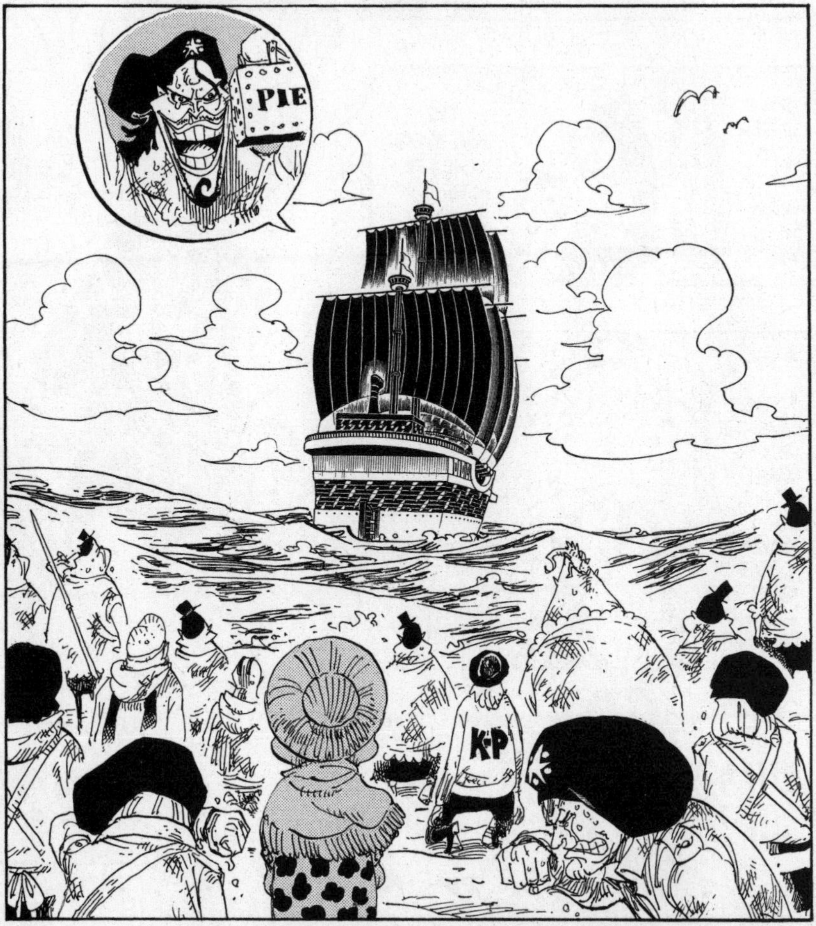

CARIBOU'S NEW WORLD KEE HEE HEE, VOL. 44:
"LIVE LONG, OLD HAG!! GABURU THE REVOLUTIONARY LEAVES TO START ANOTHER LEGEND"

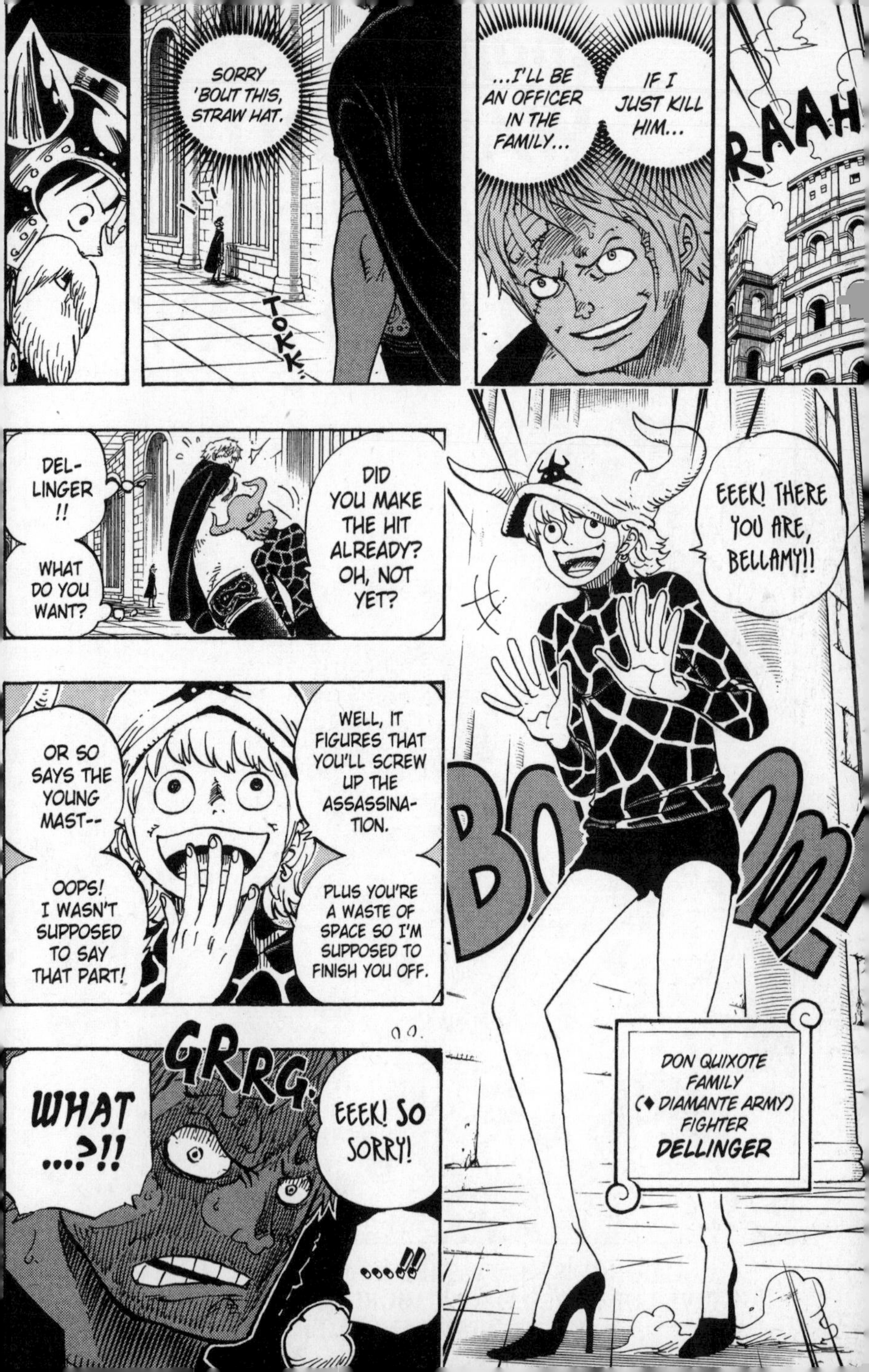
RAAH
IF I JUST KILL HIM...
...I'LL BE AN OFFICER IN THE FAMILY...
SORRY 'BOUT THIS, STRAW HAT.
TOKK
EEEK! THERE YOU ARE, BELLAMY!!
BOOM
DON QUIXOTE FAMILY (♦ DIAMANTE ARMY) FIGHTER
DELLINGER
DID YOU MAKE THE HIT ALREADY? OH, NOT YET?
DEL-LINGER!!
WHAT DO YOU WANT?
WELL, IT FIGURES THAT YOU'LL SCREW UP THE ASSASSINA-TION.
PLUS YOU'RE A WASTE OF SPACE SO I'M SUPPOSED TO FINISH YOU OFF.
OR SO SAYS THE YOUNG MAST--
OOPS! I WASN'T SUPPOSED TO SAY THAT PART!
EEEK! SO SORRY!
GRRG
WHAT ...?!!
....!!

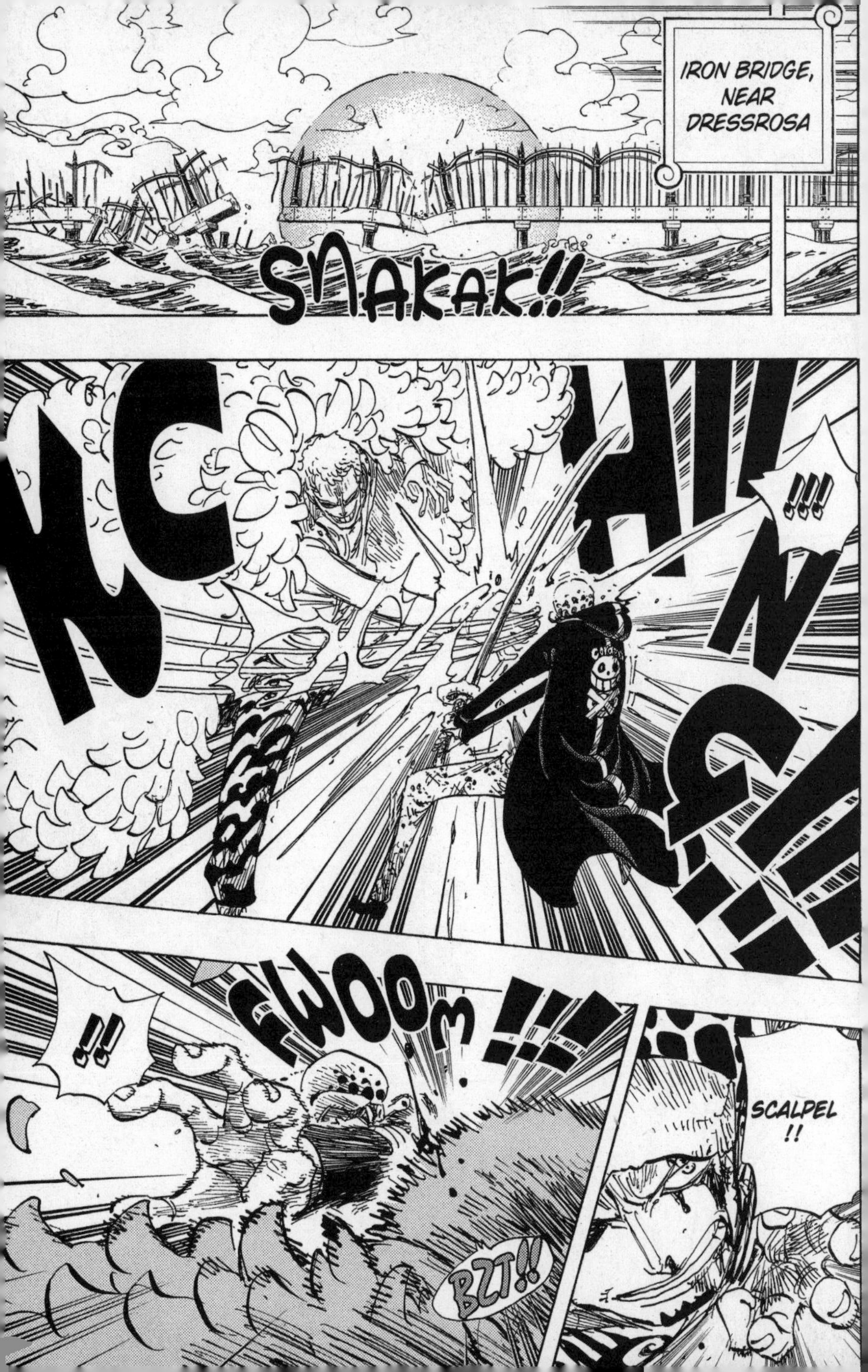
IRON BRIDGE, NEAR DRESSROSA
SNAKAK!!
!!!
KCHANG!!
SCALPEL!!
BZT!!
FWOOM!!!
!!

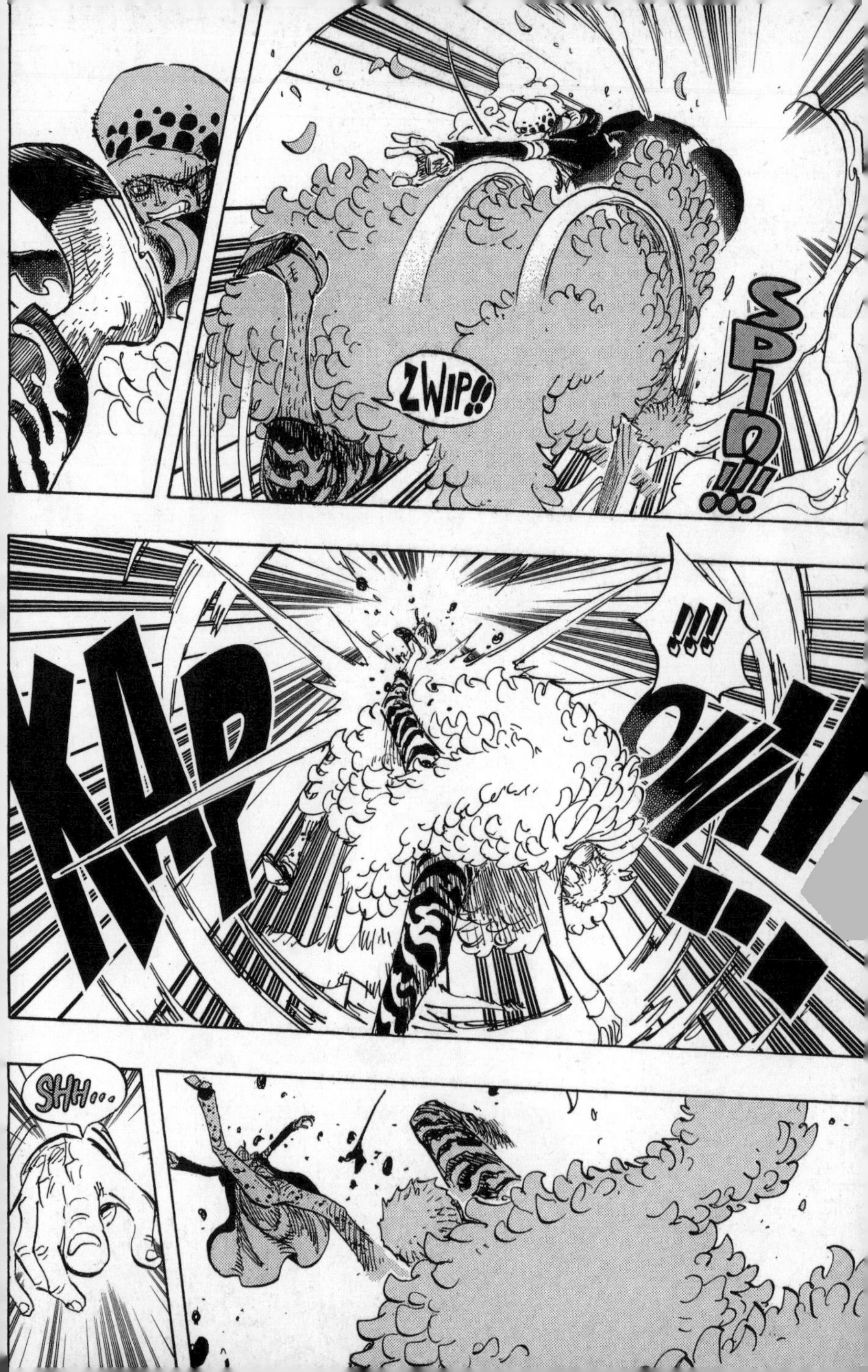
SPIN!!!
ZWIP!!
!!!
SHH...

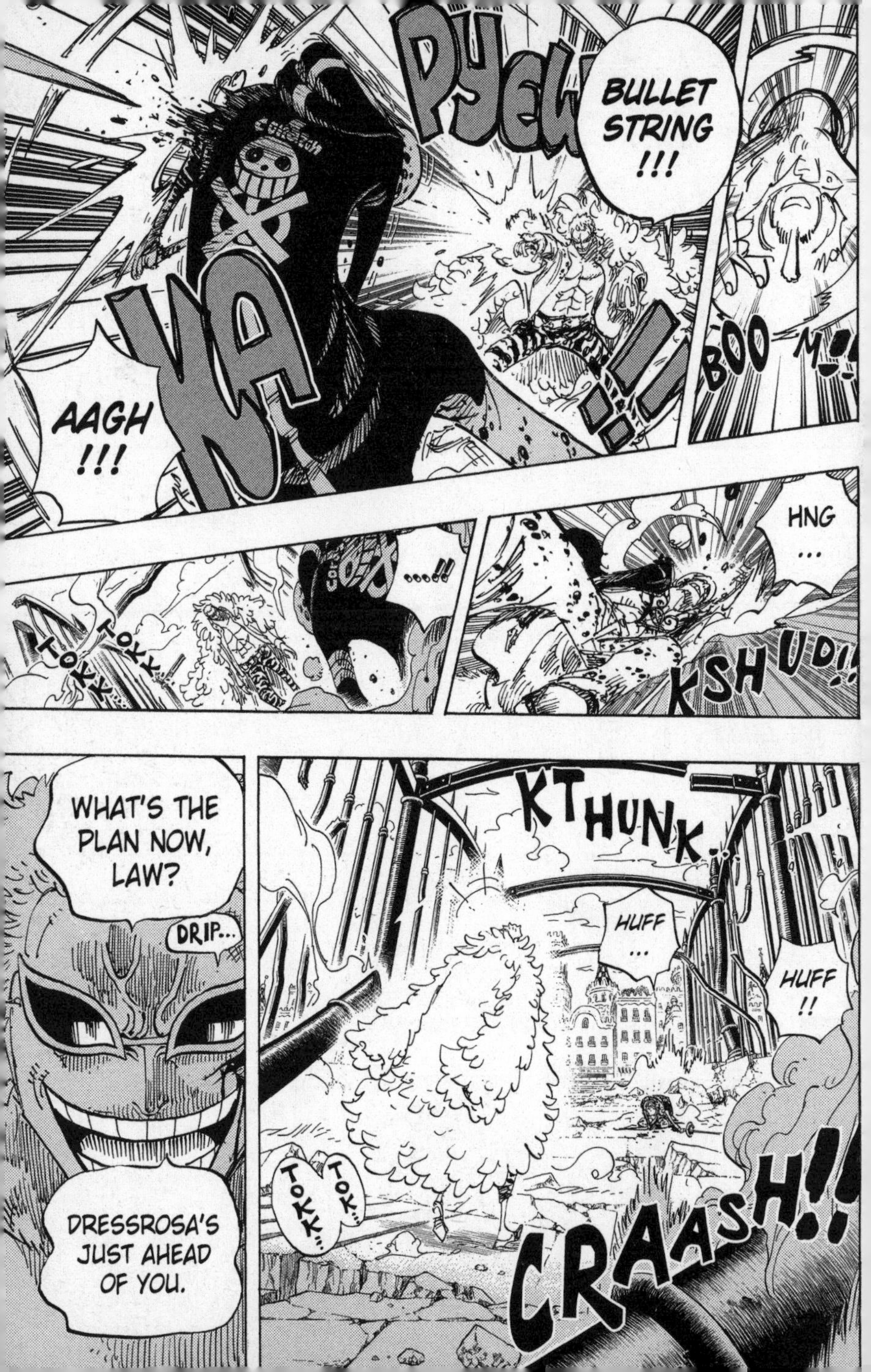
BOOM!!
BULLET STRING !!!
PYEW
!!
KA
AAGH !!!
HNG ...
KSHUD!!
....!!
TOKK TOKK...
KTHUNK...
HUFF ...
HUFF !!
TOK... TOKK...
CRAASH!!
WHAT'S THE PLAN NOW, LAW?
DRIP...
DRESSROSA'S JUST AHEAD OF YOU.

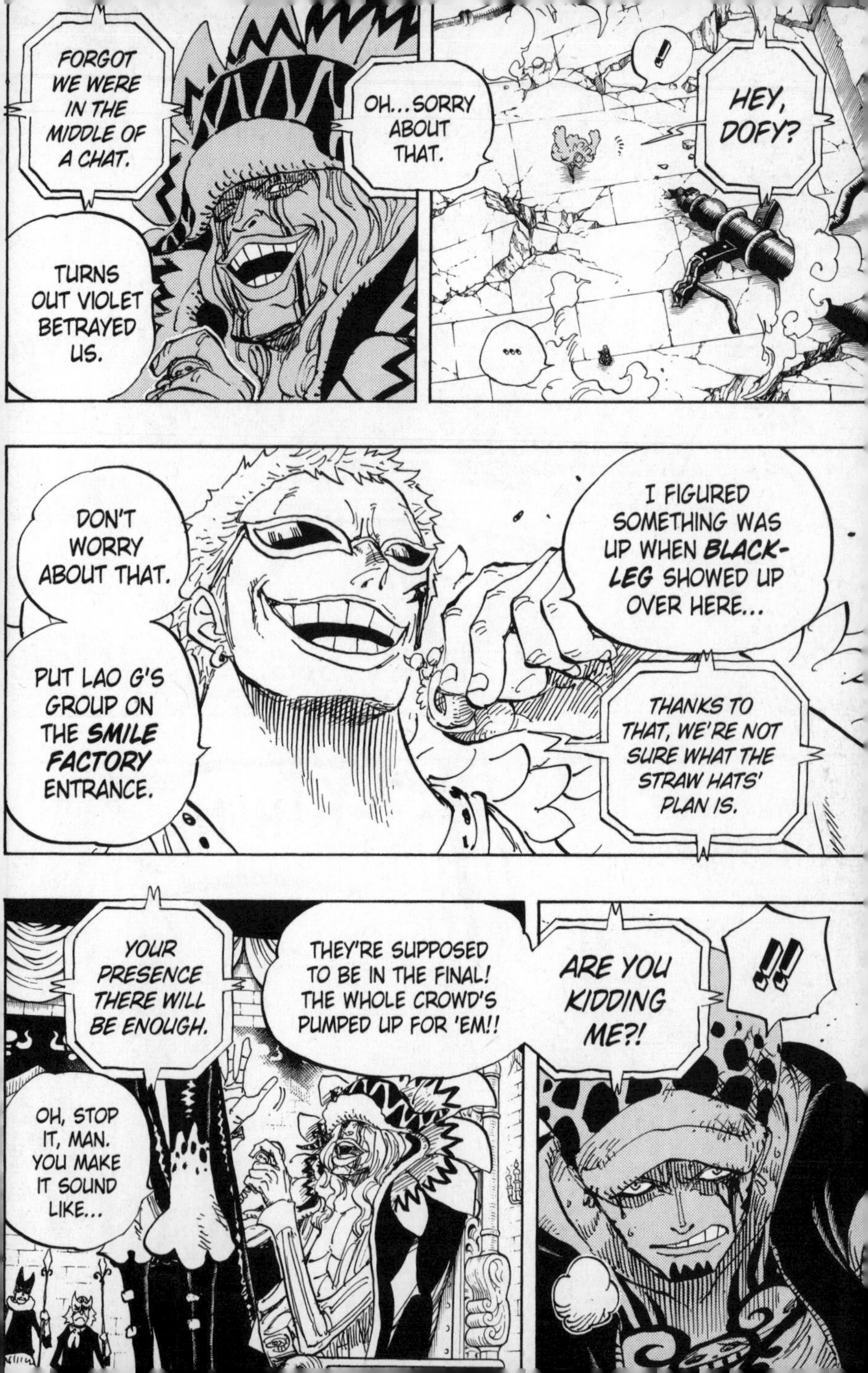
!
HEY, DOFY?
...
OH...SORRY ABOUT THAT.
FORGOT WE WERE IN THE MIDDLE OF A CHAT.
TURNS OUT VIOLET BETRAYED US.
I FIGURED SOMETHING WAS UP WHEN BLACK-LEG SHOWED UP OVER HERE...
THANKS TO THAT, WE'RE NOT SURE WHAT THE STRAW HATS' PLAN IS.
DON'T WORRY ABOUT THAT.
PUT LAO G'S GROUP ON THE SMILE FACTORY ENTRANCE.
!!
ARE YOU KIDDING ME?!
THEY'RE SUPPOSED TO BE IN THE FINAL! THE WHOLE CROWD'S PUMPED UP FOR 'EM!!
YOUR PRESENCE THERE WILL BE ENOUGH.
OH, STOP IT, MAN. YOU MAKE IT SOUND LIKE...

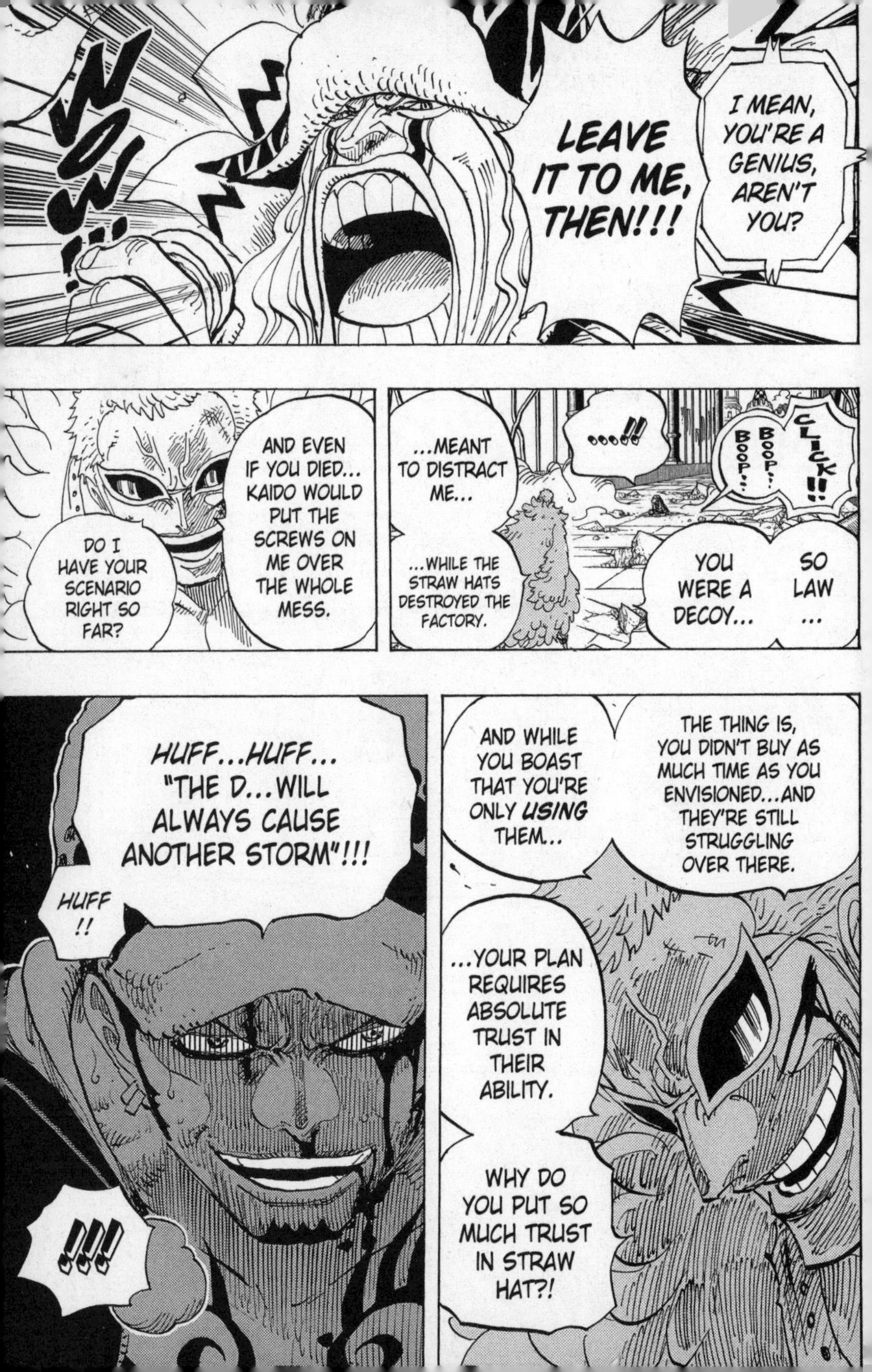
I MEAN, YOU'RE A GENIUS, AREN'T YOU?
LEAVE IT TO ME, THEN!!!
WOW!!
SO LAW...
YOU WERE A DECOY...
CLICK!!
BOOP... BOOP...
....!!
...MEANT TO DISTRACT ME...
...WHILE THE STRAW HATS DESTROYED THE FACTORY.
AND EVEN IF YOU DIED... KAIDO WOULD PUT THE SCREWS ON ME OVER THE WHOLE MESS.
DO I HAVE YOUR SCENARIO RIGHT SO FAR?
THE THING IS, YOU DIDN'T BUY AS MUCH TIME AS YOU ENVISIONED...AND THEY'RE STILL STRUGGLING OVER THERE.
AND WHILE YOU BOAST THAT YOU'RE ONLY *USING* THEM...
...YOUR PLAN REQUIRES ABSOLUTE TRUST IN THEIR ABILITY.
WHY DO YOU PUT SO MUCH TRUST IN STRAW HAT?!
HUFF...HUFF... "THE D...WILL ALWAYS CAUSE ANOTHER STORM"!!!
HUFF !!
!!!

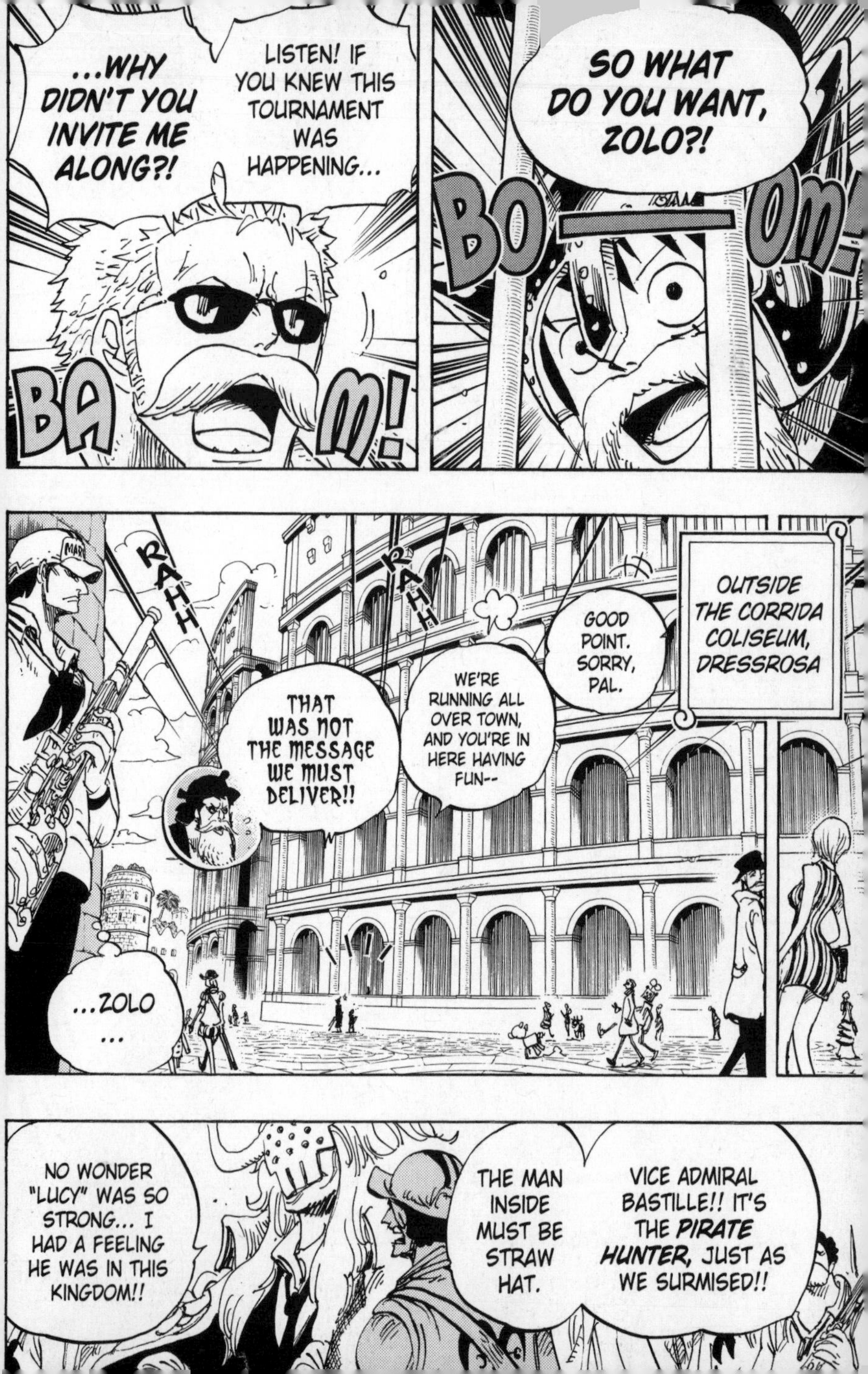
SO WHAT DO YOU WANT, ZOLO?!
BO—OM!
LISTEN! IF YOU KNEW THIS TOURNAMENT WAS HAPPENING...
...WHY DIDN'T YOU INVITE ME ALONG?!
BAM!
OUTSIDE THE CORRIDA COLISEUM, DRESSROSA
GOOD POINT. SORRY, PAL.
WE'RE RUNNING ALL OVER TOWN, AND YOU'RE IN HERE HAVING FUN--
RAHH
THAT WAS NOT THE MESSAGE WE MUST DELIVER!!
RAHH
...ZOLO ...
VICE ADMIRAL BASTILLE!! IT'S THE *PIRATE HUNTER,* JUST AS WE SURMISED!!
THE MAN INSIDE MUST BE STRAW HAT.
NO WONDER "LUCY" WAS SO STRONG... I HAD A FEELING HE WAS IN THIS KINGDOM!!

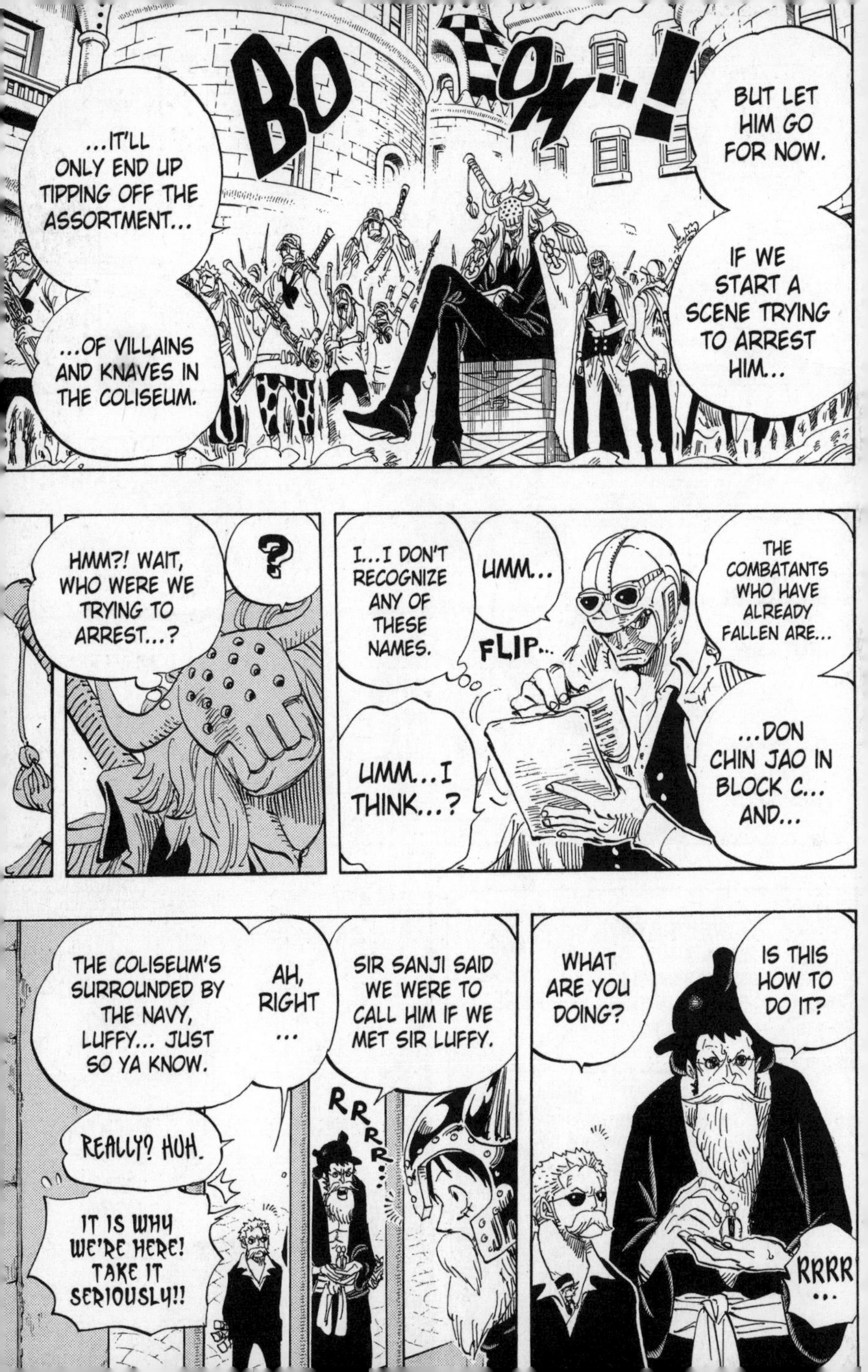
BUT LET HIM GO FOR NOW.
IF WE START A SCENE TRYING TO ARREST HIM...
BOOM!!
...IT'LL ONLY END UP TIPPING OFF THE ASSORTMENT...
...OF VILLAINS AND KNAVES IN THE COLISEUM.
THE COMBATANTS WHO HAVE ALREADY FALLEN ARE...
...DON CHIN JAO IN BLOCK C... AND...
UMM...
I...I DON'T RECOGNIZE ANY OF THESE NAMES.
FLIP...
UMM...I THINK...?
?
HMM?! WAIT, WHO WERE WE TRYING TO ARREST...?
IS THIS HOW TO DO IT?
WHAT ARE YOU DOING?
RRRR...
SIR SANJI SAID WE WERE TO CALL HIM IF WE MET SIR LUFFY.
AH, RIGHT...
RRRR...
THE COLISEUM'S SURROUNDED BY THE NAVY, LUFFY... JUST SO YA KNOW.
REALLY? HUH.
IT IS WHY WE'RE HERE! TAKE IT SERIOUSLY!!

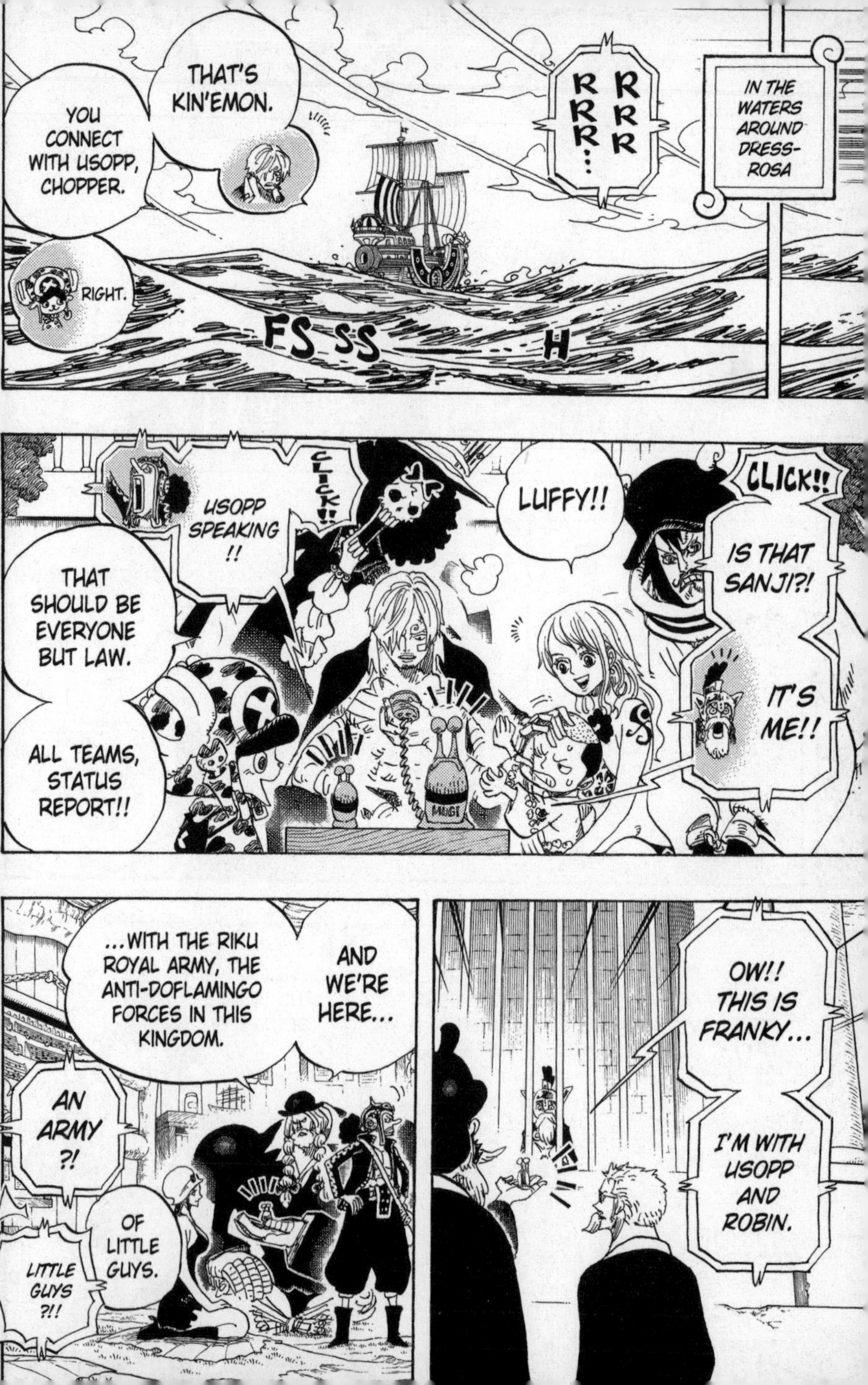
IN THE WATERS AROUND DRESS-ROSA
RRR... RRR
THAT'S KIN'EMON.
YOU CONNECT WITH USOPP, CHOPPER.
RIGHT.
FSSSH
CLICK!!
IS THAT SANJI?!
IT'S ME!!
LUFFY!!
CLICK!!
USOPP SPEAKING!!
THAT SHOULD BE EVERYONE BUT LAW.
ALL TEAMS, STATUS REPORT!!
MUGI
OW!! THIS IS FRANKY...
I'M WITH USOPP AND ROBIN.
AND WE'RE HERE...
...WITH THE RIKU ROYAL ARMY, THE ANTI-DOFLAMINGO FORCES IN THIS KINGDOM.
AN ARMY?!
OF LITTLE GUYS.
LITTLE GUYS?!!

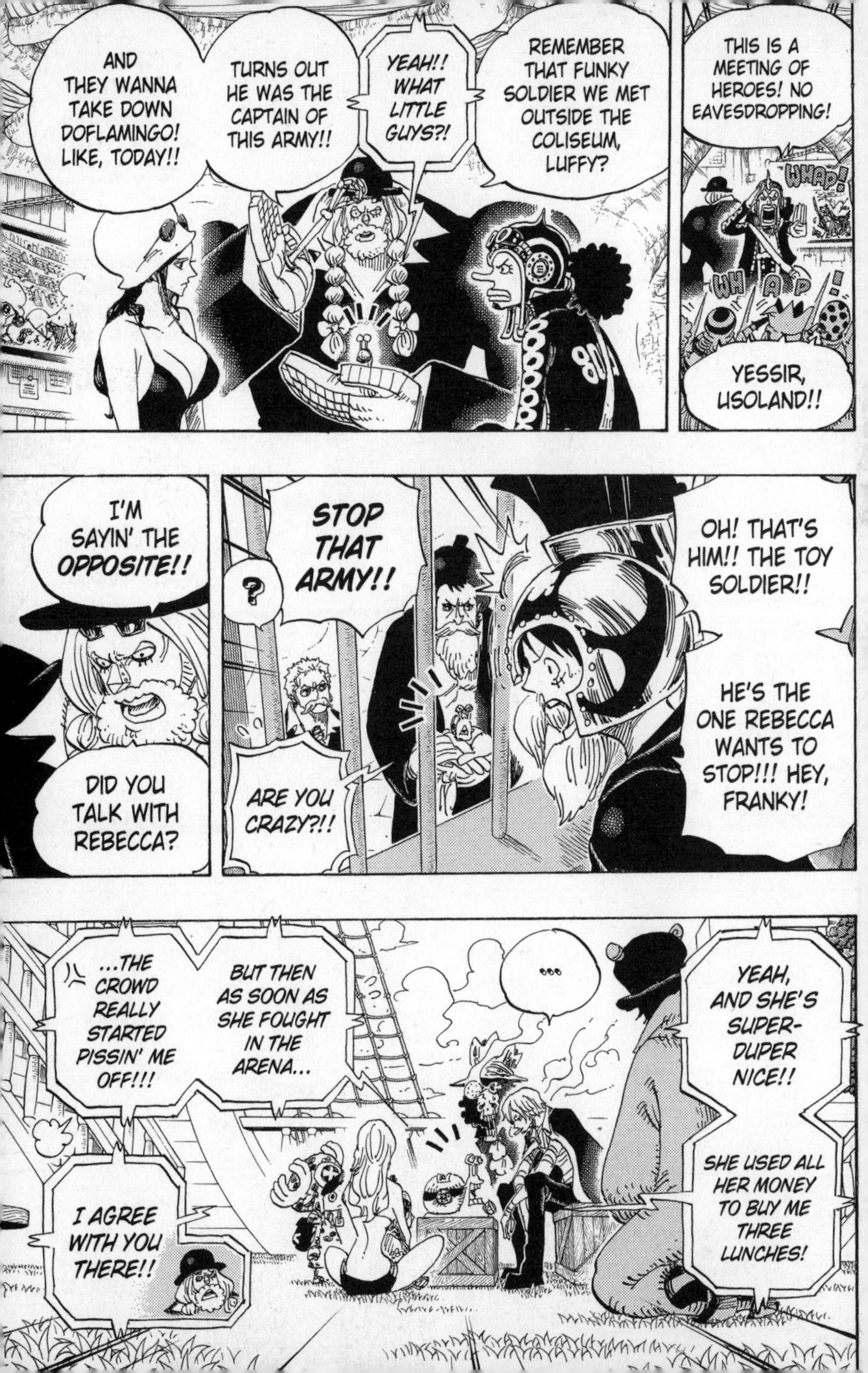
THIS IS A MEETING OF HEROES! NO EAVESDROPPING!
WHAP!
WHAP!
YESSIR, USOLAND!!
REMEMBER THAT FUNKY SOLDIER WE MET OUTSIDE THE COLISEUM, LUFFY?
YEAH!! WHAT LITTLE GUYS?!
TURNS OUT HE WAS THE CAPTAIN OF THIS ARMY!!
AND THEY WANNA TAKE DOWN DOFLAMINGO! LIKE, TODAY!!
OH! THAT'S HIM!! THE TOY SOLDIER!!
HE'S THE ONE REBECCA WANTS TO STOP!!! HEY, FRANKY!
STOP THAT ARMY!!
?
ARE YOU CRAZY?!!
I'M SAYIN' THE OPPOSITE!!
DID YOU TALK WITH REBECCA?
YEAH, AND SHE'S SUPER-DUPER NICE!!
SHE USED ALL HER MONEY TO BUY ME THREE LUNCHES!
...
BUT THEN AS SOON AS SHE FOUGHT IN THE ARENA...
...THE CROWD REALLY STARTED PISSIN' ME OFF!!!
I AGREE WITH YOU THERE!!

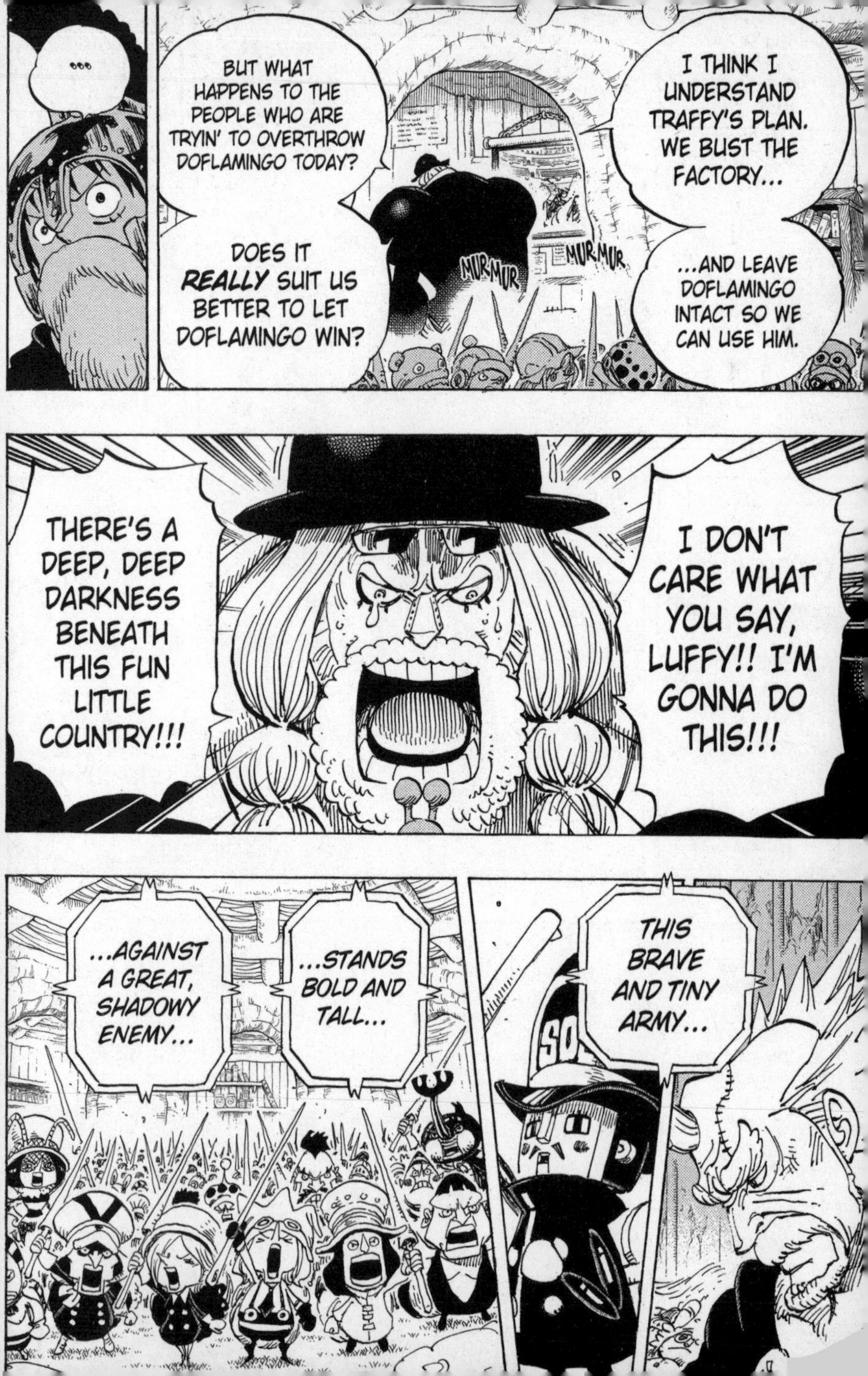
I THINK I UNDERSTAND TRAFFY'S PLAN. WE BUST THE FACTORY...
...AND LEAVE DOFLAMINGO INTACT SO WE CAN USE HIM.
BUT WHAT HAPPENS TO THE PEOPLE WHO ARE TRYIN' TO OVERTHROW DOFLAMINGO TODAY?
MUR MUR
DOES IT *REALLY* SUIT US BETTER TO LET DOFLAMINGO WIN?
MUR MUR
...
I DON'T CARE WHAT YOU SAY, LUFFY!! I'M GONNA DO THIS!!!
THERE'S A DEEP, DEEP DARKNESS BENEATH THIS FUN LITTLE COUNTRY!!!
THIS BRAVE AND TINY ARMY...
...STANDS BOLD AND TALL...
...AGAINST A GREAT, SHADOWY ENEMY...

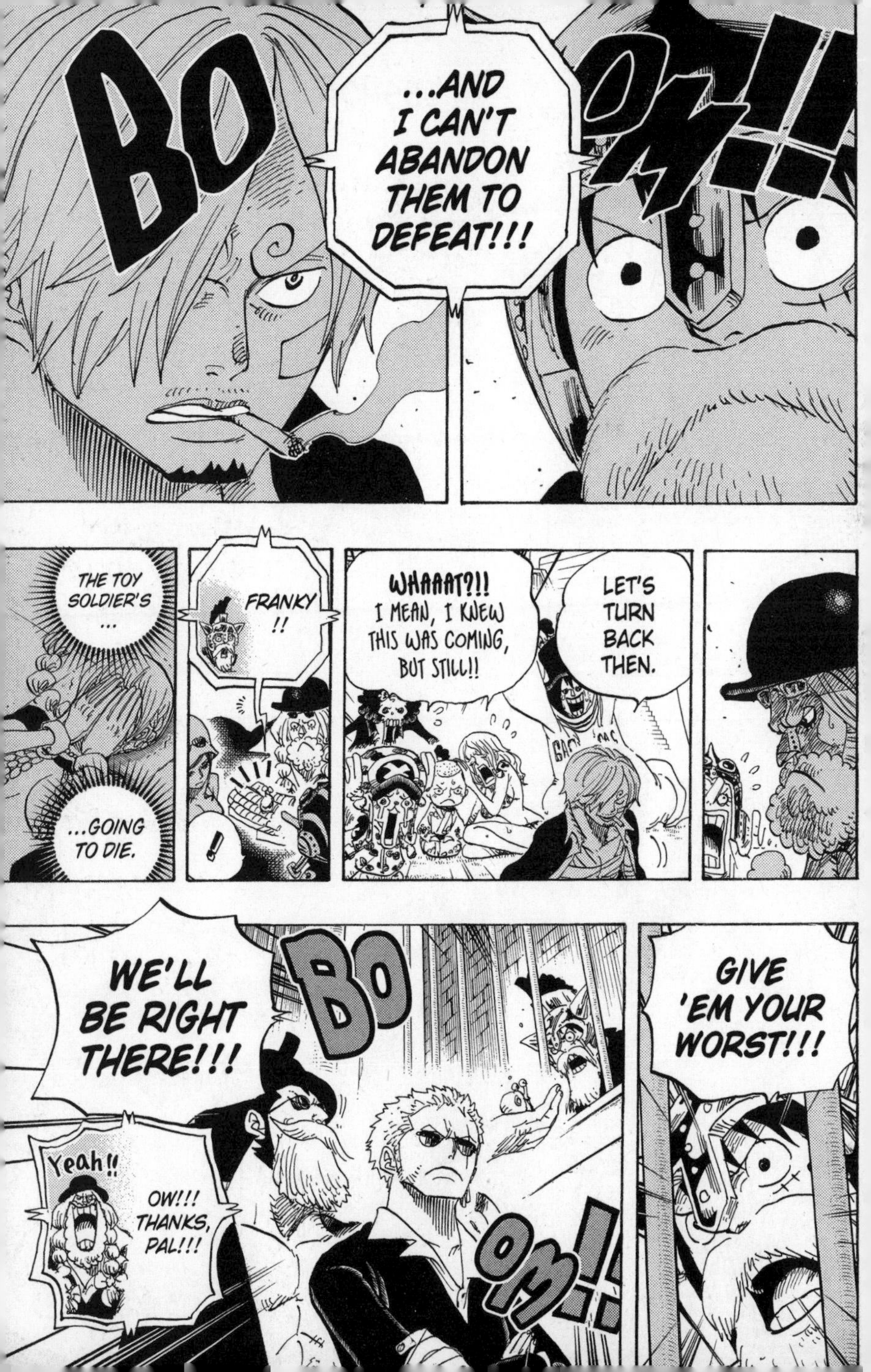
...AND I CAN'T ABANDON THEM TO DEFEAT!!!
BO
OM!!
LET'S TURN BACK THEN.
WHAAAT?!! I MEAN, I KNEW THIS WAS COMING, BUT STILL!!
FRANKY !!
!
THE TOY SOLDIER'S ...
...GOING TO DIE.
GIVE 'EM YOUR WORST!!!
WE'LL BE RIGHT THERE!!!
BO
OM!!
Yeah!!
OW!!! THANKS, PAL!!!

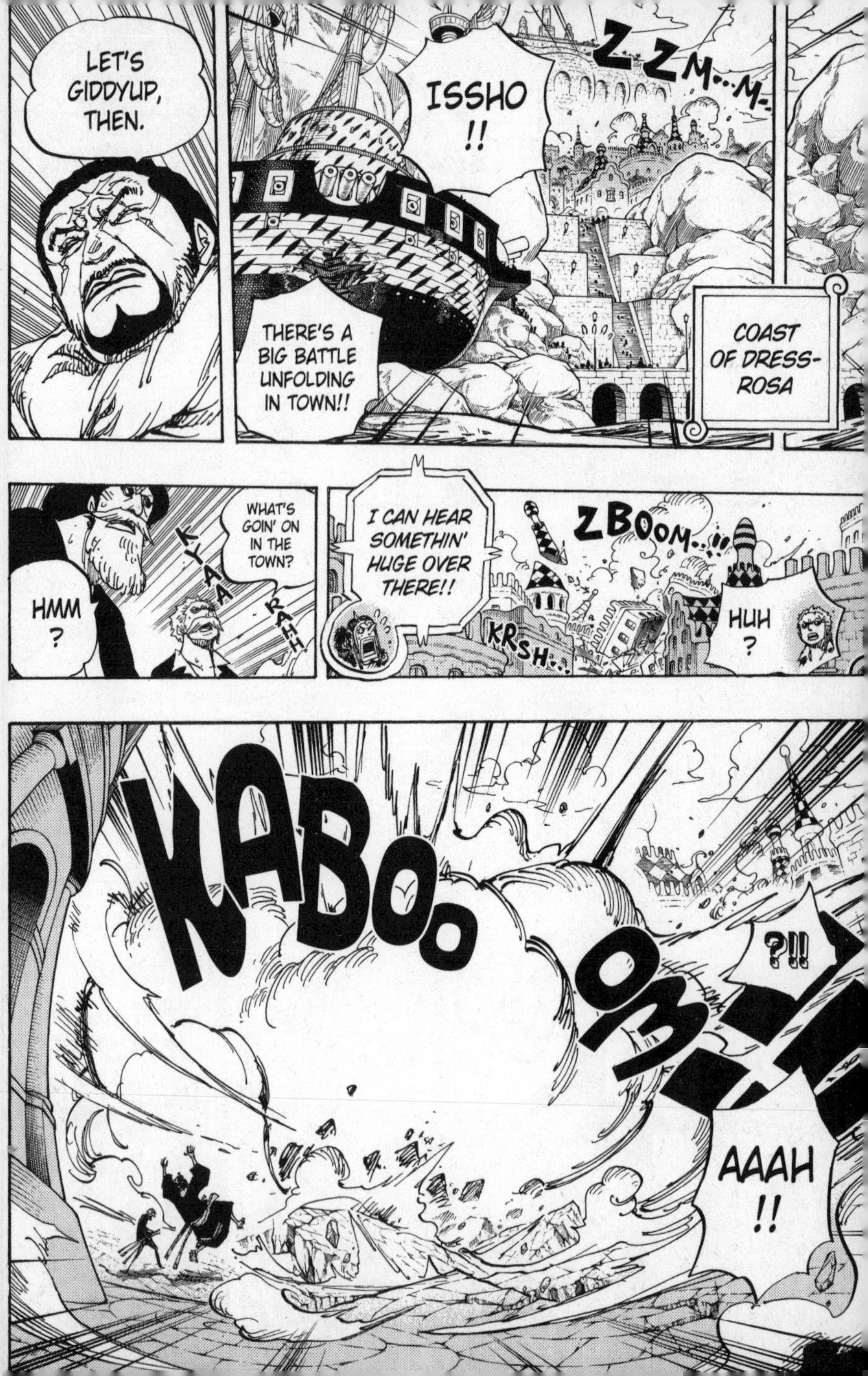
ZZM...M..
COAST OF DRESS-ROSA
ISSHO !!
THERE'S A BIG BATTLE UNFOLDING IN TOWN!!
LET'S GIDDYUP, THEN.
ZBOOM..!!
I CAN HEAR SOMETHIN' HUGE OVER THERE!!
KRSH...
HUH ?
WHAT'S GOIN' ON IN THE TOWN?
KYAAA
RAHH
HMM ?
KABOOOOM
?!!
AAAH !!

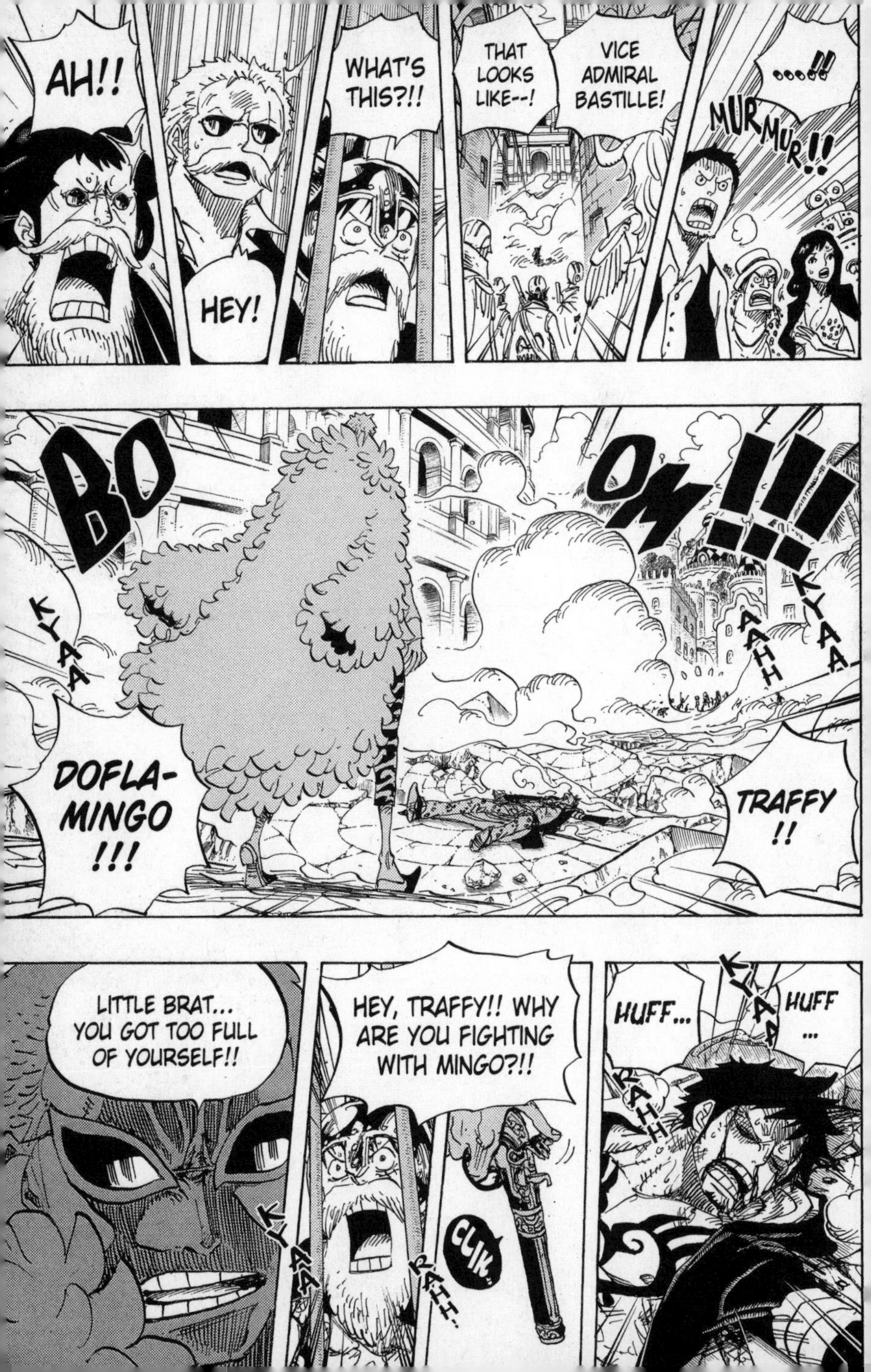
....!!
MURMUR!!
THAT LOOKS LIKE--!
VICE ADMIRAL BASTILLE!
WHAT'S THIS?!!
HEY!
AH!!
BO
OM!!!
KYAAAHH
TRAFFY!!
DOFLA-MINGO!!!
KYAA
HUFF...
HUFF...
KYAA
RAHH
HEY, TRAFFY!! WHY ARE YOU FIGHTING WITH MINGO?!!
CLIK
RAHH
LITTLE BRAT... YOU GOT TOO FULL OF YOURSELF!!
KYAA

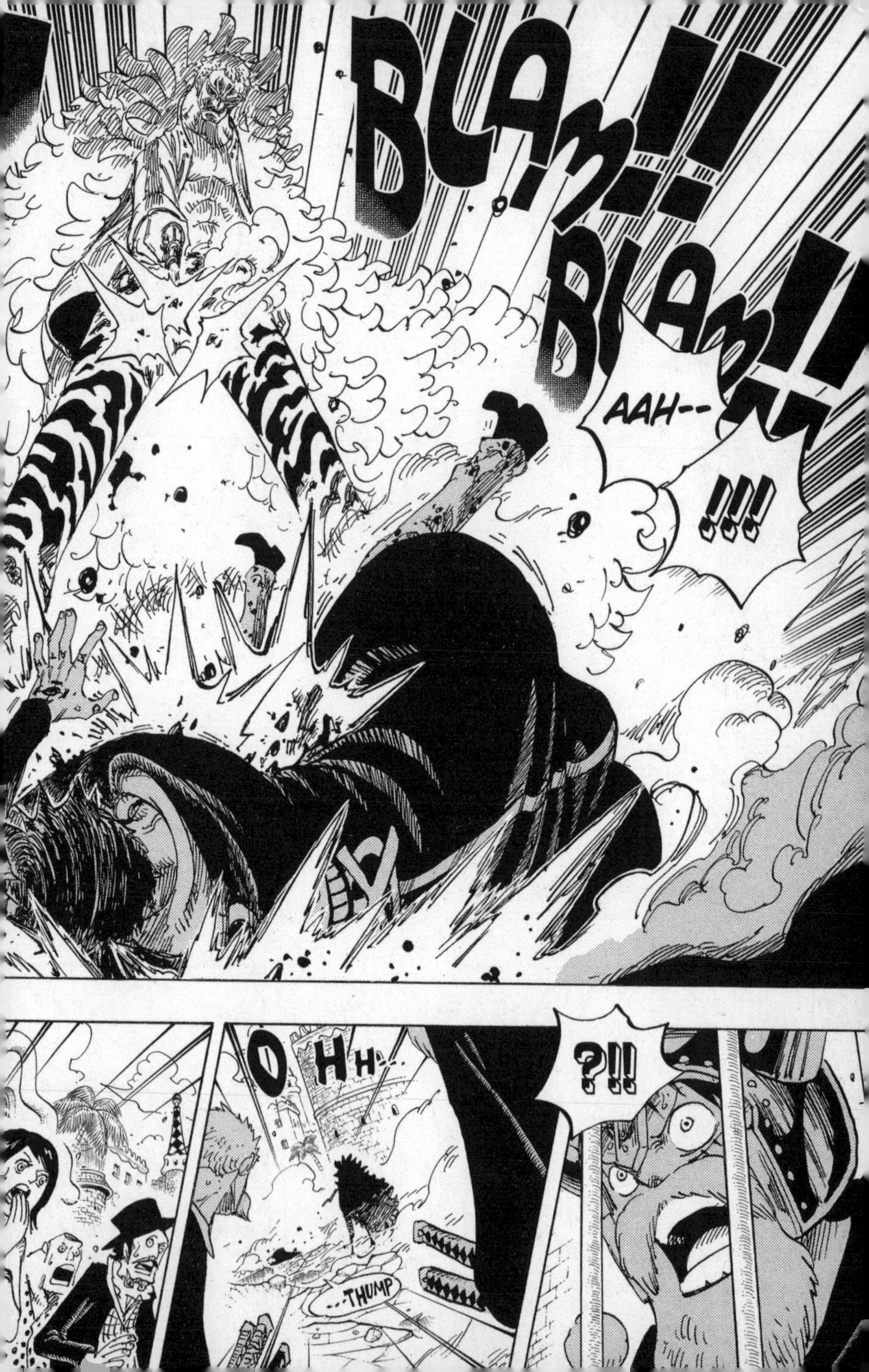
BLAM!!
BLAM!!
AAH--
!!!
?!!
OHH...
...THUMP

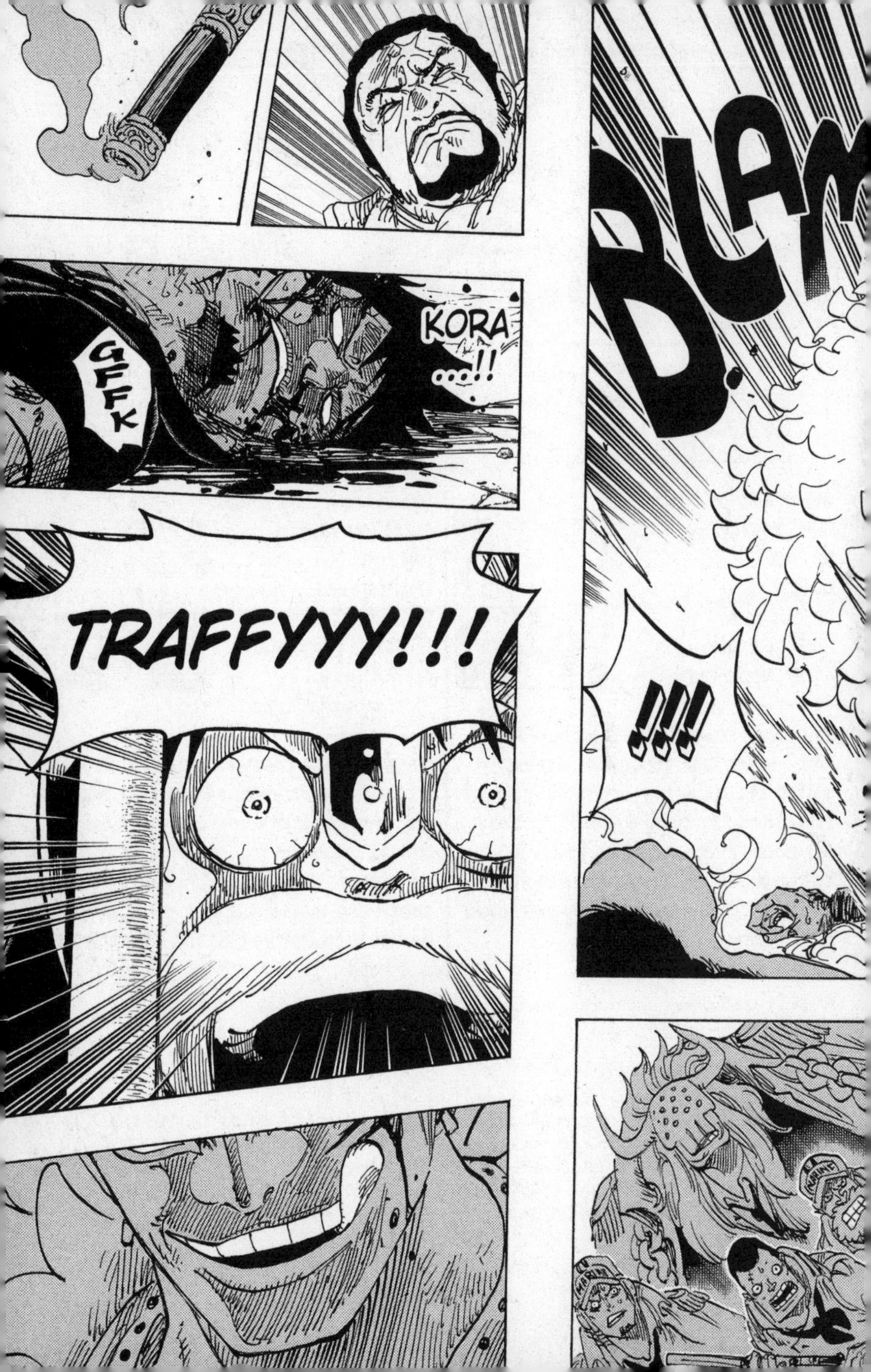
BLAM
!!!
KORA...!!
GFFK
TRAFFYYY!!!

SBS Question Corner

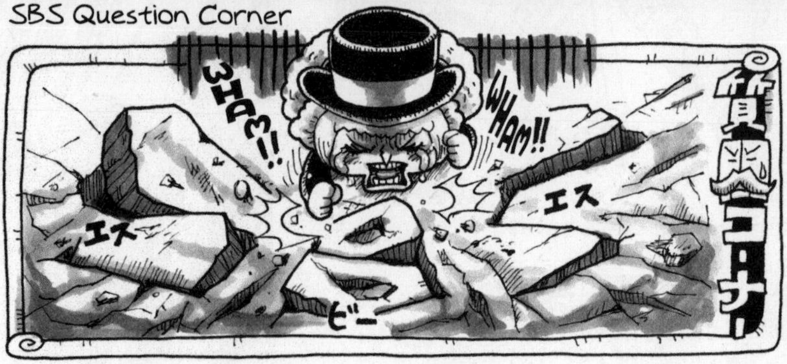
WHAM!!
WHAM!!
エス
エス
ビー
質問コーナー

(Hippo Iron, Saitama)

Q: Zolo and Sanji are always fighting! I was reading *One Piece* and thought it was odd that Zolo never seems to refer to Sanji by his name, so I went back and checked! I counted them up from Volume 5 (Sanji's introduction) to Volume 66! Here are the results, ranked by frequency!!!

(When Zolo Refers to Sanji)
(25+) You/he/him
(6) Cook
(5) Idiot
(3) Idiot cook
(2) Stupid cook,
Mr. Nosebleed

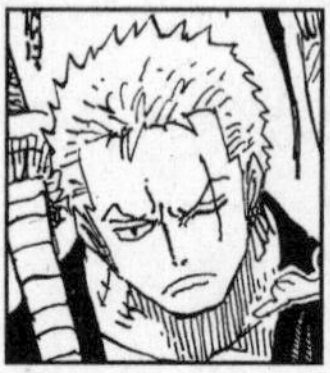

(once only) Love-struck fool, reckless idiot, rotten cook, fool, prince, useless idiot, pretty brow boy, ball-man, Prince of Stupid Kingdom, curly eyebrow, dart boy, dartboard eyebrow, stooge, Pirate A, twirly-brows, "Hgeegh," super guy, this guy, No. 7, perverted troll, liar, loser-cook, idiotic horn-dog, moron, clown

(When Sanji talks to Zolo)
(45+) You/he/him
(14) Zolo
(10) Mosshead
(5) Idiot
(3) Stupid swordsman
(2) That guy,
crappy swordsman

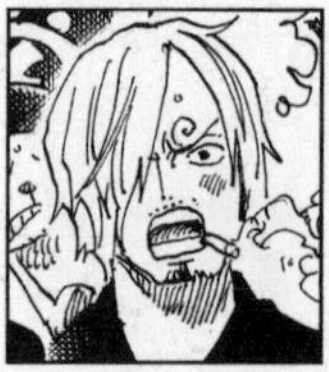

(once only) Fool, crazy kid, stupid idiot, crazy guy, muscle-bound fool, swan man, idiot mosshead, jerk, cactus head, moss, dummy, stubborn fool, scruffy-headed swordsman, idiot swordsman, green hair, that thing, moss ball, muscle-head, green, useless turd, cheeky bastard, lost little mosshead

★ In conclusion, Sanji does in fact refer to Zolo by name, but Zolo does not return the favor!

--Little Marron

A: ...Okay. Thank you very much, Little Marron!!
So you counted them all... This was very fun to read! Some of these terms made me wonder when they'd said these things. Indeed, I have trouble imagining Zolo calling him "Sanji" by name. Not once, eh? Wow. Well, they might not get along well, but they're both valuable, trustworthy men who have Luffy's back. So let's forgive them their squabbles (laughs).

[Ed. Note: In the Viz edition, Zolo does call Sanji by name a few times for the sake of context, but he does not say "Sanji" explicitly in the original Japanese.]

Chapter 730:
THREE CARDS

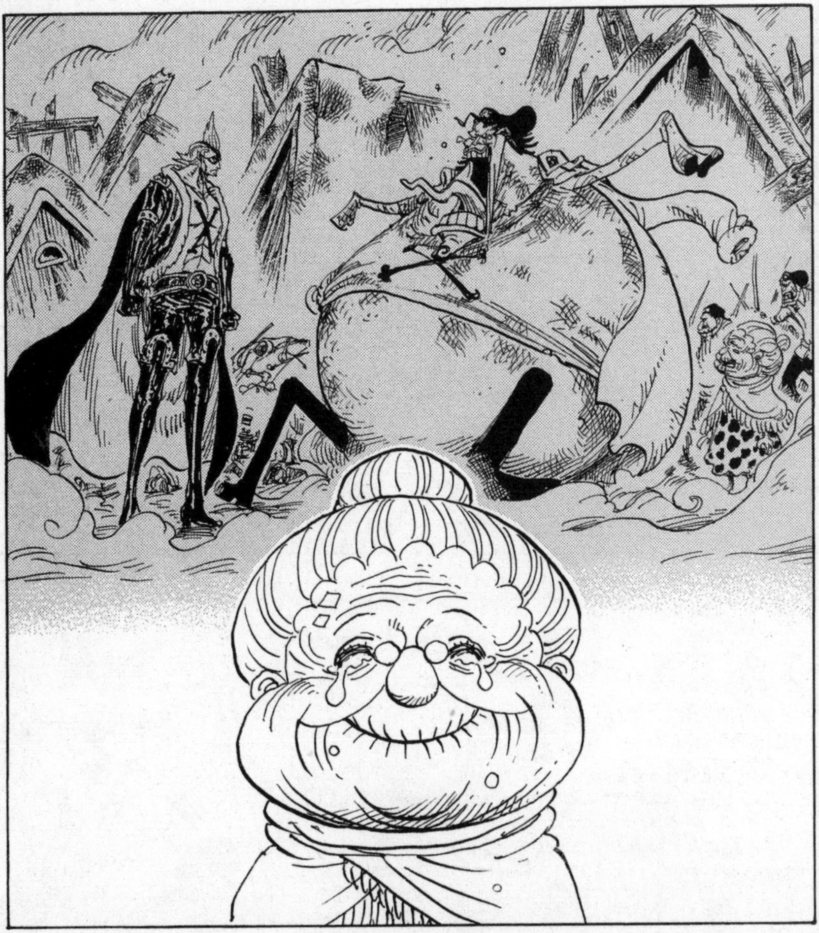

CARIBOU'S NEW WORLD KEE HEE HEE, VOL. 45: "BEFORE HE LEFT, GABURU CRIED, 'TREASURE THE GRANDMAS!!!'"

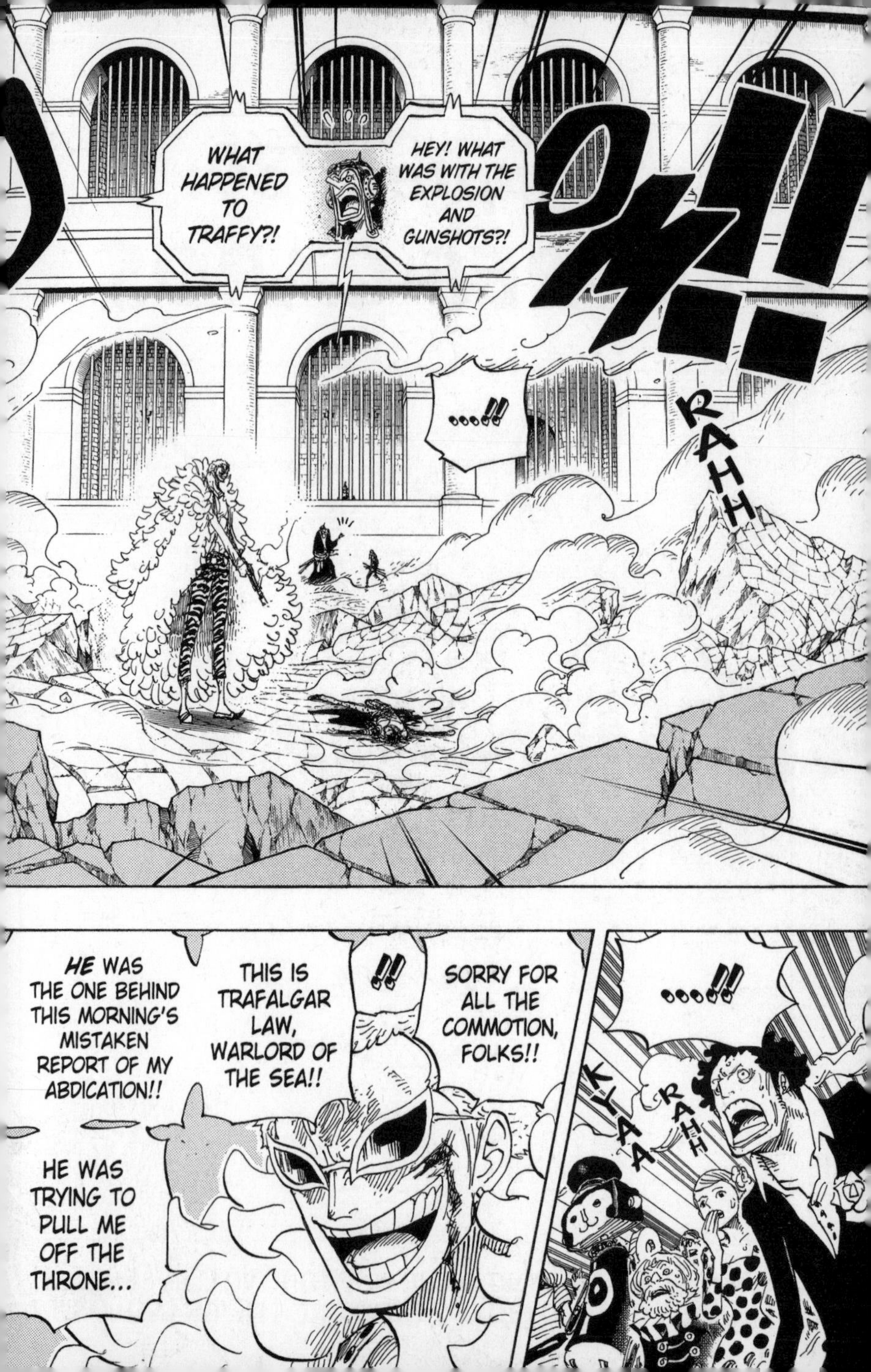
RAHH
HEY! WHAT WAS WITH THE EXPLOSION AND GUNSHOTS?!
WHAT HAPPENED TO TRAFFY?!
......!!
......!!
KYAA
RAHH
SORRY FOR ALL THE COMMOTION, FOLKS!!
!!
THIS IS TRAFALGAR LAW, WARLORD OF THE SEA!!
HE WAS THE ONE BEHIND THIS MORNING'S MISTAKEN REPORT OF MY ABDICATION!!
HE WAS TRYING TO PULL ME OFF THE THRONE...

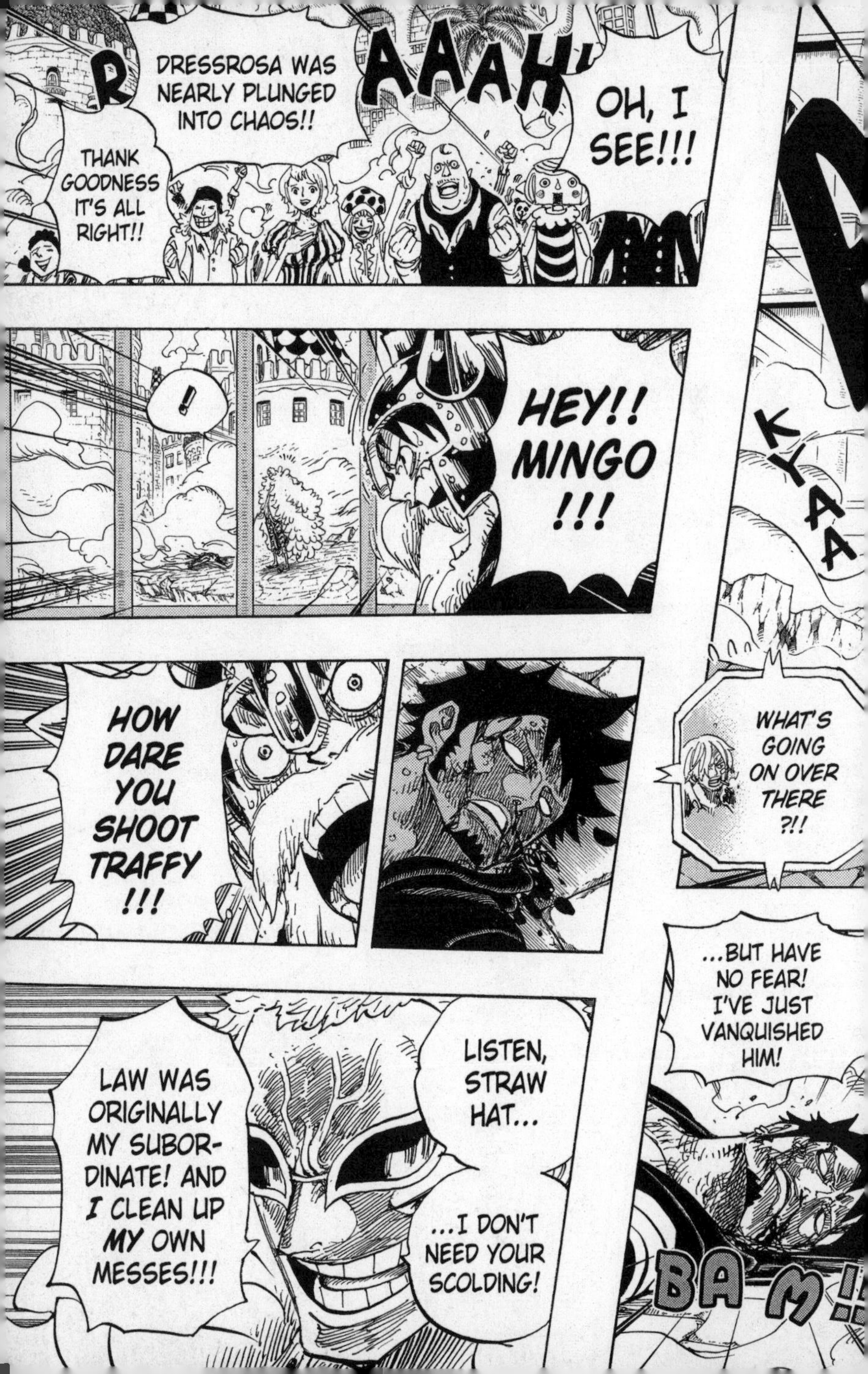
A
KYAAA
WHAT'S GOING ON OVER THERE?!!
AAAH
OH, I SEE!!!
DRESSROSA WAS NEARLY PLUNGED INTO CHAOS!!
R
THANK GOODNESS IT'S ALL RIGHT!!
!
HEY!! MINGO!!!
HOW DARE YOU SHOOT TRAFFY!!!
...BUT HAVE NO FEAR! I'VE JUST VANQUISHED HIM!
BAM!!
LISTEN, STRAW HAT...
...I DON'T NEED YOUR SCOLDING!
LAW WAS ORIGINALLY MY SUBOR-DINATE! AND I CLEAN UP MY OWN MESSES!!!

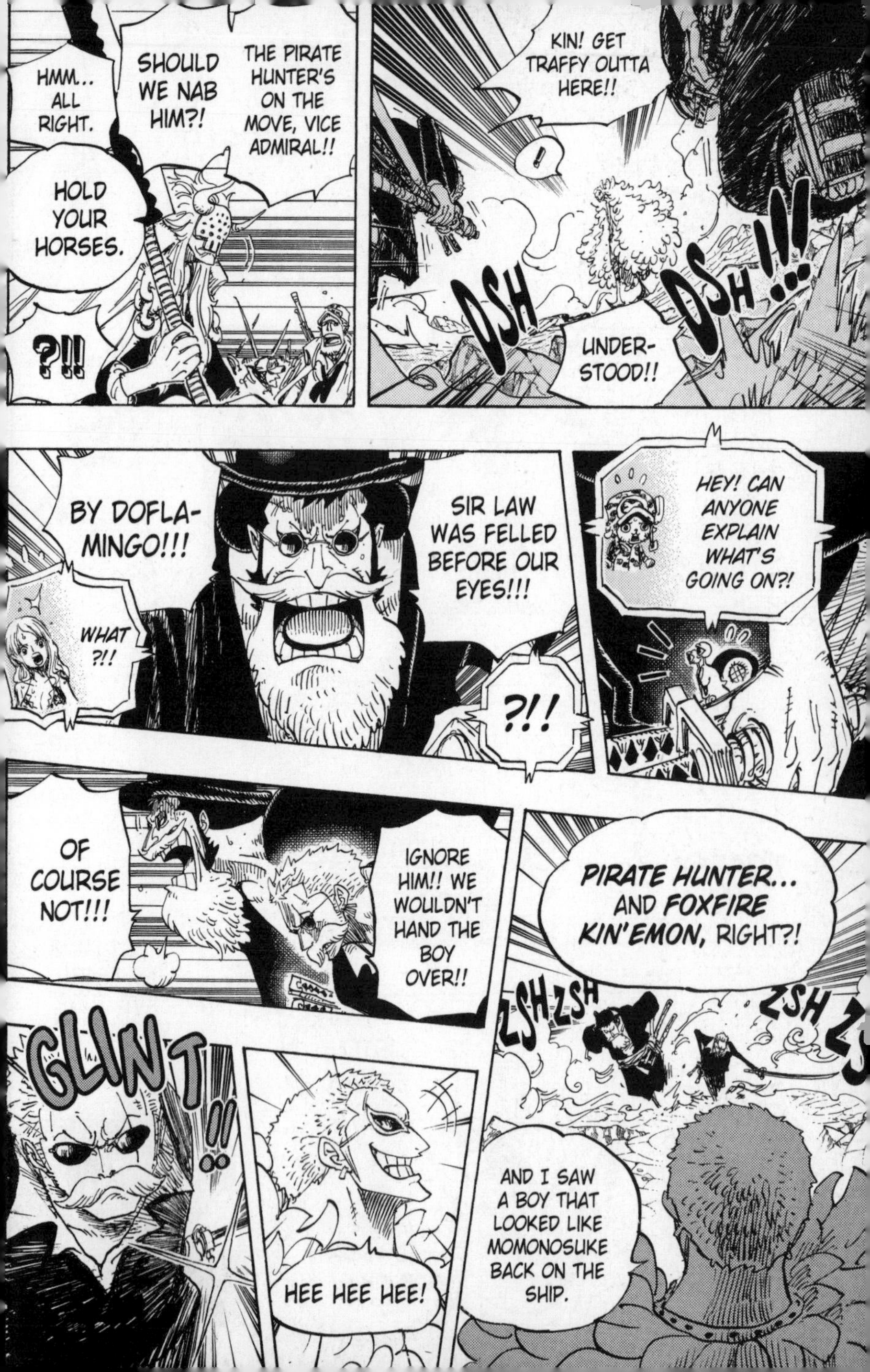
KIN! GET TRAFFY OUTTA HERE!!
!
DSH!!!
DSH
UNDER-STOOD!!
THE PIRATE HUNTER'S ON THE MOVE, VICE ADMIRAL!!
SHOULD WE NAB HIM?!
HMM... ALL RIGHT.
HOLD YOUR HORSES.
?!!
HEY! CAN ANYONE EXPLAIN WHAT'S GOING ON?!
SIR LAW WAS FELLED BEFORE OUR EYES!!!
BY DOFLA-MINGO!!!
?!!
WHAT?!!
PIRATE HUNTER... AND FOXFIRE KIN'EMON, RIGHT?!
IGNORE HIM!! WE WOULDN'T HAND THE BOY OVER!!
OF COURSE NOT!!!
ZSH
ZSH ZSH
AND I SAW A BOY THAT LOOKED LIKE MOMONOSUKE BACK ON THE SHIP.
HEE HEE HEE!
GLINT!!

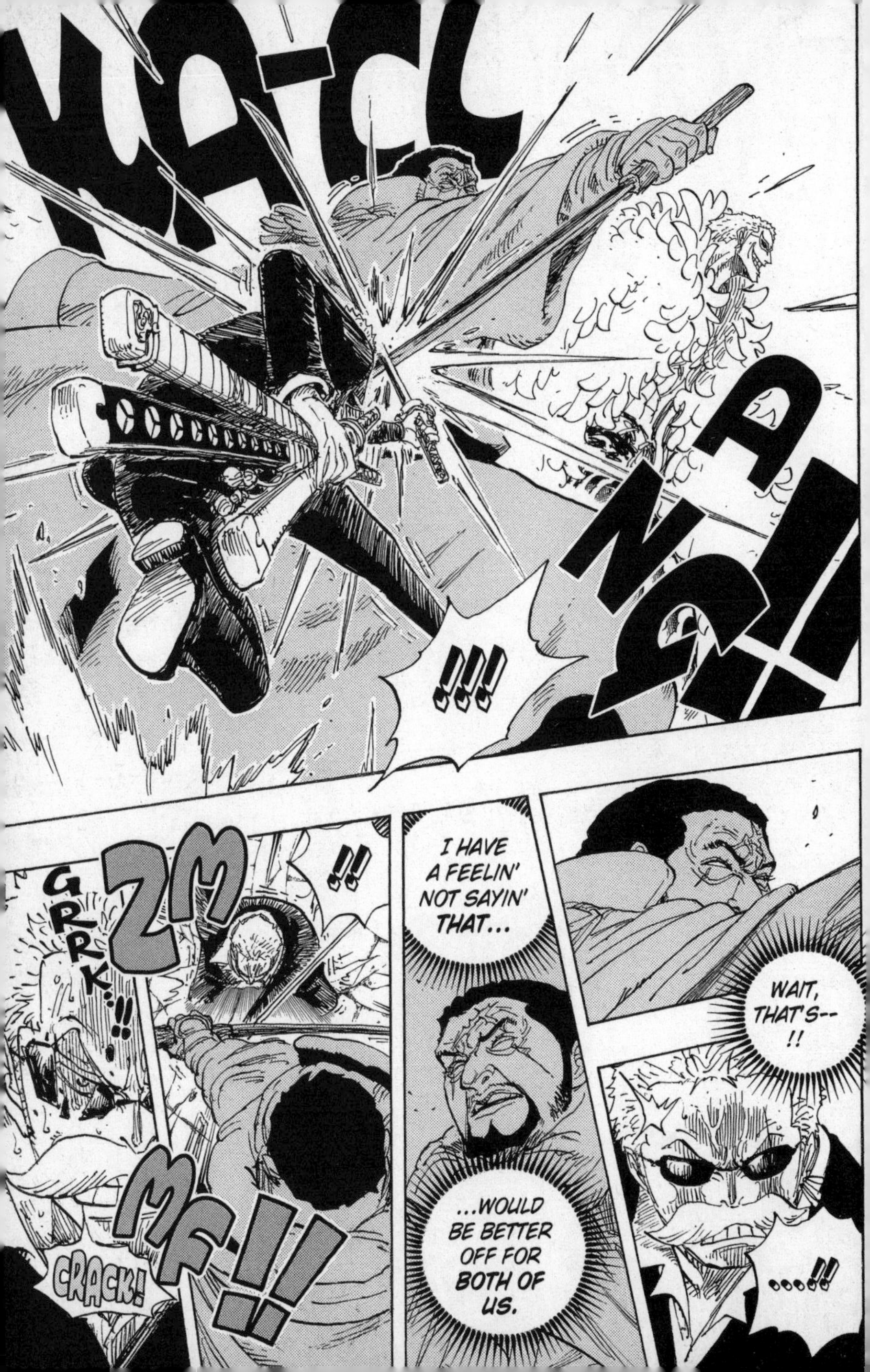
KA-CL
ANG!!
!!!
WAIT, THAT'S-- !!
...!!
I HAVE A FEELIN' NOT SAYIN' THAT...
...WOULD BE BETTER OFF FOR BOTH OF US.
!!
ZM
GRRRK..!!
MF-!!
CRACK!

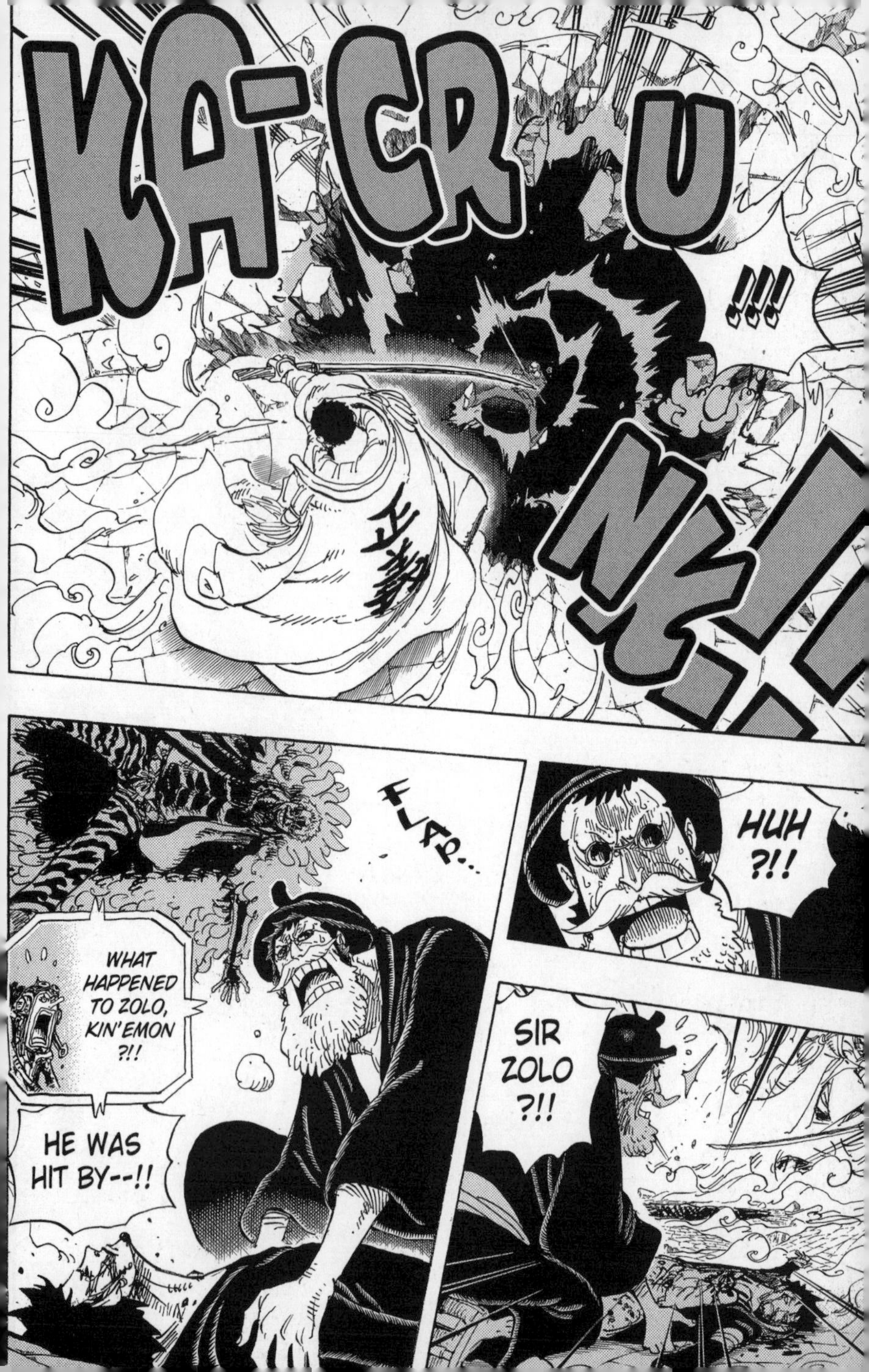
KA-CRU!!!
NN!!
HUH ?!!
SIR ZOLO ?!!
FLAP...
WHAT HAPPENED TO ZOLO, KIN'EMON ?!!
HE WAS HIT BY--!!

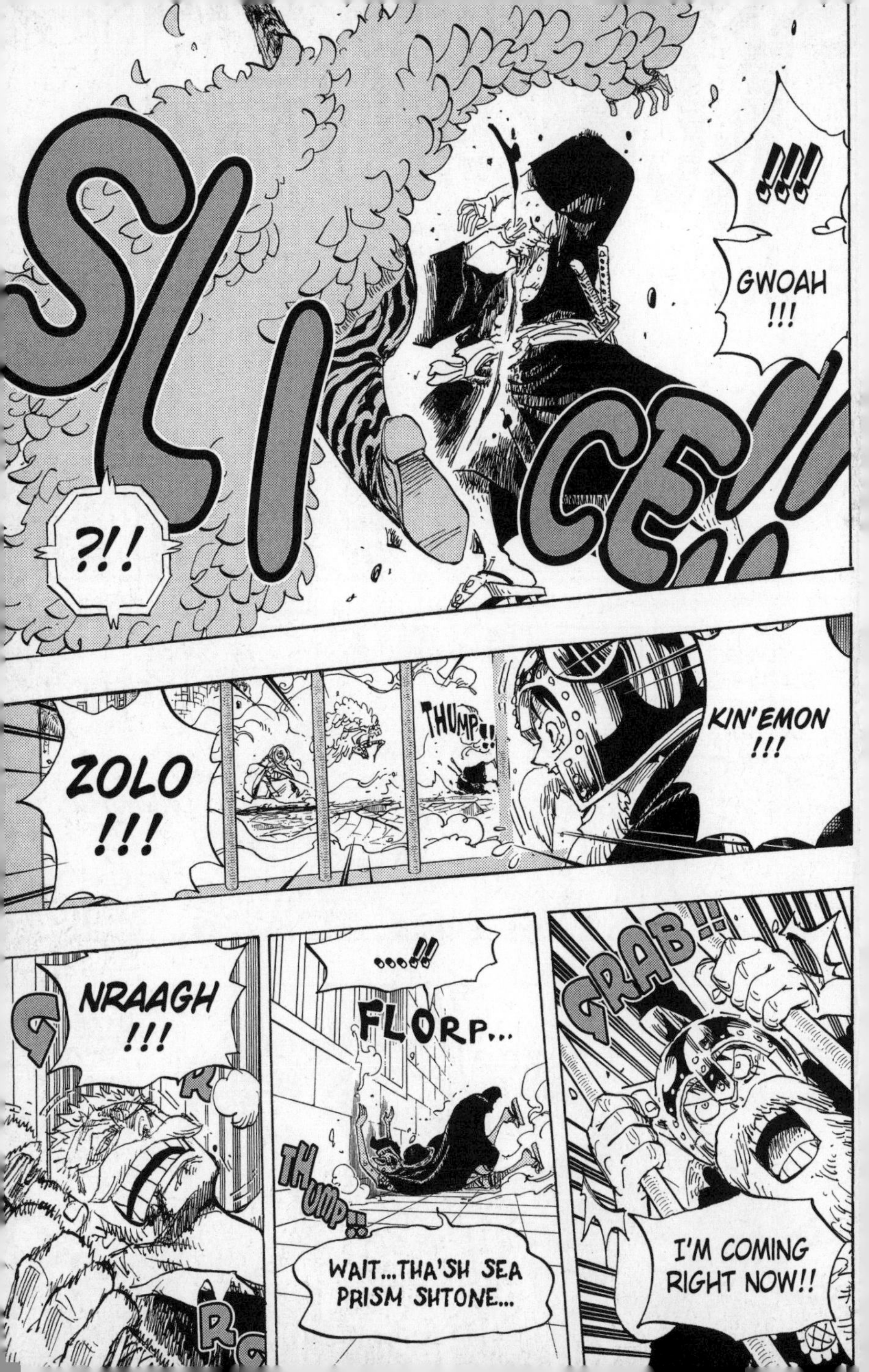
!!!
GWOAH !!!
SLI
CE
?!!
KIN'EMON !!!
THUMP!!
ZOLO !!!
GRAB!!
I'M COMING RIGHT NOW!!
...!!
FLORP...
THUMP!!
WAIT...THA'SH SEA PRISM SHTONE...
NRAAGH !!!

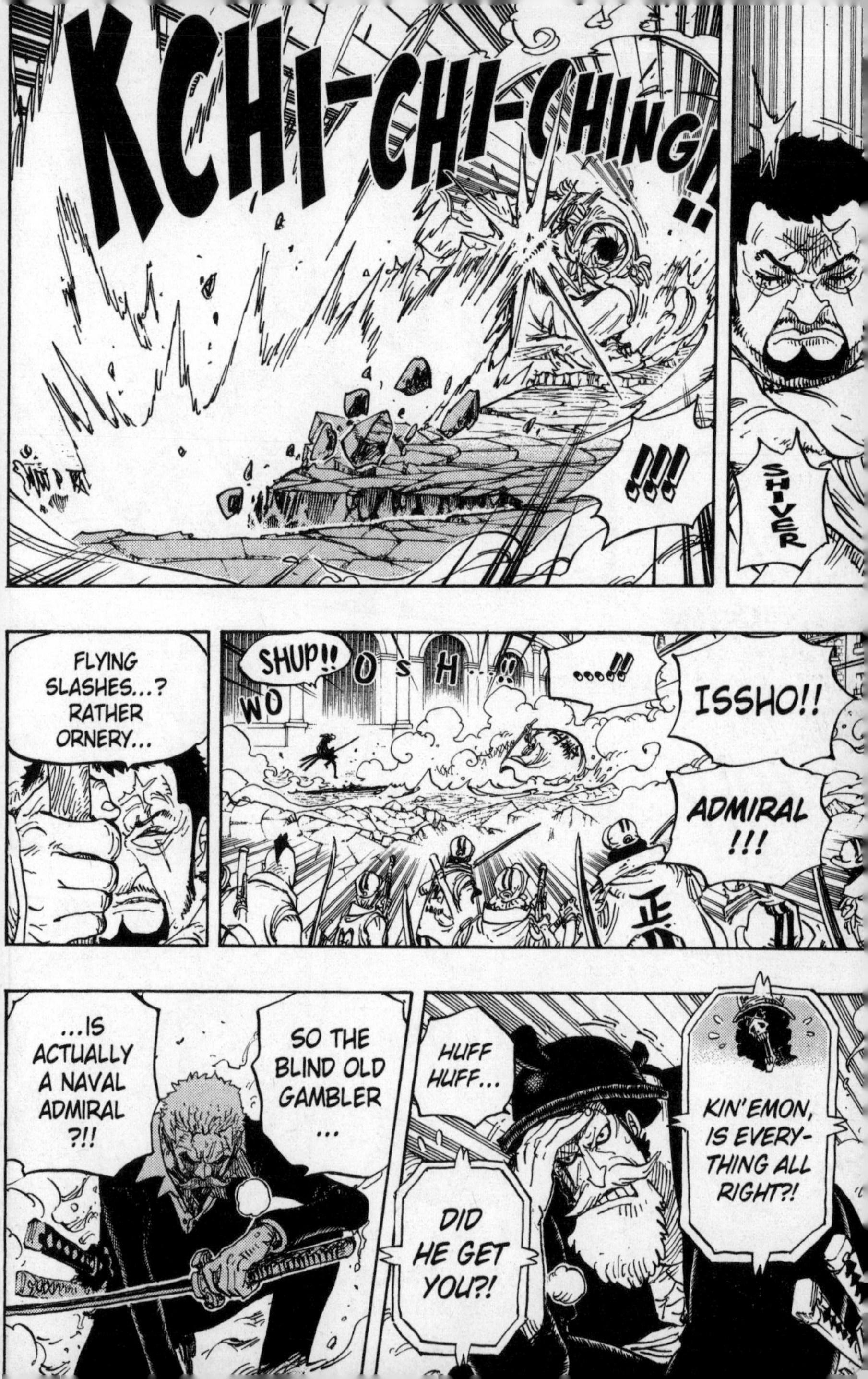
SHIVER
KCHI-CHI-CHING!!
!!!
ISSHO!!
....!!
WOOSH...!!
SHUP!!
ADMIRAL!!!
FLYING SLASHES...? RATHER ORNERY...
KIN'EMON, IS EVERYTHING ALL RIGHT?!
HUFF HUFF...
DID HE GET YOU?!
SO THE BLIND OLD GAMBLER...
...IS ACTUALLY A NAVAL ADMIRAL?!!

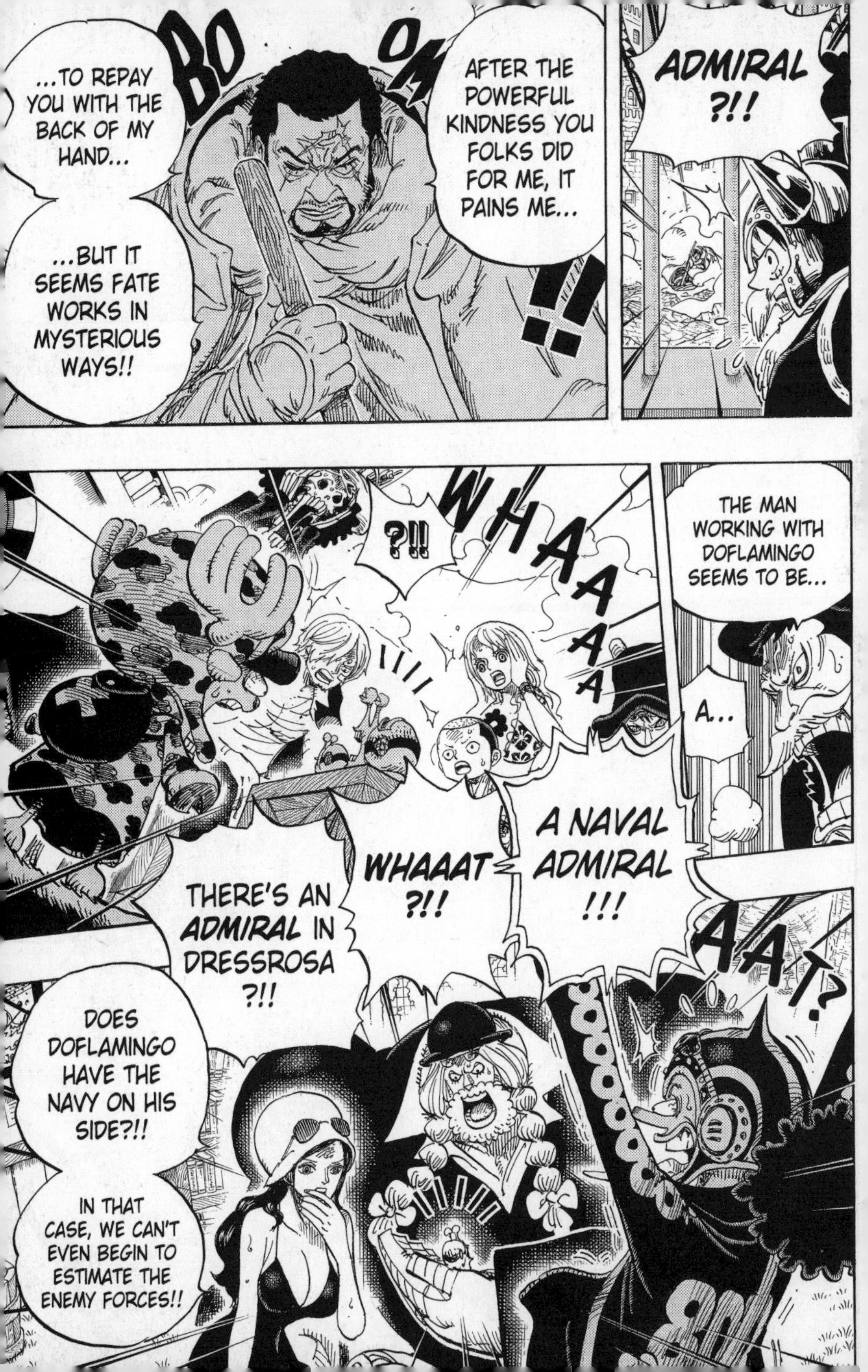
ADMIRAL ?!!
AFTER THE POWERFUL KINDNESS YOU FOLKS DID FOR ME, IT PAINS ME...
BOOM
...TO REPAY YOU WITH THE BACK OF MY HAND...
...BUT IT SEEMS FATE WORKS IN MYSTERIOUS WAYS!!
!!
THE MAN WORKING WITH DOFLAMINGO SEEMS TO BE...
A...
WHAAAAAA
?!!
A NAVAL ADMIRAL !!!
WHAAAT ?!!
THERE'S AN ADMIRAL IN DRESSROSA ?!!
AAT?
DOES DOFLAMINGO HAVE THE NAVY ON HIS SIDE?!!
IN THAT CASE, WE CAN'T EVEN BEGIN TO ESTIMATE THE ENEMY FORCES!!

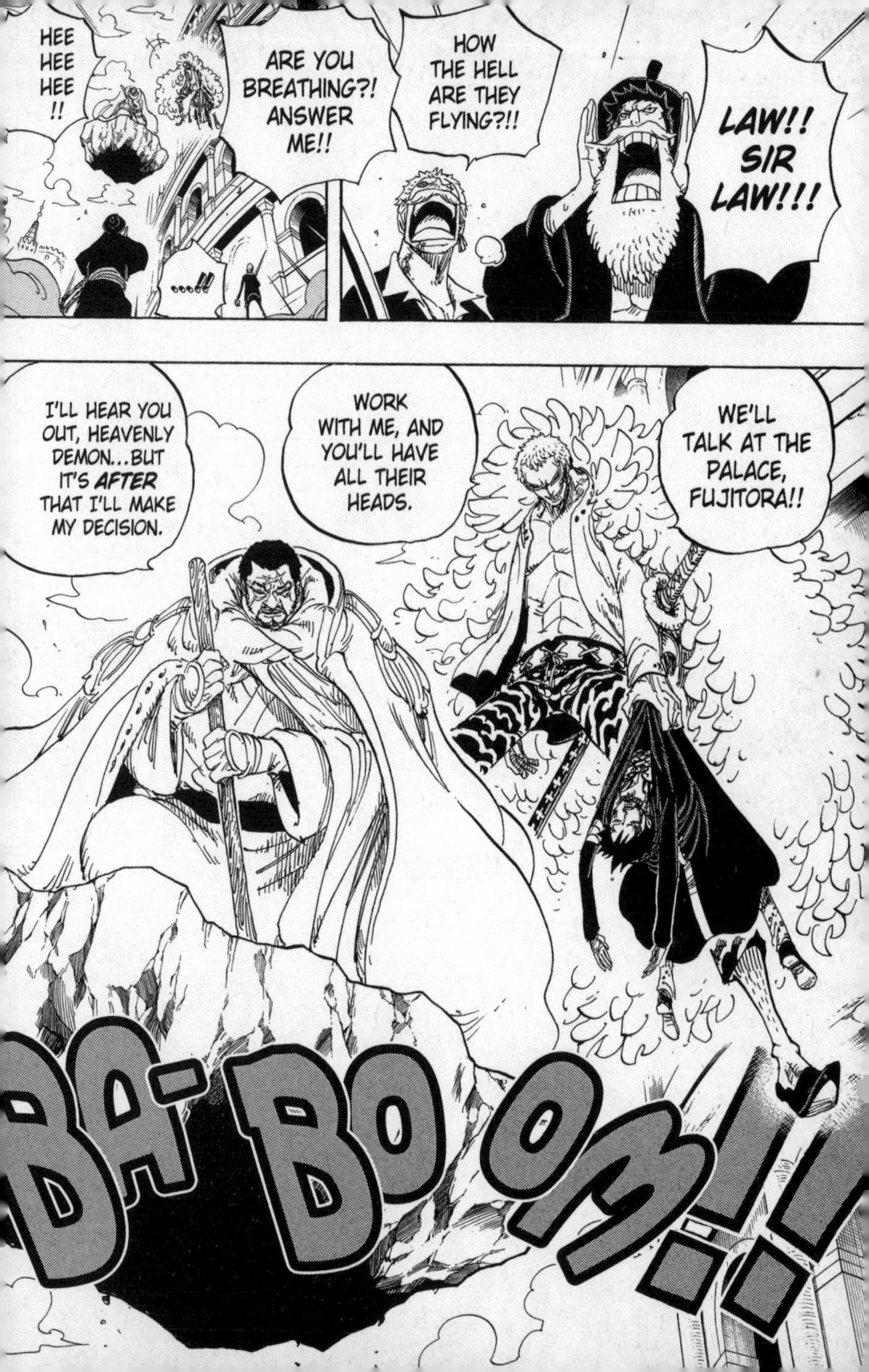
LAW!! SIR LAW!!!
HOW THE HELL ARE THEY FLYING?!!
ARE YOU BREATHING?! ANSWER ME!!
HEE HEE HEE !!
....!!
WE'LL TALK AT THE PALACE, FUJITORA!!
WORK WITH ME, AND YOU'LL HAVE ALL THEIR HEADS.
I'LL HEAR YOU OUT, HEAVENLY DEMON...BUT IT'S *AFTER* THAT I'LL MAKE MY DECISION.
BA-BOOM!!

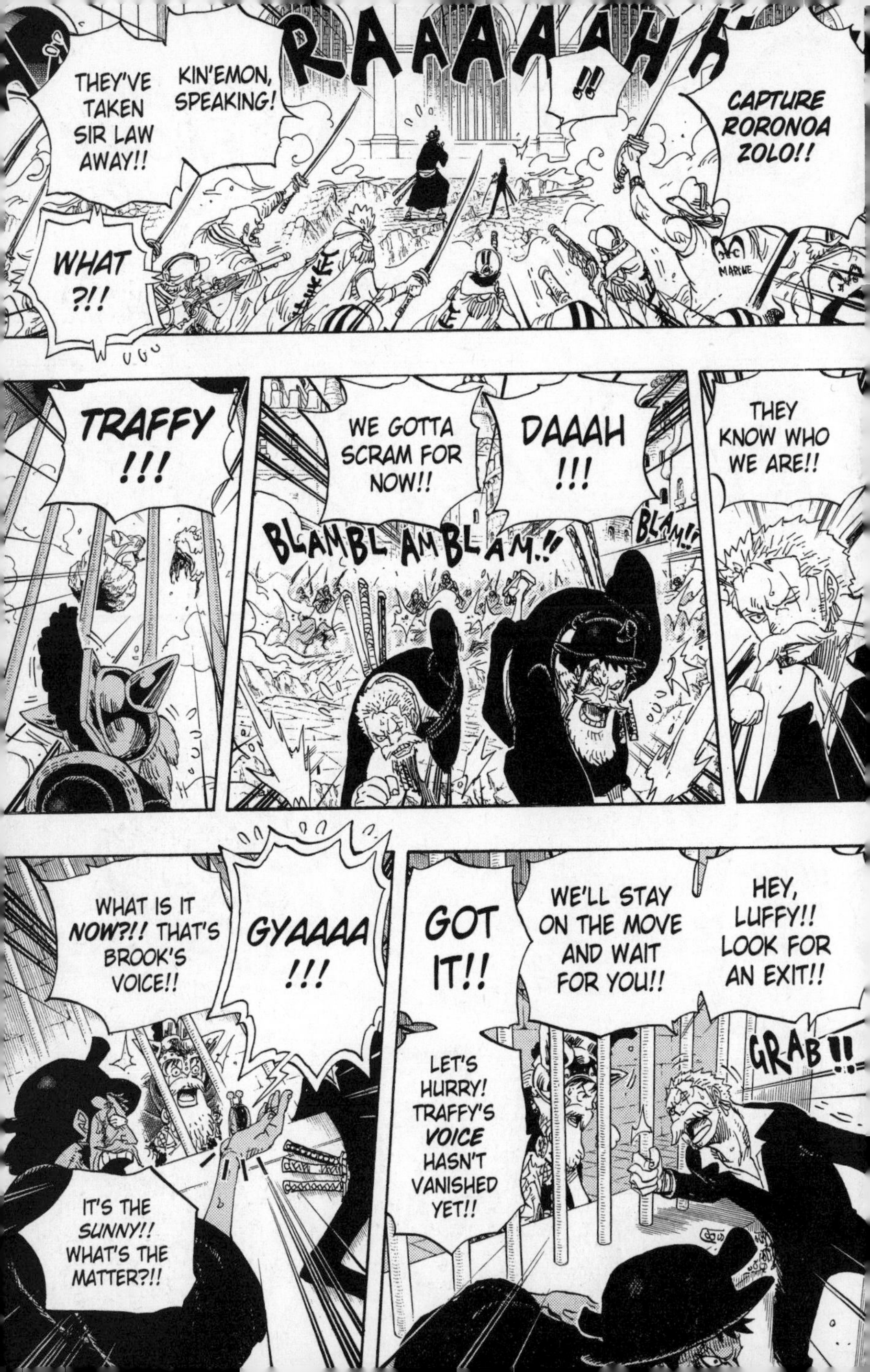
CAPTURE RORONOA ZOLO!!
RAAAAAH
!!
KIN'EMON, SPEAKING!
THEY'VE TAKEN SIR LAW AWAY!!
WHAT ?!!
THEY KNOW WHO WE ARE!!
BLAM!!
DAAAH !!!
WE GOTTA SCRAM FOR NOW!!
BLAMBLAMBLAM.!!
TRAFFY !!!
HEY, LUFFY!! LOOK FOR AN EXIT!!
GRAB!!
WE'LL STAY ON THE MOVE AND WAIT FOR YOU!!
GOT IT!!
LET'S HURRY! TRAFFY'S VOICE HASN'T VANISHED YET!!
GYAAAA !!!
WHAT IS IT NOW?!! THAT'S BROOK'S VOICE!!
IT'S THE SUNNY!! WHAT'S THE MATTER?!!

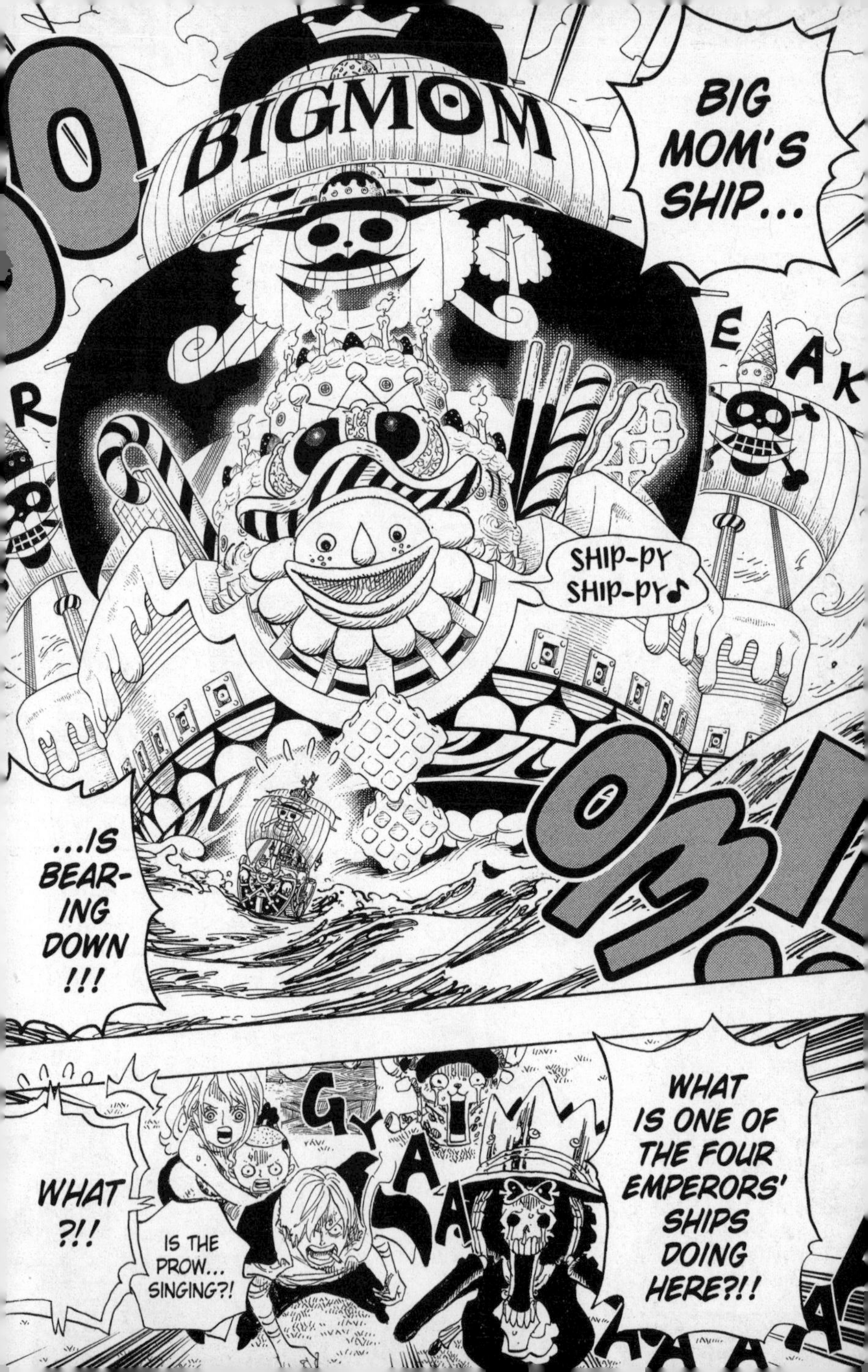
BIGMOM
BIG MOM'S SHIP...
SHIP-PY SHIP-PY♪
...IS BEAR-ING DOWN!!!
WHAT IS ONE OF THE FOUR EMPERORS' SHIPS DOING HERE?!!
IS THE PROW... SINGING?!
WHAT?!!

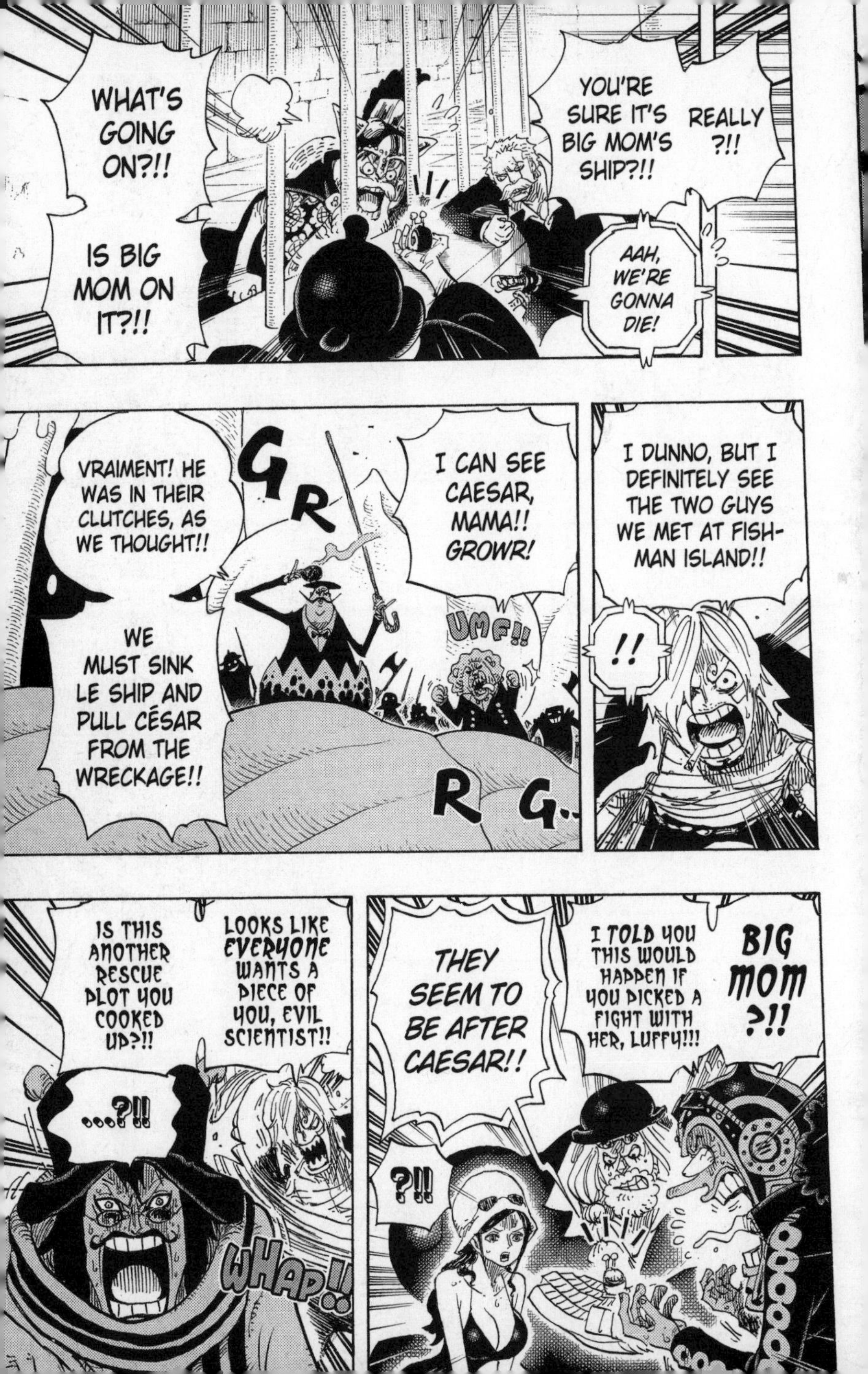
REALLY ?!!
YOU'RE SURE IT'S BIG MOM'S SHIP?!!
WHAT'S GOING ON?!!
AAH, WE'RE GONNA DIE!
IS BIG MOM ON IT?!!
I DUNNO, BUT I DEFINITELY SEE THE TWO GUYS WE MET AT FISH-MAN ISLAND!!
!!
I CAN SEE CAESAR, MAMA!! GROWR!
GR
VRAIMENT! HE WAS IN THEIR CLUTCHES, AS WE THOUGHT!!
UMF!!
WE MUST SINK LE SHIP AND PULL CÉSAR FROM THE WRECKAGE!!
R G..
BIG MOM ?!!
I TOLD YOU THIS WOULD HAPPEN IF YOU PICKED A FIGHT WITH HER, LUFFY!!!
THEY SEEM TO BE AFTER CAESAR!!
?!!
LOOKS LIKE EVERYONE WANTS A PIECE OF YOU, EVIL SCIENTIST!!
IS THIS ANOTHER RESCUE PLOT YOU COOKED UP?!!
...?!!
WHAP!!

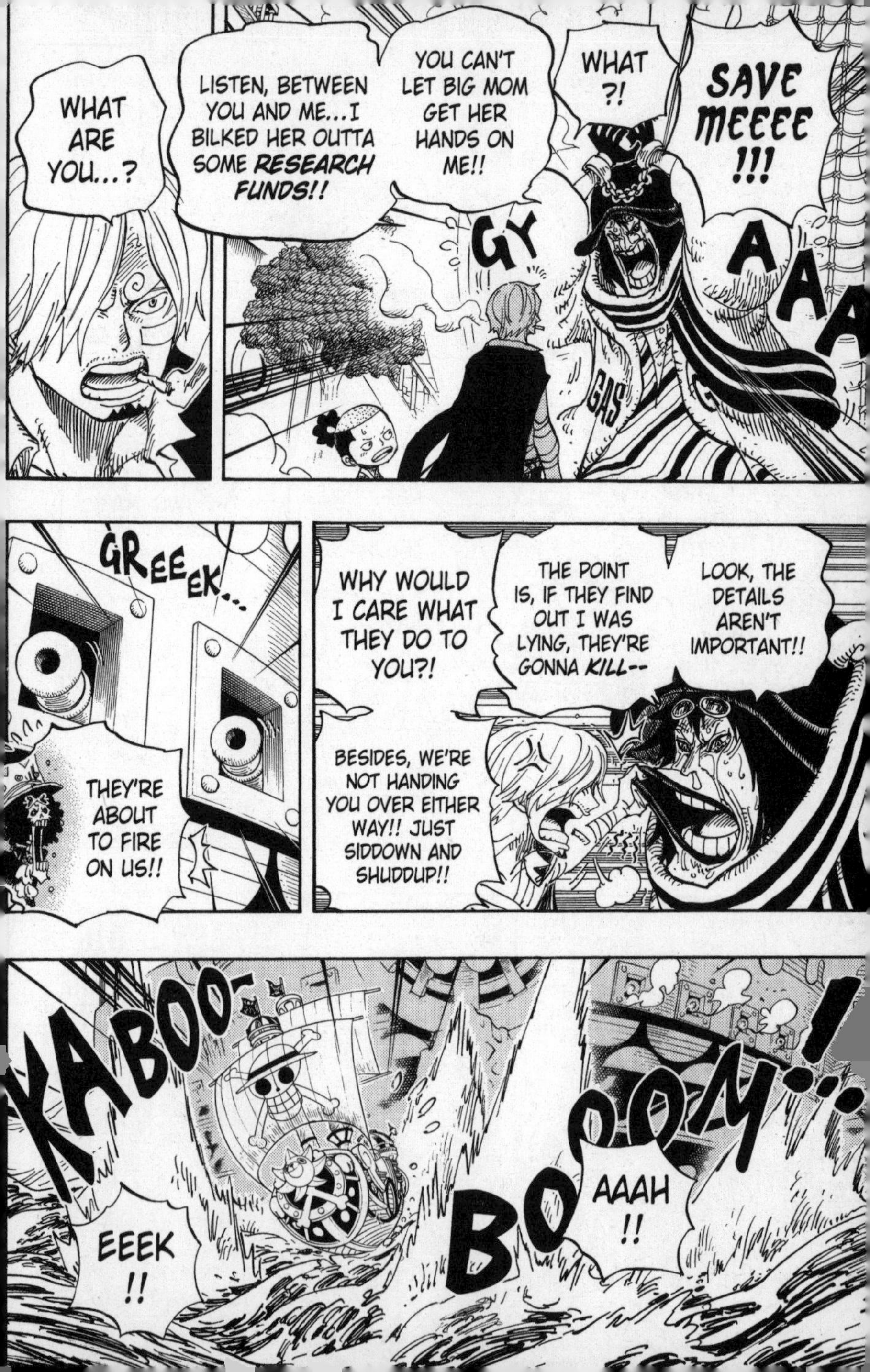
SAVE MEEEE!!!
WHAT ?!
YOU CAN'T LET BIG MOM GET HER HANDS ON ME!!
LISTEN, BETWEEN YOU AND ME...I BILKED HER OUTTA SOME RESEARCH FUNDS!!
AAA
GY
GAS
WHAT ARE YOU...?
LOOK, THE DETAILS AREN'T IMPORTANT!!
THE POINT IS, IF THEY FIND OUT I WAS LYING, THEY'RE GONNA KILL--
WHY WOULD I CARE WHAT THEY DO TO YOU?!
BESIDES, WE'RE NOT HANDING YOU OVER EITHER WAY!! JUST SIDDOWN AND SHUDDUP!!
GREEEK...
THEY'RE ABOUT TO FIRE ON US!!
KABOO-
BOOOM!!
AAAH!!
EEEK!!

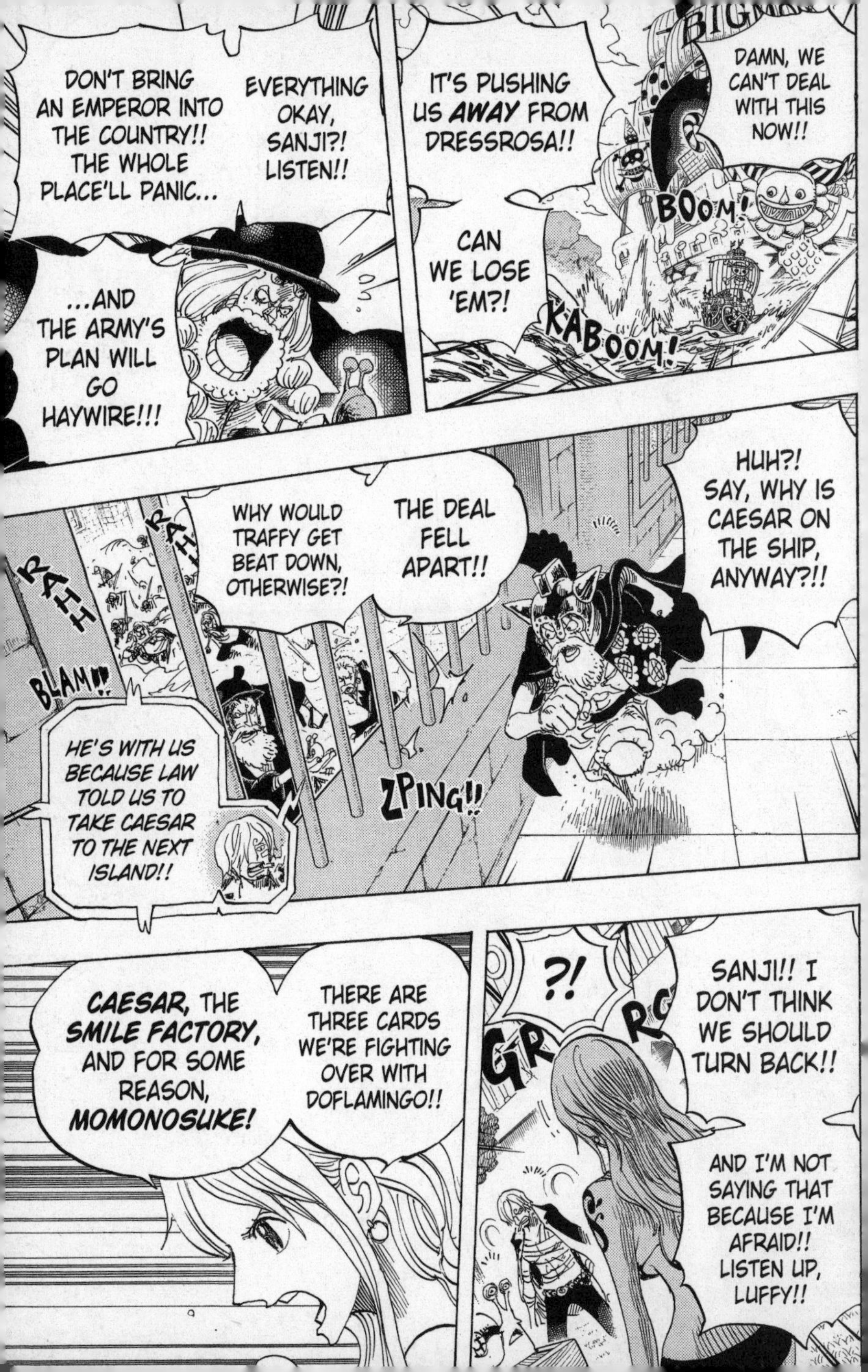
DAMN, WE CAN'T DEAL WITH THIS NOW!!
IT'S PUSHING US AWAY FROM DRESSROSA!!
BOOM!
CAN WE LOSE 'EM?!
KABOOM!
EVERYTHING OKAY, SANJI?! LISTEN!!
DON'T BRING AN EMPEROR INTO THE COUNTRY!! THE WHOLE PLACE'LL PANIC...
...AND THE ARMY'S PLAN WILL GO HAYWIRE!!!
HUH?! SAY, WHY IS CAESAR ON THE SHIP, ANYWAY?!!
THE DEAL FELL APART!!
WHY WOULD TRAFFY GET BEAT DOWN, OTHERWISE?!
RAHH
RAHH
BLAM!!
ZPING!!
HE'S WITH US BECAUSE LAW TOLD US TO TAKE CAESAR TO THE NEXT ISLAND!!
SANJI!! I DON'T THINK WE SHOULD TURN BACK!!
?!
AND I'M NOT SAYING THAT BECAUSE I'M AFRAID!! LISTEN UP, LUFFY!!
THERE ARE THREE CARDS WE'RE FIGHTING OVER WITH DOFLAMINGO!!
CAESAR, THE SMILE FACTORY, AND FOR SOME REASON, MOMONOSUKE!

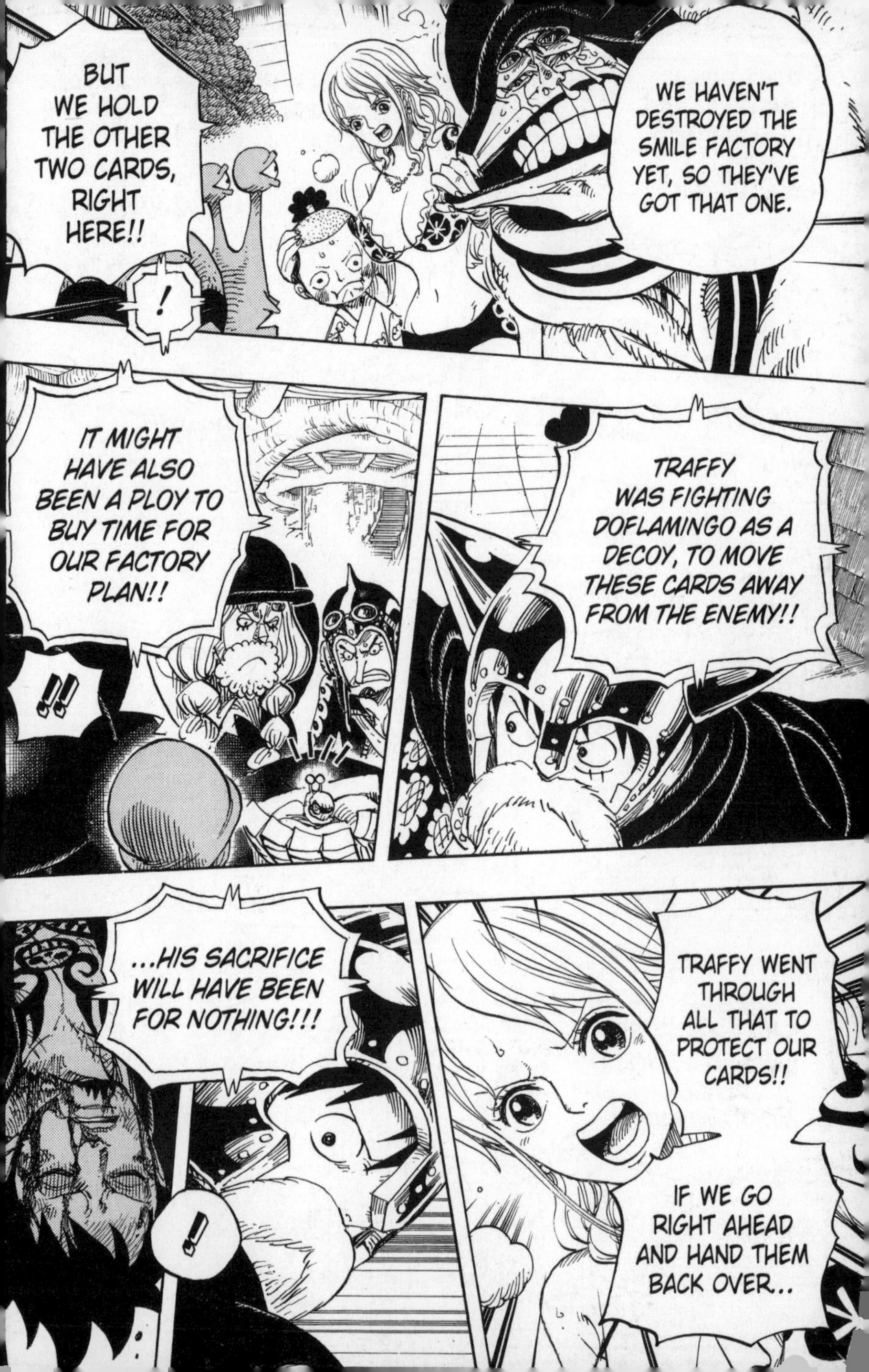
WE HAVEN'T DESTROYED THE SMILE FACTORY YET, SO THEY'VE GOT THAT ONE.
BUT WE HOLD THE OTHER TWO CARDS, RIGHT HERE!!
!
TRAFFY WAS FIGHTING DOFLAMINGO AS A DECOY, TO MOVE THESE CARDS AWAY FROM THE ENEMY!!
IT MIGHT HAVE ALSO BEEN A PLOY TO BUY TIME FOR OUR FACTORY PLAN!!
!!
TRAFFY WENT THROUGH ALL THAT TO PROTECT OUR CARDS!!
IF WE GO RIGHT AHEAD AND HAND THEM BACK OVER...
...HIS SACRIFICE WILL HAVE BEEN FOR NOTHING!!!
!

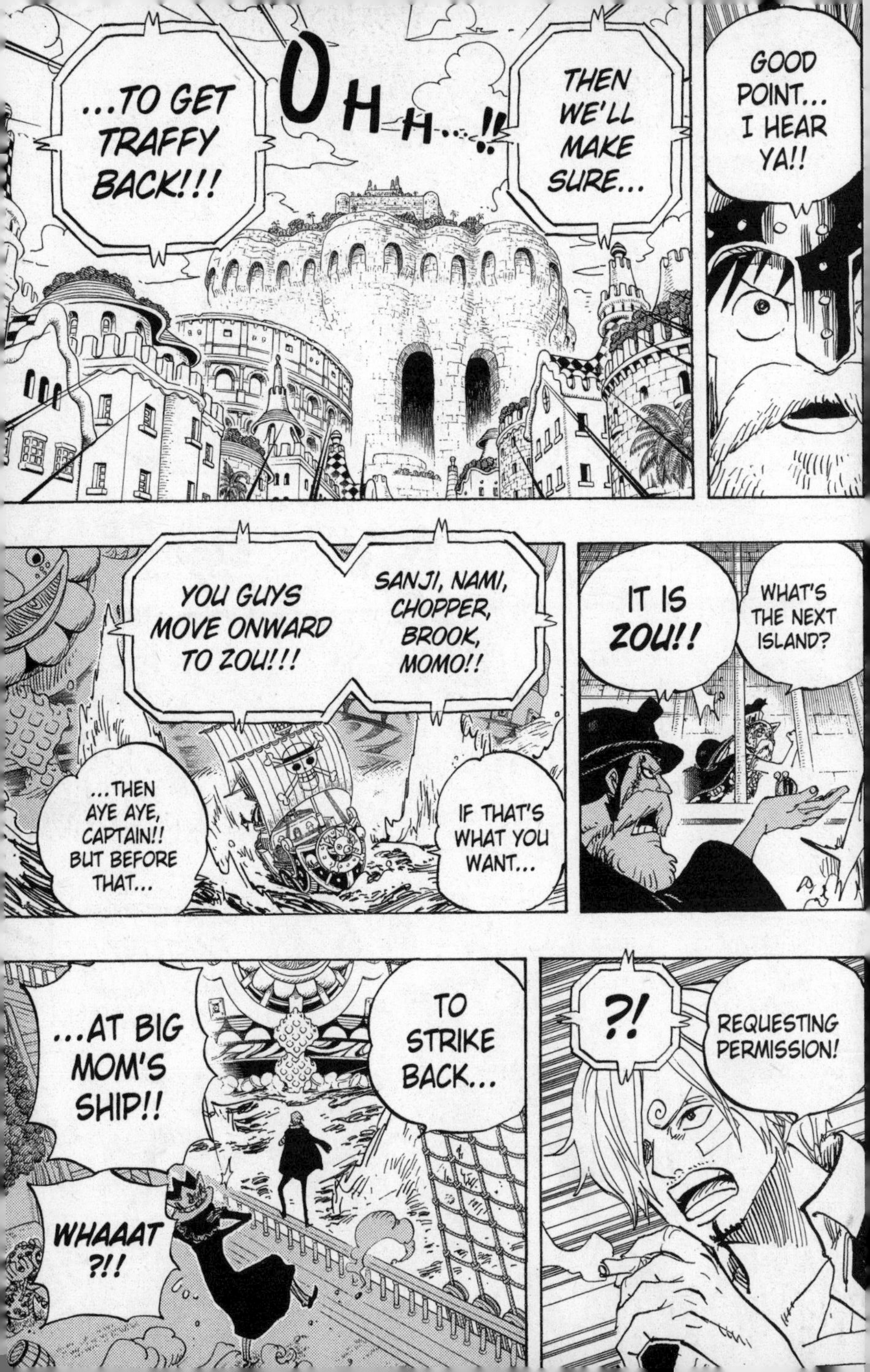
GOOD POINT... I HEAR YA!!
THEN WE'LL MAKE SURE...
OHH...!!
...TO GET TRAFFY BACK!!!
WHAT'S THE NEXT ISLAND?
IT IS ZOU!!
SANJI, NAMI, CHOPPER, BROOK, MOMO!!
YOU GUYS MOVE ONWARD TO ZOU!!!
IF THAT'S WHAT YOU WANT...
...THEN AYE AYE, CAPTAIN!! BUT BEFORE THAT...
REQUESTING PERMISSION!
?!
TO STRIKE BACK...
...AT BIG MOM'S SHIP!!
WHAAAT ?!!

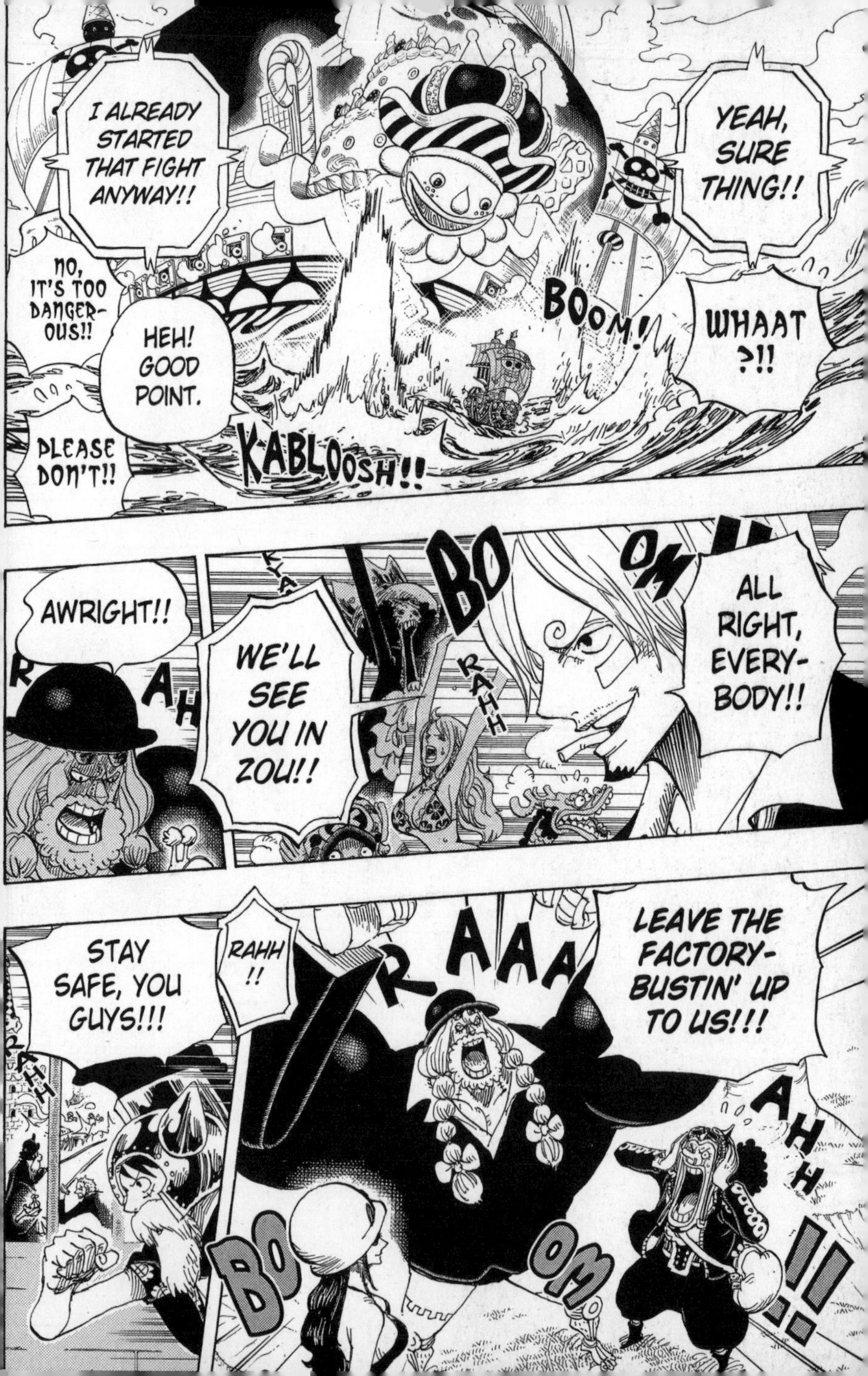
YEAH, SURE THING!!
I ALREADY STARTED THAT FIGHT ANYWAY!!
BOOM!
WHAAT ?!!
NO, IT'S TOO DANGER-OUS!!
HEH! GOOD POINT.
KABLOOSH!!
PLEASE DON'T!!
BOOM!!
ALL RIGHT, EVERY-BODY!!
RAHH
WE'LL SEE YOU IN ZOU!!
AWRIGHT!!
RAH
LEAVE THE FACTORY-BUSTIN' UP TO US!!!
RAAA
RAHH !!
STAY SAFE, YOU GUYS!!!
AHHH
RAHH
BOOM!!

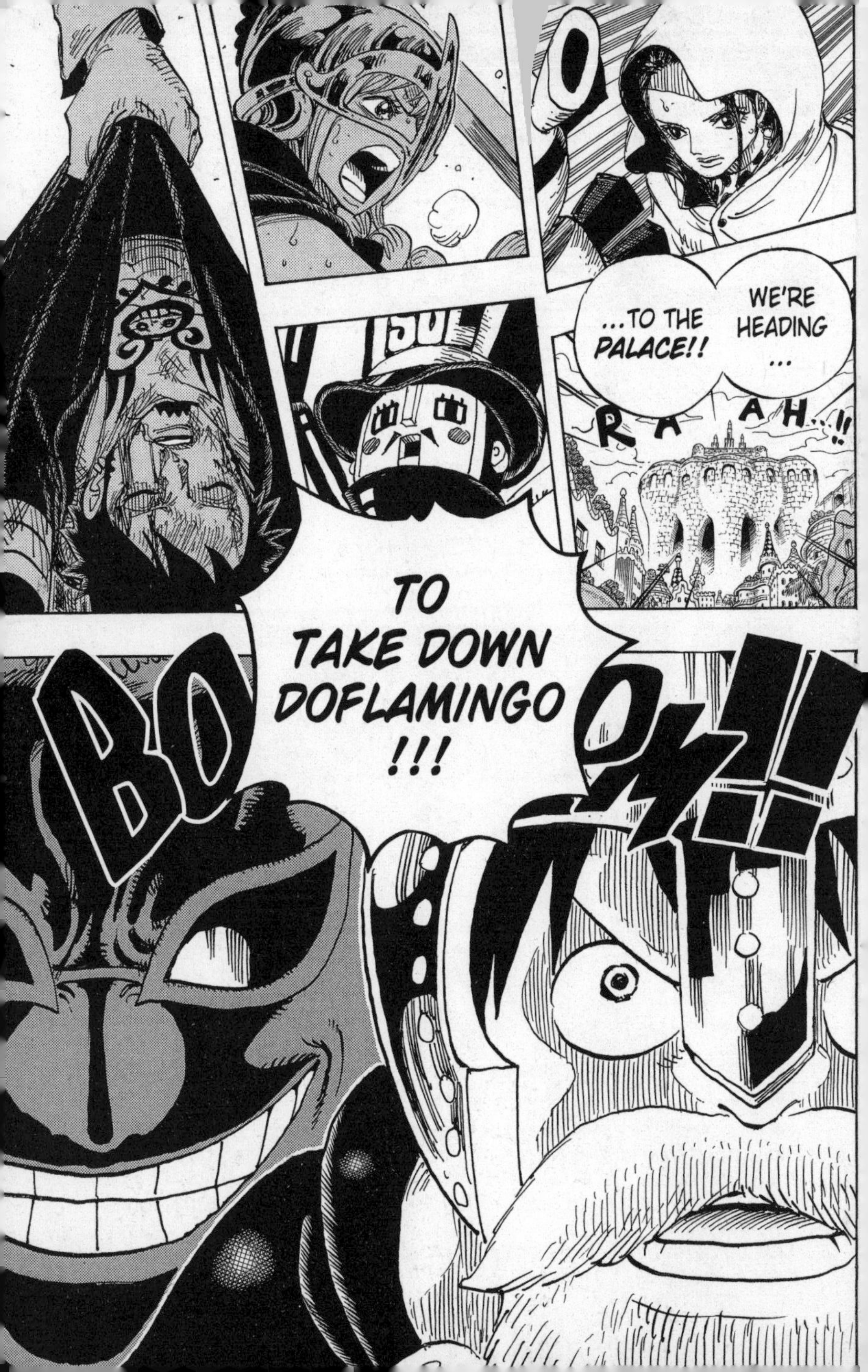
WE'RE HEADING ...
...TO THE PALACE!!
RAAH..!!
TO TAKE DOWN DOFLAMINGO !!!
BOOM!!

質問コーナー
エス
ビー
エス

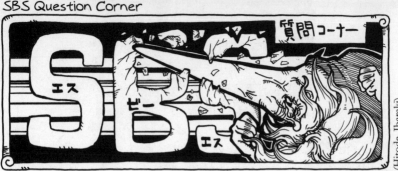

(Hitode, Ibaraki)

Q: It's nice to make your acquaintance, Oda Sensei. First of all, "You're a naughty big person!" Secondly, those little Tontattas are so gosh-darn cute. I want to know as many names and positions as possible. Please (x100) tell me.
If you don't, I godda rip off all yoh clothes!
--Beautiful Lady Swordsman Carrying Meat

A: Huh? But I'm already naked... Okay! Here you go! Some of them haven't really been drawn clearly yet, so they only get design sketches.

Head Tonta
Gancho
Tonta Captain
Leo
Vice Captains
Bomba
Rampo
Aerial Squads
Cub
Bian
Flapper
Bobomba
(Bomba's Bro)
Mousey
Nubon
Pellini
Grabba
(Leo's Gramma)
Inhel
Recon Team
Cotton
Wicka
Baxcon
Daikon

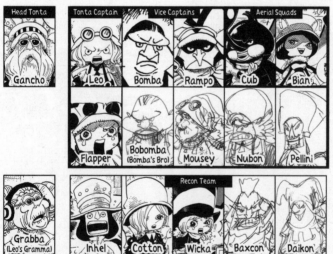

Not remembering their names won't affect your ability to understand the story. If I don't make a character's name clear enough through the story, it's not that important of a name to begin with. This answer ate up a whole page though!
Well, it's time. That's another SBS in the can! See you next volume!!

Chapter 731:
OPERATION DRESSROSA S.O.P.

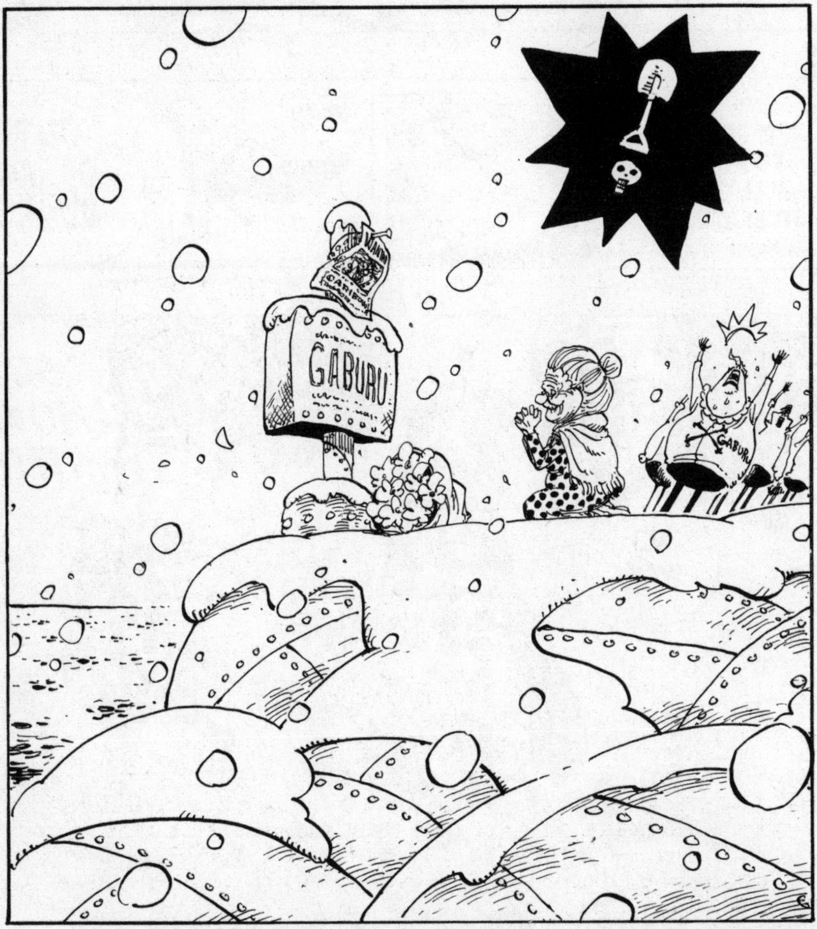
GABURU

CARIBOU'S NEW WORLD KEE HEE HEE, FINAL VOLUME:
"THANK YOU CARIBOU THE PIRATE, JUST AS SWEET AS MY REAL GRANDSON"

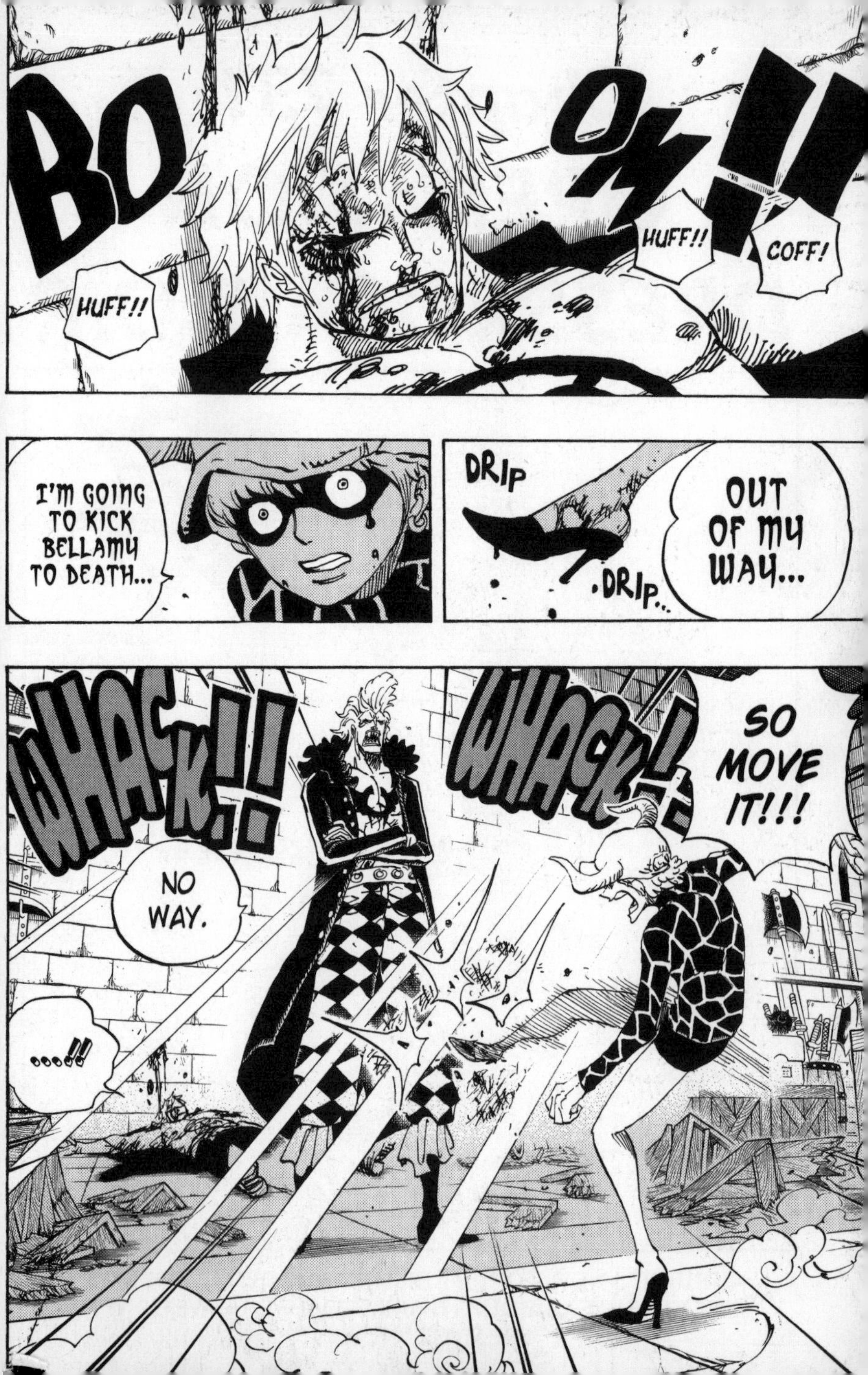
BOOM!!
COFF!
HUFF!!
HUFF!!
DRIP
OUT OF MY WAY...
DRIP...
I'M GOING TO KICK BELLAMY TO DEATH...
SO MOVE IT!!!
WHACK!!
WHACK!!
NO WAY.
....!!

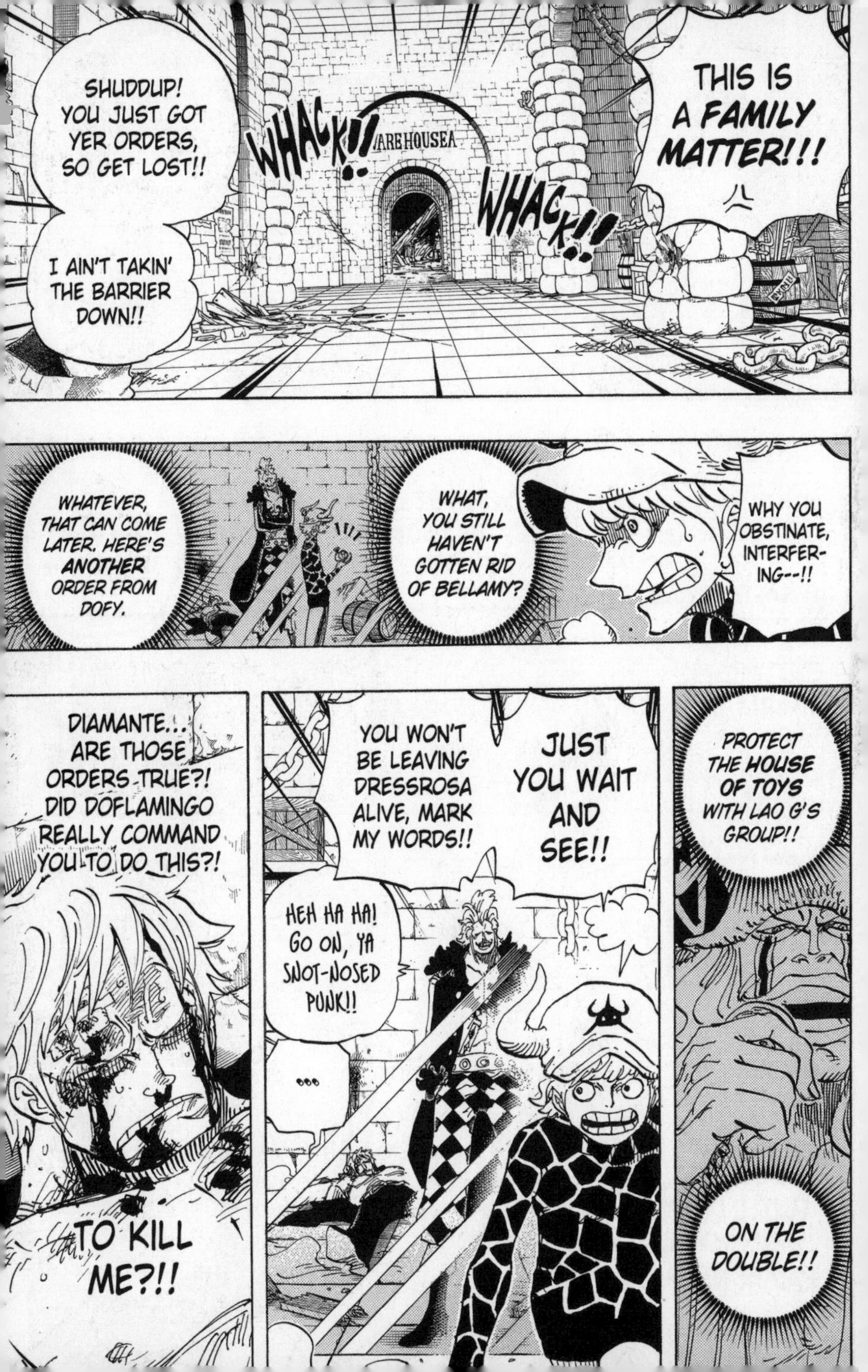
THIS IS A FAMILY MATTER!!!
WHACK!!
WHACK!!
SHUDDUP! YOU JUST GOT YER ORDERS, SO GET LOST!!
I AIN'T TAKIN' THE BARRIER DOWN!!
WHY YOU OBSTINATE, INTERFER-ING--!!
WHAT, YOU STILL HAVEN'T GOTTEN RID OF BELLAMY?
WHATEVER, THAT CAN COME LATER. HERE'S ANOTHER ORDER FROM DOFY.
PROTECT THE HOUSE OF TOYS WITH LAO G'S GROUP!!
ON THE DOUBLE!!
JUST YOU WAIT AND SEE!!
YOU WON'T BE LEAVING DRESSROSA ALIVE, MARK MY WORDS!!
HEH HA HA! GO ON, YA SNOT-NOSED PUNK!!
...
DIAMANTE... ARE THOSE ORDERS TRUE?! DID DOFLAMINGO REALLY COMMAND YOU TO DO THIS?!
TO KILL ME?!!

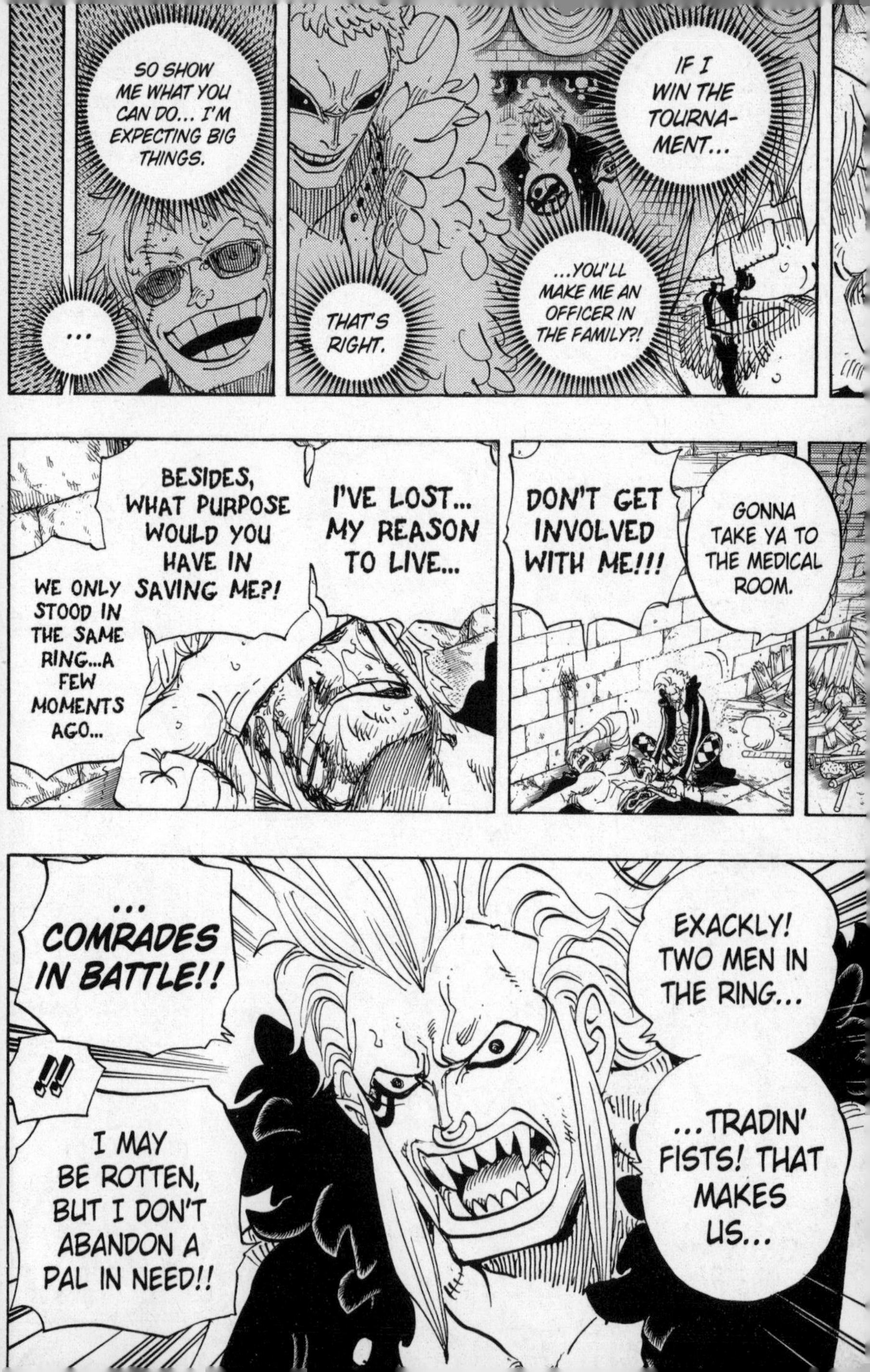
IF I WIN THE TOURNAMENT...
...YOU'LL MAKE ME AN OFFICER IN THE FAMILY?!
THAT'S RIGHT.
SO SHOW ME WHAT YOU CAN DO... I'M EXPECTING BIG THINGS.
...
GONNA TAKE YA TO THE MEDICAL ROOM.
DON'T GET INVOLVED WITH ME!!!
I'VE LOST... MY REASON TO LIVE...
BESIDES, WHAT PURPOSE WOULD YOU HAVE IN SAVING ME?!
WE ONLY STOOD IN THE SAME RING...A FEW MOMENTS AGO...
EXACKLY! TWO MEN IN THE RING...
...TRADIN' FISTS! THAT MAKES US...
...COMRADES IN BATTLE!!
!!
I MAY BE ROTTEN, BUT I DON'T ABANDON A PAL IN NEED!!

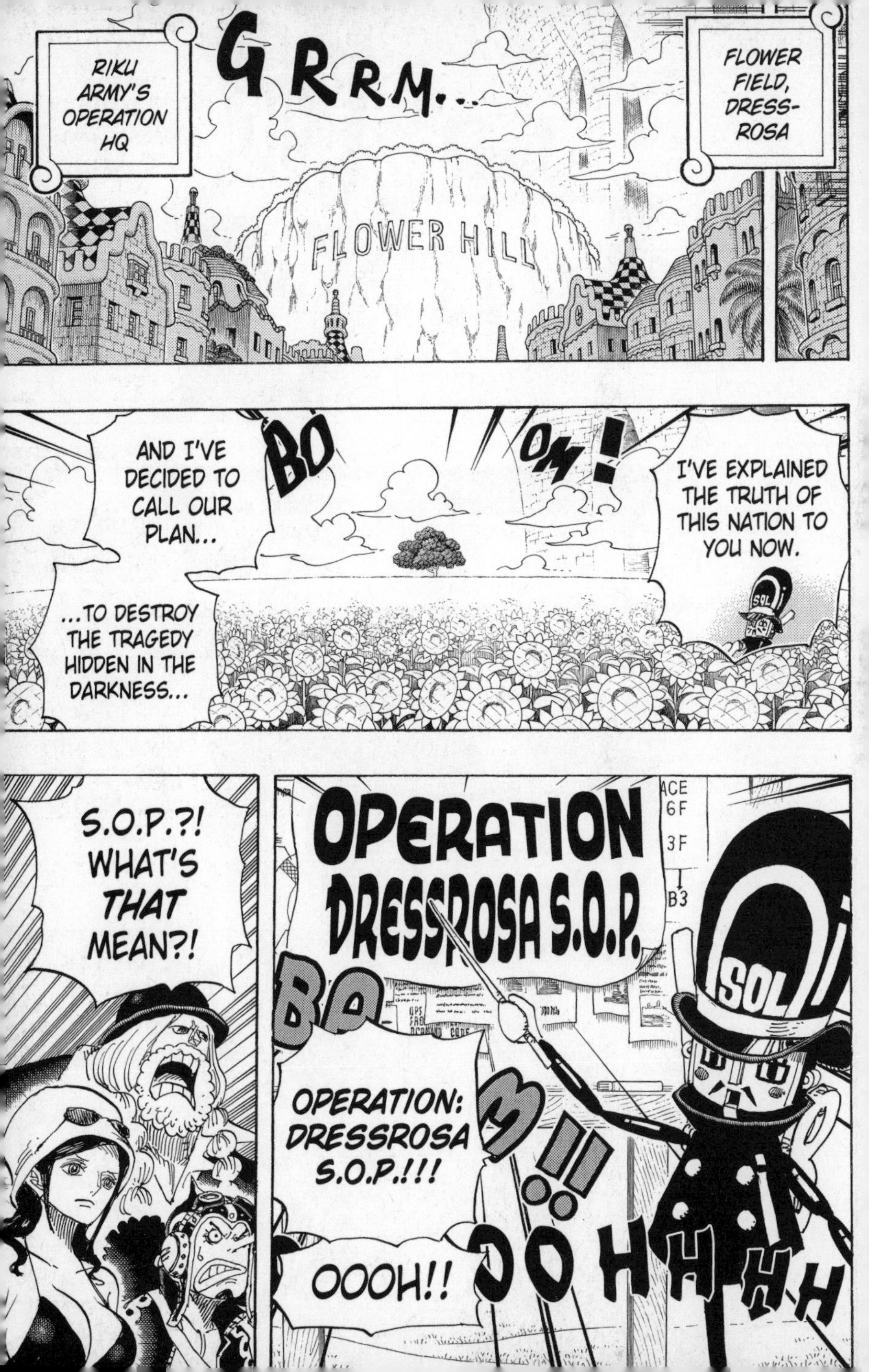
FLOWER FIELD, DRESS-ROSA
RIKU ARMY'S OPERATION HQ
GRRM...
FLOWER HILL
I'VE EXPLAINED THE TRUTH OF THIS NATION TO YOU NOW.
BOOM!
AND I'VE DECIDED TO CALL OUR PLAN...
...TO DESTROY THE TRAGEDY HIDDEN IN THE DARKNESS...
ACE
6F
3F
B3
OPERATION DRESSROSA S.O.P.
BOOM!!
OPERATION: DRESSROSA S.O.P.!!!
OOOHHHHH
OOOH!!
S.O.P.?! WHAT'S *THAT* MEAN?!

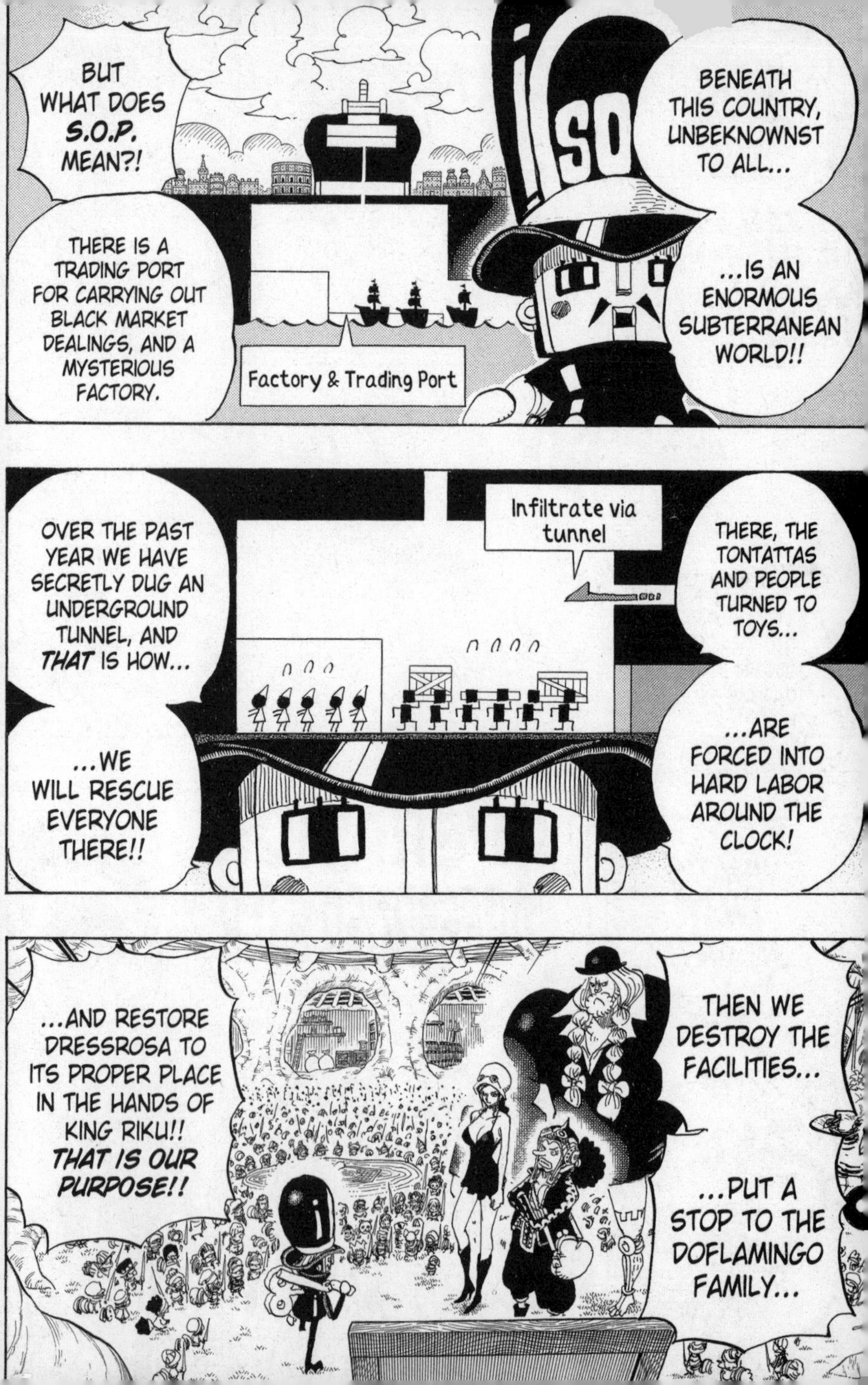

BUT WHAT DOES S.O.P. MEAN?!
BENEATH THIS COUNTRY, UNBEKNOWNST TO ALL...
...IS AN ENORMOUS SUBTERRANEAN WORLD!!
THERE IS A TRADING PORT FOR CARRYING OUT BLACK MARKET DEALINGS, AND A MYSTERIOUS FACTORY.
Factory & Trading Port
THERE, THE TONTATTAS AND PEOPLE TURNED TO TOYS...
...ARE FORCED INTO HARD LABOR AROUND THE CLOCK!
Infiltrate via tunnel
OVER THE PAST YEAR WE HAVE SECRETLY DUG AN UNDERGROUND TUNNEL, AND *THAT* IS HOW...
...WE WILL RESCUE EVERYONE THERE!!
THEN WE DESTROY THE FACILITIES...
...PUT A STOP TO THE DOFLAMINGO FAMILY...
...AND RESTORE DRESSROSA TO ITS PROPER PLACE IN THE HANDS OF KING RIKU!! ***THAT IS OUR PURPOSE!!***

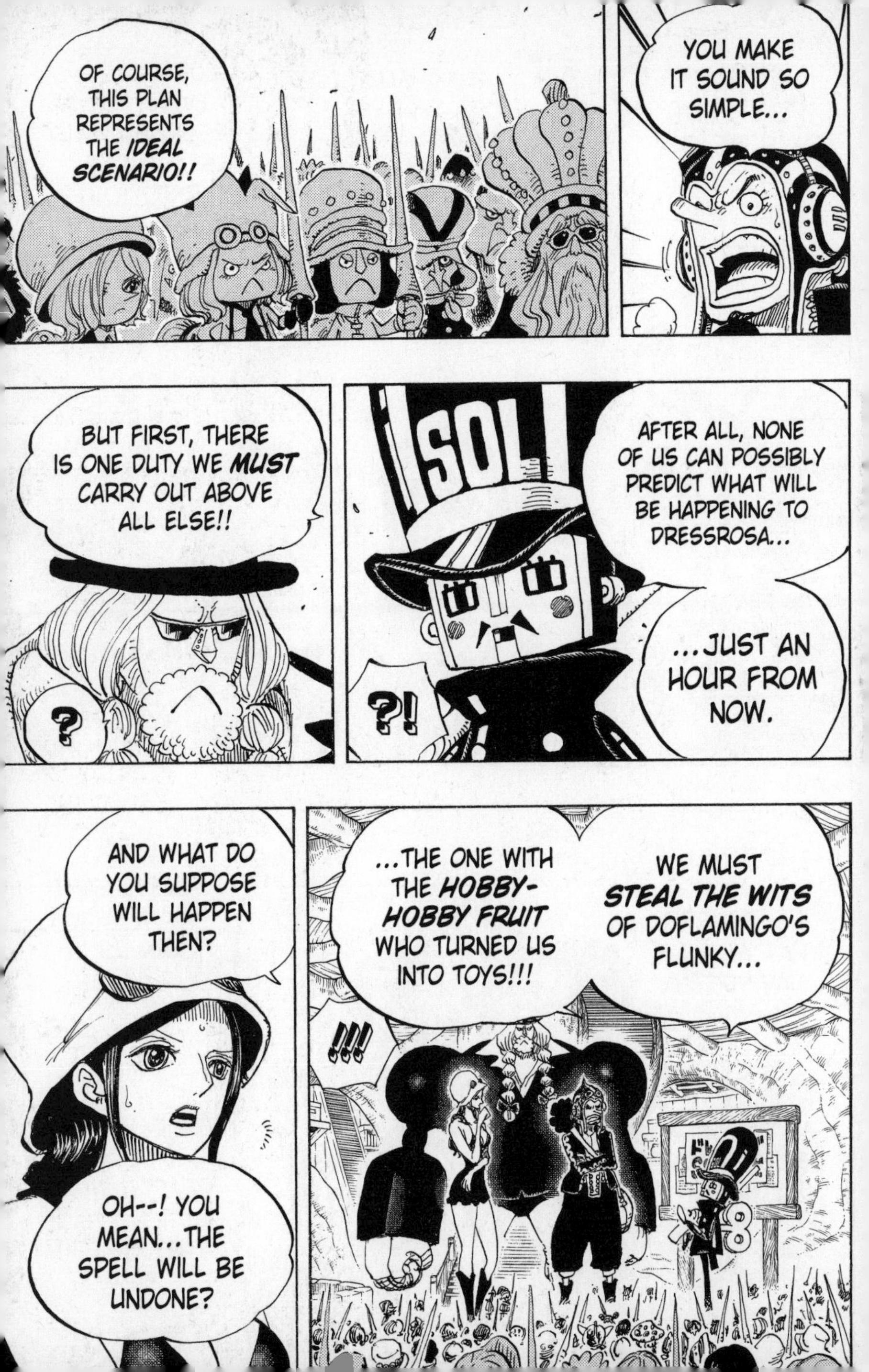
YOU MAKE IT SOUND SO SIMPLE...
OF COURSE, THIS PLAN REPRESENTS THE *IDEAL SCENARIO!!*
AFTER ALL, NONE OF US CAN POSSIBLY PREDICT WHAT WILL BE HAPPENING TO DRESSROSA...
...JUST AN HOUR FROM NOW.
?!
BUT FIRST, THERE IS ONE DUTY WE *MUST* CARRY OUT ABOVE ALL ELSE!!
?
WE MUST *STEAL THE WITS* OF DOFLAMINGO'S FLUNKY...
...THE ONE WITH THE *HOBBY-HOBBY FRUIT* WHO TURNED US INTO TOYS!!!
!!!
AND WHAT DO YOU SUPPOSE WILL HAPPEN THEN?
OH--! YOU MEAN...THE SPELL WILL BE UNDONE?

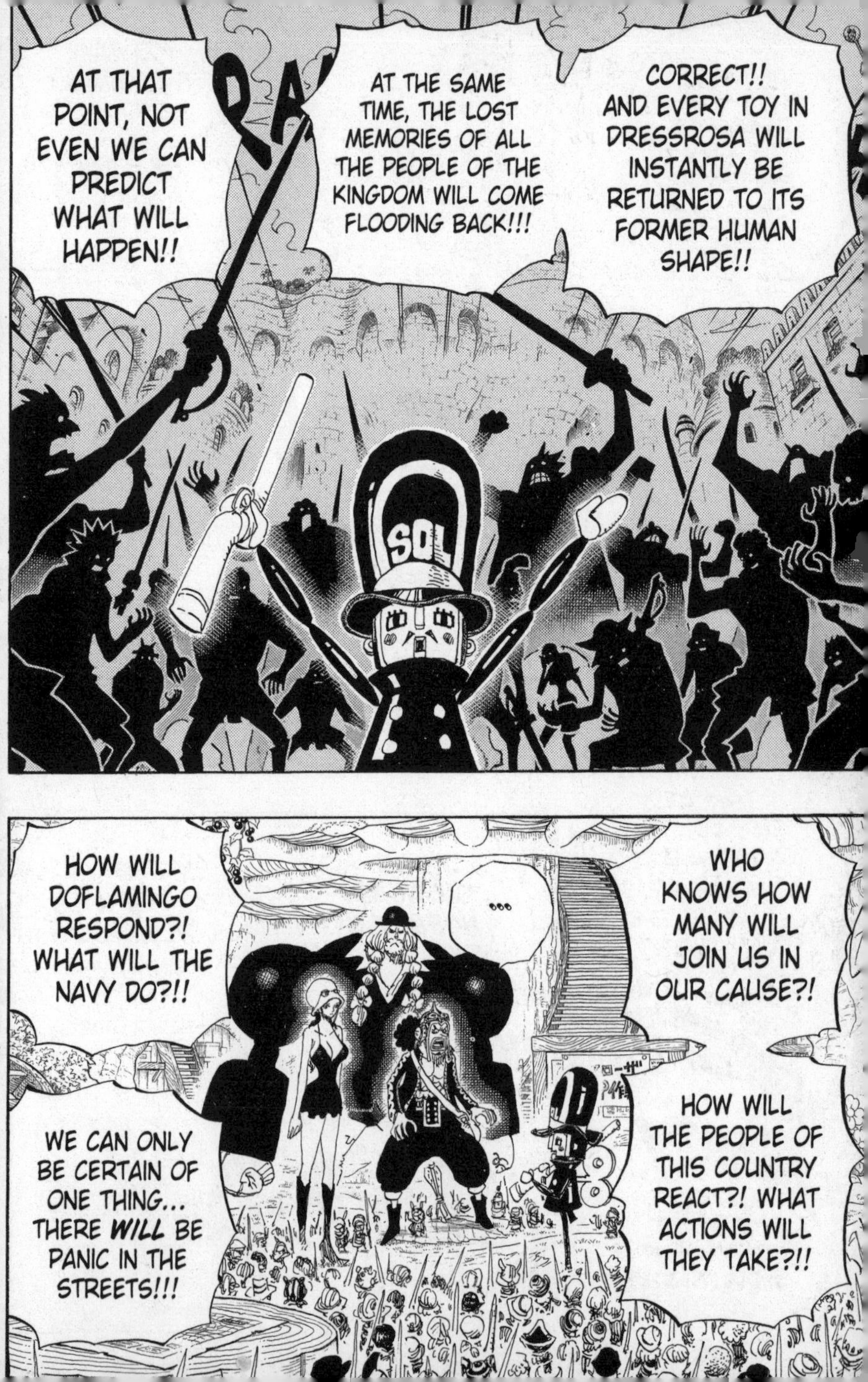
CORRECT!! AND EVERY TOY IN DRESSROSA WILL INSTANTLY BE RETURNED TO ITS FORMER HUMAN SHAPE!!
AT THE SAME TIME, THE LOST MEMORIES OF ALL THE PEOPLE OF THE KINGDOM WILL COME FLOODING BACK!!!
AT THAT POINT, NOT EVEN WE CAN PREDICT WHAT WILL HAPPEN!!
SOL
WHO KNOWS HOW MANY WILL JOIN US IN OUR CAUSE?!
...
HOW WILL DOFLAMINGO RESPOND?! WHAT WILL THE NAVY DO?!!
HOW WILL THE PEOPLE OF THIS COUNTRY REACT?! WHAT ACTIONS WILL THEY TAKE?!!
WE CAN ONLY BE CERTAIN OF ONE THING... THERE *WILL* BE PANIC IN THE STREETS!!!

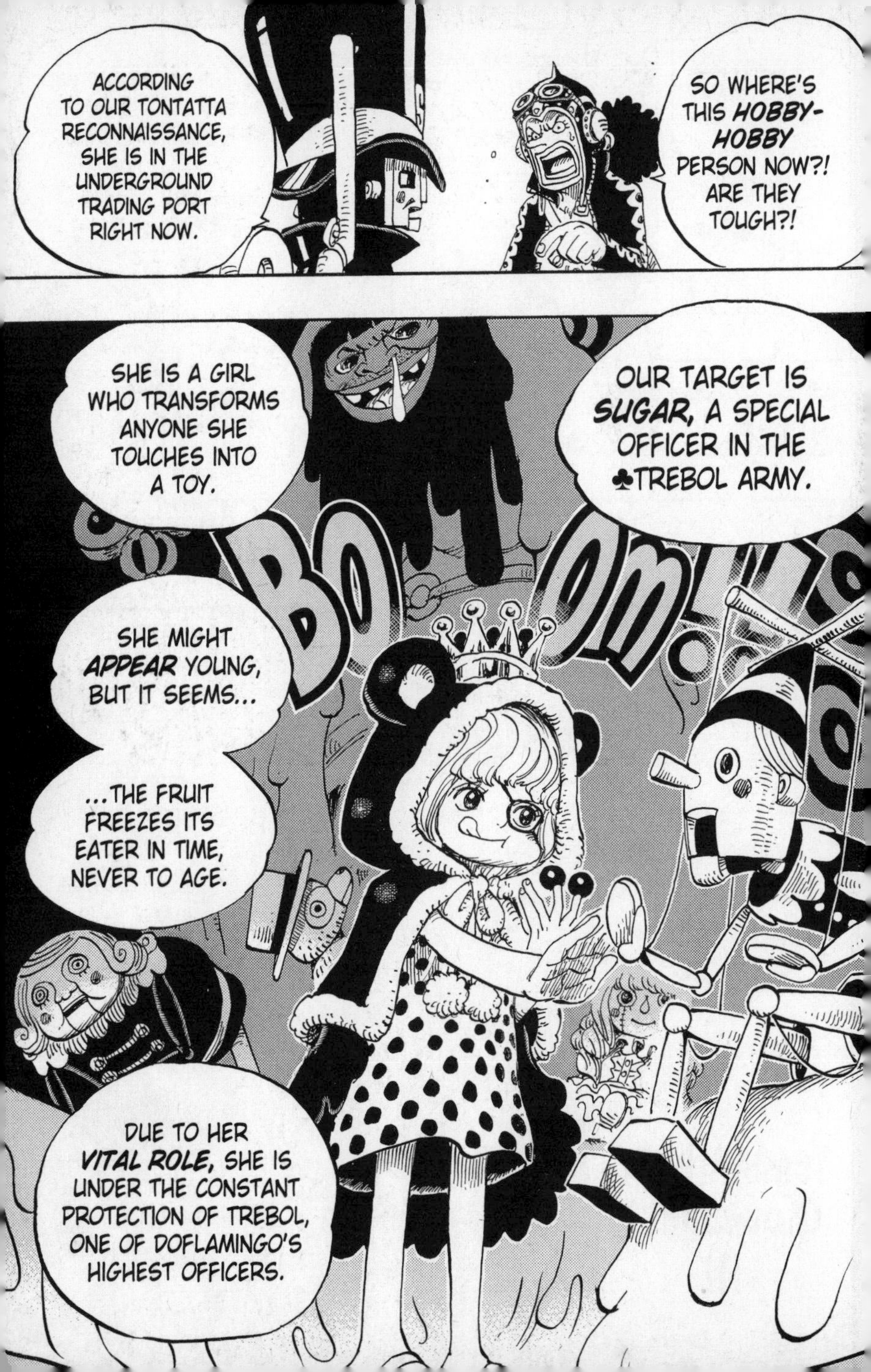
SO WHERE'S THIS *HOBBY-HOBBY* PERSON NOW?! ARE THEY TOUGH?!
ACCORDING TO OUR TONTATTA RECONNAISSANCE, SHE IS IN THE UNDERGROUND TRADING PORT RIGHT NOW.
OUR TARGET IS *SUGAR,* A SPECIAL OFFICER IN THE ♣TREBOL ARMY.
SHE IS A GIRL WHO TRANSFORMS ANYONE SHE TOUCHES INTO A TOY.
BOOM
SHE MIGHT *APPEAR* YOUNG, BUT IT SEEMS...
...THE FRUIT FREEZES ITS EATER IN TIME, NEVER TO AGE.
DUE TO HER *VITAL ROLE,* SHE IS UNDER THE CONSTANT PROTECTION OF TREBOL, ONE OF DOFLAMINGO'S HIGHEST OFFICERS.

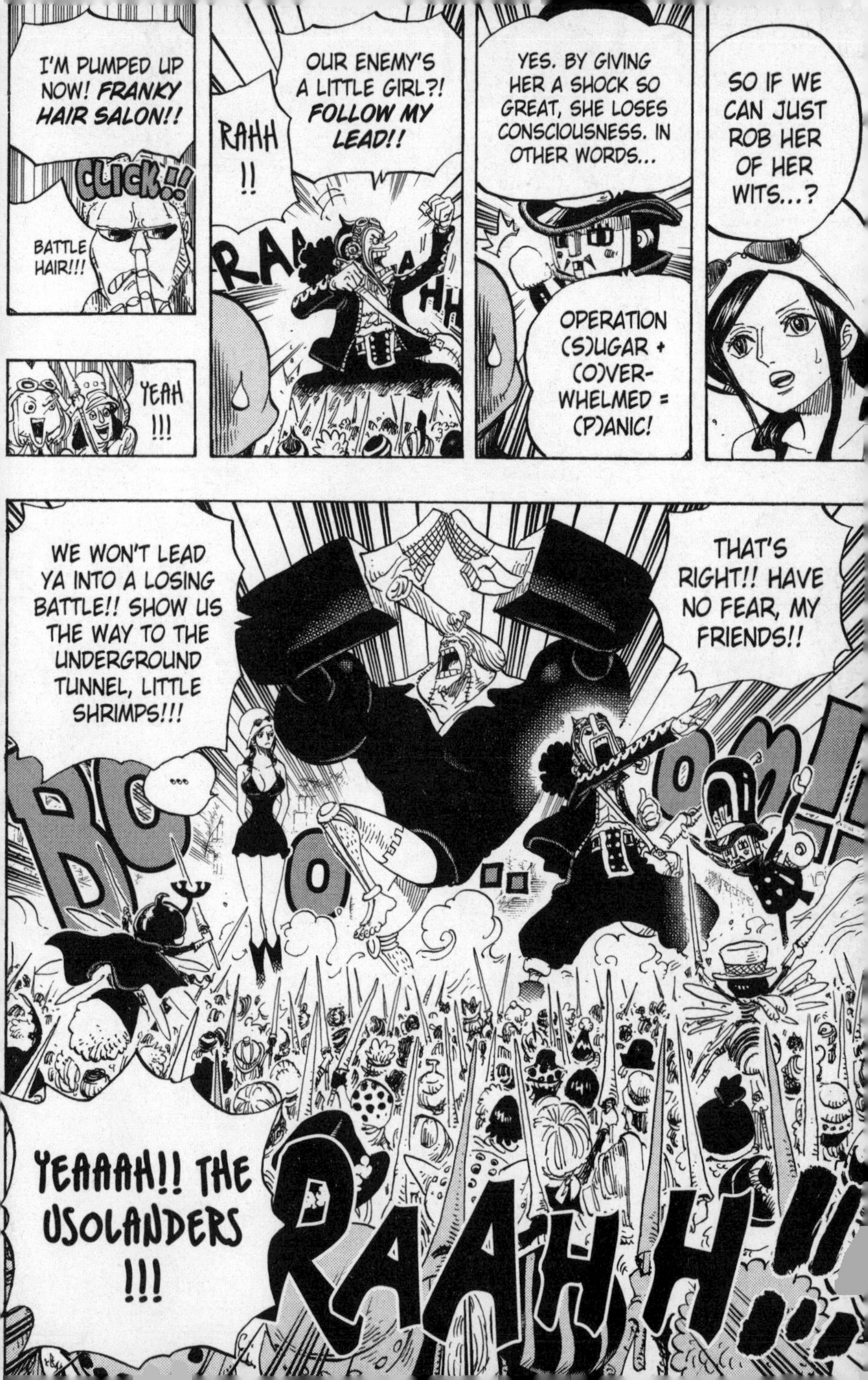
SO IF WE CAN JUST ROB HER OF HER WITS...?
YES. BY GIVING HER A SHOCK SO GREAT, SHE LOSES CONSCIOUSNESS. IN OTHER WORDS...
OPERATION (S)UGAR + (O)VER-WHELMED = (P)ANIC!
OUR ENEMY'S A LITTLE GIRL?! ***FOLLOW MY LEAD!!***
RAHH !!
I'M PUMPED UP NOW! ***FRANKY HAIR SALON!!***
CLICK!!
BATTLE HAIR!!!
YEAH !!!
THAT'S RIGHT!! HAVE NO FEAR, MY FRIENDS!!
WE WON'T LEAD YA INTO A LOSING BATTLE!! SHOW US THE WAY TO THE UNDERGROUND TUNNEL, LITTLE SHRIMPS!!!
...
YEAAAH!! THE USOLANDERS !!!
RAAHH!!

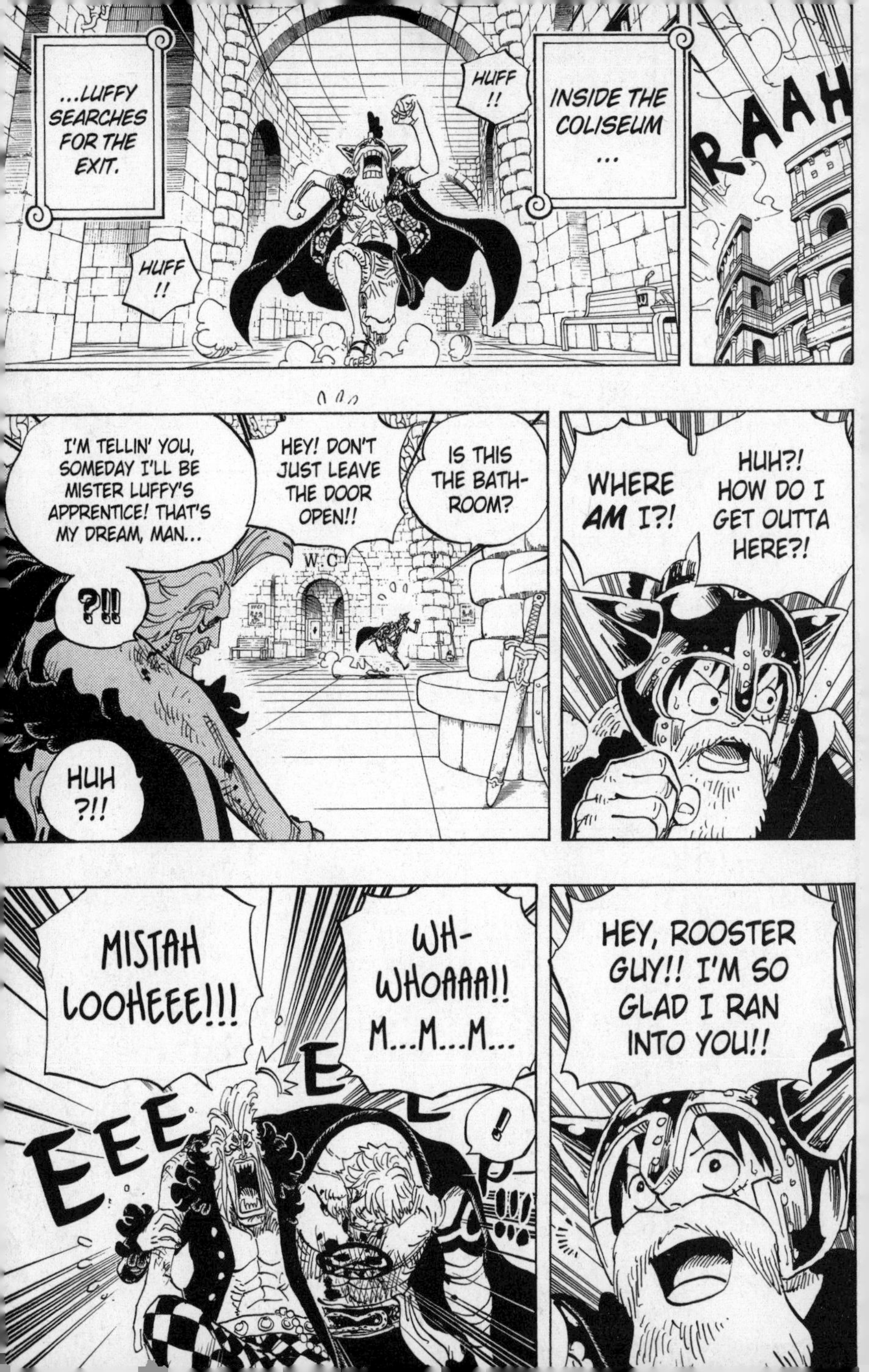
RAAH
INSIDE THE COLISEUM ...
HUFF !!
...LUFFY SEARCHES FOR THE EXIT.
HUFF !!
HUH?! HOW DO I GET OUTTA HERE?!
WHERE AM I?!
IS THIS THE BATH-ROOM?
HEY! DON'T JUST LEAVE THE DOOR OPEN!!
W.C
I'M TELLIN' YOU, SOMEDAY I'LL BE MISTER LUFFY'S APPRENTICE! THAT'S MY DREAM, MAN...
?!!
HUH ?!!
HEY, ROOSTER GUY!! I'M SO GLAD I RAN INTO YOU!!
WH- WHOAAA!! M...M...M...
!
MISTAH LOOHEEE!!!
EEE
E

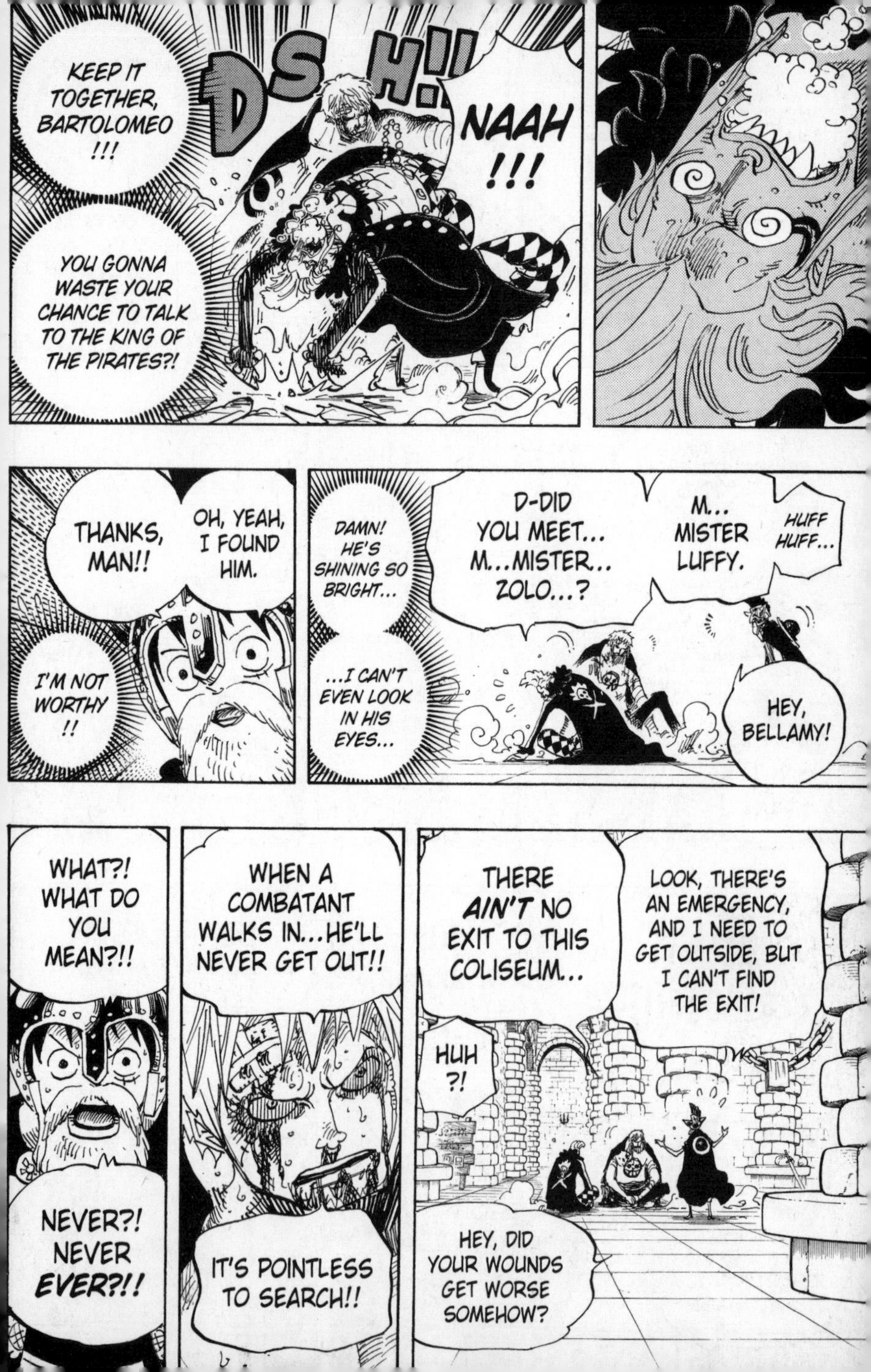

DSH!!
NAAH!!!
KEEP IT TOGETHER, BARTOLOMEO!!!
YOU GONNA WASTE YOUR CHANCE TO TALK TO THE KING OF THE PIRATES?!
HUFF HUFF...
M... MISTER LUFFY.
D-DID YOU MEET... M...MISTER... ZOLO...?
DAMN! HE'S SHINING SO BRIGHT...
HEY, BELLAMY!
...I CAN'T EVEN LOOK IN HIS EYES...
OH, YEAH, I FOUND HIM.
THANKS, MAN!!
I'M NOT WORTHY!!
LOOK, THERE'S AN EMERGENCY, AND I NEED TO GET OUTSIDE, BUT I CAN'T FIND THE EXIT!
THERE AIN'T NO EXIT TO THIS COLISEUM...
HUH?!
HEY, DID YOUR WOUNDS GET WORSE SOMEHOW?
WHEN A COMBATANT WALKS IN...HE'LL NEVER GET OUT!!
IT'S POINTLESS TO SEARCH!!
WHAT?! WHAT DO YOU MEAN?!!
NEVER?! NEVER EVER?!!

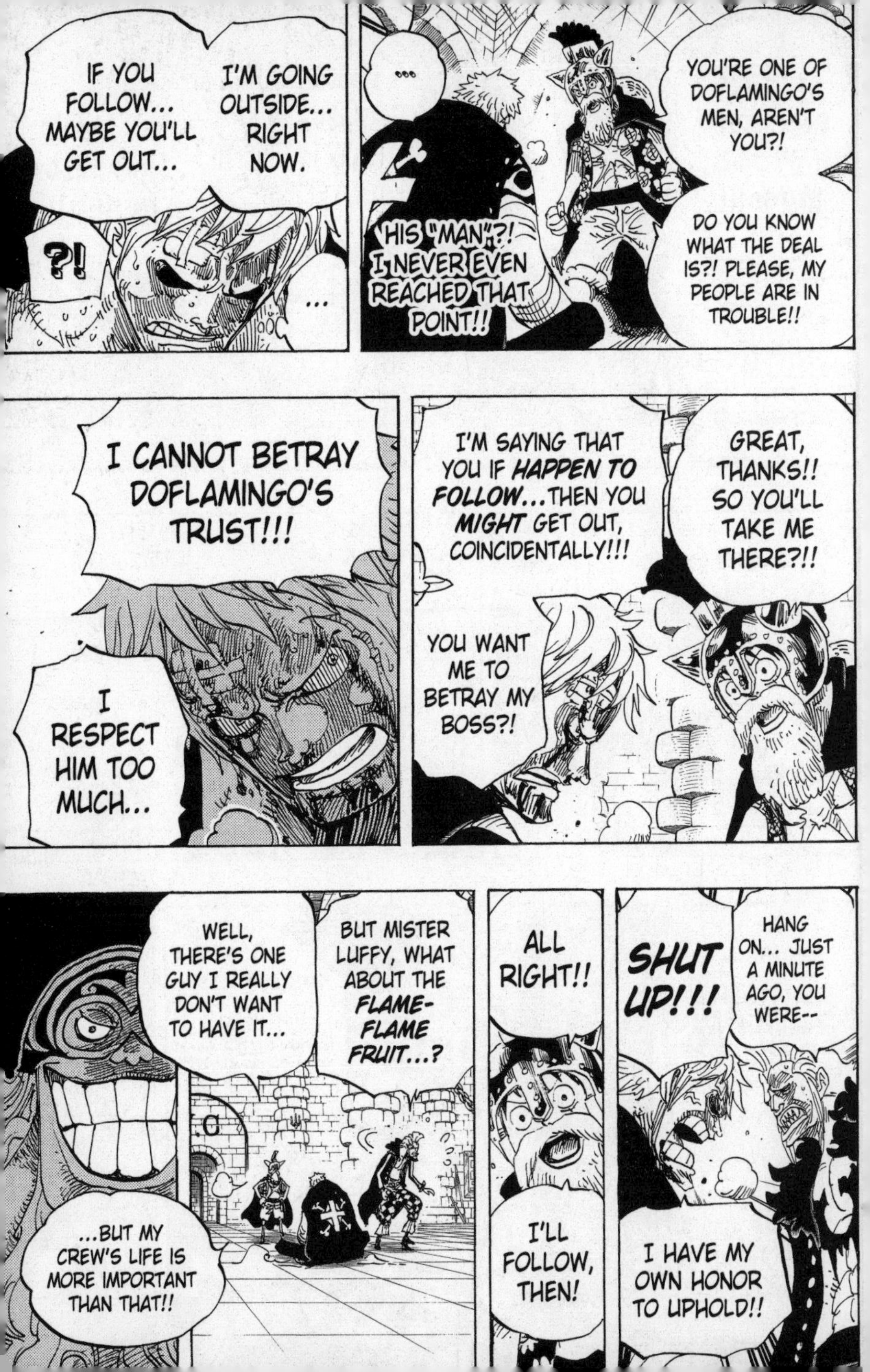
YOU'RE ONE OF DOFLAMINGO'S MEN, AREN'T YOU?!
...
DO YOU KNOW WHAT THE DEAL IS?! PLEASE, MY PEOPLE ARE IN TROUBLE!!
HIS "MAN"?! I NEVER EVEN REACHED THAT POINT!!
I'M GOING OUTSIDE... RIGHT NOW.
IF YOU FOLLOW... MAYBE YOU'LL GET OUT...
?!
...
GREAT, THANKS!! SO YOU'LL TAKE ME THERE?!!
I'M SAYING THAT YOU IF *HAPPEN TO FOLLOW*...THEN YOU *MIGHT* GET OUT, COINCIDENTALLY!!!
YOU WANT ME TO BETRAY MY BOSS?!
I CANNOT BETRAY DOFLAMINGO'S TRUST!!!
I RESPECT HIM TOO MUCH...
HANG ON... JUST A MINUTE AGO, YOU WERE--
SHUT UP!!!
I HAVE MY OWN HONOR TO UPHOLD!!
ALL RIGHT!!
I'LL FOLLOW, THEN!
BUT MISTER LUFFY, WHAT ABOUT THE *FLAME-FLAME FRUIT*...?
WELL, THERE'S ONE GUY I REALLY DON'T WANT TO HAVE IT...
...BUT MY CREW'S LIFE IS MORE IMPORTANT THAN THAT!!

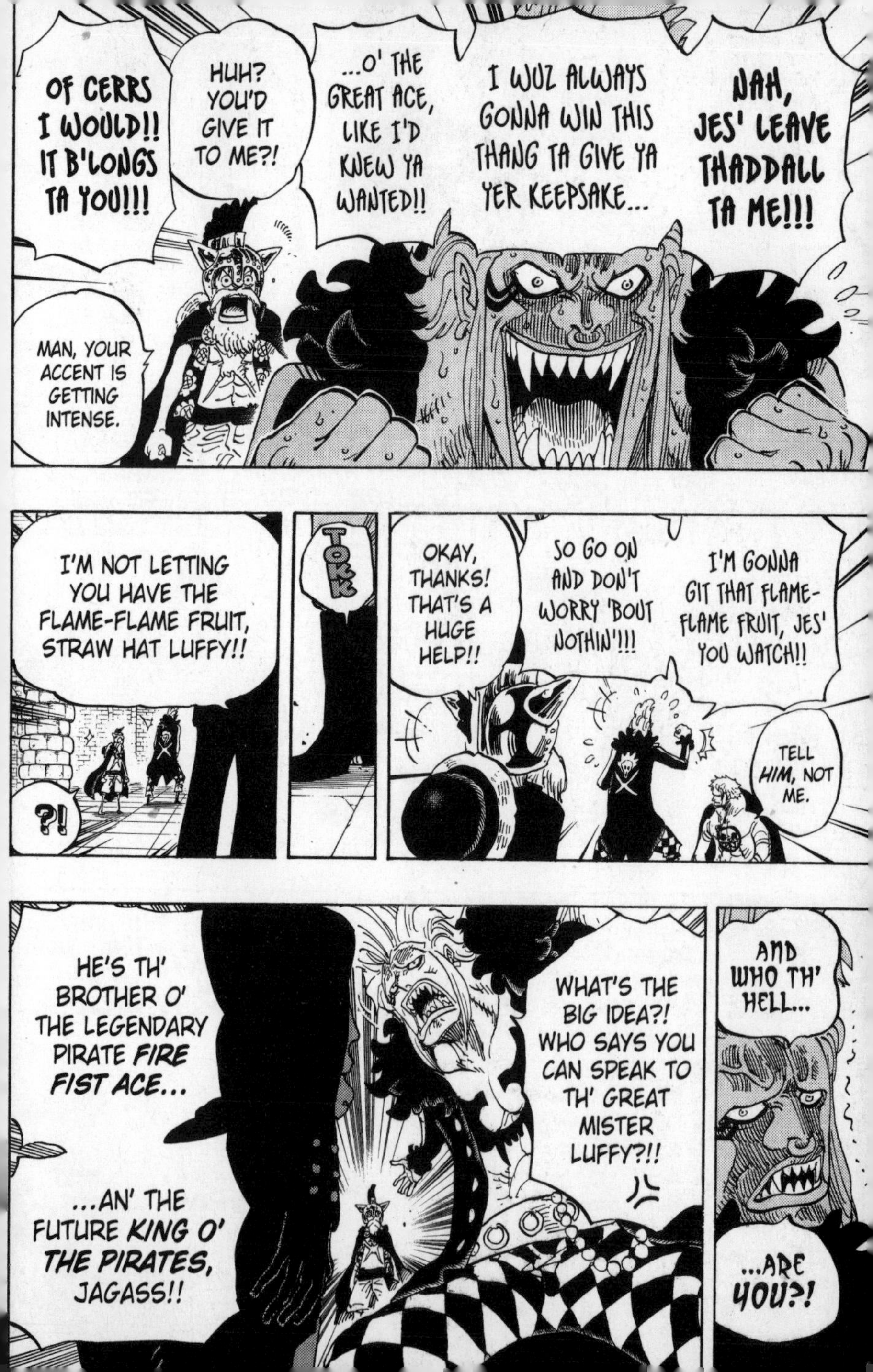
NAH, JES' LEAVE THADDALL TA ME!!!
I WUZ ALWAYS GONNA WIN THIS THANG TA GIVE YA YER KEEPSAKE...
...O' THE GREAT ACE, LIKE I'D KNEW YA WANTED!!
HUH? YOU'D GIVE IT TO ME?!
OF CERRS I WOULD!! IT B'LONGS TA YOU!!!
MAN, YOUR ACCENT IS GETTING INTENSE.
I'M GONNA GIT THAT FLAME-FLAME FRUIT, JES' YOU WATCH!!
SO GO ON AND DON'T WORRY 'BOUT NOTHIN'!!!
OKAY, THANKS! THAT'S A HUGE HELP!!
TELL HIM, NOT ME.
TOKK
I'M NOT LETTING YOU HAVE THE FLAME-FLAME FRUIT, STRAW HAT LUFFY!!
?!
AND WHO TH' HELL...
...ARE YOU?!
WHAT'S THE BIG IDEA?! WHO SAYS YOU CAN SPEAK TO TH' GREAT MISTER LUFFY?!!
HE'S TH' BROTHER O' THE LEGENDARY PIRATE FIRE FIST ACE...
...AN' THE FUTURE KING O' THE PIRATES, JAGASS!!

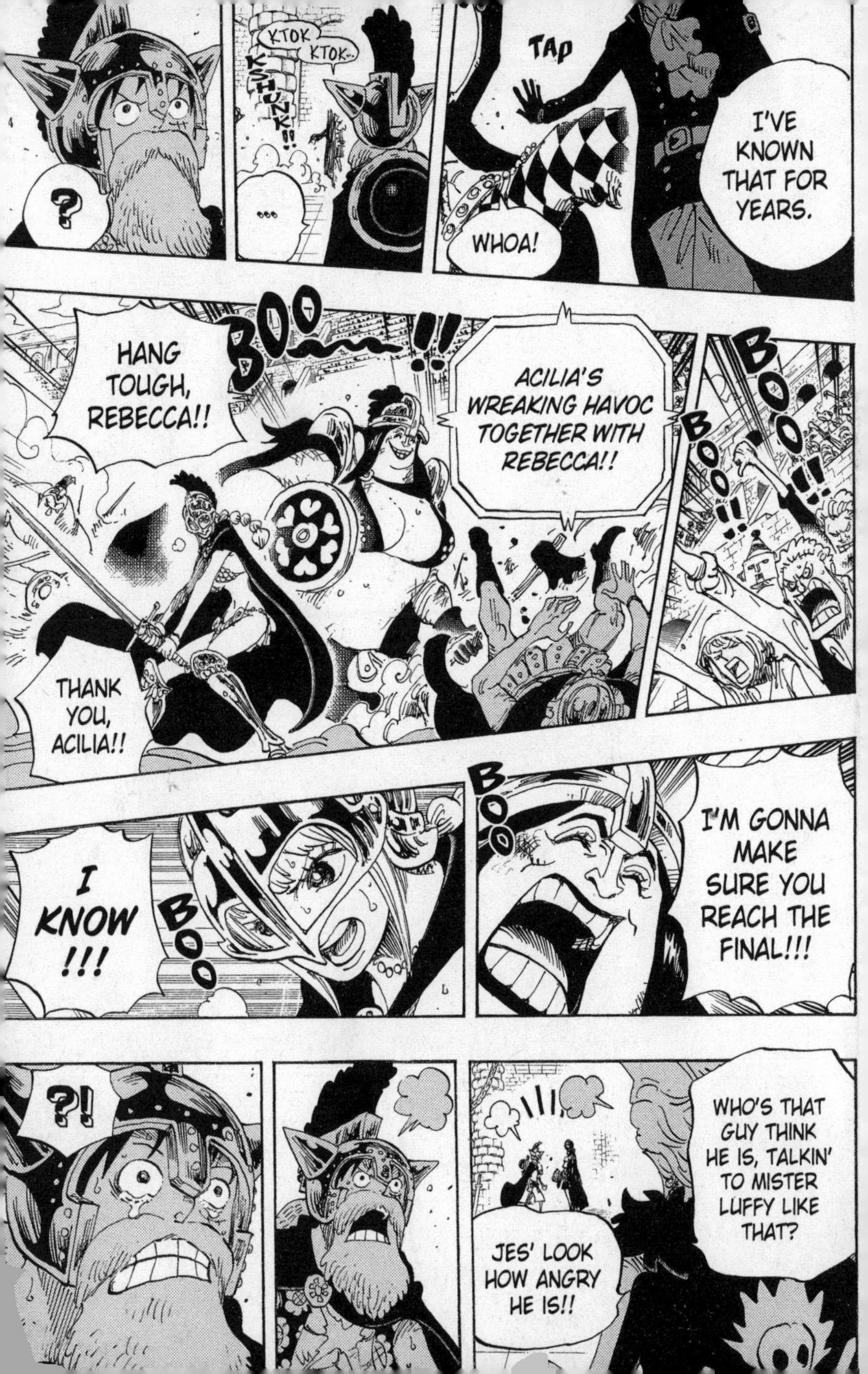
TAP
I'VE KNOWN THAT FOR YEARS.
WHOA!
KTOK KTOK..
KSHUNK!!
...
?
BOO!!
BOO!!
ACILIA'S WREAKING HAVOC TOGETHER WITH REBECCA!!
BOO!!
HANG TOUGH, REBECCA!!
THANK YOU, ACILIA!!
BOO
I'M GONNA MAKE SURE YOU REACH THE FINAL!!!
BOO
I KNOW!!!
WHO'S THAT GUY THINK HE IS, TALKIN' TO MISTER LUFFY LIKE THAT?
JES' LOOK HOW ANGRY HE IS!!
?!

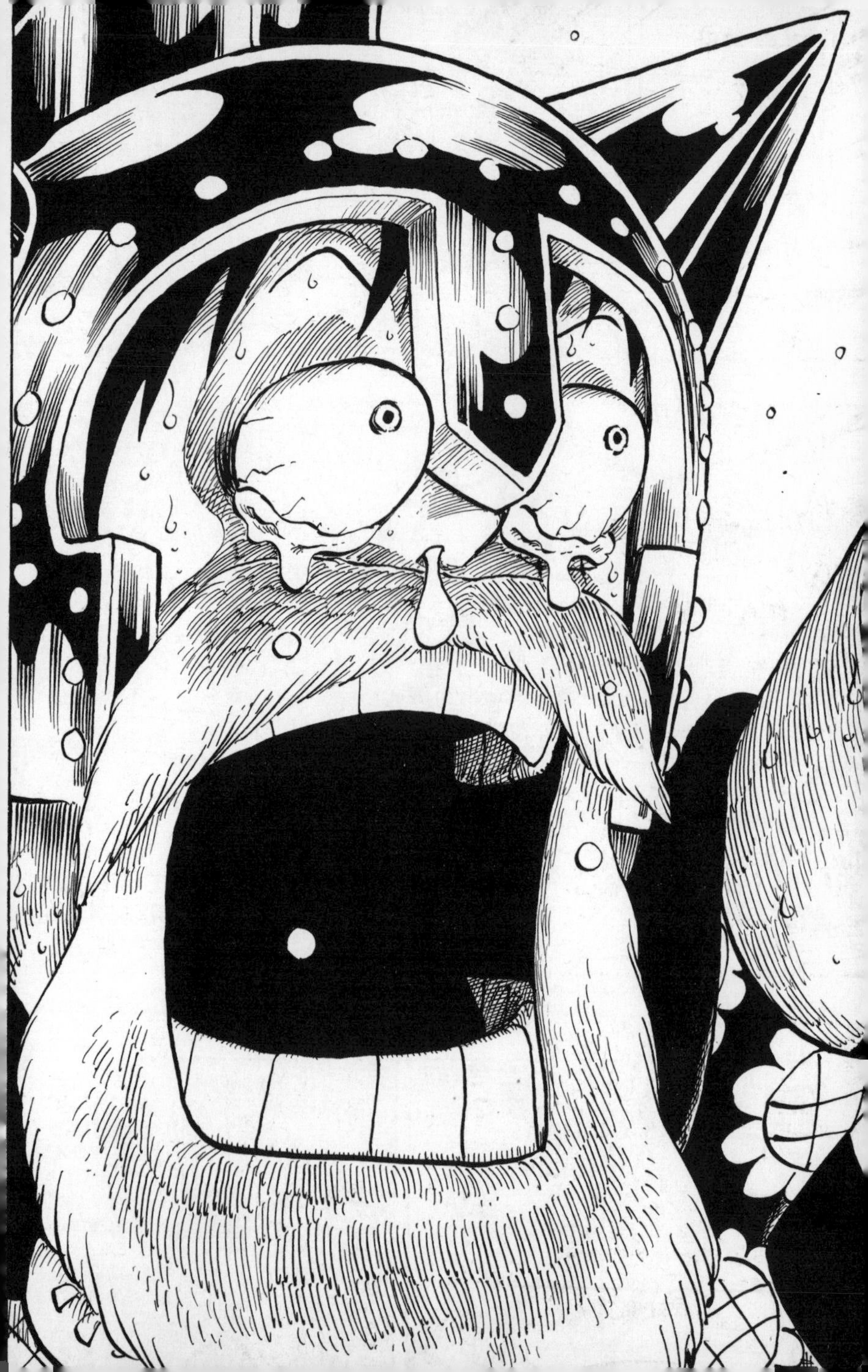

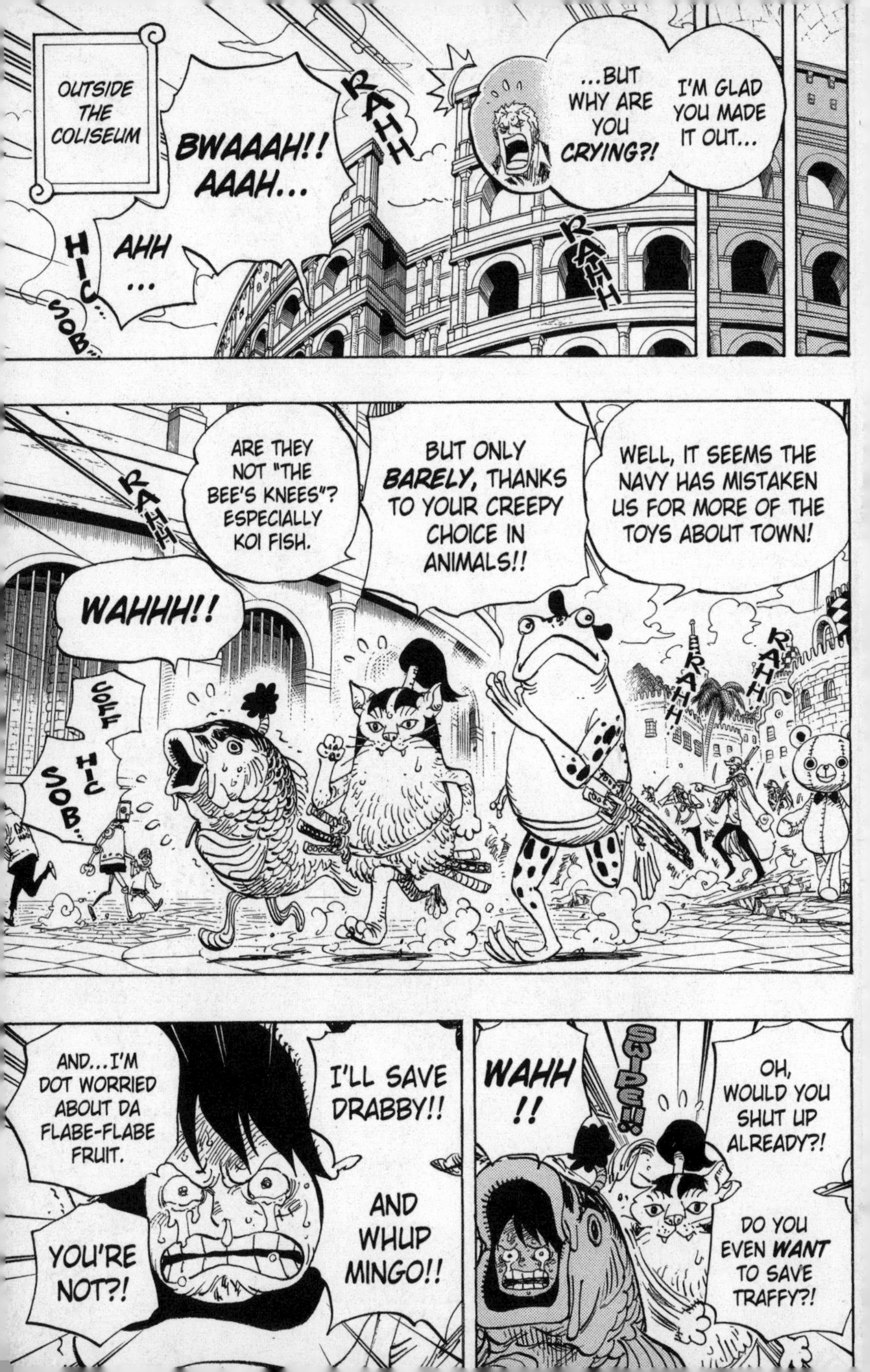

I'M GLAD YOU MADE IT OUT...
...BUT WHY ARE YOU CRYING?!
RAHH
BWAAAH!! AAAH...
OUTSIDE THE COLISEUM
RAHH
AHH...
HIC
SOB...
WELL, IT SEEMS THE NAVY HAS MISTAKEN US FOR MORE OF THE TOYS ABOUT TOWN!
RAHH
RAHH
BUT ONLY BARELY, THANKS TO YOUR CREEPY CHOICE IN ANIMALS!!
ARE THEY NOT "THE BEE'S KNEES"? ESPECIALLY KOI FISH.
RAHH
WAHHH!!
COFF
HIC
SOB...
OH, WOULD YOU SHUT UP ALREADY?!
SWIPE!!
WAHH!!
DO YOU EVEN WANT TO SAVE TRAFFY?!
I'LL SAVE DRABBY!!
AND...I'M DOT WORRIED ABOUT DA FLABE-FLABE FRUIT.
AND WHUP MINGO!!
YOU'RE NOT?!

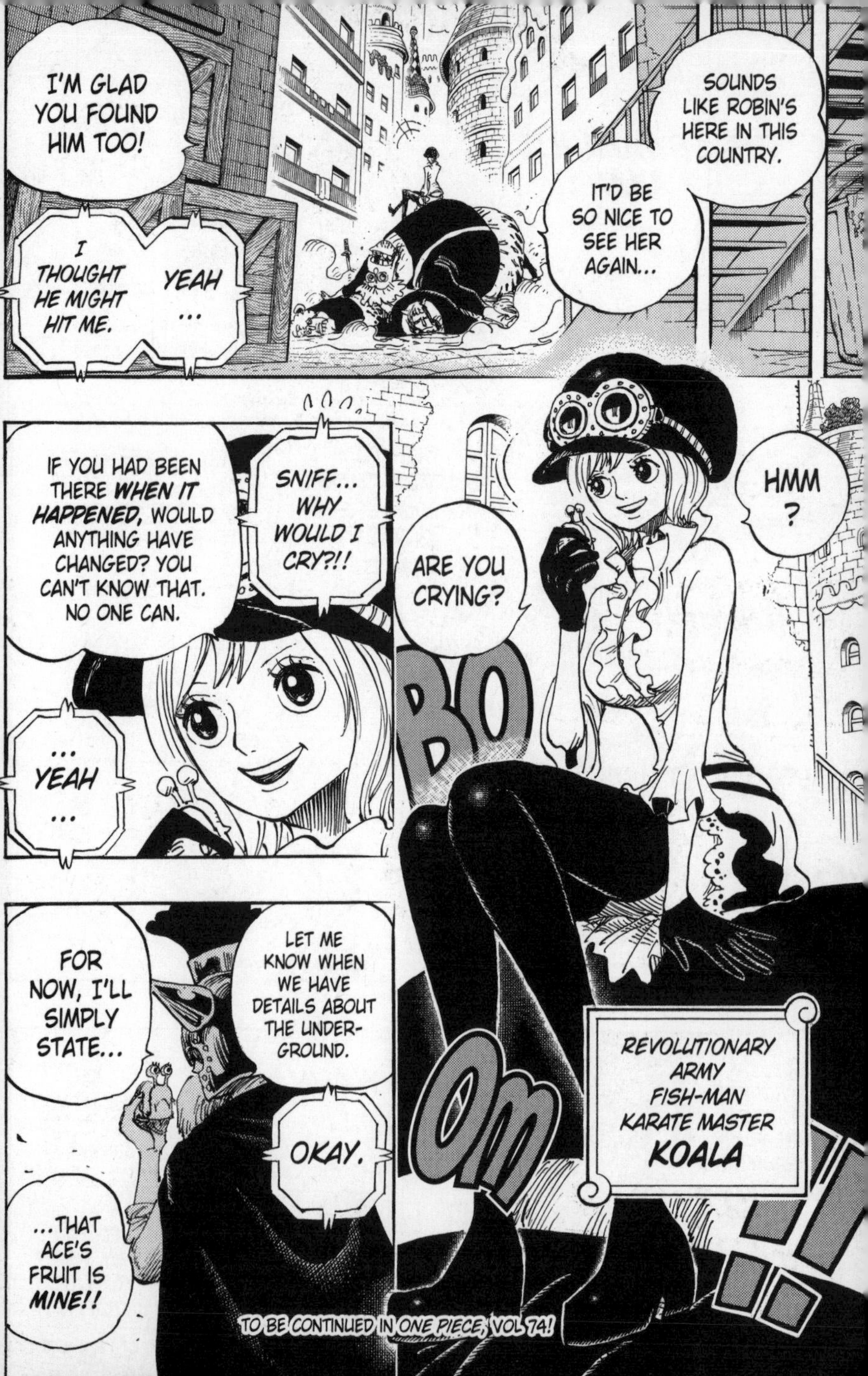
SOUNDS LIKE ROBIN'S HERE IN THIS COUNTRY.
IT'D BE SO NICE TO SEE HER AGAIN...
I'M GLAD YOU FOUND HIM TOO!
YEAH ...
I THOUGHT HE MIGHT HIT ME.
HMM ?
ARE YOU CRYING?
BOOM!!
REVOLUTIONARY ARMY FISH-MAN KARATE MASTER KOALA
SNIFF... WHY WOULD I CRY?!!
IF YOU HAD BEEN THERE *WHEN IT HAPPENED,* WOULD ANYTHING HAVE CHANGED? YOU CAN'T KNOW THAT. NO ONE CAN.
... YEAH ...
LET ME KNOW WHEN WE HAVE DETAILS ABOUT THE UNDER-GROUND.
FOR NOW, I'LL SIMPLY STATE...
OKAY.
...THAT ACE'S FRUIT IS *MINE!!*
TO BE CONTINUED IN ONE PIECE, VOL 74!

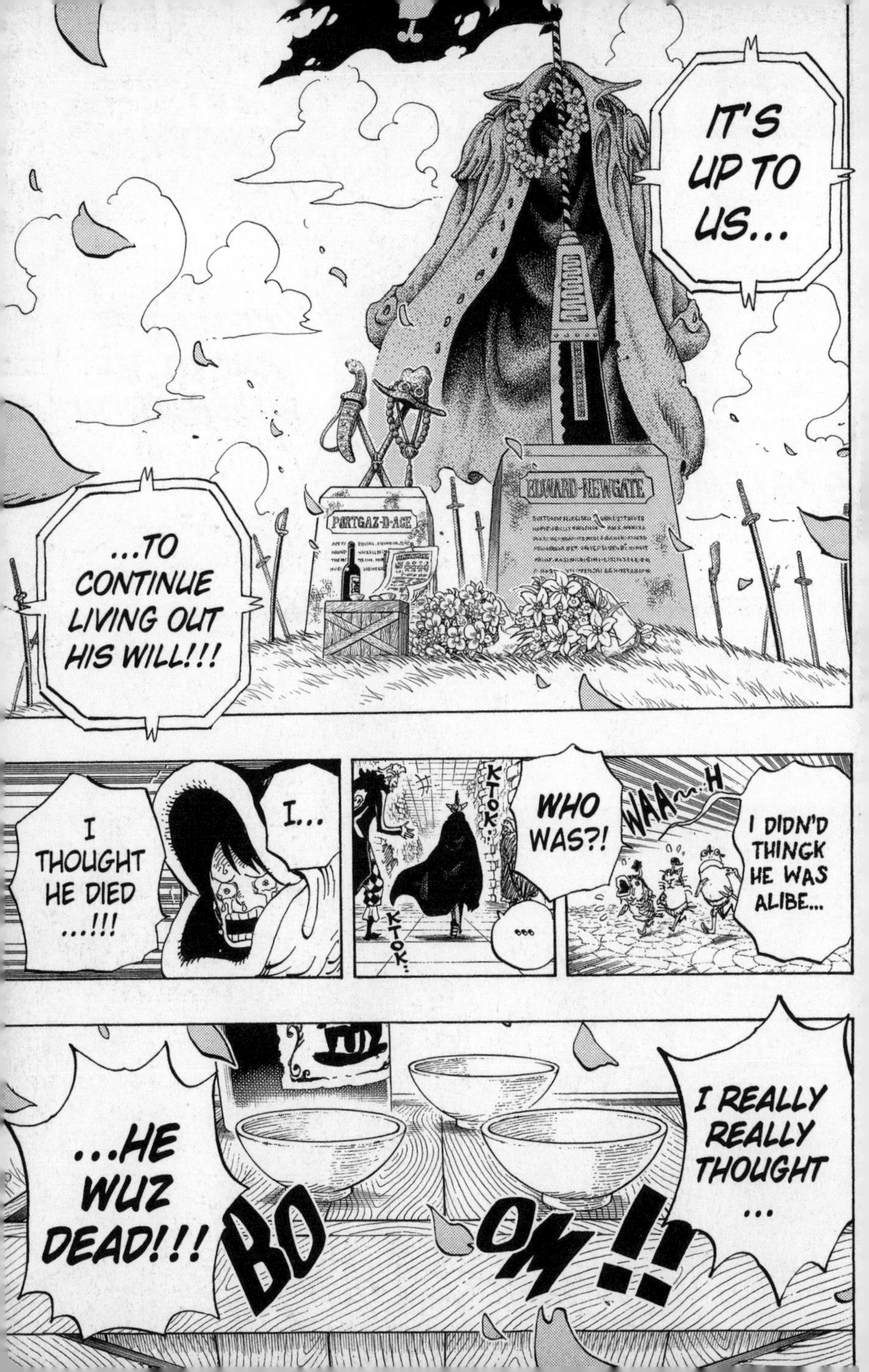
IT'S UP TO US...
EDWARD NEWGATE
PORTGAZ D ACE
...TO CONTINUE LIVING OUT HIS WILL!!!
WAA~~H
I DIDN'D THINGK HE WAS ALIBE...
WHO WAS?!
KTOK
KTOK..
...
I...
I THOUGHT HE DIED ...!!!
I REALLY REALLY THOUGHT ...
BOOM!!
...HE WUZ DEAD!!!

COMING NEXT VOLUME:

THE COMPLETE AND UTTER ERADICATION ...
...OF THE "SEVEN WARLORDS" SYSTEM!!!

Who is the mysterious stranger who has Luffy so emotional? And how will this new character impact the growing conflict on Dressrosa? Now that Luffy is out of the tournament, Doflamingo may be forced to take the offensive. And just when things start going bad for the Straw Hats, a new hero emerges!

ON SALE APRIL 2015!

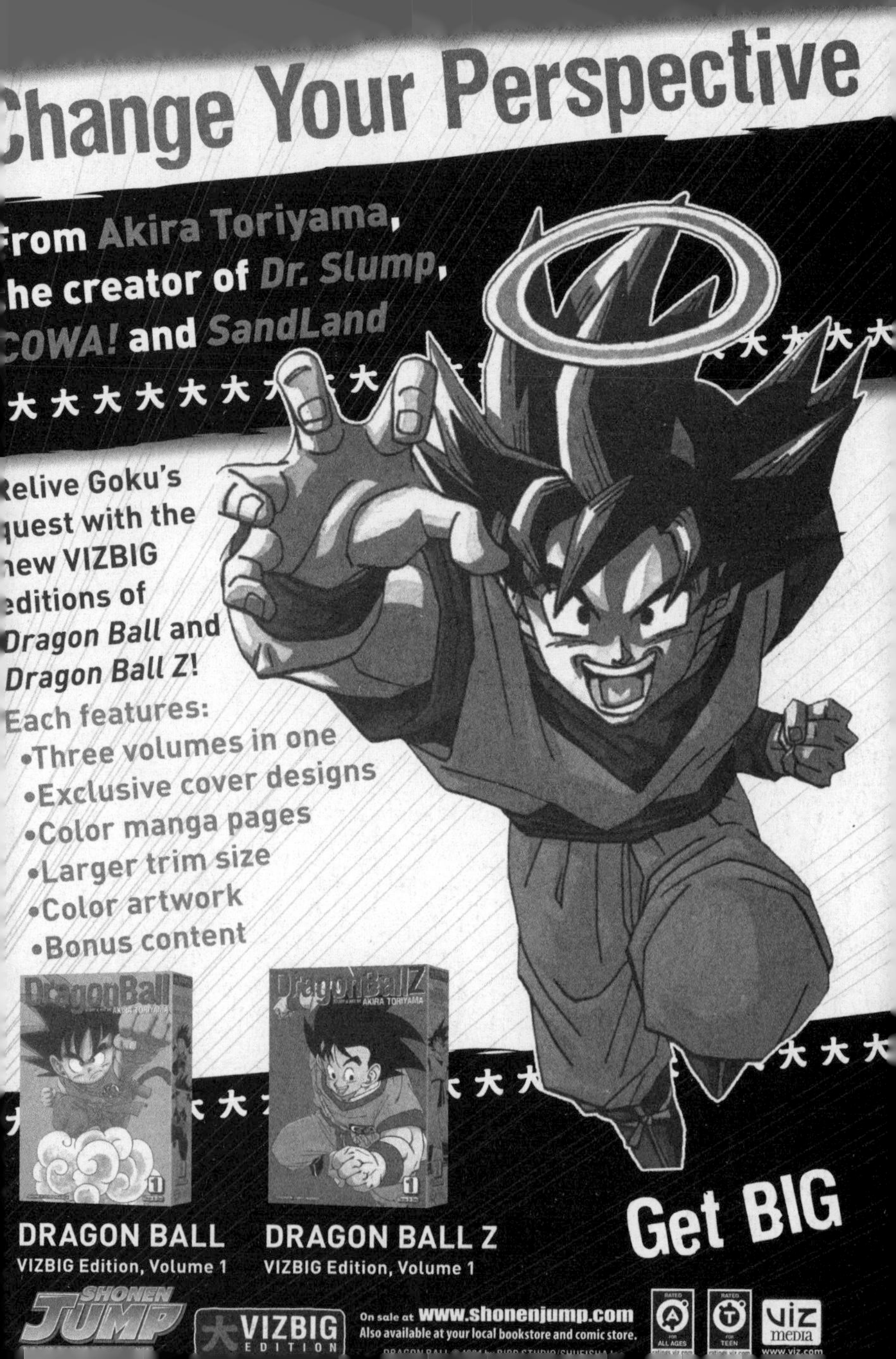
Change Your Perspective
From Akira Toriyama,
he creator of Dr. Slump,
COWA! and SandLand
Relive Goku's
quest with the
new VIZBIG
editions of
Dragon Ball and
Dragon Ball Z!
Each features:
•Three volumes in one
•Exclusive cover designs
•Color manga pages
•Larger trim size
•Color artwork
•Bonus content
DragonBall
AKIRA TORIYAMA
DragonBallZ
AKIRA TORIYAMA
DRAGON BALL
VIZBIG Edition, Volume 1
DRAGON BALL Z
VIZBIG Edition, Volume 1
Get BIG
SHONEN JUMP
VIZBIG EDITION
On sale at www.shonenjump.com
Also available at your local bookstore and comic store.
RATED A FOR ALL AGES
RATED T FOR TEEN
viz media
www.viz.com

You're Reading in the Wrong Direction!!

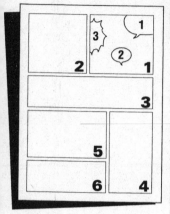

Whoops! Guess what? You're starting at the wrong end of the comic!

…It's true! In keeping with the original Japanese format, **One Piece** is meant to be read from right to left, starting in the upper-right corner.

Unlike English, which is read from left to right, Japanese is read from right to left, meaning that action, sound effects and word-balloon order are completely reversed…something which can make readers unfamiliar with Japanese feel pretty backwards themselves. For this reason, manga or Japanese comics published in the U.S. in English have sometimes been published "flopped"—that is, printed in exact reverse order, as though seen from the other side of a mirror.

By flopping pages, U.S. publishers can avoid confusing readers, but the compromise is not without its downside. For one thing, a character in a flopped manga series who once wore in the original Japanese version a T-shirt emblazoned with "M A Y" (as in "the merry month of") now wears one which reads "Y A M"! Additionally, many manga creators in Japan are themselves unhappy with the process, as some feel the mirror-imaging of their art skews their original intentions.

We are proud to bring you Eiichiro Oda's **One Piece** in the original unflopped format. For now, though, turn to the other side of the book and let the journey begin…!

—Editor